D1598089

Harley-Davidson Twin Cam 88
Service and Repair Manual

by Alan Ahlstrand

Models covered
Softail. 88 cu in (1450 cc). 2000 thru 2003
Dyna. 88 cu in (1450 cc). 1999 thru 2003
Touring models. 88 cu in (1450 cc). 1999 thru 2003

ABCDE
FGHIJ
KLMNO
PQRST

ISBN **1 56392 478 1**

British Library Cataloguing in Publication Data
A catalogue record for this book is available from the British Library.

Library of Congress Control Number 2002114287
Printed in the USA

Haynes Publishing
Sparkford, Nr Yeovil, Somerset BA22 7JJ, England

Haynes North America, Inc
861 Lawrence Drive, Newbury Park, California 91320, USA   03-256

Contents

LIVING WITH YOUR HARLEY-DAVIDSON TWIN CAM 88

Introduction

Daily (pre-ride) checks

MAINTENANCE

Routine maintenance and servicing

Contents

REPAIRS AND OVERHAUL

Engine, transmission and associated systems

Chassis and bodywork components

Electrical system

Wiring diagrams

REFERENCE

Index

Harley-Davidson
Milwaukee Magic

by Alan Ahlstrand

Milwaukee Magic

Late in the 1960s, on a typical warm summer California evening, a friend showed up at my house and announced, "Alan, if I can't make the payment, I'm coming to you for the money, because I'm *not* losing this bike."

He'd just traded his Suzuki X-6 - a 250cc 2-stroke twin with six-speed transmission, at that time being talked about as the new Harley-beater - for a new-to-him 1966 Sportster XLCH.

I'd ridden the Suzuki and laid it down on asphalt, so I wasn't invited onto the front seat of the Sportster. Instead, he gave complete instructions in back-seat riding technique for a torquey motorcycle without a sissy bar or grab strap for the passenger: "Put your hands around my waist and lock your fingers, or the bike will jet out from under you." Off we went,

ending up on newly-opened Highway 280 south of San Francisco, which was deserted at 2 a.m. Helmetless, ungoggled, dressed in jeans and t-shirts and unbridled by a sense of mortality, we cranked it up. After I'd had enough time to think "We're crazy, but yeee-haaa" more than once, he took one hand off the grip, turned around with one eye closed, the other half-closed and streaming tears, grinned, and held up one finger - we'd hit a hundred miles an hour.

Maybe the speedometer was optimistic, and it was really only 97.4 or so, but when the wind is shredding the shirt on your back and flapping your face like flags in a hurricane, the difference is academic.

Every Harley rider has done something like that - or will, when the time and place are right - and that Milwaukee magic has been the key to the company's modern success.

All of this started a century ago. In 1903

Arthur Davidson and William S. Harley finished a three-year project, building what amounted to a powered bicycle. The first Harley-Davidson engine had a single cylinder with a bore of 2-1/8 inches and a stroke of 2-7/8 inches, displacing 405 cc. The intake valve was not operated mechanically; rather, it was sucked open by the downward pull of the piston and pushed shut by the compressing fuel-air mixture on the piston's upward stroke, a design shared with contemporary automobile engines such as the Knox Porcupine. Power transmission was by a leather belt, assisted when necessary by bicycle pedals, a chain, sprockets and human effort. Braking was accomplished by pedaling backwards, bicycle-style. The front suspension was the leading-link design later to be improved and used in Springers, historic and modern. The rear suspension? There wasn't any - the bike's rigid, triangular rear frame section connected directly to the rear axle.

From 1903 to 1909, the company continued to grow, with steady improvements in the single-cylinder bike's design, steady increases in sales, and a move from the shed where the company started to a two-story factory in Milwaukee. In 1909 Harley's first V-twin, the model 5D, was introduced, and with it the company's enduring theme.

Despite diversions such as the Topper scooter and Aermacchi singles of the Sixties and Seventies, the theme continues to the present day. The heart of all Harleys, the key to what makes a motorcycle a Harley-Davidson, is the engine. The rest of the bike exists to keep the engine off the pavement. This function is performed in grand style, of course, with a near-infinite selection of customizing possibilities, but at the center of it all is a big-displacement, narrow-angle, uneven-firing, air-cooled V-twin that roars instead of wails. From the flatheads that succeeded the Model 5D, to the Knucklehead of 1936, to the Panhead of 1948, to the Shovelhead of 1966, to the Evolution of 1984, to the current Twin Cam 88, every important Harley-Davidson engine has fit that description.

(Actually, the only official designations in the list are Evolution and Twin Cam 88. Panhead, Knucklehead and Shovelhead were

The 1975 FLH1200 (Shovelhead)

informal names, based on the appearance of the cylinder heads and valve covers. For that reason, the Twin Cam 88 came dangerously close to being dubbed "Fathead.")

In addition to big piston displacement and a V-twin configuration, Harley engines share some unique characteristics. The angle between the cylinders, or "V," is 45 degrees. The crankshaft has one crankpin, with both connecting rods mounted on it. This means that the cylinders fire 90-degrees apart (at 315 and 405 degrees of crankshaft rotation). This uneven firing sequence gives the engine its signature "potato-potato" idle. In addition to being mounted on a single crankpin, the connecting rods are mounted knife-and-fork style rather than side-by-side. In this design, the bottom end of one connecting rod is an inverted Y, with the bottom end of the other connecting rod centered between the Y's branches. This allows the engine to be narrow from side to side, while the small angle between the cylinders allows it to be narrow front-to-rear.

The company continued producing new products under family ownership until 1969, when it was bought by the conglomerate AMF. The AMF years, 1969 to 1981, were widely regarded as the company's Dark Ages - sales dropped, along with the bikes' reputation for quality. My friend replaced his 1966 Sportster with a 1979 model, and then replaced a series of tachs and speedometers because the needles kept breaking off from vibration. This era ended with the company's rescue in a buyout by company executives, led by Vaughn Beals. This is one of the most successful employee buyouts in corporate history, if the company's stock price and sales are any indication - the stock has multiplied in value many times, and Harley-Davidson has for years maintained the biggest market share in the cruiser and touring bike categories.

That almost didn't happen - and Harley-Davidson nearly ended up in the recycling bin of history, as a nostalgic brand name that would-be entrepreneurs could paste onto yet another corporate startup attempt.

The buyout coincided with a downturn in the motorcycle market. Along with that, competition from Japanese bikes had become well established. The Suzuki X-6 wasn't a Harley-beater, but there were now plenty of four-cylinder Japanese 750s that were. Worse yet, the major Japanese manufacturers began to build V-twin cruisers. Faced with imminent doom, Harley-Davidson turned to the US government for help. This came in the form of a tariff, beginning in 1983, on Japanese-built motorcycles with displacements over 700 cc. The result was a sudden rash of Japanese bikes displacing 699cc, but it was enough to keep the company alive. Its fortunes even improved enough that it asked for an early end to the tariff in 1987.

The motorcycle market coasted along the bottom for several years, then finally began to

The 1974 XL1000 Sportster (Shovelhead)

The XL1200 Sportster (Evolution)

The 1993 FLSTC Heritage Softail (Evolution)

The 1993 XLH 883 Sportster Hugger (Evolution)

turn up significantly in the early 1990s. As the market revived, the audience was changing; motorcyclists were becoming older, richer, but more in need of a bad boy image (and increasingly, a bad girl image). They also needed bikes that were reliable and relatively comfortable to ride. Harley-Davidson had possessed the image for decades, even if Marlon Brando did ride a Triumph in "The Wild One." With the Evolution engine and improved quality control, the company was on its way to reliability. Comfort and simplicity had been evolving, and continued to do so.

Comfort and simplicity were no part of the Sportster XLCH, but in its day, the bike was enough of a thrill ride to make up for it. The kickstarter, operated in the wrong synchronicity with the twist-grip spark timing, could kick back and hurt you. The drum brakes stopped the bike far less capably than the engine made it go. The XLCH had no battery; its electrical system was powered by a magneto, which meant that the lights would dim if you let the engine idle. (Why no, officer, I wasn't speedshifting, I was just trying to keep the lights safely bright.)

The XLCH was intended for competition. Other Harleys were easier to ride, and had battery-based electrical systems. Electric start was introduced on the first Electra Glide in 1965. Final drive progressed from an exposed chain, to an enclosed chain, to a cogged belt that's still in use. Drum brakes were replaced by discs at front and rear. Rubber engine mounts were employed on touring bikes, and later on the Dyna. The hardtail look of early bikes was recreated with the Softail, but the Softail had a rear suspension. A well-designed sequential port fuel injection system was added as an option. Some models were designed with low seat heights to accommodate shorter riders.

The Evolution engine was a turning point in the company's history, even though it was essentially a refined top end on the Shovelhead bottom end. The iron cylinders and heads of the Shovelhead were replaced with aluminum components. The valve train's basic design was unchanged, with a single gear-driven camshaft, hydraulic lifters, pushrods and rocker arms. The change to aluminum at the top end eliminated a major source of oil leaks, at the joints of the cylinders and crankcase, because the parts now expanded and contracted at the same rate as they heated and cooled. The combination of mechanical improvement and Harley tradition was enthusiastically received by customers, first in the Big Twins for 1984 and then in the Sportster for 1986.

The Evolution engine was superseded by the Twin Cam 88, in the Touring and Dyna chassis for the 1999 model year and in Softails for 2000 (the Evo is still used in the Sportster). Unlike the Evolution, the Twin Cam 88 was a completely new design, even while it retained the basics of the traditional Harley

A hundred years old, and stronger than ever - 100th Anniversary models sport a distinctive logo

Past meets future - the Sportster is essentially unchanged, while the V-Rod is radically new

engine. Despite the name, the engine did not have overhead cams. The Twin Cam designation came about because the wide spacing between the large cylinder bores made a single camshaft impractical. The solution was to use one camshaft for each cylinder. The camshafts are mounted in a support plate on the right side of the engine, below the cylinders. The rear camshaft is driven by the crankshaft through a chain and sprockets mounted outside the camshaft support plate. The rear camshaft drives the front camshaft through a second chain and sprockets, mounted inside the camshaft support plate. As with earlier Harley engines, the camshafts operate the valves through hydraulic lifters, pushrods and rocker arms.

Engine vibration in Dyna and Touring models was handled by rubber engine mounts. In the Softail, where the engine is solidly mounted to the chassis, another solution was needed. This was the Twin Cam 88B, the balancer-equipped version of the engine that appeared in Softails in 2000. The Twin Cam 88B is the same as non-counterbalanced versions from the crankshaft up. A pair of balance shafts, one behind the crankshaft and one in front, are driven by the crankshaft through a chain and sprockets.

Thus Harley-Davidson ends its first century with a very good product line and very good prospects. What's in store for Harley's next century? Logically, the company's future cruisers and touring motorcycles should be variations of the V-Rod sport bike. The V-Rod is an attractive mix of Harley tradition and modern technology. Like traditional Harleys, the V-Rod has a V-twin engine. Unlike traditional Harleys, the V-Rod employs overhead cams, four-valve heads and liquid cooling to produce an impressive 115 horsepower. And yet, Harley customers have left V-Rods on the sales floor in record numbers while buying more Twin Cam 88s every year.

Modern Japanese bikes tend to have four-figure price tags and five-figure redlines; Harleys, traditional and V-Rod, are the other way around. Modern Harleys are well built and reliable, but so are their competitors. Why, in the face of those facts, do traditional Harleys continue to dominate their market? When Milwaukee magic applies, logic doesn't. It's as simple, and as complicated, as that.

Acknowledgements

Our thanks are due to Santa Barbara Harley Davidson, Carpinteria, California, for supplying the motorcycle used in the photographs throughout this manual. Thanks also to JIMS Tools, of Camarillo, California (www.jimsusa.com), for supplying the special tools used in some photographs. The introduction "Milwaukee Magic" was written by Alan Ahlstrand.

About this manual

The aim of this manual is to help you get the best value from your motorcycle. It can do so in several ways. It can help you decide what work must be done, even if you choose to have it done by a dealer; it provides information and procedures for routine maintenance and servicing; and it offers diagnostic and repair procedures to follow when trouble occurs.

We hope you use the manual to tackle the work yourself. For many simpler jobs, doing it yourself may be quicker than arranging an appointment to get the motorcycle into a dealer and making the trips to leave it and pick it up. More importantly, a lot of money can be saved by avoiding the expense the shop must pass on to you to cover its labor and overhead costs. An added benefit is the sense of satisfaction and accomplishment that you feel after doing the job yourself.

References to the left or right side of the motorcycle assume you are sitting on the seat, facing forward.

We take great pride in the accuracy of information given in this manual, but motorcycle manufacturers make alterations and design changes during the production run of a particular motorcycle of which they do not inform us. No liability can be accepted by the authors or publishers for loss, damage or injury caused by any errors in, or omissions from, the information given.

Buying spare parts

Once you have found all the identification numbers, record them for reference when buying parts. Since the manufacturers change specifications, parts and vendors (companies that manufacture various components on the machine), providing the ID numbers is the only way to be reasonably sure that you are buying the correct parts.

Whenever possible, take the worn part to the dealer so direct comparison with the new component can be made. Along the trail from the manufacturer to the parts shelf, there are numerous places that the part can end up with the wrong number or be listed incorrectly.

The two places to purchase new parts for your motorcycle - the accessory store and the franchised dealer - differ in the type of parts they carry. While dealers can obtain virtually every part for your motorcycle, the accessory dealer is usually limited to normal high wear items such as shock absorbers, tune-up parts, various engine gaskets, cables, chains, brake parts, etc. Rarely will an accessory outlet have major suspension components, cylinders, transmission gears, or cases.

Used parts can be obtained for considerably less than new ones, but you can't always be sure of what you're getting. Once again, take your worn part to the salvage yard for direct comparison.

Whether buying new, used or rebuilt parts, the best course is to deal directly with someone who specializes in parts for your particular make.

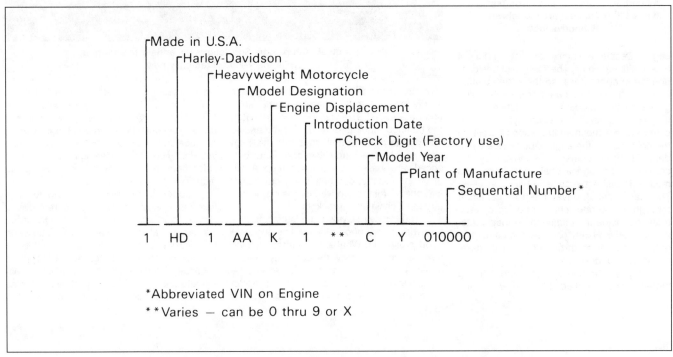

The Vehicle Identification Number (VIN) contains information about the motorcycle

Decoding the Vehicle Identification Number (VIN)

The frame serial number is stamped into the right side of the steering head and printed on a decal attached to the right frame downtube. An abbreviated frame serial number is stamped on the crankcase below the "V" of the cylinders. Both of these numbers should be recorded and kept in a safe place so they can be given to law enforcement officials in the event of a theft.

The frame serial number and engine serial number should also be kept in a handy place (such as with your driver's license) so they are always available when purchasing or ordering parts for your machine.

The Vehicle Identification Number (VIN) contains code letters and numbers that provide specific information about each motorcycle. The purpose of each letter or number is shown in the accompanying illustration. The letter and number codes are described below. **Note:** *The letters used to designate some models have been used in the past to designate different models (for example, FXSTB designates the Softail Night Train; in earlier years, it designated the Softail Bad Boy). The letters and model names listed here are correct for the years covered in this manual*

Market designation

1: Manufactured for USA
5: Manufactured for all other markets

Heavyweight motorcycle:

901 cc or greater engine displacement

Model designation (Softail)

BH: FSXT Softail Standard (carbureted)
BJ: FLSTC Softail Heritage Classic (carbureted)
BL: FXSTS Softail Springer (carbureted)
BM: FLSTF Fat Boy (carbureted)
BR: FLSTS Heritage Springer (carbureted)
BS: FXSTD Softail Deuce (carbureted)
BT: FXSTB Night Train carbureted)

BV: FXSTI Softail Standard (fuel injected)
BW: FLSTCI Softail Heritage Classic (fuel injected)
BX: FLSTFI Fat Boy (fuel injected)
BY: FLSTSI Heritage Springer (fuel injected)
BZ: FXSTSI Softail Springer (fuel injected)
JA: FXSTBI Night Train (fuel injected)
JB: FXSTDI Softail Deuce (fuel injected)

Model designation (Dyna)

GH: FXD Dyna Super Glide
GJ: FXDX Dyna Super Glide Sport
GL: FXDXT Dyna Super Glide T-Sport

GD: FXDL Dyna Low Rider
GE: FXDWG Dyna Wide Glide

continued on next page

Model designation (Touring)

DD: FLHT Electra Glide Standard (carbureted)
DG: FLHTC Shrine (carbureted)
DJ: FLHTC Electra Glide Classic (carbureted)
FB: FLHR-I Road King (fuel injected)
FC: FLHTCUI Ultra Classic Electra Glide (fuel injected)
FD: FLHR Road King (carbureted)
FF: FLHTCI Electra Glide Classic (fuel injected)
FG: FLHTCUI (fuel injected, cruise control)
FH: FLHPI Road King (Police, fuel injected)

FL: FLHTCUI Shrine (fuel injected)
FM: FLHTPI Electra Glide (police, fuel injected)
FP: FLTR Road Glide (carbureted)
FR: FLHRCI Road King Classic (fuel injected)
FS: FLTRI Road Glide (fuel injected)
FT: FLHPEI
FV: FLHTI Electra Glide standard (fuel injected)
FW: FLHRI Shrine (fuel injected)

Introduction date and special models

1: Regular introduction date
2: Mid-year introduction date

3: California model
4: Anniversary model

Engine Type

V: Twin Cam 88 (carbureted)
W: Twin Cam 88 (fuel injected)

Y: Twin Cam 88B (carbureted)
B: Twin Cam 88B (fuel injected)

VIN check digit

Varies from 0 through 9 or X

Model year

X: 1999
Y: 2000
1: 2001
2: 2002
3: 2003

Assembly plant

K: Kansas City, Missouri
Y: York, Pennsylvania

An abbreviated version of the VIN is stamped in the engine, below the "V" of the cylinders

The VIN is also printed on a decal on the right frame downtube

The VIN is stamped on the right side of the steering head

Professional mechanics are trained in safe working procedures. However enthusiastic you may be about getting on with the job at hand, take the time to ensure that your safety is not put at risk. A moment's lack of attention can result in an accident, as can failure to observe simple precautions.

There will always be new ways of having accidents, and the following is not a comprehensive list of all dangers; it is intended rather to make you aware of the risks and to encourage a safe approach to all work you carry out on your bike.

Asbestos

● Certain friction, insulating, sealing and other products - such as brake pads, clutch linings, gaskets, etc. - contain asbestos. Extreme care must be taken to avoid inhalation of dust from such products since it is hazardous to health. If in doubt, assume that they do contain asbestos.

Fire

● Remember at all times that gasoline is highly flammable. Never smoke or have any kind of naked flame around, when working on the vehicle. But the risk does not end there - a spark caused by an electrical short-circuit, by two metal surfaces contacting each other, by careless use of tools, or even by static electricity built up in your body under certain conditions, can ignite gasoline vapor, which in a confined space is highly explosive. Never use gasoline as a cleaning solvent. Use an approved safety solvent.

● Always disconnect the battery ground terminal before working on any part of the fuel or electrical system, and never risk spilling fuel on to a hot engine or exhaust.

● It is recommended that a fire extinguisher of a type suitable for fuel and electrical fires is kept handy in the garage or workplace at all times. Never try to extinguish a fuel or electrical fire with water.

Fumes

● Certain fumes are highly toxic and can quickly cause unconsciousness and even death if inhaled to any extent. Gasoline vapor comes into this category, as do the vapors from certain solvents such as trichloro-ethylene. Any draining or pouring of such volatile fluids should be done in a well ventilated area.

● When using cleaning fluids and solvents, read the instructions carefully. Never use materials from unmarked containers - they may give off poisonous vapors.

● Never run the engine of a motor vehicle in an enclosed space such as a garage. Exhaust fumes contain carbon monoxide which is extremely poisonous; if you need to run the engine, always do so in the open air or at least have the rear of the vehicle outside the workplace.

The battery

● Never cause a spark, or allow a naked light near the vehicle's battery. It will normally be giving off a certain amount of hydrogen gas, which is highly explosive.

● Always disconnect the battery ground terminal before working on the fuel or electrical systems (except where noted).

● If possible, loosen the filler plugs or cover when charging the battery from an external source. Do not charge at an excessive rate or the battery may burst.

● Take care when topping up, cleaning or carrying the battery. The acid electrolyte, even when diluted, is very corrosive and should not be allowed to contact the eyes or skin. Always wear rubber gloves and goggles or a face shield. If you ever need to prepare electrolyte yourself, always add the acid slowly to the water; never add the water to the acid.

Electricity

● When using an electric power tool, inspection light etc., always ensure that the appliance is correctly connected to its plug and that, where necessary, it is properly grounded. Do not use such appliances in damp conditions and, again, beware of creating a spark or applying excessive heat in the vicinity of fuel or fuel vapor. Also ensure that the appliances meet national safety standards.

● A severe electric shock can result from touching certain parts of the electrical system, such as the spark plug wires (HT leads), when the engine is running or being cranked, particularly if components are damp or the insulation is defective. Where an electronic ignition system is used, the secondary (HT) voltage is much higher and could prove fatal.

Remember...

✗ **Don't** start the engine without first ascertaining that the transmission is in neutral.

✗ **Don't** attempt to drain oil until you are sure it has cooled sufficiently to avoid scalding you.

✗ **Don't** grasp any part of the engine or exhaust system without first ascertaining that it is cool enough not to burn you.

✗ **Don't** allow brake fluid or antifreeze to contact the machine's paintwork or plastic components.

✗ **Don't** siphon toxic liquids such as fuel or hydraulic fluid by mouth, or allow them to remain on your skin.

✗ **Don't** inhale dust - it may be injurious to health (see Asbestos heading).

✗ **Don't** allow any spilled oil or grease to remain on the floor - wipe it up right away, before someone slips on it.

✗ **Don't** use ill-fitting wrenches or other tools which may slip and cause injury.

✗ **Don't** lift a heavy component which may be beyond your capability - get assistance.

✗ **Don't** rush to finish a job or take unverified short cuts.

✗ **Don't** allow children or animals in or around an unattended vehicle.

✗ **Don't** inflate a tire above the recommended pressure. Apart from overstressing the carcass, in extreme cases the tire may blow off forcibly.

✔ **Do** ensure that the machine is supported securely at all times. This is especially important when the machine is blocked up to aid wheel or fork removal.

✔ **Do** take care when attempting to loosen a stubborn nut or bolt. It is generally better to pull on a wrench, rather than push, so that if you slip, you fall away from the machine rather than onto it.

✔ **Do** wear eye protection when using power tools such as drill, sander, bench grinder etc.

✔ **Do** use a barrier cream on your hands prior to undertaking dirty jobs - it will protect your skin from infection as well as making the dirt easier to remove afterwards; but make sure your hands aren't left slippery. Note that long-term contact with used engine oil can be a health hazard.

✔ **Do** keep loose clothing (cuffs, ties etc. and long hair) well out of the way of moving mechanical parts.

✔ **Do** remove rings, wristwatch etc., before working on the vehicle - especially the electrical system.

✔ **Do** keep your work area tidy - it is only too easy to fall over articles left lying around.

✔ **Do** exercise caution when compressing springs for removal or installation. Ensure that the tension is applied and released in a controlled manner, using suitable tools which preclude the possibility of the spring escaping violently.

✔ **Do** ensure that any lifting tackle used has a safe working load rating adequate for the job.

✔ **Do** get someone to check periodically that all is well, when working alone on the vehicle.

✔ **Do** carry out work in a logical sequence and check that everything is correctly assembled and tightened afterwards.

✔ **Do** remember that your vehicle's safety affects that of yourself and others. If in doubt on any point, get professional advice.

● If in spite of following these precautions, you are unfortunate enough to injure yourself, seek medical attention as soon as possible.

1 Engine oil level check

Before you start:

Caution: Do not run the engine in an enclosed space such as a garage or workshop.

✔ Stop the engine and support the motorcycle on its sidestand. Allow it to stand undisturbed for a few minutes to allow the oil level to stabilize. Make sure the motorcycle is on level ground.

✔ Check the engine oil level with the bike on the sidestand. If the engine is cold, use the Cold check scale on the dipstick. If the engine is warm, let it idle for one or two minutes on the sidestand, then shut it off and check the oil.

✔ To check the oil level, remove the dipstick/filler cap from the oil tank (it's on the right side of the motorcycle on all models). Rock the cap back-and-forth to free the O-ring, then lift the dipstick out. Wipe the dipstick with a clean rag, set it back in the hole (don't push it all the way in), then lift it out and read the level on the dipstick scale.

✔ Don't confuse the engine oil cap with the transmission oil cap; the engine oil cap is above the transmission cap and is held in place by a rubber O-ring, while the transmission oil cap is unscrewed with an Allen wrench.

Bike care:

● If you have to add oil frequently, you should check whether you have any oil leaks. If there is no sign of oil leakage from the joints and gaskets the engine could be burning oil (see *Troubleshooting*).

The correct oil

● Modern, high-revving engines place great demands on their oil. It is very important that the correct oil for your bike is used.

● Always top up with a good quality oil of the specified type and viscosity and do not overfill the engine.

Oil type..	H-D rating 360 or equivalent
Oil viscosity	
Below 40-degrees F (4-degrees C)	H.D. Multi-Grade, SAE 10W-40
Above 40-degrees F (4-degrees C)	H.D. Multi-Grade, SAE 20W-50
Above 60-degrees F (16-degrees C)	H.D. Regular Heavy, SAE 50
Above 80-degrees F (27-degrees C)	H.D. Extra Heavy, SAE 60

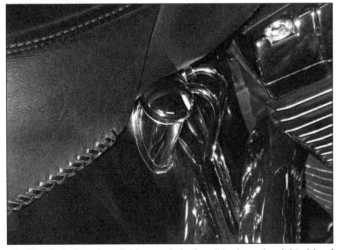

1 The Softail engine oil filler cap is in the oil tank on the right side of the bike.

2 The Dyna engine oil filler cap is on the right side, behind the rear cylinder.

3 Here's the engine oil filler cap on a Road King, between the exhaust pipe and side cover on the right side of the bike (other Touring models similar).

4 Rock the engine oil dipstick back-and-forth while pulling it out. Measure the oil level on the dipstick scale.

2 Suspension, steering and final drive checks

Suspension and Steering:
● Check that the front and rear suspension operate smoothly without binding.
● Check that the suspension is adjusted as required.
● Check that the steering moves smoothly from lock-to-lock.

Final drive:
● Check the drivebelt tension with the belt cold, the bike on the sidestand and the weight of the rider on the seat. Using a tension gauge is the best way to check, but the gauge isn't absolutely necessary. If belt tension is incorrect, adjust it (see Chapter 1). On later Dyna models, the belt is visible through a hole in the belt guard.

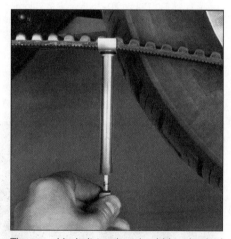

The rear drivebelt tension should be checked at the center of the upper run (Softail) or lower run (Dyna and Touring models), with the bike on the sidestand. Apply 10-pounds force to the belt (ideally, using a tension gauge) and measure the belt deflection.

3 Legal and safety checks

Lighting and signalling:
● Take a minute to check that the headlight, tail light, brake light, instrument lights and turn signals all work correctly.
● Check that the horn sounds when the switch is operated.
● A working speedometer graduated in mph is a statutory requirement in the UK.

Safety:
● Check that the throttle grip rotates smoothly and snaps shut when released, in all steering positions. Also check for the correct amount of freeplay (see Chapter 1).
● Check that the engine shuts off when the kill switch is operated.
● Check that sidestand return spring holds the stand securely up when retracted.

Fuel:
● This may seem obvious, but check that you have enough fuel to complete your journey. If you notice signs of fuel leakage - rectify the cause immediately.
● Ensure you use the correct grade unleaded fuel - see Chapter 4 Specifications.

4 Brake fluid level checks

> **Warning:** *Hydraulic fluid can harm your eyes and damage painted surfaces, so use extreme caution when handling and pouring it and cover surrounding surfaces with rag. Do not use fluid that has been standing open for some time, as it absorbs moisture from the air which can cause a dangerous loss of braking effectiveness.*

Before you start:

✔ Ensure the motorcycle is held vertical while checking the levels. Make sure the motorcycle is on level ground.

✔ Make sure you have the correct hydraulic fluid. DOT 4 is recommended. Never reuse old fluid.

✔ Wrap a rag around the reservoir being worked on to ensure that any spillage does not come into contact with painted surfaces.

Bike care:

● The fluid in the front and rear brake master cylinder reservoirs will drop slightly as the brake pads wear down.

● If any fluid reservoir requires repeated topping-up this is an indication of a hydraulic leak somewhere in the system, which should be investigated immediately.

● Check for signs of fluid leakage from the hydraulic hoses and components - if found, rectify immediately.

● Check the operation of both brakes before taking the machine on the road; if there is evidence of air in the system (spongy feel to lever or pedal), it must be bled as described in Chapter 7.

1 Check the front brake fluid level in the sight glass on top of the master cylinder. If the level is high enough, the sight glass will be dark. It lightens in color as the fluid level drops.

2 The rear master cylinder (located near the brake pedal) also has a sight glass. Fluid level is checked in the same way as for the front master cylinder.

3 If the fluid level is low in either master cylinder, remove the cover screws and lift off the cover and diaphragm. Top up to 1/8-inch (3 mm) from the gasket surface with DOT 5 brake fluid only, then reinstall the cover and diaphragm.

4 Tire checks

The correct pressures:

● The tires must be checked when **cold**, not immediately after riding. Note that low tire pressures may cause the tire to slip on the rim or come off. High tire pressures will cause abnormal tread wear and unsafe handling.
● Use an accurate pressure gauge.
● Proper air pressure will increase tire life and provide maximum stability and ride comfort.

Tire care:

● Check the tires carefully for cuts, tears, embedded nails or other sharp objects and excessive wear. Operation of the motorcycle with excessively worn tires is extremely hazardous, as traction and handling are directly affected.
● Check the condition of the tire valve and ensure the dust cap is in place.
● Pick out any stones or nails which may have become embedded in the tire tread. If left, they will eventually penetrate through the casing and cause a puncture.
● If tire damage is apparent, or unexplained loss of pressure is experienced, seek the advice of a tire fitting specialist without delay.

Tire tread depth:

● Tires incorporate wear indicators in the tread. Identify the triangular pointer or 'TWI' mark on the tire sidewall to locate the indicator bar and replace the tire if the tread has worn down to the bar.

Tire pressures*

Softail models	
FLSTC, FLSTF, FLSTS	
Rider only, front and rear	36 psi (2.5 Bar)
Rider and passenger, front	36 psi (2.5 Bar)
Rider and passenger, rear	40 psi (2.8 Bar)
FXST, FXSTB, FXSTS, FXSTD	
Rider only, front and rear	30 psi (2.0 Bar)
Rider and passenger, front	36 psi (2.5 Bar)
Rider and passenger, rear	40 psi (2.8 Bar)
Dyna models	
1999	
Rider only, front	30 psi (2.0 Bar)
Rider only, rear	36 psi (2.5 Bar)
Rider and passenger, front	36 psi (2.5 Bar)
Rider and passenger, rear	40 psi (2.8 Bar)
2000 and later	
Rider only, front and rear	30 psi (2.0 Bar)
Rider and passenger, front	36 psi (2.5 Bar)
Rider and passenger, rear	40 psi (2.8 Bar)
Touring models	
Rider only, front and rear	36 psi (2.5 Bar)
Rider and passenger, front	36 psi (2.5 Bar)
Rider and passenger, rear	40 psi (2.8 Bar)

*Listed pressures are for Dunlop tires only. If you install another brand, consult the tire dealer or manufacturer.

1 Check the tire pressures when the tires are **cold** and keep them properly inflated.

2 Measure tread depth at the center of the tire using a tread depth gauge.

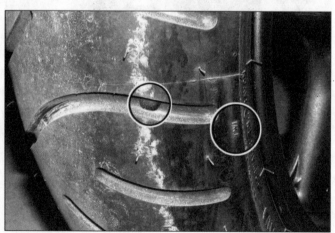

3 Tire tread wear indicator bar and its location marking (usually either an arrow, a triangle or the letters TWI) on the sidewall (arrow).

Chapter 1
Tune-up and routine maintenance

Contents

Air filter element - servicing 9
Battery - inspection 16
Brake fluid level and condition - check.................................... 24
Brake pads - wear check... 5
Brake pedal position and play - check 7
Brake system - general check 6
Choke knob (carbureted models) - check 11
Clutch - check and adjustment.. 21
Drivebelt - tension adjustment... 4
Drivebelt and sprockets - inspection...................................... 23
Electrical equipment - check 17
Engine oil and filter - change 18
Evaporative emission control system
    (California models only) - check 13
Exhaust system - check.. 29
External oil lines - check 14
Fasteners - check 15
Fluid levels - check 3
Fork oil - replacement 34

Fuel filter (fuel injected models) - replacement............................ 35
Fuel system - check.. 12
Fuel valve filter screen (carbureted models) -
    inspection and cleaning.. 33
Harley Twin Cam 88 Routine maintenance intervals 1
Idle speed (carbureted models) - check and adjustment 28
Introduction to tune-up and routine maintenance 2
Lubrication - general.. 26
Primary chain deflection - check and adjustment 22
Primary chaincase oil - change... 20
Rocker bearings (Softail Springer models) - adjustment............. 31
Spark plugs - replacement 27
Steering head bearings - check.. 30
Steering head bearings - lubrication... 25
Suspension - check 32
Throttle operation/grip freeplay - check and adjustment 10
Tires/wheels - general check 8
Transmission oil - change.. 19

Degrees of difficulty

Easy, suitable for novice with little experience 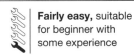	**Fairly easy,** suitable for beginner with some experience 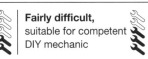	**Fairly difficult,** suitable for competent DIY mechanic	**Difficult,** suitable for experienced DIY mechanic 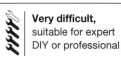	**Very difficult,** suitable for expert DIY or professional

Specifications

Engine

Spark plugs
  Type.. Harley-Davidson 6R12
  Gap.. 0.038 to 0.043 inch (0.97 to 1.09 mm)
Idle speed .... 950 to 1050 rpm
Cylinder compression pressure
  Reading .... 90 psi (6 kN/m2) or more
  Variation limit between cylinders............................ 10 per cent

Chassis

Brake pad minimum thickness (friction material)
  FLSTS and FXSTS front pads .... 0.060 inch (1.6 mm)
  All others .... 0.040 inch (1.0 mm)
Clutch freeplay (gap between cable and lever bracket) .... 1/16 to 1/8-inch (1.6 to 3.2 mm)
Drive belt slack
  Softail and Dyna models .... 5/16 to 3/8-inch (7.9 to 9.5 mm)
  Touring models
    Rear tire on ground, no rider................................ 5/16 to 3/8-inch (7.9 to 9.5 mm)
    Rear tire on ground, with rider.............................. 1/4 to 5/16-inch (6.4 to 7.9 mm)
Primary chain freeplay
  Hot engine.. 5/8 to 7/8 inch (15.9 to 22.2 mm)
  Cold engine .... 3/8 to 5/8 inch (9.5 to 15.9 mm)

1

Tire pressures*

Softail models
  FLSTC, FLSTF, FLSTS
Rider only, front and rear	36 psi (2.5 Bar)
Rider and passenger, front	36 psi (2.5 Bar)
Rider and passenger, rear	40 psi (2.8 Bar)

  FXST, FXSTB, FXSTS, FXSTD
Rider only, front and rear	30 psi (2.0 Bar)
Rider and passenger, front	36 psi (2.5 Bar)
Rider and passenger, rear	40 psi (2.8 Bar)

Dyna models
  1999
Rider only, front	30 psi (2.0 Bar)
Rider only, rear	36 psi (2.5 Bar)
Rider and passenger, front	36 psi (2.5 Bar)
Rider and passenger, rear	40 psi (2.8 Bar)

  2000 and later
Rider only, front and rear	30 psi (2.0 Bar)
Rider and passenger, front	36 psi (2.5 Bar)
Rider and passenger, rear	40 psi (2.8 Bar)

Touring models
Rider only, front and rear	36 psi (2.5 Bar)
Rider and passenger, front	36 psi (2.5 Bar)
Rider and passenger, rear	40 psi (2.8 Bar)

*Listed pressures are for Dunlop tires only. If you install another brand, consult the tire dealer or manufacturer.

Torque specifications

Air cleaner bracket screws	20 to 40 inch-lbs (2.3 to 4.5 Nm)
Air cleaner cover screw	36 to 60 inch-lbs (4.1 to 6.8 Nm)
Brake fluid reservoir cover screws	6 to 8 inch-lbs (0.7 to 0.9 Nm)
Clutch adjuster locknut (at engine)	72 to 120 inch-lbs (8.1 to 13.6 inches)
Clutch inspection cover screws	84 to 108 inch-lbs (9.5 to 12.2 mm)
Engine oil drain plug	14 to 21 ft-lbs (19.0 to 28.5 Nm)
Primary chain center bolt nut	21 to 29 ft-lbs (28.5 to 39.3 inches)
Primary chaincase cover screws	84 to 108 inch-lbs (9.5 to 12.2 mm)
Primary chaincase oil drain plug protrusion	0.160 to 0.180 inch (4.1 to 4.6 mm)*
Rear axle nut	
Initial torque	60 ft-lbs (81.3 Nm)
Maximum torque	65 ft-lbs (88.1 Nm)
Spark plugs	12 to 18 ft-lbs (16.3 to 24.4 Nm)
Transmission oil drain plug	14 to 21 ft-lbs (19.0 to 28.5 Nm)
Transmission oil filler plug	25 to 75 inch-lbs (2.8 to 8.5 Nm)
Wheel spoke nipples	40 to 50 inch-lbs (4.5 to 5.6 Nm)

*The primary chaincase drain plug is tightened until it protrudes the specified amount from the chaincase.

Recommended lubricants and fluids

Engine oil

Oil type   H-D rating 360 or equivalent
Oil viscosity
Below 40-degrees F (4-degrees C)	H.D. Multi-Grade, SAE 10W-40
Above 40-degrees F (4-degrees C)	H.D. Multi-Grade, SAE 20W-50
Above 60-degrees F (16-degrees C)	H.D. Regular Heavy, SAE 50
Above 80-degrees F (27-degrees C)	H.D. Extra Heavy, SAE 60
Oil capacity	3.5 qt (3.3 liters)

Transmission oil

Type	Harley-Davidson Transmission Lubricant or equivalent
Capacity	20 to 24 fl oz (591.5 to 709.8 cc)

Primary chaincase lubricant

Type	Harley-Davidson Primary Chaincase Lubricant or equivalent
Capacity	Approximately 26 fl oz (768.9 cc)*

Brake fluid

Type	DOT 5

Fork oil

Type .... Harley-Davidson Type E fork oil or equivalent
Amount
    Softail models
        FLSTF, FLSTC .... 12.9 fl oz (382 cc)
        FXST, FXSTB, FXSTC .... 12.0 fl oz (356 cc)
        FXSTD .... 11.6 fl oz (343 cc)
    Dyna models
        FXDWG .... 12.0 fl oz (360 cc)
        FXD, FXL models .... 10.6 fl oz (310 cc)
    Touring models (except Road King)
        Left fork.. 10.0 fl oz (295 cc)
        Right fork .... 11.1 fl oz (328 cc)
    Road King (both forks) .... 11.1 fl oz (328 cc)
Level
    Softail models
        FLSTF, FLSTC .... 4.72 inches (119.9 mm)
        FXST, FXSTB, FXSTC .... 7.28 inches (184.9 mm)
        FXSTD .... 7.48 inches (189.9 mm)
    Dyna models
        FXDWG .... 7.28 inches (184.9 mm)
        FXD, FXL models .... 6.69 inches (169.6 mm)
    Touring models (except Road King)
        Left fork.. 4.21 inches (107 mm)
        Right fork .... 5.24 inches (133 mm)
    Road King (both forks) .... 5.24 inches (133 mm)
*Fill to correct level (see text).

Miscellaneous

Steering head bearings.. Harley-Davidson Special Purpose Grease or equivalent
Sidestand.. Loctite Aerosol Anti-Seize or equivalent
Swingarm pivot bearings*.. Medium weight, lithium-based multi-purpose grease
Throttle grip .... Graphite grease
Cables and lever pivots .... Harley-Davidson Super Oil or equivalent
Brake pedal/shift lever pivots .... Medium weight, lithium-based multi-purpose grease
*Some models use permanently sealed swingarm bearings, which require no lubrication (see Chapter 5).

1

Component locations - right-hand side (Softail FXSTF shown)

1	Engine oil tank filler cap	4	Rear master cylinder brake fluid	7	Transmission oil drain plug
2	Front master cylinder brake fluid		reservoir	8	Battery (under seat)
	reservoir	5	Air cleaner	9	Engine oil tank drain plug
3	Right fork oil drain screw	6	Transmission oil filler plug	10	Right drivebelt adjuster

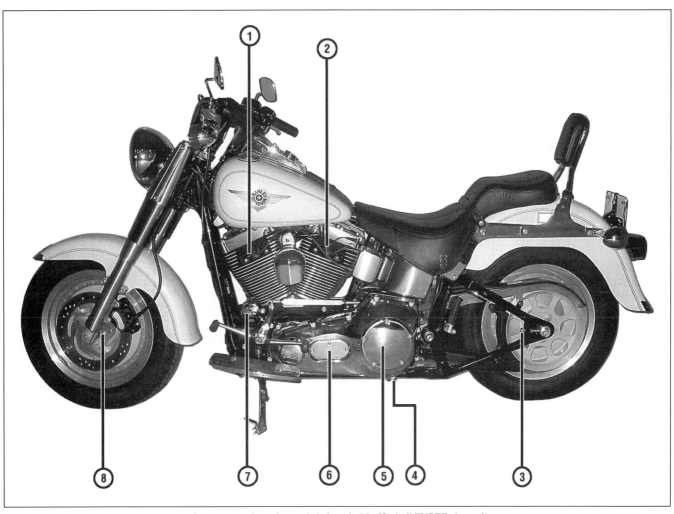

Component locations - left-hand side (Softail FXSTF shown)

1	Front cylinder spark plug	4	Primary chaincase drain plug	7	Engine oil filter
2	Rear cylinder spark plug	5	Clutch inspection cover	8	Left fork drain plug
3	Left drivebelt adjuster	6	Primary chain inspection cover		

1

1 Harley Twin Cam 88 Routine maintenance intervals

Note: *The pre-ride inspection outlined in the owner's manual covers checks and maintenance that should be carried out on a daily basis. It's condensed and included here to remind you of its importance. Always perform the pre-ride inspection at every maintenance interval (in addition to the procedures listed). The intervals listed below are the shortest intervals recommended by the manufacturer for each particular operation during the model years covered in this manual. Your owner's manual may have different intervals for your model.*

Daily or before riding

- ☐ Check the engine oil level
- ☐ Check the fuel level and inspect for leaks
- ☐ Check the operation of both brakes - also check the fluid level and look for leakage
- ☐ Check the tires for damage, the presence of foreign objects and correct air pressure
- ☐ Check the throttle for smooth operation and correct freeplay
- ☐ Check the operation of the clutch - make sure the freeplay is correct
- ☐ Make sure the steering operates smoothly, without looseness and without binding
- ☐ Check for proper operation of the headlight, taillight, brake light, turn signals, indicator lights, speedometer and horn
- ☐ Make sure the sidestand returns to its fully up position and stays there under spring pressure
- ☐ Make sure the engine STOP switch works properly
- ☐ Check deflection of the drivebelt

After the initial 1,000 miles (1,600 km) (all except Springer models) or 500 miles (800 km) (Springer models)

This service is usually performed by a dealer service department, since the bike is still under warranty. It consists of all of the daily checks plus:

- ☐ All of the 5000 mile checks
- ☐ Springer rocker bearing inspection
- ☐ Fastener torque check
- ☐ Sidestand lubrication

Every 2,500 miles (4,000 km)

- ☐ Check engine oil level (Section 3)
- ☐ Check transmission oil level (Section 3)
- ☐ Check the drivebelt tension (Section 4)
- ☐ Inspect the brake pads and discs (Section 5)
- ☐ Check the brake lines for leaks (Section 6)
- ☐ Check the brake pedal position and freeplay (Section 7)
- ☐ Inspect the wheels and tires (Section 8)

- ☐ Inspect and clean the air filter element (Section 9)
- ☐ Check/adjust the throttle operation and freeplay (Section 10)
- ☐ Check/adjust choke knob tension (carbureted models) (Section 11)
- ☐ Check the fuel system for leaks (Section 12)
- ☐ Check the evaporative emission control system (California models) (Section 13)
- ☐ Check the external oil lines for leaks (Section 14)
- ☐ Check tightness of all fasteners except head bolts (Section 15)
- ☐ Inspect the battery (Section 16)
- ☐ Operate and check all electrical equipment (Section 17)

Every 5,000 miles (8,000 km)

- ☐ Change the engine oil and filter (Section 18)
- ☐ Change the transmission oil (Section 19)
- ☐ Change the primary chaincase oil (Section 20)
- ☐ Adjust the clutch freeplay (Section 21)
- ☐ Check the primary chain deflection (Section 22)
- ☐ Check the drivebelt and sprockets for wear (Section 23)
- ☐ Check the brake fluid level and condition (Section 24)
- ☐ Lubricate the steering head bearings through the grease fitting (Section 25)
- ☐ Lubricate the cables and lever pivots (Section 26)
- ☐ Inspect the spark plugs (Section 27)
- ☐ Check/adjust the idle speed (Section 28)

Every 10,000 miles (16,000 km)

All of the items above plus:

- ☐ Replace the spark plugs (Section 27)
- ☐ Check the exhaust system for leaks and check the tightness of the fasteners (Section 29)
- ☐ Adjust the steering head bearings (Section 30)
- ☐ Adjust the rocker bearings (Springer models) (Section 31)
- ☐ Check the suspension (Section 32)

Every 20,000 miles (32,000 km)

- ☐ Inspect the fuel supply valve filter screen (carbureted models) (Section 33)
- ☐ Change the fork oil (Section 34)

Every 30,000 miles (48,000 km)

- ☐ Replace the fuel filter (fuel injected models) (Section 35)

2 Introduction to tune-up and routine maintenance

1   This Chapter covers in detail the checks and procedures necessary for the tune-up and routine maintenance of your motorcycle. Section 1 includes the routine maintenance schedule, which is designed to keep the machine in proper running condition and prevent possible problems. The remaining Sections contain detailed procedures for carrying out the items listed on the maintenance schedule, as well as additional maintenance information designed to increase reliability.

2   Since routine maintenance plays such an important role in the safe and efficient operation of your motorcycle, it is presented here as a comprehensive checklist. For the rider who does all of the bike's maintenance, these lists outline the procedures and checks that should be done on a routine basis.

3   Maintenance and safety information is printed on decals in various locations on the motorcycle **(see illustration)**. If the information on the decals differs from that included here, use the information on the decal.

4   Deciding where to start or plug into the routine maintenance schedule depends on several factors. If you have a motorcycle whose warranty has recently expired, and if it has been maintained according to the warranty standards, you may want to pick up routine maintenance as it coincides with the next mileage or calendar interval. If you have owned the machine for some time but have never performed any maintenance on it, then you may want to start at the nearest interval and include some additional procedures to ensure that nothing important is overlooked. If you have just had a major engine overhaul, then you may want to start the maintenance routine from the beginning. If you have a used machine and have no knowledge of its history or maintenance record, you may desire to combine all the checks into one large service initially and then settle into the maintenance schedule prescribed.

5   The Sections which outline the inspection and maintenance procedures are written as step-by-step comprehensive guides to the performance of the work. They explain in detail each of the routine inspections and maintenance procedures on the check list. References to additional information in applicable Chapters are also included and should not be overlooked.

2.3 Decals in various locations include safety, emissions and maintenance information

6   Before beginning any maintenance or repair, the machine should be cleaned thoroughly, especially around the oil filter, spark plugs, valve covers, side covers, carburetor or induction module, etc. Cleaning will help ensure that dirt does not contaminate the engine and will allow you to detect wear and damage that could otherwise easily go unnoticed.

Every 2,500 miles (4,000 km)

3 Fluid levels - check

Engine oil

1   Engine oil level should be checked before every ride as described in *Daily (pre-ride) checks* at the beginning of this manual, as well as at the specified maintenance intervals.

Transmission oil

2   Transmission oil level should be checked at the specified maintenance intervals.

3   Support the bike securely upright.

4   Unscrew the transmission dipstick and pull it out **(see illustration)**.

5   Wipe the dipstick clean with a lint-free cloth and put it back in the hole (just let it rest on the threads, don't screw it in).

6   Pull the dipstick out and check fluid level **(see illustration)**. If it's below the A

(add) mark, add oil of the type listed in this Chapter's Specifications. Don't overfill the transmission.

7   Check the dipstick O-ring for damage and replace it if necessary.

8   Thread the dipstick into the hole and tighten it to the torque listed in this Chapter's Specifications.

Brake fluid

9   Fluid level in the front and rear brake master cylinders should be checked before every ride as described in *Daily (pre-ride) checks* at the beginning of this manual, as well as at the specified maintenance intervals.

4 Drivebelt - tension adjustment

1   Drivebelt tension should be checked, and adjusted if necessary before every ride as described in *Daily (pre-ride) checks* at the beginning of this manual, as well as at the specified maintenance intervals.

2   The tension should be checked and adjusted with the bike on the ground and weight equivalent to the rider on the seat. The belt should be cold, so don't check ten-

3.4 Unscrew the filler plug/dipstick from the transmission

3.6 Measure oil level on the dipstick scale

1

sion or make the adjustment right after the bike has been ridden.

3   Harley-Davidson recommends using a tension gauge to prevent the belt from being set too loose. This can allow the belt to jump one or more sprocket teeth, which will damage the belt.

4   To check belt tension, apply 10 lbs. (4.54 kg) upward pressure on the center of the belt run and measure the amount the belt moves (upper belt run on Softail; lower belt run on Dyna and Touring models). Write this measurement down.

5   Roll the bike to change the belt position and repeat the measurement along every few inches of the belt. Do this along the entire belt until you locate the tightest point (where the belt moves least). At this point, compare the measurement to the range listed in this Chapter's Specifications. On later Dyna models, the belt is visible through a slot in the belt guard.

6   If the belt is not within the specified range, adjust it.

Softail models

7   Pull the clip out of the axle nut, then loosen the nut (see illustration).

8   Loosen the locknut on each belt adjuster bolt.

9   Turn the belt adjuster bolts in equal amounts until the belt tension is correct, then tighten the locknuts. Be sure to tighten or loosen the adjusters evenly so the rear wheel isn't cocked sideways.

10   Tighten the rear axle locknut to the initial torque listed in this Chapter's Specifications, then install the clip.

11   Try to install the clip through the axle and locknut. If necessary, tighten the nut just enough to align the holes so the clip can be installed, but don't exceed the maximum torque listed in this Chapter's Specifications.

 Warning: Overtightening the nut could cause the rear wheel bearings to seize, resulting in loss of control of the motorcycle.

Dyna and 1999 through 2001 Touring models

12   Pull the clip out of the axle nut, then loosen the nut (see illustration).

13   Turn the belt adjuster bolts (the Allen bolts at the rear of the swingarm) in equal amounts until the belt tension is correct, then tighten the locknuts. Be sure to tighten or loosen the adjusters evenly so the rear wheel isn't cocked sideways.

14   Check the belt tension. On Dyna models so equipped, use the measuring lines next to the hole in the belt guard (see illustration).

15   Tighten the rear axle locknut to the initial torque listed in this Chapter's Specifications, then install the clip.

16   Try to install the clip through the axle and locknut. If necessary, tighten the nut just

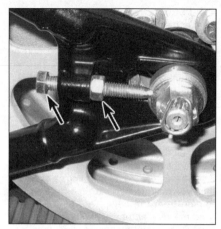

4.7 On Softails, loosen the locknut (left arrow) and turn the drivebelt adjuster (right arrow)

enough to align the holes so the clip can be installed, but don't exceed the maximum torque listed in this Chapter's Specifications.

 Warning: Overtightening the nut could cause the rear wheel bearings to seize, resulting in loss of control of the motorcycle.

2002 and later Touring models

17   Before you start, buy a new clip for the right-hand end of the axle. The clip must be replaced whenever it's removed.

18   Remove the right saddlebag and muffler (see Chapters 7 and 4).

19   Pry the clip out of the right-hand end of the axle. Loosen the axle nut, then retighten it to 15 to 20 ft-lbs (20 to 27 Nm).

20   If the belt is too loose, adjust it with the motorcycle on the ground. If it's too tight, jack up the motorcycle and support it securely upright with the rear wheel off the ground.

21   Place a socket over the welded nut on

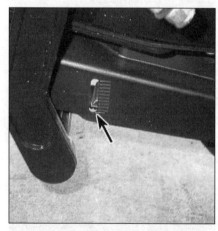

4.14 Later Dyna models have a viewing slot to check belt tension - each line on the scale equals 1/8-inch (3 mm) of freeplay

4.12 On Dynas, remove the clip from the end of the axle and loosen the axle nut (left arrow), then turn the adjuster (right arrow)

the left end of the axle. Turning the nut will rotate the snail-type belt tension adjusters on both sides of the axle (see illustration).

22   Turn the nut to set the belt tension correctly. If you loosened the belt, push the rear wheel forward so the adjusters once again touch their contact points on the ends of the axle.

23   If the motorcycle is jacked up, lower it to the ground.

24   Recheck belt tension (note that the specified tension is different, depending on whether the motorcycle is jacked up or resting on the rear wheel). If it's incorrect, repeat the above steps to adjust it.

25   Hold the axle securely with a socket on the left end and tighten the nut on the right end to the torque listed in this Chapter's Specifications. **Note:** *Don't move the axle forward or rearward while tightening, or the whole procedure will have to be done over.*

26   Install a new clip on the end of the axle.

27   Install all components removed for access.

4.21 On Touring models, drivebelt tension is adjusted by rotating the snail-type adjusters on each side of the axle (arrow)

5.2a Look at the pad friction material to see if it's worn - this is a front four-piston caliper . . .

5.2b . . . and this is a rear caliper

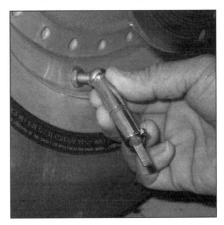

8.4 Use an accurate gauge to check the air pressure in the tires

5 Brake pads - wear check

1   Disc brake pads should be checked at the recommended intervals and replaced with new ones when worn beyond the limit listed in this Chapter's Specifications.
2   Brake pad wear can be checked without removing the calipers **(see illustrations)**. The brake pads should have at least the specified minimum amount of lining material remaining on the metal backing plate.
3   If the pads are worn excessively, they must be replaced with new ones (see Chapter 6).

6 Brake system - general check

1   A routine general check of the brakes will ensure that any problems are discovered and remedied before the rider's safety is jeopardized.
2   Check the brake lever and pedal for loose connections, excessive play, bends, and other damage. Replace any damaged parts with new ones (see Chapter 6).
3   Make sure all brake fasteners are tight. Check the brake pads for wear (see Section 5) and make sure the fluid level in the reservoir is correct (see *Daily (pre-ride) checks* at the beginning of this manual). Look for leaks at the hose connections and check for cracks in the hoses. If the lever is spongy, bleed the brakes as described in Chapter 6.
4   Make sure the brake light operates when the front brake lever is depressed.
5   Make sure the brake light is activated when the rear brake pedal is depressed.
6   Neither brake light switch is adjustable. If a front switch fails to operate properly, replace it with a new one (see Chapter 8). If a rear switch, which detects hydraulic pressure in the rear brake line, fails to operate

properly, bleed the rear brake (see Chapter 6). If that doesn't solve the problem, replace the switch with a new one (see Chapter 8).

7 Brake pedal position and play - check

1   Rear brake pedal position and play are not adjustable.
2   Operate the brake pedal and check for excessive play. If you find this problem, bleed the brakes (see Chapter 6). If that doesn't help, overhaul the rear master cylinder and caliper (see Chapter 6).
3   On Dyna models, you can make minor adjustments in pedal height for rider preference by loosening the locknut on the master cylinder pushrod and rotating the pushrod.

> ⚠ **Warning: Do not allow more than six threads of the pushrod to be exposed.**

8 Tires/wheels - general check

1   Routine tire and wheel checks should be made with the realization that your safety depends to a great extent on their condition.
2   Check the tires carefully for cuts, tears, embedded nails or other sharp objects and excessive wear. Operation of the motorcycle with excessively worn tires is extremely hazardous, as traction and handling are directly affected. Check the wear indicators molded into the tire, referring to the illustration in *Daily (pre-ride) checks* at the beginning of this manual, and replace worn tires with new ones when the indicators are worn away.
Note: *In the UK, tread depth must be at least 1 mm over 3/4 of the tread breadth all the way around the tire, with no bald patches.*
3   Repair or replace punctured tires as soon as damage is noted. Do not try to patch

a torn tire, as wheel balance and tire reliability may be impaired.
4   Check the tire pressures when the tires are cold and keep them properly inflated **(see illustration)**. Proper air pressure will increase tire life and provide maximum stability and ride comfort. Keep in mind that low tire pressures may cause the tire to slip on the rim or come off, while high tire pressures will cause abnormal tread wear and unsafe handling.

Cast wheels

5   The cast wheels used on some models are virtually maintenance free, but they should be kept clean and checked periodically for cracks and other damage. Never attempt to repair damaged cast wheels; they must be replaced with new ones.
6   Check the valve stem locknuts to make sure they are tight. Also, make sure the valve stem cap is in place and tight. If it is missing, install a new one made of metal or hard plastic.

Wire wheels

7   The wire wheels used on some models should be checked periodically for cracks, bending, loose spokes and corrosion. Never

8.7 Check the tension of the spokes periodically, but don't over-tighten them

1

9.1 Remove the center screw and take off the air cleaner cover . . .

9.2 . . . then remove the three screws, the bracket and the filter element

9.3 Wipe the inside of the housing with a clean rag, then place a clean rag in the opening to keep out dirt and foreign objects

attempt to repair damaged wheels; they must be replaced with new ones. Loose spokes can be tightened with a spoke wrench **(see illustration)**, but be careful not to overtighten and distort the wheel rim.

9 Air filter element - servicing

1   Remove the cover screw and lift off the air filter cover and its O-ring **(see illustration)**.
2   Remove the Torx screws and take off the air filter bracket **(see illustration)**. Disconnect the breather tubes from the back of the element, then remove the element and gasket.
3   Wipe out the housing and cover with a clean rag, then place a clean rag in the carburetor or throttle body opening to keep out dirt **(see illustration)**.
4   Wash the element in soap and lukewarm water. Don't tap the element on a hard surface to remove the dirt. Finish cleaning by blowing low-pressure compressed air from the inside of the element to the outside, or else let it air dry.

5   After cleaning, hold the element up to a bright light. The light should pass evenly through the element (any darker areas are still dirty).
6   Check the gasket, cover O-ring and breather tubes for damage or deterioration and replace them as needed. If you're working on a carbureted California model, make sure the door for the evaporative emission control system moves freely.
7   Reinstall the filter by reversing the removal procedure. Make sure the element is seated properly and securely connected to the breather tubes in the filter housing before installing the cover.

10 Throttle operation/grip freeplay - check and adjustment

Check

1   With the engine stopped, make sure the throttle grip rotates easily from fully closed to fully open with the front wheel turned at various angles. The grip should return automatically from fully open to fully closed when released. If the throttle sticks, check the

throttle cables for cracks or kinks in the housings. Also, make sure the inner cables are clean and well-lubricated.
2   Check for a small amount of freeplay at the grip and compare the freeplay to the value listed in this Chapter's Specifications.

Adjustment

Note: *These motorcycles use two throttle cables - a throttle (pull) cable and an idle (push) cable.*
3   Start freeplay adjustments at the throttle end of the cables. Loosen the locknut on each cable where it leaves the handlebar **(see illustrations)**. Turn the adjusters to eliminate all throttle grip play, but leave the locknuts loose for the time being.
4   While holding the throttle wide open, make sure the cam on the throttle pulley just touches its stop. If necessary, turn the adjuster on the throttle cable to change the position of the throttle pulley cam. Once this is done, tighten the throttle cable locknut.
5   Release the throttle grip and turn the handlebars all the way to full right lock.
6   Turn the idle cable adjuster at the handlebar while watching the cable housing at

10.3a Pull back the rubber covers from the throttle cable adjusters (arrow) . . .

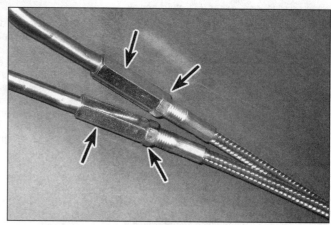

10.3b . . . loosen the locknuts (right arrows) and turn the adjusters (left arrows)

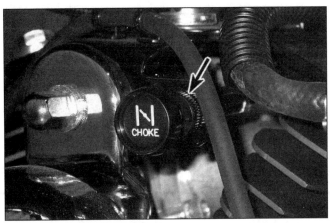

11.1 Loosen the hex nut behind the bracket, then turn the
knurled nut (arrow) to set choke knob tension

12.1 Check the fuel valve (carbureted models) and
its line for leaks

the carburetor or throttle body. The adjustment is correct when the cable housing just touches the spring inside the cable tube on the cable bracket.

7   Make sure the throttle pulley returns to idle when the throttle grip is in the closed throttle position.

 Warning: Turn the handlebars all the way through their travel with the engine idling. Idle speed should not change. If it does, the cables may be routed incorrectly. Correct this condition before riding the bike.

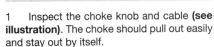
11 Choke knob (carbureted models) - check

1   Inspect the choke knob and cable **(see illustration)**. The choke should pull out easily and stay out by itself.
2   If the knob doesn't operate correctly, loosen the hex nut behind the mounting bracket. Hold the cable with a wrench on the cable flats and adjust the knob's tension with the plastic knurled nut behind the knob. If this doesn't help, check the plunger bushing for wear or damage and replace as necessary. Don't lubricate the cable.

12 Fuel system - check

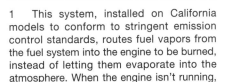

Warning 1: Gasoline is extremely flammable, so take extra precautions when you work on any part of the fuel system. Don't smoke or allow open flames or bare light bulbs near the work area, and don't work in a garage where a natural gas-type appliance (such as a water heater or clothes dryer) is present. If you spill any fuel on your skin, rinse it off immediately with soap and water. When

you perform any kind of work on the fuel system, wear safety glasses and have a fire extinguisher suitable for a class B type fire (flammable liquids) on hand.

Warning 2: Before disconnecting any fuel lines on fuel injected models, relieve fuel system pressure (see Chapter 3).

1   Check the fuel tank, the fuel supply valve (carbureted models only), the lines and the carburetor or fuel rail and injectors for leaks and evidence of damage **(see illustration)**. **Note:** *Injectors may also leak fuel into the engine, which won't be visible from the outside. Refer to Chapter 3 to test the injectors for internal leaks.*
2   If carburetor gaskets are leaking, the carburetor(s) should be disassembled and rebuilt by referring to Chapter 3.
3   If the fuel supply valve is leaking on carbureted models, tightening the screws may help. If leakage persists, the valve should be disassembled and repaired or replaced with a new one.
4   If the fuel lines are cracked or otherwise deteriorated, replace them with new ones.

13 Evaporative emission control system (California models only) - check

1   This system, installed on California models to conform to stringent emission control standards, routes fuel vapors from the fuel system into the engine to be burned, instead of letting them evaporate into the atmosphere. When the engine isn't running, vapors are stored in a carbon canister.

Hoses
2   To begin the inspection of the system, remove the seat and fuel tank (see Chapters 3 and 7 if necessary). Inspect the hoses from the fuel tank, carburetor or throttle body and air cleaner housing (carbureted models) to the canister for cracking, kinks or other signs of deterioration.

Component inspection
3   Label and disconnect the hoses, then remove the canister from the machine (see Chapter 3).
4   Inspect the canister for cracks or other signs of damage. Tip the canister so the nozzles point down. If fuel runs out of the canister, the liquid/vapor separator is probably bad. The fuel inside the canister has probably caused damage, so it would be a good idea to replace it.

14 External oil lines - check

1   Follow the external lines from the oil tank to the engine and check them for leaks.
2   If the bike is equipped with rubber hoses, replace them if they're cracked or deteriorated. Use new hose clamps.
3   If leaks can be seen on a bike equipped with metal lines, disconnect the lines with a hose disconnection tool (see Chapter 2) and check the fitting O-rings. Replace as needed.

15 Fasteners - check

1   Since vibration of the machine tends to loosen fasteners, all nuts, bolts, screws, etc. should be periodically checked for proper tightness.
2   Pay particular attention to the following:

Spark plugs
Oil drain plugs
Oil filter
Gearshift lever
Footpegs and sidestand
Engine mount bolts
Shock absorber mount bolts
Front axle and clamp bolt(s)
Rear axle nut

3   If a torque wrench is available, use it along with the torque specifications at the beginning of this, or other, Chapters.

1

16 Battery - inspection

⚠️ **Warning: Be extremely careful when handling or working around the battery. The electrolyte is very caustic and an explosive gas (hydrogen) is given off when the battery is charging.**

Maintenance free battery

1   All of these motorcycles except 1999 Touring models use a maintenance free battery. Do not open the cell caps at any time. If the electrolyte level is low, replace the battery.
2   Remove the seat (see Chapter 7). If you're working on a Dyna, remove the top cover from the battery box.
3   Check the top of the battery for dirt, electrolyte and the white material that indicates oxidation **(see illustration)**. If any of these are found, remove and clean the battery (see Chapter 8).
4   Check the terminals and cable ends for corrosion and damage. Clean or replace damaged parts. Make sure the cable ends are tight.
5   Check the battery case for damage, including cracks, warpage and leaks. Replace the battery if any of these problems are found.

Fillable battery

⚠️ **Warning: Be extremely careful when handling or working around the battery. The electrolyte is very caustic and an explosive gas (hydrogen) is given off when the battery is charging.**

6   This procedure applies to fillable batteries, installed as original equipment on 1999 Touring models. The maintenance-free batteries used on other models do not require periodic checks of the electrolyte level.
7   Remove the seat (see Chapter 7).
8   Unbolt and move aside any electrical components mounted near the battery that obstruct battery removal, then unbolt the battery retainer and lift it off. Note the position of the battery vent tube.
9   Remove the bolts securing the battery cables to the battery terminals (remove the negative cable first, positive cable last). Pull the battery straight up to remove it. The elec-

16.3 Check the top of the battery, the cable end and the terminals for corrosion or dirt

16.12 On 1999 Touring models, check the specific gravity with a hydrometer

trolyte level will now be visible through the translucent battery case - it should be between the Upper and Lower level marks.
10   If it is low, remove the cell caps and fill each cell to the upper level mark with distilled water. Do not use tap water (except in an emergency), and do not overfill. The cell holes are quite small, so it may help to use a plastic squeeze bottle with a small spout to add the water. If the level is within the marks on the case, additional water is not necessary.
11   Next, check the specific gravity of the electrolyte in each cell with a small hydrometer made especially for motorcycle batteries. These are available from most dealer parts departments or motorcycle accessory stores.
12   Remove the caps, draw some electrolyte from the first cell into the hydrometer **(see illustration)** and note the specific gravity. Compare the reading to the Specifications listed in this Chapter. **Note:** *Add 0.004 points to the reading for every 10-degrees F above 68-degrees F (20-degrees C) - subtract 0.004 points from the reading for every 10-degrees below 68-degrees F (20-degrees C).* Return the electrolyte to the appropriate cell and repeat the check for the remaining cells. When the check is complete, rinse the hydrometer thoroughly with clean water.
13   If the specific gravity of the electrolyte in each cell is as specified, the battery is in good condition and is apparently being charged by the machine's charging system.
14   If the specific gravity is low, the battery is not fully charged. This may be due to cor-

roded battery terminals, a dirty battery case, a malfunctioning charging system, or loose or corroded wiring connections. On the other hand, it may be that the battery is worn out, especially if the machine is old, or that infrequent use of the motorcycle prevents normal charging from taking place.
15   Be sure to correct any problems and charge the battery if necessary. Refer to Chapter 8 for additional battery maintenance and charging procedures.
16   Install the battery cell caps, tightening them securely. Reconnect the cables to the battery, attaching the positive cable first and the negative cable last. Be very careful not to pinch or otherwise restrict the battery vent tube, as the battery may build up enough internal pressure during normal charging system operation to explode.

17 Electrical equipment - check

1   Turn on the lights and make sure all of them work.
2   Operate the turn signals and make sure all of them blink steadily.
3   Sound the horn.
4   With the key on, operate the brake pedal and lever separately. Each of them should illuminate the brake light.
5   Check the instruments and indicator lamps for correct operation.
6   If any problems are found, repair them (see Chapter 8).

Every 5,000 miles (8,000 km)

18 Engine oil and filter - change

1   Consistent routine oil and filter changes

are the single most important maintenance procedure you can perform on a motorcycle. The oil not only lubricates the internal parts of the engine, but it also acts as a coolant, a cleaner, a sealant, and a protectant. Because of these demands, the oil takes a terrific amount of abuse and should be

replaced often with new oil of the recommended grade and type. Saving a little money on the difference in cost between a good oil and a cheap oil won't pay off if the engine is damaged.
2   Before changing the oil and filter, warm up the engine so the oil will drain easily. Be

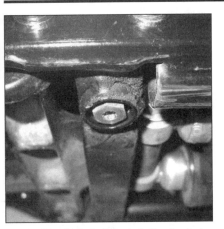

18.4a The Softail oil tank drain plug is in the frame

18.4b The Dyna engine oil drain plug (lower arrow) and transmission oil drain plug (upper arrow) are both mounted in the engine oil tank below the transmission

18.4c The Touring model engine oil drain plug (right) and transmission drain plug (left) are mounted in the oil tank; don't confuse the engine drain plug with the pipe plug next to it

careful when draining the oil, as the exhaust pipes, the engine, and the oil itself can cause severe burns.

3   Prop the motorcycle upright over a clean drain pan. Remove the oil filler cap from the oil tank to act as a reminder that there is no oil in the engine (see *Daily (pre-ride) checks* at the front of this manual for dipstick location if necessary.

4   Remove the oil tank drain plug from the underside of the frame (Softail), from the left rear corner of the oil pan (Dyna) or from the left front corner of the oil pan (Touring models) and allow the oil to drain into the pan **(see illustrations)**. **Note:** *The transmission drain pan on Dyna and Touring models is on the right-hand side of the oil pan, about halfway along its length. Don't confuse this with the engine oil drain plug.* Discard the sealing washer on the drain plug; it should be replaced whenever the plug is removed.

5   As the oil is draining, remove the oil filter **(see illustration)**. If additional maintenance is planned for this time period, check or service another component while the oil is allowed to drain completely.

6   Wipe any remaining oil off the filter sealing area of the crankcase.

7   Check the condition of the drain plug threads.

8   Coat the gasket on a new filter with clean engine oil **(see illustration)**. Install the filter and tighten it to the amount listed in this Chapter's Specifications.

9   Slip a new sealing washer over the drain plug, then install and tighten the plug to the torque listed in this Chapter's Specifications. Avoid overtightening, as damage to the oil tank will result.

10   Before refilling the engine, check the old oil carefully. If the oil was drained into a clean pan, small pieces of metal or other material can be easily detected. If the oil is very metallic colored, then the engine is experiencing wear from break-in (new engine) or from insufficient lubrication. If there are flakes or chips of metal in the oil, then something is drastically wrong internally and the engine will have to be disassembled for inspection and repair.

11   If the inspection of the oil turns up nothing unusual, refill the oil tank or pan to the proper level with the recommended oil and install the filler cap. Start the engine and let it run for two or three minutes. Shut it off, wait a few minutes, then check the oil level. If necessary, add more oil to bring the level up

to the Maximum mark. Check around the drain plug and filter housing for leaks.

12   The old oil drained from the engine cannot be reused in its present state and should be disposed of. Check with your local refuse disposal company, disposal facility or environmental agency to see whether they will accept the oil for recycling. Don't pour used oil into drains or onto the ground. After the oil has cooled, it can be drained into a suitable container (capped plastic jugs, topped bottles, milk cartons, etc.) for transport to one of these disposal sites.

19 Transmission oil - change

1

1   Before changing the transmission oil, warm up the transmission by riding the bike so the oil will drain easily. Be careful when draining the oil, as the exhaust pipes, the engine, and the oil itself can cause severe burns.

2   Prop the motorcycle upright over a clean drain pan. Remove the transmission oil

18.5 Unscrew the oil filter with a filter wrench

18.8 Smear a film of clean oil onto the gasket surface

19.3 The Softail transmission drain plug is in the underside of the transmission

filler cap to act as a reminder that there is no oil in the transmission.

3   Remove the transmission drain plug from the underside of the transmission and allow the oil to drain into the pan **(see illustration 18.4b, 18.4c or the accompanying illustration)**. Discard the sealing washer on the drain plug; it should be replaced whenever the plug is removed.

4   Check the condition of the drain plug threads.

5   Slip a new O-ring over the drain plug, then install and tighten the plug to the torque listed in this Chapter's Specifications. Avoid overtightening, as damage to the transmission will result.

6   Before refilling the engine, check the old oil carefully. If the oil was drained into a clean pan, small pieces of metal or other material can be easily detected. If the oil is very metallic colored, then the transmission is experiencing wear from break-in (new transmission) or from insufficient lubrication. If there are flakes or chips of metal in the oil, then something is drastically wrong internally and the transmission will have to be disassembled for inspection and repair.

7   If the inspection of the oil turns up nothing unusual, refill the transmission to the proper level with the recommended oil. Place the filler cap/dipstick in the hole (don't screw it in), then remove it and check the oil level. If necessary, add more oil to bring the level up to the F mark on the dipstick. Check around the drain plug for leaks.

8   The old oil drained from the transmission cannot be reused in its present state and should be disposed of. Check with your local refuse disposal company, disposal facility or environmental agency to see whether they will accept the oil for recycling. Don't pour used oil into drains or onto the ground. After the oil has cooled, it can be drained into a suitable container (capped plastic jugs, topped bottles, milk cartons, etc.) for transport to one of these disposal sites.

20 Primary chaincase oil - change

1   Before changing the chaincase oil, warm up the oil by riding the bike so the oil will drain easily. Be careful when draining the oil, as the exhaust pipes, the engine, and the oil itself can cause severe burns.

2   Prop the motorcycle upright over a clean drain pan. Remove the clutch inspection cover (see Section 21).

3   Remove the chaincase drain plug (from the underside or bottom side of the chaincase depending on model)and allow the oil to drain into the pan **(see illustration)**.

4   Check the condition of the drain plug threads. Also look for metallic particles on the drain plug magnet; if there are many, then something is wrong internally and the chain-

20.3 The primary chaincase drain plug is in the underside (shown) on some models; on other models it's in the side of the chaincase next to the bottom

case cover will have to be removed for inspection and repair. Also check the old oil carefully. If the oil was drained into a clean pan, small pieces of metal or other material can be easily detected. If the oil is very metallic colored, then the chaincase components are experiencing wear from break-in (new components) or from insufficient lubrication.

5   If there are pieces of fiber-like material in the oil, the clutch is experiencing excessive wear and should be checked.

6   Install and tighten the plug until it protrudes the distance listed in this Chapter's Specifications. Avoid overtightening, as damage to the chaincase will result.

7   If the inspection of the oil turns up nothing unusual, refill the chaincase to the proper level with the recommended oil. Pour the new oil in through the inspection cover opening, referring to this Chapter's Specifications for the amount. The level is correct when you can see the oil between the clutch and the chaincase cover **(see illustration)**. The top of the oil should be level with the bottom of the clutch diaphragm spring.

8   Reinstall the clutch inspection cover (see Section 21).

9   The old oil drained from the transmission cannot be reused in its present state and

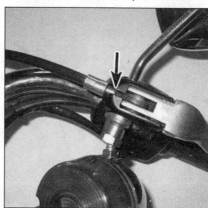

21.2 Pull on the cable and measure the clearance between the cable end and bracket

20.7 The chaincase oil level is correct when the oil is visible between the clutch and chaincase, even with the bottom of the clutch diaphragm spring (arrow)

should be disposed of. Check with your local refuse disposal company, disposal facility or environmental agency to see whether they will accept the oil for recycling. Don't pour used oil into drains or onto the ground. After the oil has cooled, it can be drained into a suitable container (capped plastic jugs, topped bottles, milk cartons, etc.) for transport to one of these disposal sites.

21 Clutch - check and adjustment

1   Correct clutch freeplay is necessary to ensure proper clutch operation and reasonable clutch service life. Freeplay normally changes because of cable stretch and clutch wear, so it should be checked and adjusted periodically.

2   Clutch cable freeplay is checked at the handlebar end of the cable. Slowly pull on the cable until resistance is felt, then note how far the cable end has moved away from the clutch lever bracket **(see illustration)**. Compare this distance with the value listed in this Chapter's Specifications. Too little freeplay may result in the clutch not engag-

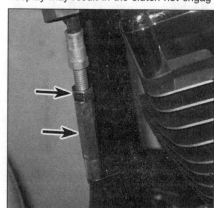

21.3 Loosen the locknut (arrow) and turn the midline cable adjuster to adjust the clutch cable

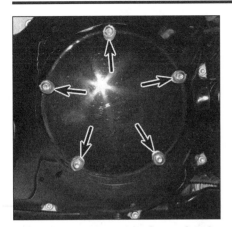

21.4 Remove the screws (arrows) and take the clutch inspection cover off the primary chaincase

21.5 Loosen the locknut with a box wrench and turn the adjusting screw with an Allen wrench

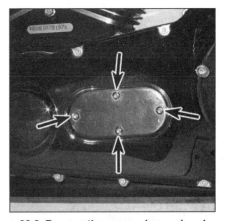

22.2 Remove the screws (arrows) and take the primary chain inspection cover off the chaincase (Softail shown)

ing completely. If there is too much freeplay, the clutch might not release fully.

3   Loosen the locknut on the mid-line cable adjuster, then loosen the mid-line cable adjuster as far as possible, so there is slack in the clutch cable **(see illustration)**.

4   Loosen the clutch cover screws evenly, in a criss-cross pattern, then remove the screws and clutch cover **(see illustration)**.

5   Loosen the locknut on the clutch adjusting screw, then turn the screw all the way in until it seats lightly (don't bottom the screw hard) **(see illustration)**. Back out the screw one-half to one full turn, then hold the screw with an Allen wrench and tighten the locknut to the torque listed in this Chapter's Specifications.

6   Pull the clutch lever all the way to the handlebar, then release it. Do this three times to set the release mechanism.

7   Turn the mid-line cable adjuster away from the locknut to eliminate all play in the clutch lever. Check cable free-play as described in Step 2. If it's not within the range listed in this Chapter's Specifications, turn the mid-line cable adjuster to correct it.

8   If the proper amount of freeplay still can't be obtained, the cable must be replaced (see Chapter 2).

9   Once cable freeplay is correct, tighten the locknut on the mid-line cable adjuster and reposition the rubber boot.

10   Remove the sealing ring from the clutch cover and check it for damage or deterioration. Replace it if problems are found. If you're reusing the old sealing ring, wipe it clean of oil.

11   Install the sealing ring in the cover groove, then install the cover on the engine. Tighten the cover screws evenly, in a criss-cross pattern, to the torque listed in this Chapter's Specifications.

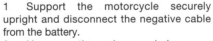

22 Primary chain deflection - check and adjustment

1   Support the motorcycle securely upright and disconnect the negative cable from the battery.

2   Unscrew the primary chain cover screws and take the cover off the chaincase **(see illustration)**. If necessary, pry it loose with a taped screwdriver, taking care not to scratch the chaincase surface.

3   Remove all traces of gasket from the chaincase opening, taking care not to let any

22.3 Remove all traces of the cover gasket and install a new one

pieces fall into the chaincase **(see illustration)**. The gasket must be replaced with a new one whenever the cover is removed.

4   Move the top run of the primary chain up-and-down and measure the amount of movement **(see illustration)**. If it's not within the range listed in this Chapter's Specifications, adjust the chain (the amount of movement varies depending on whether the engine is cold or hot).

5   To make the adjustment, loosen the center nut (but don't remove it) **(see illustra-**

22.4 Measure play along the top run of the chain (chaincase cover removed for clarity)

22.5 Adjust the primary chain by loosening the nut (arrow) and raising or lowering the tensioner pad

1

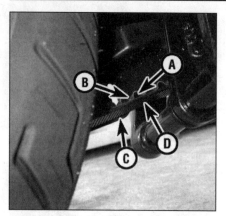

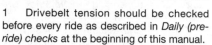

23.2 Check the belt for wear and damage

A) Hairline cracks and minor chipping in the internal areas of the teeth (not the outer surface) are acceptable, but check the belt often

B) Cracks or other damage to the tooth surfaces (B) require belt replacement

C) Frayed edges or a beveled outer edge are acceptable, but check the belt often

D) Stone damage in the center of the belt is acceptable, but replace the belt if stone damage is on the edge

tion). Slide the tensioner pad up or down until the chain has the correct amount of play, then tighten the center nut to the torque listed in this Chapter's Specifications.

6   Install the cover, using a new gasket, and tighten the screws to the torque listed in this Chapter's Specifications.

7   Reconnect the negative cable to the battery.

23 Rear drivebelt and sprockets - inspection

1   Drivebelt tension should be checked before every ride as described in Daily (pre-ride) checks at the beginning of this manual.

2   Place the transmission in neutral and support the bike with the rear wheel off the ground. Rotate the rear wheel slowly and check each belt and sprocket tooth for wear or damage (see illustration). The following conditions don't require belt replacement, but the belt should be given frequent, complete inspections:

a) Hairline cracks in the internal portion of the belt teeth (if the cracks don't penetrate the outer layer of the tooth - the layer that contacts the sprocket)

b) Minor chips in the internal tooth material at the ends of teeth

c) Frayed fabric along the edges, with strands of cord exposed

d) Bevel wear of the outer edge of the belt

e) Stone damage in the middle of the belt

3   The following conditions require belt replacement:

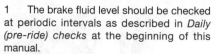

25.1 If the bike is equipped with a steering head grease fitting (arrow) , lubricate the steering head bearings with a grease gun

a) Cracks that penetrate the outer layer of a tooth

b) Missing teeth

c) Hook (uneven) wear of teeth

d) Outer layer of teeth worn through

e) Stone damage on the edge of the belt

4   Check the sprocket teeth for chips and other damage, especially if the damaged area has sharp edges. If the damage is severe enough that it has left a pattern on the belt, replace the belt and sprockets.

5   If teeth are missing or heavily damaged, replace the belt and sprockets.

6   Check the chrome surface of the sprockets for wear. If you can't tell whether the chrome has worn off, drag a sharp tool (knife tip or nail) across the surface in the valley between two teeth. If the chrome is good, it won't be visibly scratched by the tool. If the chrome has worn away and the aluminum is exposed, the tool will leave a shiny scratch. In this case, replace the belt and sprockets.

24 Brake fluid level and condition - check

1   The brake fluid level should be checked at periodic intervals as described in Daily (pre-ride) checks at the beginning of this manual.

2   Also check the brake fluid for signs of contamination. If the fluid is contaminated, bleed all of it out and replace it with new fluid (see Chapter 6).

25 Steering head bearings - lubrication

1   If the motorcycle is equipped with a grease fitting on the steering head in the frame, use it and a grease gun to lubricate the steering head bearings (see illustration).

2   On all models, the steering head bear-

26.3a Lubricating a cable with a pressure lube adapter (make sure the tool seats around the inner cable)

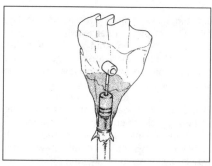

26.3b Lubricating a control cable with a makeshift funnel and motor oil

ings should be periodically removed and repacked with grease (see Chapter 5).

26 Lubrication - general

1   Since the controls, cables and various other components of a motorcycle are exposed to the elements, they should be lubricated periodically to ensure safe and trouble-free operation.

2   The footpegs, clutch and brake lever and sidestand pivot should be lubricated frequently. In order for the lubricant to be applied where it will do the most good, the component should be disassembled. However, if chain and cable lubricant is being used, it can be applied to the pivot joint gaps and will usually work its way into the areas where friction occurs. If motor oil or light grease is being used, apply it sparingly as it may attract dirt (which could cause the controls to bind or wear at an accelerated rate). Note: One of the best lubricants for the control lever pivots is a dry-film lubricant (available from many sources by different names).

3   The clutch cable should be separated from the handlebar lever and bracket before it is lubricated (see Chapter 2). This is a convenient time to inspect the bushing at the end of the cable. The cable should be treated with motor oil or a commercially

available cable lubricant which is specially formulated for use on motorcycle control cables. Small adapters for pressure lubricating the cables with spray can lubricants are available and ensure that the cable is lubricated along its entire length **(see illustration)**. If motor oil is being used, tape a funnel-shaped piece of heavy paper or plastic to the end of the cable, then pour oil into the funnel and suspend the end of the cable upright **(see illustration)**. Leave it until the oil runs down into the cable and out the other

end. When attaching the cable to the lever, be sure to lubricate the barrel-shaped fitting at the end with high-temperature grease. **Note:** *While you're lubricating, check the barrel end of the cable for fraying. Replace frayed cables*.

4   To lubricate the throttle cables, disconnect the cables at the lower end, then lubricate the cable with a pressure lube adapter **(see illustration 26.3a)**.

5   The speedometer cable (if equipped) should be removed from its housing and

lubricated with motor oil or cable lubricant.

6   Refer to Chapter 5 for the swingarm bearing lubrication procedure where applicable.

7   The brake pedal pivot on early Softail models has a grease nipple and can be lubricated with a grease gun. Later Softail models use permanently lubricated bushings. On all other models, remove the brake pedal and lubricate the shaft with a light coat of Harley-Davidson Wheel Bearing Grease or equivalent.

Every 10,000 miles (16,000 km)

27 Spark plugs - replacement

1   Disconnect the spark plug caps from the spark plugs **(see illustration)**. If available, use compressed air to blow any accumulated debris from around the spark plugs. Remove the plugs with a spark plug socket.

2   Inspect the electrodes for wear. Both the center and side electrodes should have square edges and the side electrode should be of uniform thickness. Look for excessive deposits and evidence of a cracked or chipped insulator around the center electrode. Compare your spark plugs to the color spark plug reading chart. Check the threads, the washer and the ceramic insulator body for cracks and other damage.

3   If the electrodes are not excessively worn, and if the deposits can be easily removed with electrical contact cleaner, the plugs can be re-gapped and reused (if no cracks or chips are visible in the insulator). If in doubt concerning the condition of the plugs, replace them with new ones, as the expense is minimal.

4   If you're going to reuse the plugs, use a fine file to square the edges of the electrodes.

5   Before installing new plugs, make sure they are the correct type and heat range. Check the gap between the electrodes, as they are not preset. For best results, use a wire-type gauge rather than a flat gauge to check the gap **(see illustration)**. If the gap must be adjusted, bend the side electrode only and be very careful not to chip or crack the insulator nose **(see illustration)**. Make sure the washer is in place before installing each plug.

6   Since the cylinder heads are made of aluminum, which is soft and easily damaged, thread the plugs into the heads by hand. Since the plugs are quite recessed, slip a short length of hose over the end of the plug to use as a tool to thread it into place. The hose will grip the plug well enough to turn it, but will start to slip if the plug begins to cross-thread in the hole - this will prevent damaged threads and the accompanying repair costs.

7   Once the plugs are finger tight, the job can be finished with a socket. If a torque wrench is available, tighten the spark plugs to the torque listed in this Chapter's Specifications. If you do not have a torque wrench,

tighten the plugs finger tight (until the washers bottom on the cylinder head) then use a wrench to tighten them an additional 1/4 turn. Regardless of the method used, do not over-tighten them.

8   Reconnect the spark plug caps.

28 Idle speed (carbureted models) - check and adjustment

1   The idle speed on carbureted models should be checked and adjusted at the specified maintenance intervals and when it is obviously too high or too low. Before adjusting the idle speed, make sure the spark plug gaps are correct. Also, turn the handlebars back-and-forth and see if the idle speed changes as this is done. If it does, the accelerator cable may not be adjusted correctly, or it may be worn out. Be sure to correct this problem before proceeding.

2   The engine should be at normal operating temperature, which is usually reached after 10 to 15 minutes of stop and go riding. Prop the motorcycle securely upright. Make

1

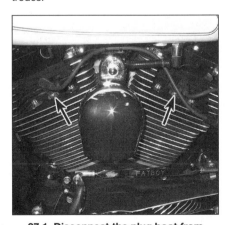

27.1 Disconnect the plug boot from each spark plug

27.5a Spark plug manufacturers recommend using a wire type gauge when checking the gap - if the wire doesn't slide between the electrodes with a slight drag, adjustment is required

27.5b To change the gap, bend the side electrode only, as indicated by the arrows, and be very careful not to crack or chip the ceramic insulator surrounding the center electrode

30.7 Loosen the lower triple clamp bolts (arrows) from the front of the bike (shown) or from the rear, depending on model

32.3 Check above and below the fork seals (arrows) for signs of oil leakage

sure the transmission is in Neutral.

3   If you have a scan tool (Harley-Davidson Scanalyzer or equivalent), connect it to the data link connector (see Chapter 3). If not, connect a tune-up tachometer to the negative terminal of the ignition coil.

4   Start the engine and let it idle. Make sure the choke knob is pushed all the way in.

5   Turn the idle speed screw with an idle adjuster (Harley tools HD-33413 and HD33413-2 or equivalent), until the idle speed listed in this Chapter's Specifications is obtained.

6   Snap the throttle open and shut a few times, then recheck the idle speed. If necessary, repeat the adjustment procedure.

7   If a smooth, steady idle can't be achieved, the fuel/air mixture may be incorrect. Refer to Chapter 3 for additional carburetor information.

29 Exhaust system - check

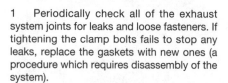

1   Periodically check all of the exhaust system joints for leaks and loose fasteners. If tightening the clamp bolts fails to stop any leaks, replace the gaskets with new ones (a procedure which requires disassembly of the system).

2   The exhaust pipe flange nuts at the cylinder heads are especially prone to loosening, which could cause damage to the head. Check them frequently and keep them tight.

30 Steering head bearings - check

1   These motorcycles are equipped with

tapered roller steering head bearings which can become dented, rough or loose during normal use of the machine. In extreme cases, worn or loose steering head bearings can cause steering wobble that is potentially dangerous.

2   To check the bearings, support the motorcycle securely upright. Block the machine so the front wheel is raised off the ground.

3   Point the wheel straight ahead and slowly move the handlebars from side-to-side. Dents or roughness in the bearing races will be felt and the bars will not move smoothly.

4   Next, grasp the fork legs and try to move the wheel forward and backward. Any looseness in the steering head bearings will be felt. If play is felt in the bearings, adjust them as described in Chapter 5.

5   If you're working on a Touring model, remove any non-stock equipment from the handlebars. Turn the handlebars all the way to the left, then let them go. The handlebars should swing by themselves to the right, back to the left, then back to the right (three swings total). The second and third swings can be partial, but there must be three. If the handlebars swing only once or twice, the bearings are too tight. If the handlebars swing four times, the bearings are too loose. In either case, adjust them as described in Chapter 5.

31 Rocker bearings (Softail Springer models) - adjustment

The rocker bearing turning torque on Softail Springer models should be adjusted at the specified interval. This is a somewhat complicated procedure that requires partial

disassembly of the fork legs. Refer to Chapter 5 for the procedure and pay careful attention to the safety warnings.

32 Suspension - check

1   The suspension components must be maintained in top operating condition to ensure rider safety. Loose, worn or damaged suspension parts decrease the vehicle's stability and control.

2   While standing alongside the motorcycle, lock the front brake and push on the handlebars to compress the forks several times. See if they move up-and-down smoothly without binding. If binding is felt, the forks should be disassembled and inspected as described in Chapter 5.

3   Carefully inspect the area around the fork seals for any signs of fork oil leakage (see illustration). If leakage is evident, the seals must be replaced as described in Chapter 5.

4   Check the tightness of all suspension nuts and bolts to be sure none have worked loose.

5   Inspect the rear shock absorbers for fluid leakage and tightness of the mounting nuts. If leakage is found, the shocks should be replaced. Replace both shocks as a pair.

6   Prop the bike securely upright. Grab the swingarm on each side, just ahead of the axle. Rock the swingarm from side to side - there should be no discernible movement at the rear. If there's a little movement or a slight clicking can be heard, make sure the pivot shaft nuts are tight. If the pivot nuts are tight but movement is still noticeable, the swingarm will have to be removed and the bearings replaced as described in Chapter 5.

Every 20,000 miles (32,000 km)

33 Fuel valve filter screen (carbureted models) - inspection and cleaning

1   Make sure the fuel control valve is in the Off position. Disconnect the hose from the fuel outlet fitting, then connect a length of hose to the fitting and place the end in an approved gasoline container.
2   Turn the fuel valve handle to reserve.
3   Disconnect the hose from the vacuum fitting and attach a vacuum pump to the fitting. Apply vacuum (1 to 10inches Hg) to the fitting, which will allow the gasoline from the tank to flow into the drain hose.
Caution: Don't apply any more vacuum than necessary to make the gasoline flow.
4   Unscrew the hex nut on the bottom of the fuel tank **(see illustration 12.1 and the accompanying illustration)**. The screen-type filter is attached to the fuel control valve **(see illustration)**.
5   Thoroughly clean the filter. It can be removed from the valve to be cleaned or

replaced if it's damaged.
6   If the fuel valve leaks, it's impractical to attempt to repair it. The complete unit should be replaced with a new one.
7   Apply thread sealant (Loctite Pipe Sealant with Teflon or equivalent) to the threads before installing the valve on the fuel tank.

34 Fork oil - replacement

1   This procedure applies to the damper rod forks used on Softails and all Dyna models except the FXDX and FXDX-T. Changing the fork oil on cartridge forks (used on FXDX,FXDX-T and the left fork leg on FLHT models) requires partial disassembly of the fork (see Chapter 5).
2   Prop the motorcycle securely upright. Position a jack with a block of wood on the jack head under the engine to support the motorcycle when the fork caps are removed.
3   Unscrew the fork tube caps (all except

Dyna FXDL) or center plugs (Dyna FXDL), taking care to release the spring pressure slowly **(see illustration)**.
4   Place a pan beneath the drain screw, then remove the drain screw and washer **(see illustration)**.

> ⚠️ *Warning: Do not allow the fork oil to contact the brake disc, pads or tire. If it does, clean the disc with brake system cleaner, wipe off the tire, and replace the pads with new ones before riding the motorcycle.*

5   After most of the oil has drained, slowly compress and release the forks to pump out the remaining oil. An assistant will most likely be required to do this procedure.
6   Check the drain screw gasket for damage and replace it if necessary. Clean the threads of the drain screw with solvent and let it dry, then install the screw and gasket, tightening it securely.
7   Pour the type and amount of fork oil, listed in this Chapter's Specifications, into the fork tube through the opening at the top **(see illustration)**. Remove the jack from

1

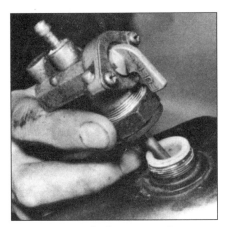

33.4a Loosen the large nut and remove the fuel valve from the tank . . .

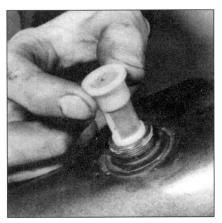

33.4b . . . to gain access to the screen-type filter for cleaning

34.3 Unscrew the cap from the top of the fork leg

34.4 Remove the drain plug (arrow) from the bottom of the fork leg

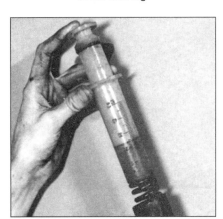

34.7 Fill the fork legs with the specified amount of fork oil (a baby bottle or measuring cup will make it easier to measure the amount)

under the engine and slowly pump the forks a few times to purge the air from the upper and lower chambers.

8   Check the plug seal and replace it if it's damaged or deteriorated **(see illustration)**. Install the cap, push it down against the spring pressure, and tighten it to the torque listed in this Chapter's Specifications.

9   Repeat the procedure on the other fork. Note that it is essential that the oil quantity and level is identical in each fork.

34.8 Replace the fork cap seal (arrow) if it's damaged

Every 30,000 miles (48,000 km)

35 Fuel filter (fuel injected models) - replacement

The fuel filter on fuel injected models is mounted inside the tank. It should be replaced at the specified maintenance interval (see Chapter 3).

Chapter 2 Part A
Engine

Contents

Degrees of difficulty

Easy, suitable for novice with little experience	**Fairly easy,** suitable for beginner with some experience	**Fairly difficult,** suitable for competent DIY mechanic	**Difficult,** suitable for experienced DIY mechanic	**Very difficult,** suitable for expert DIY or professional

Specifications

General

Bore	3.75 inches (95.25 mm)
Stroke	4.00 inches (101.6 mm)
Displacement..	88 cubic inches (1450 cc)
Cylinder compression pressure	
Reading..	90 psi (6 kN/m2) or more
Variation limit between cylinders.......................	10 per cent
Oil pressure..	30 to 38 psi (207 to 262 kN/m2) at 2000 rpm, engine warmed up to 230-degrees F (110-degrees C)

Rocker arms

End clearance	
Standard..	0.003 to 0.013 inches (0.08 to 0.33 mm)
Limit..	0.025 inch (0.635 mm)
Shaft-to-bushing clearance	
Standard..	0.0005 to 0.0020 inch (0.013 to 0.051 mm)
Limit..	0.0035 inch (0.089 mm)
Shaft-to-support plate clearance	
Standard..	0.0007 to 0.0022 inches
Limit..	0.0035 inch (0.089 mm)

Lifters

Clearance in bore
    Standard .... 0.0008 to 0.0020 inches (0.02 to 0.05 mm)
    Limit .... 0.003 inch (0.076 mm)
Roller fit (limit) .... 0.0015 inch (0.038 mm)
Roller end clearance limit .... 0.026 inch (0.660 mm)

Cylinder head, valves and valve springs

Cylinder head warpage limit .... 0.006 inch (0.0152 mm)
Valve seat width (intake and exhaust) .... 0.040 to 0.062 inch (1.02 to 1.58 mm)
Valve spring free length
    Inner .... 1.926 to 1.996 inches (48.9 to 50.7 mm)
    Outer .... 2.105 to 2.177 inches (53.47 to 55.30 mm)

Cylinders

Bore diameter limit
    Standard bore .... 3.753 inches (95.326 mm)
    0.005 inch (0.127 mm) oversize .... 3.758 inches (95.453 mm)
    0.010 inch (0.25 mm) oversize .... 3.763 inches (95.58 mm)
    0.020 inch (0.50 mm) oversize* .... 3.773 inches (95.834 mm)
    0.030 inch (0.76 mm) oversize* .... (3.783 inches (96.088 mm)
Taper limit .... 0.002 inch (0.05 mm)
Out-of-round limit .... 0.003 inch (0.08 m)
Gasket and base surface warpage limit .... 0.008 inches (0.20 mm)

*1999 through 2002 models only.

Pistons

Piston-to-cylinder clearance
    1999 through 2002
        Standard .... 0.0006 to 0.0016 inch (0.15 to 0.41 mm)
        Limit .... 0.0053 inch (0.135 mm)
    Early 2003*
        Standard .... 0.0006 to 0.0017 inch (0.015 to 0.043 mm)
        Limit .... 0.003 inch (0.076 mm)
    Late 2003* .... 0.0014 to 0.0025 inch (0.036 to 0.064 mm)
        Limit .... 0.003 inch (0.076 mm)

*Early and late pistons can be identified by the coating material on the piston skirt. On early 2003 pistons, the coating material is uninterrupted, with no patches of bare aluminum. Late 2003 model pistons have an oval opening in the coating material on each side of the piston, exposing a patch of bare aluminum, 90-degrees from the piston pin bore.

Piston rings

1999 through 2002 models

Top ring side clearance
    Standard .... 0.002 to 0.0045 inch (0.051 to 0.114 mm)
    Limit .... 0.0037 inch (0.09 mm)
Second ring side clearance
    Standard .... 0.0016 to 0.0041 inch (0.041 to 0.104 mm)
    Limit .... 0.0037 inch (0.09 mm)
Oil ring side clearance (standard) .... 0.0016 to 0.0076 inch (0.041 to 0.193 mm)
Top ring gap
    Standard .... 0.007 to 0.020 inch (0.178 to 0.508 mm)
    Limit .... 0.020 inch (0.51 mm)
Second ring gap
    Standard .... 0.007 to 0.020 inch (0.178 to 0.508 mm)
    Limit .... 0.024 inch (0.61 mm)
Oil ring rail gap
    Standard .... 0.009 to 0.052 inch (0.23 to 1.32 mm)
    Limit .... 0.050 inch (1.27 mm)

2003 models

Compression ring side clearance (top and second)
    Standard .... 0.0012 to 0.0037 inch (0.030 to 0.094 mm)
    Limit .... 0.0045 inch (0.11 mm)
Oil ring side clearance
    Standard .... Not specified
    Limit .... 0.010 inch (0.25 mm)

Top ring gap
    Standard... 0.010 to 0.020 inch (0.254 to 0.508 mm)
    Limit... 0.030 inch (0.76 mm)
Second ring gap
    Standard... 0.014 to 0.024 inch (0.356 to 0.610 mm)
    Limit... 0.034 inch (0.86 mm)
Oil ring rail gap
    Standard... Not specified
    Limit... 0.050 inch (1.27 mm)

Oil pump

Oil pump clearance limit (inner to outer rotor) .... 0.004 inch (0.10 mm)

Torque specifications

Softail engine mounts
    Engine mount through-bolt nuts .... 70 to 80 ft-lbs (122.0 to 149.1 Nm)
    Upper mount bracket to cylinder head bolts .... 28 to 35 ft-lbs (38.0 to 47.5 Nm)
    Upper mount bracket to frame bolt.............................. 45 to 50 ft-lbs (61.0 to 67.8 Nm)
Dyna engine mounts
    Crankcase to front engine mounting bracket bolts........................... 33 to 38 ft-lbs (44.7 to 51.5 Nm)
    Front isolator mounting bolts .... 21 to 27 ft-lbs (28.5 to 36.6 Nm)
    Stabilizer link bolt .... 18 to 22 ft-lbs (24.4 to 29.8 Nm)
    Cylinder head bracket bolts
        1999 through 2002... 28 to 35 ft-lbs (38.0 to 47.5 Nm)
        2003 .... 25 to 30 ft-lbs (33.9 to 40.7 Nm)
Touring model engine mounts
    Upper mounting bracket to cylinder heads....................................... 25 to 30 ft-lbs (33.9 to 40.7 Nm)
    Upper engine mounting bracket to stabilizer link.............................. 18 to 22 ft-lbs (24.4 to 29.8 Nm)
    Crankcase to front engine mounting bracket bolts........................... 33 to 38 ft-lbs (44.7 to 51.5 Nm)
Transmission-to-engine bolts... 30 to 35 ft-lbs (40.7 to 47.5 Nm)
Valve cover bolts .... 15 to 18 ft-lbs (20.3 to 24.4 Nm)
Breather bolts .... 90 to 120 inch-lbs (10.2 to 13.6 Nm)
Rocker support plate bolts .... 15 to 18 ft-lbs (20.3 to 34.4 Nm)
Camshaft outer cover screws... 20 to 30 inch-lbs (2.3 to 3.4 Nm)
Camshaft cover bolts .... 90 to 120 inch-lbs (10.2 to 13.6 Nm)
Camshaft support plate bolts .... 90 to 120 inch-lbs (10.2 to 13.6 Nm)
Bearing retainer plate to camshaft support plate .... 20 to 30 inch-lbs (2.3 to 3.4 Nm)
Camshaft sprocket bolt
    Initial torque... 15 ft-lbs (20.3 Nm)
    Final torque .... 34 ft-lbs (46.1 Nm)
Crankshaft sprocket bolt
    Initial torque... 15 ft-lbs (20.3 Nm)
    Final torque .... 24 ft-lbs (32.4 Nm)
Cylinder head bolts
    First step .... 84 to 108 inch-lbs (9.5 to 12.2 Nm)
    Second step .... 144 to 168 inch-lbs (16.3 to 18.9 Nm)
    Third step .... 1/4-turn past second step
Cylinder studs... 120 inch-lbs (13.6 Nm)
Valve lifter cover bolts .... 90 to 120 inch-lbs (10.2 to 13.6 Nm)
Oil line fittings (Softail) .... 120 to 168 inch-lbs (13.6 to 19.0 Nm)
Oil pump bolts
    First step .... 40 to 45 inch-lbs (4.5 to 5.1 Nm)
    Second step (replacing one alignment tool with bolt)...................... 40 to 45 inch-lbs
    Third step (replacing second alignment tool with bolt) .... 40 to 45 inch-lbs
    Fourth step (all bolts)... 90 to 120 inch-lbs (10.2 to 13.6 Nm)
Oil passage pipe plug .... 120 to 144 inch-lbs (13.6 to 16.3 Nm)
Oil jet screws .... 25 to 35 inch-lbs (2.8 to 4.0 Nm)
Crankcase bolts.. 15 to 19 ft-lbs (20.3 to 25.8 Nm)
Balancer sprocket nuts (Softail)... 78 to 82 ft-lbs (105.7 to 111.2 Nm)
Balancer housing bolts (Softail) .... 18 to 22 ft-lbs (24.4 to 29.8 Nm)

2A

1 General information

The engine on all models is an air-cooled V-twin. The valves are operated by two separate camshafts (one for the front cylinder and one for the rear), pushrods and rocker arms. The camshafts are chain driven off the crankshaft. The engine/transmission assembly is constructed from aluminum alloy. The crankcase is divided vertically.

The crankcase incorporates a dry sump, pressure-fed lubrication system which uses an external oil tank, dual-rotor oil pump, oil filter, relief valve and oil pressure switch. The oil pump, which has separate rotors for scavenging and pressure feed, is driven directly by the crankshaft. The balancer shafts (on Softail models only) are inside the crankcase.

Power from the crankshaft is routed to the transmission via the clutch and primary drive chain. The clutch is of the wet, multi-plate type and is direct-driven off the crankshaft. The transmission is a five-speed, constant-mesh unit. The clutch and primary drive chain are contained in the primary drive housing on the left side of the engine. The transmission is mounted on the back of the engine. Service procedures for the clutch, primary drive and transmission are covered in Part B of this Chapter.

2 Cylinder compression - check

1   Among other things, poor engine performance may be caused by leaking valves, incorrect valve clearances, a leaking head gasket, or worn pistons, rings and/or cylinder walls. A cylinder compression check will help pinpoint these conditions and can also indicate the presence of excessive carbon deposits in the cylinder heads.
2   The only tools required are a compression gauge and a spark plug wrench.

2.5 A compression gauge with a threaded (12 mm) fitting for the spark plug hole is preferred over the type that requires hand pressure to retain the seal

Depending on the outcome of the initial test, a squirt-type oil can may also be needed.
3   Run the engine until it reaches normal operating temperature. Place the motorcycle on the jiffy stand or prop it securely upright. Remove the spark plugs (see Chapter 1, if necessary). Work carefully - don't strip the spark plug hole threads and don't burn your hands.
4   Disable the ignition by unplugging the primary wires from the coil (see Chapter 4). Be sure to mark the locations of the wires before detaching them.
5   Install the compression gauge in one of the spark plug holes **(see illustration)**. Hold or block the throttle wide open.
6   Crank the engine over for five to seven revolutions (or until the gauge reading stops increasing) and observe the initial movement of the compression gauge needle as well as the final total gauge reading. Repeat the procedure for the other cylinder and compare the results to the value listed in this Chapter's Specifications.
7   If the compression in both cylinders built up quickly and evenly to the specified amount, you can assume the engine upper end is in reasonably good mechanical condition. Worn or sticking piston rings and worn cylinders will produce very little initial movement of the gauge needle, but compression will tend to build up gradually as the engine spins over. Valve and valve seat leakage, or head gasket leakage, is indicated by low initial compression which does not tend to build up.
8   To further confirm your findings, add a small amount of engine oil to each cylinder by inserting the nozzle of a squirt-type oil can through the spark plug holes. The oil will tend to seal the piston rings if they are leaking. Repeat the test for the other cylinder.
9   If the compression increases significantly after the addition of the oil, the piston rings and/or cylinders are definitely worn. If the compression does not increase, the pressure is leaking past the valves or the head gasket. Leakage past the valves may be due to insufficient valve clearances, burned, warped or cracked valves or valve seats, or valves that are hanging up in the guides.
10   If compression readings are considerably higher than specified, the combustion chambers are probably coated with excessive carbon deposits. It is possible (but not very likely) for carbon deposits to raise the compression enough to compensate for the effects of leakage past rings or valves. Remove the cylinder heads and carefully decarbonize the combustion chambers (see Section 14).

3 Operations possible with the engine in the frame

The components and assemblies listed below can be removed without having to remove the engine from the frame. If, how-

ever, a number of areas require attention at the same time, removal of the engine is recommended.

Clutch, primary drive and transmission (see Part B of this Chapter)
Valve covers
Breather assemblies
Rocker arms, pushrods and lifters
Cylinder heads and valves
Cylinders and pistons
Cam support plate and camshafts
Oil pump
Starter motor
Alternator

4 Operations requiring engine removal

1   It is necessary to remove the engine from the frame and separate the crankcase halves to gain access to the following components:

Balancers (Softail models)
Crankshaft, connecting rods and bearings

5 Major engine repair - general note

1   It is not always easy to determine when or if an engine should be completely overhauled, as a number of factors must be considered.
2   High mileage is not necessarily an indication that an overhaul is needed, while low mileage, on the other hand, does not preclude the need for an overhaul. Frequency of servicing is probably the single most important consideration. An engine that has regular and frequent oil and filter changes, as well as other required maintenance, will most likely give many miles of reliable service. Conversely, a neglected engine, or one which has not been broken in properly, may require an overhaul very early in its life.
3   Exhaust smoke and excessive oil consumption are both indications that piston rings and/or valve guides are in need of attention. Make sure oil leaks are not responsible before deciding that the rings and guides are bad. Refer to Section 2 and perform a cylinder compression check to determine for certain the nature and extent of the work required.
4   If the engine is making obvious knocking or rumbling noises, the connecting rod and/or main bearings are probably at fault.
5   Loss of power, rough running, excessive valve train noise and high fuel consumption rates may also point to the need for an overhaul, especially if they are all present at the same time. If a complete tune-up does not remedy the situation, major mechanical work is the only solution.
6   An engine overhaul generally involves

6.8 Remove the shift arm, transmission case brackets and transmission-to-engine bolts (arrows, left side shown)

6.14 Unbolt the Softail upper engine mounting bracket from both cylinder heads and the frame

6.17a The left end of the Softail upper engine mounting bolt has a collar (arrow) but no spacers . . .

6.17b . . . the left end of the lower mounting bolt has a collar outside the frame and a spacer inside . . .

restoring the internal parts to the specifications of a new engine. During an overhaul the piston rings are replaced and the cylinder walls are bored and/or honed. If a rebore is done, then new pistons are also required. The crankshaft and connecting rods are replaced as a complete assembly if problems are found with any of them. Generally the valves are serviced as well, since they are usually in less than perfect condition at this point. While the engine is being overhauled, other components such as the carburetor (if equipped) and starter motor can be rebuilt also. The end result should be a like-new engine that will give as many trouble-free miles as the original.

7   Before beginning the engine overhaul, read through all of the related procedures to familiarize yourself with the scope and requirements of the job. Overhauling an engine is not all that difficult, but it is time consuming. Plan on the motorcycle being tied up for a minimum of two weeks. Check on the availability of parts and make sure that any necessary special tools, equipment and supplies are obtained in advance.

8   Most work can be done with typical shop hand tools, although a number of precision measuring tools are required for inspecting parts to determine if they must be replaced. Often a dealer service department or motorcycle repair shop will handle the inspection of parts and offer advice concerning reconditioning and replacement. As a general rule, time is the primary cost of an overhaul so it doesn't pay to install worn or substandard parts.

9   As a final note, to ensure maximum life and minimum trouble from a rebuilt engine, everything must be assembled with care in a spotlessly clean environment.

Note: *These engines use a number of O-rings, some of them very close to each other in size. Make sure O-rings are labeled when you buy them, or else have the parts supplier label them for you. Don't remove the labels until you're ready to install the O-rings.*

6   Engine - removal and installation

Note: *Engine removal and installation should be done with the aid of an assistant to avoid damage or injury that could occur if the engine is dropped. A hydraulic floor jack should be used to support and lower the engine if possible (they can be rented at low cost).*

Removal

Softail and Dyna models

1   Prop the motorcycle securely upright and disconnect the battery (negative cable first). Drain the oil from the oil tank and primary chaincase (see Chapter 1).
2   Remove the seat (see Chapter 7).

Softail models

3   Remove the floorboards (see Chapter 7). Unbolt the inner rear fender, so it can be lifted up later in the procedure when you remove the swingarm pivot bolt.
3   Remove the air cleaner, fuel tank and exhaust system (see Chapter 3).
4   Remove the primary chaincase assembly (see Chapter 2B).
5   Remove the oil tank (see Section 21).
6   Remove the ignition coil together with the seat post (see Chapter 4).
7   Support the engine with a jack, using a wooden block between the jack and engine to protect the engine.
8   Remove the transmission shift arm (see Chapter 2B) and both of the transmission case-to-frame brackets **(see illustration)**.
9   Remove all four transmission-to-engine bolts **(see illustration 6.8)**.
10   Disconnect the clutch cable at the handlebar (see Chapter 2B). Tie a string to the cable to show its routing, then release the cable from the retainer and pull it out of the frame, leaving it connected to the transmission.

11   If you're working on a California model, disconnect the evaporative emission system canister hoses (see Chapter 3). On all models, remove the hose bracket from the back of the transmission housing.
12   Remove the swingarm pivot shaft (see Chapter 5).
13   Move the electrical panel to make room for transmission removal, then disconnect the neutral switch wires and pull the transmission out of the frame to the right side of the bike.
14   Remove the horn bracket and upper engine mount **(see illustration)**.
15   If you're working on a carbureted model, disconnect the MAP sensor connector. If you're working on a fuel injected model, disconnect the induction module connector. Remove the air cleaner and disconnect the throttle cables (see Chapter 3).
16   Disconnect the electrical connectors for the voltage regulator, crankshaft position sensor and oil pressure sending unit (see Chapters 4 and 8, if necessary).
17   With the engine supported, remove the two front mounting bolts, spacers and collars **(see illustrations)**.

2A

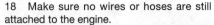

6.17c ... the right side of the upper mounting bolt has a collar and spacer inside the frame and a washer outside ...

6.17d ... as does the right side of the lower mounting bolt

6.27 On Dynas, remove the engine stabilizer and horn bracket

6.32 Remove the front mounting bolts (arrows)

18 Make sure no wires or hoses are still attached to the engine.

19 With the help of at least one assistant, separate the engine from the transmission, then slowly and carefully guide the engine out the right side, away from the bike.

Dyna models

20 Remove the air cleaner, fuel tank and exhaust system and disconnect the throttle cables from the carburetor (see Chapter 3).

21 Remove both footpegs and their brackets (see Chapter 7).

22 Remove the oil line cover from the right side of the crankcase and disconnect the oil lines.

23 Disconnect the electrical connectors for the crankshaft position sensor, camshaft position sensor (if so equipped), MAP sensor (carbureted models), oil pressure sending unit and alternator (see Chapters 3, 4 and 8 if necessary).

24 Remove the transmission shift arm (see Chapter 2B) and both of the transmission case-to-frame brackets.

25 Remove the primary chaincase assembly (see Chapter 2B).

26 Disconnect the spark plug wires (see Chapter 1).

27 Remove the right-hand engine stabilizer and horn bracket (see illustration).

28 Disconnect the clutch cable at the handlebar (see Chapter 2B). Tie a string to the cable to show its routing, then release the cable from the retainer and pull it out of the frame, leaving it connected to the transmission.

29 Support the engine with a jack, using a wooden block between the jack and engine to protect the engine. Pad the frame tubes with duct tape or similar material so they aren't scratched.

30 Tie the transmission in place with a ratcheting tie-down strap wrapped around the top and bottom of the transmission. Remove all four transmission-to-engine bolts.

31 Remove the oil filter base unit from the crankcase. Locate the O-rings.

32 With the engine supported, remove the two front mounting bolts, spacers and collars (see illustration).

33 Work the engine oil dipstick free of the oil tank and set it aside.

34 Make sure no wires or hoses are still attached to the engine.

35 With the help of at least one assistant, separate the engine from the transmission, then slowly and carefully guide the engine out the right side, away from the bike. It may be necessary to rotate the engine counterclockwise to free it from the transmission-to-engine dowels.

Touring models

36 Remove the air cleaner, fuel tank and exhaust system and disconnect the throttle cables from the carburetor or induction module (see Chapter 3). If you're working on a carbureted model, free the choke knob from its bracket and disconnect the electrical connector from the MAP sensor. If you're working on a fuel injected module, disconnect the electrical connectors from the induction module and engine temperature sensor.

37 Remove the saddlebags, side covers and right floorboard (see Chapter 7). If you're working on an FLHTCU, remove the screw that secures each lower fairing to the engine guard.

38 If the motorcycle is equipped with cruise control, disconnect the cable (see Chapter 8).

39 Disconnect the electrical connectors for the crankshaft position sensor, camshaft position sensor (if so equipped), oil pressure sending unit and alternator (see Chapters 3, 4 and 8 if necessary). Remove the crankshaft position sensor. Free the sensor harness from its retainers, all the way back to the retainer under the camshaft cover on the right side of the engine, and lay it out of the way under the frame.

40 Remove the ignition coil and bracket (see Chapter 4).

41 Remove the hose cover from the oil hoses on the right-hand side of the engine, then disconnect them. Disconnect the breather hose from the right side of the engine behind the lifter cover and tuck it back out of the way.

42 Disconnect the electrical connectors form the alternator and voltage regulator. Free the wiring harnesses from their retainers and place them out of the way. Detach the voltage regulator from its mounting studs and let it hang by the wires.

43 Remove the primary chaincase assembly (see Chapter 2B).

44 Disconnect the spark plug wires and remove the spark plugs (see Chapter 1).

45 Support the engine oil tank (located beneath the transmission) with a jack. Use a block of wood between jack and tank so the tank won't be damaged.

46 Remove the upper engine mounting bracket, engine stabilizer and horn bracket.

47 Disconnect the clutch cable at the handlebar (see Chapter 2B). Tie a string to the cable to show its routing, then release the cable from the retainer and pull it out of the frame, leaving it connected to the transmission.

48 Support the engine with a jack, using a wooden block between the jack and engine to protect the engine. Pad the frame tubes, valve covers and rear master cylinder reservoir with duct tape or similar material so they aren't scratched.

6.50a Unbolt the front engine mount . . .

6.50b . . . and engine stabilizer (touring models)

49   Support the transmission with a cargo strap and rubber-coated hooks attached to both sides of the transmission.

50   Unbolt the engine mount and stabilizer **(see illustrations)**. Remove all four transmission-to-engine bolts.

51   Make sure no wires or hoses are still attached to the engine.

52   With the help of at least one assistant, separate the engine from the transmission, then slowly and carefully guide the engine out the right side, away from the bike.

Installation

20   Installation is the reverse of removal. Note the following points:

a) *Don't tighten any of the engine mounting bolts until they all have been installed.*

b) *Use new gaskets at all exhaust pipe connections.*

c) *Don't forget the dowels in the two lower transmission case bolt holes.*

d) *Tighten the engine mounting bolts to the torque listed in this Chapter's Specifications.*

e) *Adjust the drivebelt, throttle cables and clutch cable following the procedures in Chapter 1.*

f) *Fill the oil tank and check the engine oil level (see Chapter 1).*

7 Engine disassembly and reassembly - general information

1   Before disassembling the engine, clean the exterior with a degreaser and rinse it with water. A clean engine will make the job easier and prevent the possibility of getting dirt into the internal areas of the engine.

2   In addition to the precision measuring tools mentioned earlier, you will need a torque wrench, a valve spring compressor, oil gallery brushes, a piston ring removal and installation tool, a piston ring compressor. Some new, clean engine oil of the correct grade and type, some engine assembly lube

(or moly-based grease) and a tube of RTV (silicone) sealant will also be required.

3   An engine support stand made from short lengths of 2 x 4's bolted together will facilitate the disassembly and reassembly procedures **(see illustration)**. The perimeter of the mount should be just big enough to accommodate the engine oil pan. If you have an automotive-type engine stand, an adapter plate can be made from a piece of plate, some angle iron and some nuts and bolts.

4   When disassembling the engine, keep "mated" parts together (including gears, cylinders, pistons, etc. that have been in contact with each other during engine operation). These "mated" parts must be reused or replaced as an assembly.

5   Engine/transmission disassembly should be done in the following general order with reference to the appropriate Sections.

> *Remove the valve covers*
> *Remove the breathers*
> *Remove the rocker arms, pushrods and lifters*
> *Remove the cylinder heads*
> *Remove the cylinders*
> *Remove the pistons*
> *Remove the camshafts*
> *Remove the oil pump*
> *Remove the primary drive housing*

8.4a Slip a screwdriver into the removal slot of the spring cap retainer and push down . . .

> *(see Chapter 2B)*
> *Remove the alternator rotor/stator coils and starter jackshaft (see Chapter 8)*
> *Separate the crankcase halves*
> *Remove the balancer chain and shafts (Softail)*
> *Remove the crankshaft and connecting rods*

6   Reassembly is accomplished by reversing the general disassembly sequence.

8 Top Dead Center (TDC) - locating

1   Various procedures in this manual require placing one of the pistons at TDC on its compression stroke.

2   Remove the spark plugs (see Chapter 1).

3   Select a method to rotate the crankshaft as follows:

a) *With the primary cover installed, support the bike with the rear wheel off the ground. Place the transmission in fifth gear and turn the rear wheel in the forward direction.*

b) *With the primary cover removed, place the transmission in neutral and turn the compensating sprocket with a 1-1/2-inch socket.*

c) *With the engine out of the bike, weld a 1/2-inch drive, 13/16-inch socket to a compensating sprocket shaft extension (Harley-Davidson part on. HD-40266-85). Slip the tool over the compensating sprocket shaft and use a breaker bar to rotate the engine counterclockwise.*

Caution: Don't rotate the engine by the crankshaft or primary camshaft sprocket bolts. They may snap off.

4   Slip a screwdriver into the removal slot of the spring cap retainer on the intake pushrod (this is the pushrod closest to the center of the engine, on either front or rear cylinder). Push down on the screwdriver and pry outward to remove the spring cap retainer **(see illustrations)**.

8.4b . . . and pry outward to remove the spring cap retainer

2A

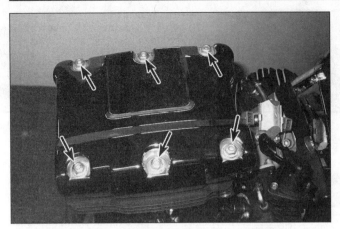

9.7 Loosen the valve cover bolts (arrows) evenly, then remove them

10.2 Unscrew the breather bolts (arrows) and lift off the breather . . .

5   Lift the lower pushrod cover to expose the intake lifter. Place a finger on the lifter so you can feel it rise and fall, then rotate the crankshaft as described above. Let the intake lifter rise, then fall, indicating that the intake valve has closed, which means the piston has traveled downward on the intake stroke.

6   Place a finger over the spark plug hole and turn the engine as described above. This will cause air pressure to build up against your finger as the piston rises on the compression stroke. Keep turning until the pressure stops building, then look into the spark plug hole with a flashlight. Turn the engine back and forth slightly while watching the top of the piston, which will go up and down slightly. Center the piston at the top of its stroke.

9   Valve covers - removal and installation

Removal

1   Support the bike securely upright.
2   Remove the seat and right floorboard (see Chapter 7).

10.3 . . . early models use separate components, shown here, and later models use a one-piece breather assembly

3   Disconnect the negative cable from the battery.
4   Remove the exhaust system, fuel tank and air cleaner housing. Disconnect the throttle cables and remove the carburetor or EFI induction module (see Chapter 3).
5   Remove the spark plugs (see Chapter 1).
6   Unbolt the upper engine mount from the frame. If you're working on a carbureted model, detach the choke cable from the horn bracket. Remove the upper engine mount and horn bracket together.
7   Unscrew the valve cover mounting bolts **(see illustration)**. The bolts have both an internal Allen fitting and an external hex, so you can use an Allen wrench or socket, depending on how much room there is for access. **Note:** *The bolts have been secured with non-permanent thread locking agent, so they may be difficult to remove.*
8   Lift the cover off the cylinder head. If it's stuck, don't attempt to pry it off - tap around the sides with a plastic hammer to dislodge it.
9   If the gasket didn't come off with the valve cover, remove it from the engine.

Installation

10   Peel the rubber gasket from the cover if it's stuck there. Always replace it with a new one whenever it's removed.
11   Clean the mating surfaces of the cylin-

der head and the valve cover with lacquer thinner, acetone or brake system cleaner.
12   Install the gasket to the cover. Make sure its indented side is on the correct side of the cylinder head.
13   Position the cover on the cylinder head, making sure the gasket doesn't slip out of place.
14   Apply non-permanent thread locking agent to the threads of the bolts and install all of them loosely (be sure to install the three long bolts and three short bolts on the correct sides of the cover). Tighten the bolts evenly to the torque listed in this Chapter's Specifications.

Caution: The three bolts on the left side of the rear valve cover must be torqued with 3/8-inch drive torque wrench and adapter (Snap-On part no. FRDH 141 or equivalent) or else the bolts will be overtightened, distorting the cover.

18   The remainder of installation is the reverse of removal.

10   Breather - removal, inspection and installation

1   Remove the valve cover and gasket (see Section 9).

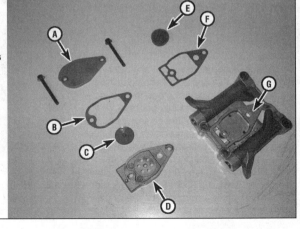

10.5 Breather components (early models)

a) Cover
b) Gasket
c) Umbrella valve
d) Baffle
e) Filter
f) Gasket
g) Rocker support plate

11.3a Unscrew the rocker support plate bolts and lift off the plate

11.3b There's an O-ring under the support plate; install a new one on reassembly

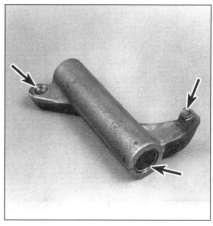

11.7 Check the rocker arm bushings, the pushrod recesses and the valve stem pads for wear and damage (arrows)

2   Unscrew the breather bolts **(see illustration)**.
3   If you're working on an early model with a multi-piece breather, remove the breather cover, gasket, umbrella valve, baffle, filter element and lower gasket **(see illustration)**.
4   If you're working on a later model with a one-piece breather assembly, remove the breather assembly from the rocker support plate.
5   Remove the breather filter **(see illustration)**. It should be replaced with a new one whenever it's removed. Don't try to clean it with solvent or compressed air.
6   Installation is the reverse of the removal steps.

11 Rocker arms, pushrods and lifters - removal, inspection and installation

Support plate and rocker arms

Removal

1   Remove the valve cover and breather (see Sections 9 and 10).
2   Place the piston of the cylinder you're working at TDC compression (see Section 8).

Caution: Complete work on one cylinder, then place the remaining cylinder at TDC compression before working on it.

3   Loosen the support plate bolts evenly, 1/4-turn at a time, then lift the support plate and rocker arms off the cylinder head, together with the bolts **(see illustration)**. Locate the breather plate O-ring **(see illustration)**.

Inspection

4   Measure rocker arm end play with a feeler gauge. If it's beyond the limit listed in this Chapter's Specifications, replace the rocker arms or support plate, whichever is worn.
5   Pull the bolts out of the support plate, together with their washers. Tag the rocker arms with their locations, then carefully tap the rocker arm shafts out of the bores from

the left side. As each shaft begins to leave its bore, place a tag on it so it can be returned to its original location.
6   Keep all of the parts in order so they can be reinstalled in their original locations. **Note:** *A container such as an egg carton with numbers written on the compartment is a convenient way to keep the parts in order.*
7   Clean all of the components with solvent and dry them off. Blow through the oil passages in the rocker arms with compressed air, if available. Inspect the rocker arm faces for pits, spalling, score marks and rough spots. Look for cracks in each rocker arm. If the faces of the rocker arms are damaged, the rocker arms and pushrods should be replaced as a set **(see illustration)**.
8   Measure the outer diameter of each rocker shaft and the inner diameter of the rocker arms with a micrometer and compare the measurements to the values listed in this Chapter's Specifications. If the shafts are worn, replace them. If the rocker arm bushings are worn, have them pressed out and new ones pressed in by a dealer service department or other qualified shop.

Installation

9   Coat the rocker shaft and rocker arm bores with moly-based grease. Install the rocker arms and shaft, making sure the rocker arms are returned to their original locations if you're reusing the old ones. As you install the rocker shaft, align its notch with the bolt hole **(see illustration)**.
10   Make sure the cylinder being worked on is still at TDC on its compression stroke (see Section 8).
11   Lay the support plate and rocker arms on the rocker housing. Install the bolts and washers, with the two long bolts on the right side of the engine and the two short bolts on the left side of the engine.
12   Install the breather on the rocker support plate and install its bolts, but don't tighten them yet (see Section 9).
13   Tighten the support plate bolts in the specified sequence, 1/4-turn at a time, until

they're snug. Then tighten them in the same sequence to the torque listed in this Chapter's Specifications.

Caution: The bolt on the left rear corner of the rear cylinder must be torqued with 3/8-inch drive torque wrench and adapter (Snap-On part no. FRDH 161 or equivalent) or else the bolts will be overtightened, distorting the rocker housing.

14   Pull up on the lower pushrod covers to expose the pushrods of the cylinder you're working on. Twist the pushrods with fingers and make sure they rotate freely. If they don't, find the problem before continuing. It may be that the engine has been rotated so the piston is not at TDC compression.
15   Reinstall the pushrod tubes.
16   Slip the upper end of each spring cap retainer into its slot in the cylinder head. Using a screwdriver and your finger, push the bottom end of the spring cap retainer into line with its slot in the upper pushrod cover, then push it down so it seats securely against the pushrod cover.
17   The remainder of installation is the reverse of the removal steps.

2A

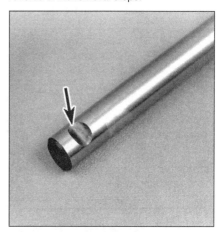

11.9 Check the bushing contact areas on the shafts for wear; on assembly, align the shaft cutouts (arrow) with the bolt holes

11.18a Label the pushrods for cylinder (front or rear) and location (intake or exhaust)

Pushrods and lifters

Removal

18 Label the pushrods and covers so they can be returned to their original locations (front or rear cylinder, intake or exhaust) **(see illustrations)**.
19 Remove the rocker support plate as

11.20a Lift the pushrod tubes against the spring tension and pull them out

11.20b Lift the pushrods out of the engine

11.18b Pushrod tube locations
a) *Front cylinder exhaust*
b) *Front cylinder intake*
c) *Rear cylinder exhaust*
d) *Rear cylinder intake*

described above.
20 Remove the upper pushrod covers (see Section 8). Remove the lower pushrod covers **(see illustration)**. Take the pushrods out **(see illustrations)**.
21 Unbolt the lifter cover from the engine and take it off **(see illustration)**. Remove the lifter cover gasket **(see illustration)**.
22 Remove the anti-rotation pin and take the lifters out of the engine **(see illustration)**. Label them as they're removed for cylinder (front or rear) and valve (intake or exhaust) **(see illustration)**.

Inspection

23 Pull the upper and lower pushrod covers apart. Remove the upper, lower and center O-rings, spring cap, spring and flat washer **(see illustration 11.20c)**.
24 Clean all parts except the lifters in sol-

vent. Remove all old gasket material from the lifter cover and its mating surface on the engine.

Inspection

25 Check the pushrod ends for wear or scoring **(see illustration)**. Roll the pushrods on a flat surface such as a piece of plate glass and check them for bending. Replace the pushrods if problems are visible. Don't disassemble them.
26 Measure the diameter of the lifters and lifter bores, using a micrometer and bore gauge. Calculate the difference and compare it to the value listed in this Chapter's Specifications. If it's beyond the specified range, replace the lifters or the crankcase, whichever is worn.
27 Make sure the rollers on the lifters turn freely, with no play on their pins. If you find

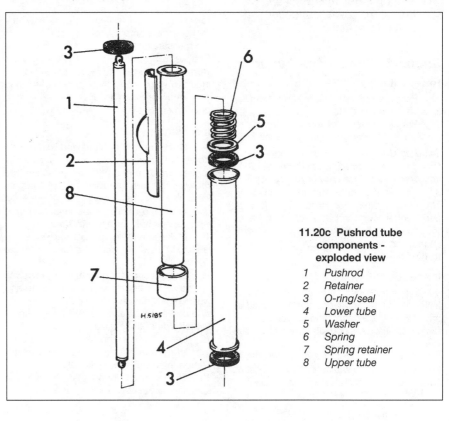

11.20c Pushrod tube components - exploded view
1 Pushrod
2 Retainer
3 O-ring/seal
4 Lower tube
5 Washer
6 Spring
7 Spring retainer
8 Upper tube

11.21a Unbolt the lifter cover (arrows) . . .

11.21b . . . lift it off and remove the gasket

11.22a Remove the anti-rotation pin (arrow)

either problem, replace the lifter.
28 Check the lifters for worn pushrod sockets. Make sure the plunger inside the lifter is fully in contact with the lifter C-clip. Operate the plunger inside the lifter and make sure it moves freely. Replace the lifter if problems are found.
29 Place the lifters in clean engine oil and keep them in a covered container until they're reinstalled.

Installation

30 Installation is the reverse of the removal steps, with the following additions:

a) Use new O-rings on the pushrod tubes.
b) Lubricate all parts with clean engine oil on assembly.

12 Cylinder head and rocker housing - removal and installation

Caution: The engine must be completely cool before beginning this procedure, or the cylinder head may become warped.
Note: *This procedure can be performed with*

11.22b Label the lifters and pull them out of the bores

the engine in the frame. If the engine has been removed, ignore the steps which don't apply.

Removal

1 Support the bike securely upright.
2 Remove the valve cover, breather and

11.25 Check the pushrod ends for wear and make sure the oil holes are clear

rocker support plate from the cylinder you're working on (see Sections 9, 10 and 11).
3 Loosen the rocker housing bolts evenly, in the correct sequence, until they're all loose, then remove them **(see illustration)**. Lift the rocker housing off the cylinder head and remove the gasket **(see illustration)**.

2A

12.3a Rocker housing bolt TIGHTENING sequence

12.3b Lift off the rocker housing and remove the gasket

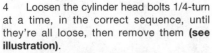

12.4 Cylinder head bolt TIGHTENING sequence

12.6 Lift off the cylinder head, note the O-ring locations (arrows) and remove the gasket

12.9 Install the O-rings on the dowels, fitting them inside the gasket holes

4   Loosen the cylinder head bolts 1/4-turn at a time, in the correct sequence, until they're all loose, then remove them **(see illustration)**.

5   Lift the cylinder head off the cylinder. If the head is stuck, use two wooden dowels inserted into the intake or exhaust ports to lever the head off. Don't attempt to pry the head off by inserting a screwdriver between the head and the cylinder block - you'll damage the sealing surfaces.

6   Lift the head gasket off the cylinder and remove the O-rings **(see illustration)**. **Note:** *The head gaskets and O-rings should always be replaced with new ones whenever they're removed. However, if you're planning to do your own measurements of the cylinder bore using torque plates (see Section 15), save the head gasket and O-rings for use with the torque plates.*

7   Check the cylinder head gasket and the mating surfaces on the cylinder head and cylinder for signs of leakage, which could indicate warpage. Refer to Section 14 and check the flatness of the cylinder head.

8   Clean all traces of old gasket material from the cylinder head and cylinder. Be careful not to let any of the gasket material fall

into the crankcase, the cylinder bores or the oil passages.

Installation

9   Coat new O-rings with oil. Make sure the dowels are in place, then place the new O-rings on them **(see illustration)**. **Note:** *It's important to install the O-rings before the head gasket to ensure proper head gasket alignment.*

10   Place the new head gasket on the cylinder with its part number up. Never reuse the old gasket and don't use any type of gasket sealant.

11   Clean the threads of the head bolts, using a die if necessary. Lightly coat the head bolt threads and contact surfaces with clean engine oil (H-D 20W-50 or equivalent).

12   Look for the Front or Rear mark cast into the cylinder head **(see illustration)**, then carefully position the cylinder head on the correct cylinder with the indentation in the cooling fins toward the right side of the engine.

13   Insert the head bolts into their holes, but don't tighten them yet. The two long bolts go on the right side of the engine and the two short bolts on the left side.

14   Tighten all four head bolts finger-tight.

15   Tighten the head bolts to the initial torque listed in this Chapter's Specifications, following the tightening sequence.

16   Go through the same sequence again, this time tightening all four bolts to the second-step torque listed in this Chapter's Specifications.

17   Mark the heads of the bolts and the head next to the bolts with a felt pen **(see illustration)**. Using the marks as a guide, tighten the bolts an additional 90-degrees (+/-5-degrees).

18   Install a new rocker housing gasket, making sure it's right side up (covering the breather channel) **(see illustration)**. Installing the gasket upside down (leaving the breather channel uncovered) will allow large quantities of oil to leak out when the engine is started. Make sure the gasket is installed on the correct cylinder head **(see illustration)**.

19   Position the rocker housing on the cylinder head with its indented side toward the front of the engine.

20   Make sure the rocker housing bolts holes are aligned with those in the gasket. Apply non-permanent thread locking agent to the threads of the rocker housing bolts

12.12 Use the Front or Rear labels (arrow) to make sure the heads are installed on the correct cylinders

12.17 Mark the head bolts, mark the heads at 90-degrees from the head bolt marks, then tighten the bolts to align the marks

12.18a Make sure the rocker housing gasket is right side up so it covers the breather channel . . .

12.18b ... install the gasket labeled Front Head on the front cylinder head ...

12.18c ... and install the gasket labeled Rear Head on the rear cylinder head

14.7a Compress the springs with a valve spring compressor, then remove the keepers (arrows) with a magnet or needle-nose pliers

and install them in the engine. The four short bolts go in the center holes and the two long bolts go in the left holes. Tighten the bolts evenly, following the correct sequence, to the torque listed in this Chapter's Specifications. **Note:** *If the engine is in the bike, you'll need a 1/4-inch drive torque wrench to tighten the left rear bolt on the rear cylinder.*

21   Coat a new oil baffle O-ring with clean engine oil and install in on top of the rocker housing.
22   The remainder of installation is the reverse of the removal steps.
23   Change the engine oil (see Chapter 1).

13 Valves/valve seats/valve guides - servicing

1   Because of the complex nature of this job and the special tools and equipment required, servicing of the valves, the valve seats and the valve guides (commonly known as a valve job) is best left to a professional.
2   The home mechanic can, however, remove and disassemble the head, do the initial cleaning and inspection, then reassemble and deliver the head to a dealer service department or properly equipped motorcycle repair shop for the actual valve servicing. Refer to Section 14 for those procedures.
3   The dealer service department will remove the valves and springs, recondition or replace the valves and valve seats, replace the valve guides, check and replace the valve springs, spring retainers and keepers (as necessary), replace the valve seals with new ones and reassemble the valve components.
4   After the valve job has been performed, the head will be in like-new condition. When the head is returned, be sure to clean it again very thoroughly before installation on the engine to remove any metal particles or abrasive grit that may still be present from the valve service operations. Use compressed air, if available, to blow out all the holes and passages.

14 Cylinder head and valves - disassembly, inspection and reassembly

1   As mentioned in the previous Section, valve servicing and valve guide replacement should be left to a dealer service department or motorcycle repair shop. However, disassembly, cleaning and inspection of the valves and related components can be done (if the necessary special tools are available) by the home mechanic. This way no expense is incurred if the inspection reveals that service work is not required at this time.
2   To properly disassemble the valve components without the risk of damaging them, a valve spring compressor is absolutely necessary. This special tool can usually be rented, but if it's not available, have a dealer service department or motorcycle repair shop handle the entire process of disassembly, inspection, service or repair (if required) and reassembly of the valves.

Disassembly

3   Remove the cylinder head from the engine (see Section 12).
4   Before the valves are removed, scrape away any traces of gasket material from the head gasket sealing surface. Work slowly and do not nick or gouge the soft aluminum of the head. Gasket removing solvents, which work very well, are available at most motorcycle shops and auto parts stores.
5   Carefully scrape all carbon deposits out of the combustion chamber area. A hand held wire brush or a piece of fine emery cloth can be used once the majority of deposits have been scraped away. Do not use a wire brush mounted in a drill motor, or one with extremely stiff bristles, as the head material is soft and may be eroded away or scratched by the wire brush.
6   Before proceeding, arrange to label and store the valves along with their related components so they can be kept separate and reinstalled in the same valve guides they are

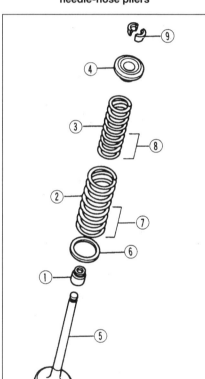

14.7b Valve components - exploded view

*1   Oil seal
2   Outer spring
3   Inner spring
4   Valve spring retainer
5   Valve
6   Outer spring seat
7   Tightly wound coils
8   Tightly wound coils
9   Keepers*

removed from (again, plastic bags work well for this).
7   Compress the valve spring on the first valve with a spring compressor, then remove the keepers **(see illustrations)** and the

2A

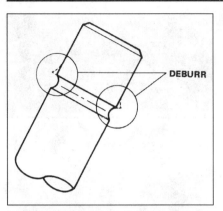

14.7c If the valve binds in the guide, deburr the area above the keeper groove

retainer from the valve assembly. Do not compress the springs any more than is absolutely necessary. Carefully release the valve spring compressor and remove the springs and the valve from the head. If the valve binds in the guide (won't pull through), push it back into the head and deburr the area around the keeper groove with a very fine file or whetstone **(see illustration)**.

8   Repeat the procedure for the remaining valves. Remember to keep the parts for each valve together so they can be reinstalled in the same location.
9   Once the valves have been removed and labeled, pull off the valve stem seals with pliers and discard them (the old seals should never be reused), then remove the spring seats.
10   Next, clean the cylinder head with solvent and dry it thoroughly. Compressed air will speed the drying process and ensure that all holes and recessed areas are clean.
11   Clean all of the valve springs, keepers, retainers and spring seats with solvent and dry them thoroughly. Do the parts from one valve at a time so that no mixing of parts between valves occurs.
12   Scrape off any deposits that may have formed on the valve, then use a motorized wire brush to remove deposits from the valve heads and stems. Again, make sure the valves do not get mixed up.

Inspection

13   Inspect the head very carefully for cracks and other damage. If cracks are found, a new head will be required.
14   Using a precision straightedge and a feeler gauge, check the head gasket mating surface for warpage. Lay the straightedge lengthwise, across the head and diagonally (corner-to-corner), intersecting the head bolt holes. Try to slip a feeler gauge of the same thickness as the warpage limit listed in this Chapter's Specifications under it, on either side of the combustion chamber **(see illustration)**. If the feeler gauge can be inserted between the head and the straightedge, the head is warped and must either be machined or, if warpage is excessive, replaced with a new one.
15   Examine the valve seats **(see illustration)**. If they are pitted, cracked or burned, the head will require valve service that is beyond the scope of the home mechanic. Measure the valve seat width and compare it to this Chapter's Specifications **(see illustration)**. If it is not within the specified range, or if it varies around its circumference, valve service work is required.
16   Clean the valve guides to remove any carbon buildup, then measure the inside diameters of the guides (at both ends and

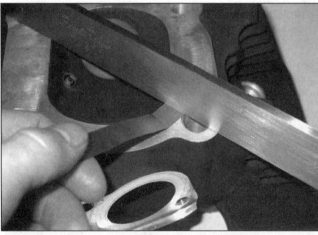

14.14 Lay a precision straightedge across the cylinder head and try to slide a feeler gauge of the specified thickness (equal to the maximum allowable warpage) under it

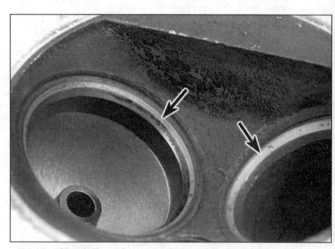

14.15a Check the valve seats (arrows) in each head - look for pits, cracks and burned areas

14.15b Measuring the valve seat width

14.16a Measure the valve guide with a small hole gauge . . .

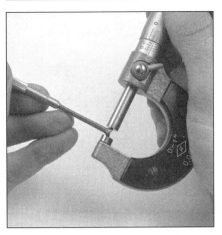

14.16b ... then measure the gauge with a micrometer

14.17a Check the valve face and margin for wear and cracks

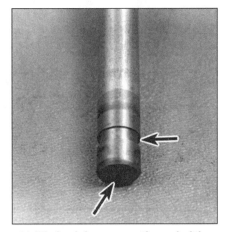

14.17b Look for wear on the end of the valve stem and make sure the keeper groove isn't distorted in any way

14.18 Measure the valve stem diameter with a micrometer

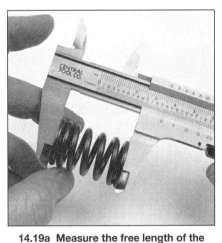

14.19a Measure the free length of the valve springs

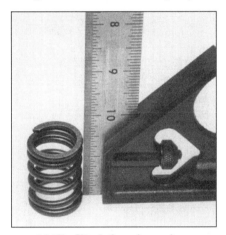

14.19b Check the valve springs for squareness

2A

the center of the guide) with a small hole gauge and a 0-to-1-inch micrometer **(see illustrations)**. If the guides exceed the maximum value given in the Chapter's Specifications, they must be replaced. The guides are measured at the ends and at the center to determine if they are worn in a bell-mouth pattern (more wear at the ends). If they are, guide replacement is an absolute must.

17 Carefully inspect each valve face for cracks, pits and burned spots **(see illustration)**. Check the valve stem and the keeper groove area for cracks **(see illustration)**. Rotate the valve and check for any obvious indication that it is bent. Check the end of the stem for pitting and excessive wear. The presence of any of the above conditions indicates the need for valve servicing.

18 Measure the valve stem diameter and replace if it exceeds the minimum value listed in this Chapter's Specifications **(see illustration)**. Also check the valve stem for bending. Set the valve in a V-block with a dial indicator touching the middle of the stem. Rotate the valve and note the reading on the gauge. If the stem runout exceeds the value listed in this Chapter's Specifications, replace the valve.

19 Check the end of each valve spring for wear and pitting. Measure the free length **(see illustration)** and compare it to this Chapter's Specifications. Any springs that are shorter than specified have sagged and should not be reused. Stand the spring on a flat surface and check it for squareness **(see illustration)**.

20 Check the spring retainers and keepers for obvious wear and cracks. Any questionable parts should not be reused, as extensive damage will occur in the event of failure during engine operation.

21 If the inspection indicates that no service work is required, the valve components can be reinstalled in the head.

Reassembly

22 Before installing the valves in the head, they should be lapped (1999 through 2002 models only) to ensure a positive seal between the valves and seats. Valves should not be lapped on 2003 models. This procedure requires fine valve lapping compound (available at auto parts stores) and a valve lapping tool. If a lapping tool is not available, a piece of rubber or plastic hose can be slipped over the valve stem (after the valve

has been installed in the guide) and used to turn the valve.

23 Apply a small amount of fine lapping compound to the valve face **(see illustration)**, then slip the valve into the guide. **Note:** *Make sure the valve is installed in the correct guide and be careful not to get any lapping compound on the valve stem.*

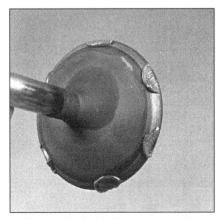

14.23 Apply the lapping compound very sparingly, in small dabs, to the valve face only

14.24a Rotate the lapping tool or hose back-and-forth between the palms of your hands

14.24b Lift the tool and valve periodically to redistribute the lapping compound on the valve face and seat

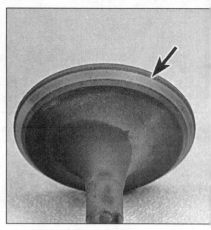

14.24c After lapping, the valve face should exhibit a uniform, unbroken contact pattern (arrow). . .

14.24d . . . and the seat should be the specified width (arrow) with a smooth, unbroken appearance

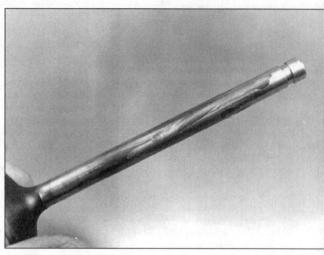

14.27a Lubricate the valve stem with moly-base grease before installing the valve in the cylinder head

24 Attach the lapping tool (or hose) to the valve and rotate the tool between the palms of your hands **(see illustration)**. Use a back-and-forth motion rather than a circular motion. Lift the valve off the seat and turn it at regular intervals to distribute the lapping compound properly **(see illustration)**. Continue the lapping procedure until the valve face and seat contact area is of uniform width and unbroken around the entire circumference of the valve face and seat **(see illustrations)**.

25 Carefully remove the valve from the guide and wipe off all traces of lapping compound. Use solvent to clean the valve and wipe the seat area thoroughly with a solvent soaked cloth. Repeat the procedure for the remaining valves.

26 Lay the spring seats in place in the cylinder head, then install new valve stem seals on each of the guides. Use an appropriate size deep socket to push the seals into place until they are properly seated. Don't twist or cock them, or they will not seal properly against the valve stems. Also, don't

remove them again or they will be damaged.

27 Coat the valve stems with assembly lube or moly-based grease **(see illustration)**, then install one of them into its guide. Next, install the spring seats, springs and retainers, compress the springs and install the keepers. When compressing the springs with the valve spring compressor, depress them only as far as is absolutely necessary to slip the keepers into place. Apply a small amount of grease to the keepers **(see illustration)** to help hold them in place as the pressure is released from the springs. Make certain that the keepers are securely locked in their retaining grooves.

28 Support the cylinder head on blocks so the valves can't contact the workbench top, then very gently tap each of the valve stems with a soft-faced hammer. This will help seat the keepers in their grooves.

29 Once all of the valves have been installed in the head, check for proper valve sealing by pouring a small amount of solvent into each of the valve ports. If the solvent leaks past the valve(s) into the combustion chamber area,

disassemble the valve(s) and repeat the lapping procedure, then reinstall the valve(s) and repeat the check. Repeat the procedure until a satisfactory seal is obtained.

14.27b A small dab of grease will help hold the keepers in place on the valve spring while the valve is released

15.1 Slip pieces of rubber tubing over the cylinder studs

15.4 Pack clean rags into the crankcase opening to keep out debris

15.5a Remove the cylinder base O-ring . . .

15 Cylinders - removal, inspection and installation

Removal

1   Before you start, obtain four six-inch lengths of 1/2-inch inside diameter tubing for each cylinder. You'll need these to slip over the studs **(see illustration)**.
2   Following the procedure given in Section 12, remove the cylinder head. Make sure the crankshaft is positioned at Top Dead Center (TDC) for the cylinder you're working on (see Section 8).
3   Remove the valve cover, breather, rocker support, rocker plate and cylinder head (see Sections 9 through 12).
4   Lift the cylinder straight up just until you can stuff clean shop towels around the piston, in the space between the cylinder and crankcase **(see illustration)**. If the cylinder is stuck, tap around its perimeter with a soft-faced hammer. Don't attempt to pry between the cylinder and the crankcase, as you will ruin the sealing surfaces.
5   Lift the cylinder straight off the studs. Remove the cylinder base O-ring and dowel O-rings **(see illustrations)**.

15.5b . . . and the cylinder dowel O-ring

Inspection

Caution: Don't attempt to separate the liner from the cylinder.
6   Check the cylinder walls carefully for scratches and score marks.
7   The cylinders tend to distort slightly when they're removed from the engine, so bore measurements will be off unless the cylinders are clamped. Harley-Davidson manufactures a set of torque plates for this

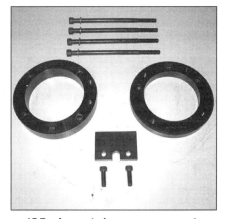

15.7a Accurate bore measurements require a set of torque plates to clamp the cylinder (this is the JIMS tool)

purpose. These are heavy metal plates that are attached to the top and bottom of the cylinder by studs that go through the cylinder stud passages. JIMS tools also supplies an equivalent tool **(see illustrations)**. If you don't have these or the equivalent, or the necessary bore gauge, have the measurements done by a dealer service department or other qualified shop.

2A

15.7b Lay one plate over the top of the cylinder . . .

15.7c . . . and attach the other plate and mounting base with the bolts, then tighten the nuts

8   Using the appropriate precision measuring tools, check each cylinder's diameter 1/2-inch down from the top, halfway down the ring travel area, and at the bottom of the ring travel area, parallel to the crankshaft axis **(see illustrations)**. Next, measure each cylinder's diameter at the same three locations across the crankshaft axis. Compare the results to this Chapter's Specifications. If the cylinder walls are tapered, out-of-round, worn beyond the specified limits, or badly scuffed or scored, have them rebored and honed by a dealer service department or a motorcycle repair shop. If a rebore is done, oversize pistons and rings will be required as well. Oversize pistons are listed in this Chapter's Specifications. Remove the torque plates after taking the measurements.

9   Lay a straightedge across the cylinder top surface and measure any gap between the straightedge and surface with a feeler gauge **(see illustration)**. Repeat the measurement on the cylinder bottom O-ring surface. If either surface is warped beyond the limit listed in this Chapter's Specifications, replace the cylinder and piston.

10   If they are in reasonably good condition and not worn to the outside of the limits, and if the piston-to-cylinder clearances can be maintained properly (see Section 6), then the cylinders do not have to be rebored; honing is all that is necessary.

11   To perform the honing operation you will need the proper size flexible hone with fine stones, or a "bottle brush" type hone, plenty of light oil or honing oil, some shop towels and an electric drill motor. Harley-Davidson recommends a bottle-brush type hone with 240-grit stones. Hold the cylinder block in a vise (cushioned with soft jaws or wood blocks) when performing the honing operation. Mount the hone in the drill motor, compress the stones and slip the hone into the cylinder. Lubricate the cylinder thoroughly, turn on the drill and move the hone up and down in the cylinder at a pace which will produce a fine crosshatch pattern on the cylinder wall with the crosshatch lines inter-

15.8a Measure the cylinder bore with a micrometer

secting at a 60-degree angle - the angle is important to obtain good ring seating. Be sure to use plenty of lubricant and do not take off any more material than is absolutely necessary to produce the desired effect. Do not withdraw the hone from the cylinder while it is running. Instead, shut off the drill and continue moving the hone up and down in the cylinder until it comes to a complete stop, then compress the stones and withdraw the hone. Wipe the oil out of the cylinder and repeat the procedure on the remaining cylinder. Remember, do not remove too much material from the cylinder wall. If you do not have the tools, or do not desire to perform the honing operation, a dealer service department or motorcycle repair shop will generally do it for a reasonable fee.

12   Next, the cylinders must be thoroughly washed with warm soapy water to remove all traces of the abrasive grit produced during the honing operation. Be sure to run a brush through the bolt holes and flush them with running water. After rinsing, dry the cylinders thoroughly and apply a coat of light, rust-preventative oil to all machined surfaces.

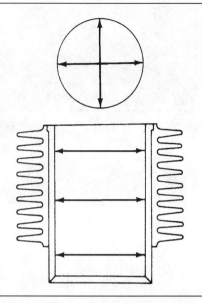

15.8b Measure the cylinder diameter in two directions, at the top, center and bottom of travel

Installation

13   Lubricate the cylinder bore, piston and rings with plenty of clean engine oil. Apply a thin film or oil to the new cylinder base O-ring and the two cylinder dowel O-rings.

14   Install the dowel pins, then place the new cylinder base O-ring on the cylinder **(see illustration)**.

15   Slowly rotate the crankshaft until the piston is at top dead center. Install a support tool under the piston (HD-42322, JIMS or equivalent) **(see illustration)**. With the tool securely in place, lower the piston until it rests securely ion the tool.

16   Attach a piston ring compressor to the piston and compress the piston rings **(see illustration)**. A large hose clamp can be used instead - just make sure it doesn't scratch the piston, and don't tighten it too much.

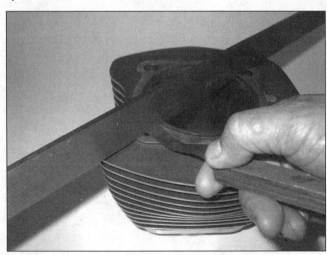

15.9 Check flatness of the cylinder top surface with a straightedge and feeler gauge

15.14 Install the cylinder base O-ring (shown) and dowel O-ring

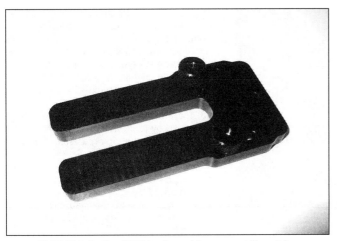

15.15 This is the JIMS tool used to support the piston while it's removed

15.16 Clamp the rings with a ring compressor and slip the cylinder over the piston

16.3a Using a sharp scribe, scratch the cylinder position (front or rear) into the piston crowns - also note the arrow, which must point to the front

16.3b Wear eye protection and pry the circlip out of the groove with a pointed tool

16 Pistons - removal, inspection and installation

1   The pistons are attached to the connecting rods with piston pins that are a slip fit in the pistons and rods.

2   Before removing the pistons from the rods, stuff a clean shop towel into each crankcase hole, around the connecting rod **(see illustration 15.4)**. This will prevent the circlips from falling into the crankcase if they are inadvertently dropped.

Removal

3   Using a sharp scribe, scratch the position of each piston (front or rear cylinder) into its crown. Each piston should also have an arrow pointing toward the front of the engine **(see illustration)**. If not, scribe an arrow into the piston crown before removal. Support the piston and remove the circlip with needle-nose pliers or a pointed tool **(see illustration)**. Push the piston pin out with fingers **(see illustration)**. If the pin won't come out, fabricate a piston pin removal tool from threaded stock (stud), nuts, washers and a piece of pipe **(see illustration)**.

4   Push the piston pin out from the opposite end to free the piston from the rod. You

17   Install the cylinder over the piston with the indentation in the cooling fins toward the right (valve lifter) side of the engine and carefully lower it down until the piston crown fits into the cylinder liner. Push down on the cylinder, making sure the piston doesn't get cocked sideways, until the bottom of the

cylinder liner slides down past the piston rings. A wood or plastic hammer handle can be used to gently tap the cylinder down, but don't use too much force or the piston will be damaged.

18   Remove the piston ring compressor or hose clamp, being careful not to scratch the piston. Raise the piston enough to remove the support tool.

19   The remainder of installation is the reverse of removal.

16.3c Push the piston pin part-way out, then pull it the rest of the way

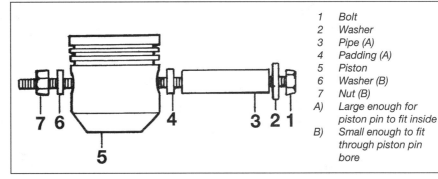

1	Bolt
2	Washer
3	Pipe (A)
4	Padding (A)
5	Piston
6	Washer (B)
7	Nut (B)
A)	Large enough for piston pin to fit inside
B)	Small enough to fit through piston pin bore

16.3d The piston should come out with hand pressure - if it doesn't, this tool can be fabricated from readily available parts

2A

16.6 Remove the piston rings with a ring removal and installation tool

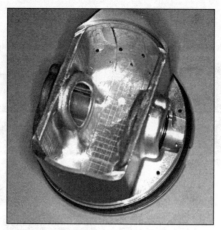

16.11 Check the piston pin bore and the piston skirt for wear, and make sure the internal holes are clear

may have to deburr the area around the groove to enable the pin to slide out (use a triangular file for this procedure). Repeat the procedure for the other piston.

Inspection

5   Before the inspection process can be carled out, the plstons must be cleaned and the old piston rings removed.

6   Using a piston ring installation tool, carefully remove the rings from the pistons **(see illustration)**. Do not nick or gouge the pistons in the process.

7   Scrape all traces of carbon from the tops of the pistons. A hand-held wire brush or a piece of fine emery cloth can be used once most of the deposits have been scraped away. Do not, under any circumstances, use a wire brush mounted in a drill motor to remove deposits from the pistons; the piston material is soft and will be eroded away by the wire brush.

8   Use a piston ring groove cleaning tool to remove any carbon deposits from the ring grooves. If a tool is not available, a piece broken off the old ring will do the job. Be very

careful to remove only the carbon deposits. Do not remove any metal and do not nick or gouge the sides of the ring grooves.

9   Once the deposits have been removed, clean the pistons with solvent and dry them thoroughly. Make sure the oil return holes below the oil ring grooves are clear.

10   If the pistons are not damaged or worn excessively and if the cylinders are not rebored, new pistons will not be necessary. Normal piston wear appears as even, vertical wear on the thrust surfaces of the piston and slight looseness of the top ring in its groove. New piston rings, on the other hand, should always be used when an engine is rebuilt.

11   Carefully inspect each piston for cracks around the skirt, at the pin bosses and at the ring lands **(see illustration)**.

12   Look for scoring and scuffing on the thrust faces of the skirt, holes in the piston crown and burned areas at the edge of the crown. If the skirt is scored or scuffed, the engine may have been suffering from overheating and/or abnormal combustion, which caused excessively high operating temperatures. The oil pump should be checked thor-

oughly. A hole in the piston crown, an extreme to be sure, is an indication that abnormal combustion (pre-ignition) was occurring. Burned areas at the edge of the piston crown are usually evidence of spark knock (detonation). If any of the above problems exist, the causes must be corrected or the damage will occur again.

13   Measure the piston ring-to-groove clearance by laying a new piston ring in the ring groove and slipping a feeler gauge in beside it **(see illustration)**. Check the clearance at three or four locations around the groove. Be sure to use the correct ring for each groove; they are different. If the clearance is greater than specified, new pistons will have to be used when the engine is reassembled.

14   Check the piston-to-bore clearance by measuring the bore (see Section 15) and the piston diameter. Make sure that the pistons and cylinders are correctly matched. On 1999 through 2002 models, measure the piston across the skirt on the thrust faces at a 90-degree angle to the piston pin, about 1/2-inch (13 mm) up from the bottom of the skirt **(see illustration)**. On 2003 models, measure at the two small openings in the coating material on the piston skirt (where the bare aluminum is exposed). These openings are very small, so you'll need ball anvil adapters for the micrometer. Subtract the piston diameter from the bore diameter to obtain the clearance. If it is greater than specified, the cylinders will have to be rebored and new oversized pistons and rings installed. If the appropriate precision measuring tools are not available, the piston-to-cylinder clearances can be obtained, though not quite as accurately, using feeler gauge stock. Feeler gauge stock comes in 12-inch lengths and various thicknesses and is generally available at auto parts stores. To check the clearance, select a piece of feeler gauge stock equal to the piston-to-cylinder clearance listed in this Chapter's Specifications. Slip the gauge into the cylinder alongside of the piston. The cylinder should be upside down

16.13 Measure the piston ring-to-groove clearance with a feeler gauge

16.14 Measure the piston diameter with a micrometer

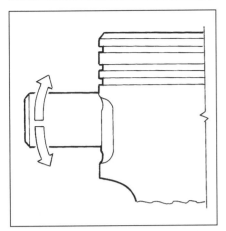

16.15 Slip the pin into the piston and try to wiggle it back-and-forth; if it's loose, replace the piston and pin

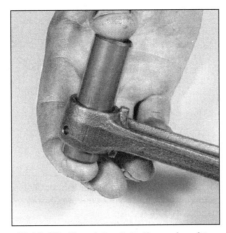

16.16 Slip the piston into the rod and try to rock it back-and-forth to check for looseness

16.18 Make sure both piston pin circlips are securely seated in the piston grooves

and the piston must be positioned exactly as it normally would be. Place the feeler gauge between the piston and cylinder on one of the thrust faces (90-degrees to the piston pin bore). The piston should slip through the cylinder (with the feeler gauge in place) with moderate pressure. If it falls through, or slides through easily, the clearance is excessive and a new piston will be required. If the piston binds at the lower end of the cylinder and is loose toward the top, the cylinder is tapered, and if tight spots are encountered as the feeler gauge is placed at different points around the cylinder, the cylinder is out-of-round. Repeat the procedure for the remaining piston and cylinder. Be sure to have the cylinders and pistons checked by a dealer service department or a motorcycle repair shop to confirm your findings before purchasing new parts.

15 Apply clean engine oil to the pin, insert it into the piston and check for freeplay by rocking the pin back-and-forth **(see illustration)**. If the pin is loose, new pistons and pins must be installed.

16 Repeat Step 15, this time inserting the pin into the connecting rod **(see illustration)**. If the pin is loose, measure the pin diameter and the pin bushing bore in the connecting rod (or have this done by a dealer service department or machine shop). Replace the piston and pin if the pin is worn; have the pin bushing pressed out and a new one pressed in if it's worn.

17 Refer to Section 17 and install the rings on the pistons.

Installation

18 Install the piston in its original location (front or rear cylinder) with the arrow pointing to the front of the engine. Lubricate the pin and the rod bore with clean engine oil. Install a new circlip in the piston groove on one side of the pistons (don't reuse the old circlips). Push the pin into position from the opposite side and install a new circlip. Compress the circlips only enough for them to fit in the pis-

ton. Make sure the circlips are properly seated in the grooves **(see illustration)**.
19 Repeat the procedure to install the other piston.

17 Piston rings - installation

1 Before installing the new piston rings, the ring end gaps must be checked.
2 Lay out the pistons and the new ring sets so the rings will be matched with the same piston and cylinder during the end gap measurement procedure and engine assembly.
3 Insert the top (No. 1) ring into the bottom of the cylinder and square it up with the cylinder walls by pushing it in with the top of the piston **(see illustration)**. The ring should be about one inch above the bottom edge of the cylinder. To measure the end gap, slip a feeler gauge between the ends of the ring and compare the measurement to the Specifications.

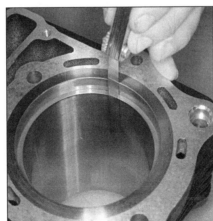

17.3 Check the piston ring end gap with a feeler gauge -measure at the bottom of the ring travel area if the cylinder looks worn

4 If the gap is larger or smaller than specified, double check to make sure that you have the correct rings before proceeding.
5 If the gap is too small, it must be enlarged or the ring ends may come in contact with each other during engine operation, which can cause serious damage. The end gap can be increased by filing the ring ends very carefully with a fine file **(see illustration)**. When performing this operation, file only from the outside in.
6 Excess end gap is not critical unless it is greater than 0.040 in (1 mm). Again, double check to make sure you have the correct rings for your engine.
7 Repeat the procedure for each ring that will be installed in the first cylinder and for each ring in the remaining cylinder. Remember to keep the rings, pistons and cylinders matched up.
8 Once the ring end gaps have been checked/corrected, the rings can be installed on the pistons.
9 The oil control ring (lowest on the piston) is installed first. It is composed of three separate components. Slip the expander into

2A

17.5 If the end gap is too small, clamp a file in a vise and file the ring ends (from the outside in only) to enlarge the gap slightly

17.9a Installing the oil ring expander -
make sure the ends don't overlap

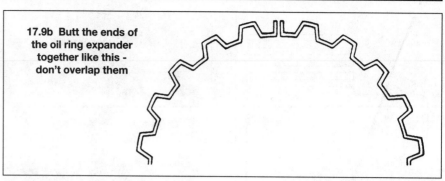

17.9b Butt the ends of
the oil ring expander
together like this -
don't overlap them

14   Repeat the procedure for the remaining
piston and rings. Be very careful not to confuse the middle and top rings.
15   Once the rings have been properly
installed, stagger the end gaps, including
those of the oil ring side rails (see illustrations).

18 Camshafts and timing chains - removal, inspection and installation

Removal

1   Support the bike securely upright.
2   Remove the seat and right floorboard
(see Chapter 7).
3   Disconnect the negative cable from the
battery.
4   Remove the exhaust system, fuel tank
and air cleaner housing. Disconnect the
throttle cables and remove the carburetor or
EFI induction module (see Chapter 3).
5   Remove the spark plugs (see Chapter 1).
6   Unbolt the upper engine mount from the
frame. If you're working on a carbureted
model, detach the choke cable from the horn
bracket. Remove the upper engine mount
and horn bracket together.
7   Remove the breather, rocker arms and

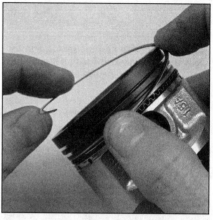

17.9c Installing an oil ring side rail - don't
use a ring installation tool to do this

the groove, then install the upper side rail
(see illustrations). Do not use a piston ring
installation tool on the oil ring side rails as
they may be damaged. Instead, place one
end of the side rail into the groove between
the spacer expander and the ring land. Hold
it firmly in place and slide a finger around the
piston while pushing the rail into the groove.
Next, install the lower side rail in the same
manner.
10   After the three oil ring components have
been installed, check to make sure that both
the upper and lower side rails can be turned
smoothly in the ring groove.
11   Install the second compression ring
(middle ring) next. Do not mix the top and
middle rings.
12   To avoid breaking the ring, use a piston
ring installation tool and make sure that the
identification mark is facing up. Fit the ring
into the middle groove on the piston. Do not
expand the ring any more than is necessary
to slide it into place.
13   Finally, install the top compression ring
in the same manner. Make sure the identifying mark is facing up.

support plate and pushrods (see Sections 10, 11 and 12). The valve lifters don't
have to be removed completely; instead,
support them at the top of their travel with
the spring from a large binder clip (available
at office supply stores).
8   Remove the bolts and take the cam
cover off the engine (see illustration).
9   Mark a directional arrow on the primary
cam chain if you plan to reuse it (see illustration).

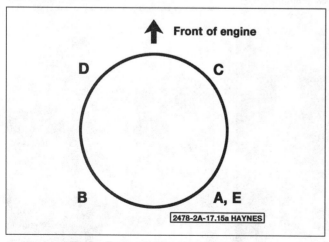

17.15a Front cylinder ring gap locations

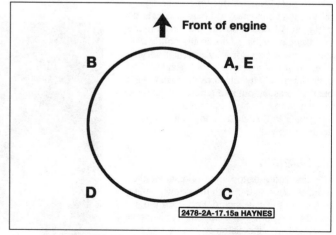

17.15b Rear cylinder ring gap locations

A	Oil ring spacer	D	Second compression ring
B	Oil ring lower rail	E	Top compression ring
C	Oil ring upper rail		

18.8 Remove the bolts (arrows) and take off the outer cam cover

18.9 Camshaft sprocket and support plate details

1 through 6 - Camshaft support plate bolt loosening AND tightening sequence

A through D - Oil pump bolt loosening AND tightening sequence (bolts B and D hidden behind sprocket)

7   Primary cam chain tensioner

8   Primary cam chain guide

9   Camshaft sprocket timing mark

10 Crankshaft sprocket timing mark (hidden behind washer)

18.12a These are the JIMS tools used to retract and hold the cam chain tensioners

18.12b Place the tool over the tensioner . . .

18.12c . . . turn it with a wrench or socket and insert the pin to hold it in the retracted position

2A

10 Unscrew the crankshaft sprocket bolt and remove the washer.

11 Unscrew the rear camshaft sprocket bolt and remove the washer. **Note:** *The bolt is secured with Loctite and can be difficult to remove. If it won't come off with a standard breaker bar, carefully heat the bolt with a propane torch, taking care not to heat any other components. Don't heat the bolt enough to turn it blue. Don't use a large breaker bar to loosen the bolt or it may break.*

12 Retract the primary cam chain tensioner with a tensioner unloader (HD-42313 or equivalent, such as JIMS 1283-1) **(see illustration).** Insert a retaining pin through the tensioner hole to hold it in the retracted position **(see illustrations).**

13 Carefully pry the camshaft sprocket off with a tool such as a seal remover. Work around the sprocket as you pry.

14 Remove the crankshaft sprocket in the same manner (you'll need a smaller prying

tool for the crankshaft sprocket). Remove the crankshaft and camshaft sprockets together with the chain, them remove the spacer from the camshaft.

15 Squeeze the tabs of the chain guide toward each other and pull the chain guide out of the support plate.

⚠️ *Warning: Don't remove the camshaft retainer pin after removing the camshaft support plate in the following Steps. It's strong enough to cause possible injury and may damage itself or the tensioner pad if released suddenly.*

16 Loosen the oil pump Allen bolts evenly until they're all loose, then unscrew them.

17 Loosen the Allen bolts that secure the camshaft support plate evenly until they're all loose, then remove them **(see illustration 18.9).**

18 Carefully pry the camshaft support plate from the crankcase, using a small pry bar located next to each of the two dowels, then take off the support plate and remove the dowel pins **(see illustration).**

19 Remove the O-rings from the oil feed hole and chain guide screen **(see illustration 18.18).** Don't remove the screen yet.

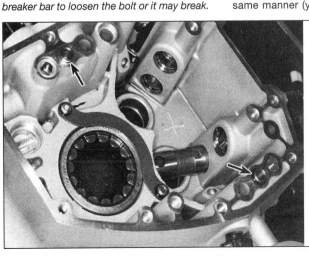

18.18 Remove the cam support plate from the right crankcase half, then remove the O-rings and dowels (arrows)

Inspection

Note: *Before replacing camshafts because of damage, check with local machine shops specializing in motorcycle engine work. It may be possible for cam lobes to be welded, reground and hardened, at a cost far lower than that of new camshafts.*

20   Check the camshaft lobes for heat discoloration (blue appearance), score marks, chipped areas, flat spots and spalling **(see illustration)**. If damage is noted or wear is excessive, the camshafts must be replaced. Also, be sure to check the condition of the lifters (see Section 11). Replacement of the camshafts and secondary chain requires a hydraulic press and support tools and should be done by a dealer service department or other qualified shop.

21   Turn the camshafts and check their needle roller bearings in the cam support plate for roughness or looseness. If problems are found, have the bearings replaced by a dealer service department or other qualified shop.

22   Check the camshaft inner needle roller bearings in the right crankcase for rough or noisy rotation and for visible damage **(see illustration 18.18)**. If problems are found, disassemble the crankcase halves (see Section 22). Have the bearings pressed out and new ones pressed in by a dealer service department or other qualified shop.

23   To inspect the chain tensioners, compress them as described above, remove the retainer pins and release the tensioner. Remove the tensioner snap-ring and slide the tensioner off its post. Check the chain tensioner for wear or damage. If the tensioner pad is worn to less than half its original thickness, or if it's damaged, replace the tensioner. If the tensioner is worn or damaged, the chain may be worn out. Inspect it carefully, along with the sprockets, and replace them as a set if necessary.

24   Check the crankshaft bushing in the cam support plate for wear or damage. If problems are found, have it pressed out and a new one pressed in by a dealer service department or other qualified shop.

25   Remove and clean the chain guide screen. Install the screen, using a new O-ring.

Installation

26   Wipe a thin layer of clean engine oil onto new O-rings for the oil feed hole and crankcase hole, then install them on the crankcase.

27   Place the cam support plate in a soft-jawed vise. Unload the secondary cam chain tensioner with HD-42313 or equivalent and secure it with the retaining pin. Apply clean engine oil to the camshaft needle roller bearings.

28   With the tensioner unloaded, lay a straightedge across the camshafts. The straightedge should align with the camshaft marks and the centers of both camshafts. If not, rotate the camshafts until it does. Leave the retaining pin in place, holding the ten-

18.20 Check the lobes of the camshaft for wear - here's a good example of a camshaft which will require replacement (or repair) of the camshaft

sioner in the unloaded position, until the cam support plate is installed on the engine.

29   Place the cam support plate unto the crankcase, aligning it with the dowels and crankshaft. Don't let the O-rings fall out of place. Once the support plate is in position, seat it on the engine by tapping with a rubber mallet.

30   Install the six Allen bolts, then tighten them evenly, in the correct sequence, to the torque listed in this Chapter's Specifications.

31   Install alignment tools (HD-33443 or equivalent) into two of the oil pump holes and install Allen bolts into the remaining two holes. The alignment tools are taped shafts, threaded on one end to fit into the oil pump bolt holes (1/4 x 1.0-inch threads). Have an assistant rotate the engine to center the oil pump. While rotating, evenly tighten the alignment tools and screws just until they're snug.

32   Tighten the alignment tools and screws in the correct sequence to the torque listed in this Chapter's Specifications (the sequence numbers are cast in the support plate next to the bolt holes).

33   Unscrew the alignment tools and install the remaining two bolts in their place. Tighten all four bolts, again following the sequence, to the torque listed in this Chapter's Specifications.

34   Remove the retaining pin to unload the secondary cam chain tensioner.

35   Install the chain guide in the cam support plate. Squeeze its tabs together as you push it into the hole, then release the tabs.

36   Install the sprocket spacer on the rear camshaft with its letters facing the engine.

37   If you've install a new crankshaft, camshafts, support plate, chain or sprockets, you'll need to select a new spacer for the rear cam sprocket as described below. If all of the original parts are being reinstalled, skip to Step 46.

38   Bolt the sprocket to the rear camshaft.

39   Install the sprocket on the crankshaft, using a washer with the same inside diameter as the original washer, but a smaller outside diameter. This leaves room for a straightedge on the face of the crankshaft sprocket.

40   Install both sprockets without the primary cam chain. Prevent the sprockets from rotating with a tool (HD-42314 or equivalent) between the sprockets. Tighten both sprocket bolts to 15 ft-lbs, then remove the tool.

41   Push the rear camshaft into the engine to take up any end play.

42   Lay a straightedge across both sprocket faces. If there's any gap between either sprocket face and the straightedge, try to insert a 0.010-inch feeler gauge into it. If it won't fit, the sprockets are aligned correctly. Skip the next step.

43   If the gap between the feeler gauge and primary cam sprocket is more than 0.010-inch, remove the cam sprocket and install the next size thicker spacer.

44   If the gap between the feeler gauge and crankshaft sprocket is more than 0.010-inch, remove the cam sprocket and install the next size thinner spacer. **Note:** *Only change spacers one size at a time, then repeat the check.*

45   Once the correct spacer has been selected, remove the sprocket bolts and the small washer under the crank sprocket bolt. Reinstall the correct crank sprocket washer.

46   Place the sprockets in the primary cam chain. If you're reinstalling the original chain, place the directional mark made during disassembly so it will be to the outside when the chain and sprockets are installed. Align the sprocket timing marks so they're directly toward each other when the chain and sprockets are installed.

47   Oil the splines of the rear camshaft and install the sprockets. Align the camshaft key with the sprocket slot, and align the flat in the crankshaft with the matching flat in the crank sprocket.

48   Check the alignment of the sprocket marks with a straightedge. The straightedge should align with both timing marks and the centers of the camshaft and crankshaft. If not, rotate the camshaft and crankshaft until the marks align. If you can't get them to align, remove the sprockets and reposition the chain on the sprocket teeth, then reinstall the sprockets.

49   Clean any remaining non-permanent thread locking agent from the sprocket bolt threads inside the camshaft and crankshaft, using a thread chaser.

50   Install new sprocket bolts, using the correct washers. These are specially sized and hardened, so don't use substitute parts. Note that the bolts and washers are not the same size.

51   If you can't get new sprocket bolts, remove all old thread locking agent from the old ones, and install them, using a small amount of semi-permanent thread locking agent on the threads. Don't use too much or the bolts will be difficult to remove.

52   Install the sprocket bolts and tighten them to the initial torque listed in this Chapter's Specifications.

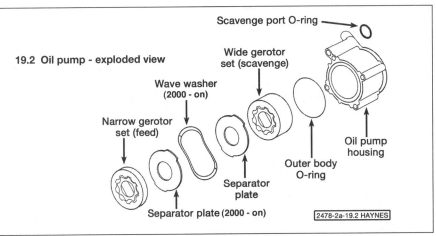

19.2 Oil pump - exploded view

Scavenge port O-ring
Wide gerotor set (scavenge)
Wave washer (2000 - on)
Narrow gerotor set (feed)
Oil pump housing
Outer body O-ring
Separator plate
Separator plate (2000 - on)

2478-2a-19.2 HAYNES

53   Loosen each bolt one full turn.
54   Tighten the cam sprocket bolt, then the crank sprocket bolt, to the torque listed in this Chapter's Specifications.
55   Unload the primary chain tensioner and pull out the retaining pin, then slowly release the tensioner.
56   Lubricate the sprockets with clean engine oil.
57   Make sure all old gasket has been removed from the cam cover and support plate. Install a new gasket. Install the bolts and tighten them evenly, in sequence, to the torque listed in this Chapter's Specifications.
Caution: Run a tap through the bolt holes before installing the bolts. Any oil or other foreign material in the holes may cause the right crankcase half to crack when the bolts are installed.
58   The remainder of installation is the reverse of the removal steps.

19 Oil pump - removal, inspection and installation

Removal

1   Remove the camshaft support plate (see Section 18).

20.3 Remove the retaining pin with a punch

2   Remove the outer O-ring from the oil pump. Pull the oil pump off the crankshaft and remove the two inner O-rings **(see illustration)**.

Inspection

3   Wash all the components in solvent, then dry them off. Check the pump body, the rotors and the shaft for scoring and wear. Measure clearance between the rotors (both sets) with a feeler gauge. If the measurements exceed the amount listed in this Chapter's Specifications, replace the rotors as a set. Also measure the thickness of the inner and outer feed (narrow) rotors. If they aren't exactly the same, replace them as a set.

Installation

4   Smear new inner O-rings with clean engine oil and install them on the engine. Don't use too much oil.
5   Install the oil pump housing over the crankshaft and push it against the engine, making sure the O-rings stay in place. Push against the scavenge port stub to make sure it's securely seated in the bore.
6   Lubricate the scavenge (wide) rotors with clean engine oil, mesh them together and install them over the crankshaft, all the way into the oil pump housing.
7   Install the inner separator plate (all

21.5a Pull back the fitting cover . . .

models), wave washer and outer separator plate (2000 and later).
8   Lubricate the feed (narrow) rotors with clean engine oil, mesh them together and install them in the oil pump housing.
9   The remainder of installation is the reverse of the removal steps.

20 Oil pressure relief valve - disassembly, inspection and reassembly

1   Remove the cam support plate and primary cam chain tensioner (see Section 18).
2   Place the cam support plate in a soft-jawed vise.
3   Tap the retaining pin out of the plate with a 1/8-inch pin punch **(see illustration)**. Remove the spring and valve body.
4   Check the pin for damage or corrosion and the spring for weakness. Replace them if problems are found.
5   Installation is the reverse of the removal steps. Lubricate the pin with clean engine oil and use a new roll pin.

21 Oil tank and lines - removal and installation

Softail models
Removal

1   Drain the oil tank (see Chapter 1).
2   Remove the seat and inner rear fender (see Chapter 7).
3   Remove the rear exhaust pipe (see Chapter 3).
4   Disconnect both battery cables, negative cable first, and unbolt the electrical panel from the rear of the oil tank.
5   Disconnect the vent and return lines from the front of the oil tank, using a coupling disconnect tool (HD-44455 or equivalent). This is similar to the tools used to disconnect fuel injection lines **(see illustrations)**.

2A

21.5b . . . and insert the tool (this is a JIMS tool) to disconnect the line from the tank

21.7a Remove two bolts at the rear of the oil tank (arrows, hidden) . . .

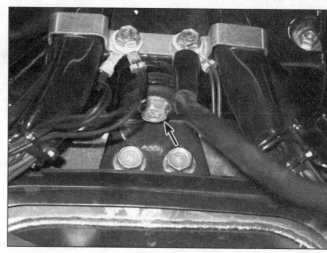

21.7b . . . and remove the tank front bracket (arrows)

6   Unbolt the fuse block and move it out of the way.
7   Remove the oil tank front and rear mounting bolts (see illustrations).
8   Remove the rubber pad from the battery tray.

9   Remove the retainers from the lower drain hose and oil feed hose (see illustration). You'll need to cut the retainers on the

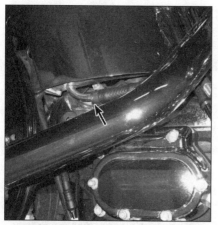

21.9 Disconnect the hoses from the underside of the tank (arrow) . . .

21.10 . . . and remove the tank from the right side of the motorcycle

21.11 Remove the snap-ring to free the oil line from the engine fitting

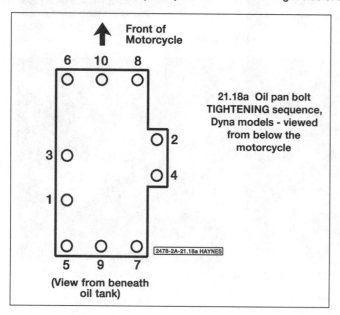

21.18a Oil pan bolt TIGHTENING sequence, Dyna models - viewed from below the motorcycle

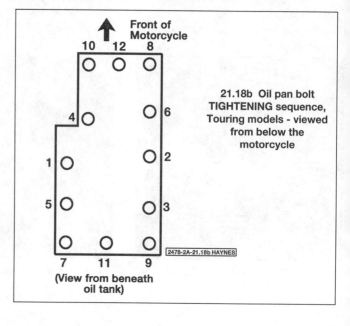

21.18b Oil pan bolt TIGHTENING sequence, Touring models - viewed from below the motorcycle

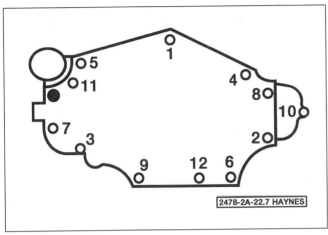

22.7 Crankcase bolt TIGHTENING sequence

22.12 Here are the crankcase dowel holes in the left case half (arrows) - the dowels stayed in the right case half

oil feed hose.

10 Remove the oil tank from the right side of the bike, feeding the battery positive cable through the tank as you remove it (see illustration).

11 If the oil line fittings have been leaking, remove them using HD 44455 or an equivalent such as a JIMS tool (see illustration). The O-rings and spacer are not available separately, so you'll need to replace the entire fitting.

12 Install the new fitting, using the same tool used for removal.

13 Installation is the reverse of the removal steps, with the following additions:

a) Use a new clamp on the oil feed hose.
b) Position the drain hose to the outside of the electrical panel and to the inside of the brake line and wiring harness.
b) Special tools are not needed to connect the vent and return lines to the tank. Just push them straight into the fittings, taking care not to damage the O-rings.
c) The fender extension goes over the tab on the frame.
d) Connect the positive battery cable first and the negative cable last.
e) Fill the oil tank and check oil level (see Chapter 1).

Dyna and Touring models

14 The Dyna and Touring engine oil tank is a pan mounted under the transmission. A passage cast into the right side of the tank connects the transmission oil drain plug to the transmission case.

15 Support the motorcycle securely upright.

16 Drain the engine and transmission oil (see Chapter 1).

17 If you're working on a Touring model, remove the rear wheel (see Chapter 5).

18 Remove the oil tank mounting bolts (see illustrations). Lower the pan away from the motorcycle. If it won't come easily, tap it with a rubber mallet to free it. Don't pry against the gasket surfaces or they will be damaged.

19 On Touring models, remove the tank to

the rear through the space left open by removing the rear wheel.

20 If necessary, remove the spring and baffle from inside the tank.

21 Installation is the reverse of the removal steps, with the following additions:

a) Tighten the pan bolts evenly, following the correct sequence, to the torque listed in this Chapter's Specifications.
b) Fill the oil tank and transmission and check oil level in both units (see Chapter 1).

22 Crankcase - disassembly and reassembly

1 To examine and repair or replace the crankshaft, connecting rods, bearings and balancer shafts (Softail models), the crankcase must be split into two parts.

2 Remove the engine from the motorcycle (see Section 6).

Disassembly

3 Remove the valve covers, breathers, rocker support plates, cylinder heads, cylinders, pistons, camshaft support plate and oil pump (see Sections 9, 10, 11, 16, 18 and 19).

4 Remove the alternator rotor (see Chapter 8). The stator need not be removed unless the crankcase halves are being replaced.

5 Remove the primary drive gear housing (see Chapter 2B).

6 Remove the oil filter (see Chapter 1). Remove the oil filter base and O-rings.

7 Remove the twelve crankcase bolts from the left side of the crankcase, in the reverse of the tightening sequence (see illustration).

8 Carefully pry the crankcase apart. Don't pry between the mating surfaces or they'll be damaged.

9 Separate the crankcase halves and remove the dowels and O-rings.

10 Refer to Sections 23 through 25 for information on the internal components of the crankcase.

Reassembly

11 Remove all traces of sealant from the crankcase mating surfaces. Be careful not to let any fall into the case as this is done.

12 Check to make sure the two dowel pins are in place in their holes in the mating surface of the crankcase half (see illustration). Wipe the dowel pin O-rings with a thin film of oil and install them on the dowel pins.

13 Make sure the following components are in place inside the crankcase:

a) Balancer shafts and rubber interconnect tube (Softail models)
b) Crankshaft, connecting rods and all case bearings

14 Apply a 1/16-inch wide bead of non-hardening gasket sealant (HD-99650-81, 3M 800 or equivalent) to the crankcase mating surface.

Caution: Don't apply an excessive amount of sealant, as it will ooze out when the case halves are assembled.

15 Slip a protective sleeve (HD 42326 or equivalent) over the end of the crankshaft to protect the bearing.

16 Place the right case half in position on the left case half and remove the sleeve from the crankshaft.

17 Install the case bolts and tighten them in sequence until all are finger-tight. Go through the sequence again, tightening to the initial torque listed in this Chapter's Specifications. Go through the sequence one more time, this time tightening them to the final torque listed in this Chapter's Specifications.

18 Take the crankcase to a dealer service department or other qualified shop and have a leakdown test performed.

19 Make sure the crankshaft turns freely.

20 The remainder of assembly is the reverse of disassembly.

2A

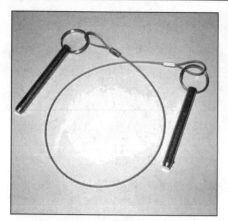

24.2a These are the JIMS retaining pins used for the balancers on Softail models

24.2b Insert the pins into the housing holes . . .

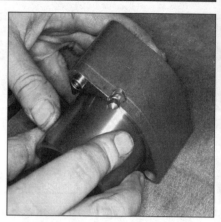

24.2c . . . and engage them with the balancer notches like this (balancer and housing removed for clarity)

23 Crankcase components - inspection and servicing

1   After the crankcases have been separated and the crankshaft (and balancer shafts on Softail models) removed, the crankcases should be cleaned thoroughly with solvent and dried with compressed air.
2   All traces of old gasket sealant should be removed from the crankcase mating surfaces. Minor damage to the surfaces can be cleaned up with a fine sharpening stone.

Caution: Be very careful not to nick or gouge the crankcase mating surfaces or leaks will result. Check both crankcase sections very carefully for cracks and other damage.

4   If any damage is found that can't be repaired, replace the crankcase halves as a set.

Bearing replacement

5   The left crankshaft bearing is covered in Section 25. The balancer bearings on Softail

models are covered in Section 24.
6   Check the right crankcase bearing and camshaft inner bearings for wear or damage (see illustration). Rotate the bearings with fingers and check for roughness, looseness or noise. Replace bearings that are in doubtful condition.
7   Unbolt the bearing retainer from the right crankshaft bearing. Drive the bearing out with a socket or bearing driver having a diameter slightly smaller than the bearing outer race.
8   The inner camshaft needle roller bearings can be pulled out with a blind hole puller. Drive in new bearings with a shouldered bearing driver that fits inside the bearings and bears against the bearing outer race.

Piston jets

9   Each cylinder has an oil jet that lubricates the piston, located on the inside of the crankcase beneath the cylinder opening.
10   Remove the Torx screws and take the jet off. Remove its O-ring.
11   Check the oil jet for clogging and clean it if necessary. If it can't be cleaned com-

pletely, replace it.
12   Wipe a new O-ring with a thin film of engine oil and install it on the crankcase. Install the oil jet and tighten its screws to the torque listed in this Chapter's Specifications.
13   Repeat Steps 10 through 12 for the other oil jet.

24 Balancers (Softail) - removal, bearing replacement and installation

Removal

1   Remove the engine from the motorcycle and separate the crankcase halves (see Sections 6 and 22).
2   Turn the crankshaft, guiding the connecting rods so they don't catch on the crankcase, until the balancer notches align with the retention pin holes. Slip the retention pins into the holes and balancer notches to keep the balancers from rotating (see illustrations).

24.3a Compress the tensioner, then slip a retaining tool onto the tensioner like this (JIMS tool shown)

24.3b Install one tool on each tensioner

24.4 Loosen the balancer nuts (arrow, rear balancer shown)

24.5 Pry the tensioner guide clip (arrow) free of its post and pry the guide off

3   Compress the balancer chain tensioner with HD-44063 or a small bar clamp. Slip a tensioner retainer (HD-44408) over the lip of each tensioner to hold it compressed, then remove the compression tool **(see illustrations)**.

4   Loosen the balancer nuts but don't remove them yet **(see illustration)**. **Note:** *The nuts are secured with Loctite and can be difficult to remove. If they won't come off with a standard breaker bar, carefully heat the nuts with a propane torch, taking care not*

to heat any other components. Don't heat the nuts enough to turn them blue. Don't use a large breaker bar to loosen the nuts or the balancer shafts may break.

5   Pry the clip on each tensioner guide free of its post with a small screwdriver **(see illustration)**. Pry the guide up and off its post, then repeat the procedure on the other tensioner guide.

6   Disengage the tabs of the lower chain guide from the crankcase and remove the chain guide **(see illustration)**.

7   Unscrew the balancer nuts and remove the washers.

8   Carefully pry the sprockets off and remove them together with the chain.

9   Remove the spacer from the front balancer shaft **(see illustration)**.

10   Unscrew the Torx screws that secure the balance shaft housing **(see illustration)**. Take the housing off the engine, together with the tensioners.

11   Remove the balance shaft housings and locate the dowels; they may come off with the support or stay in the crankcase **(see illustrations)**.

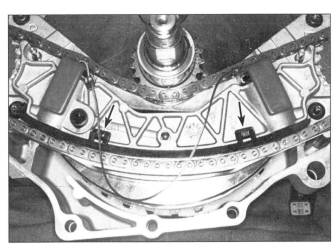

24.6 Disengage the lower chain guide tabs (arrows) and remove the guide

24.9 Remove the spacer (arrow) from the front balancer shaft

2A

24.10 Remove the Torx screws (arrows) and take the housing cover off the engine

24.11a Remove the balance shaft housing (arrow) . . .

24.11b . . . and locate the dowels (arrows)

24.13 Check the bearing and remove it
with a blind hole puller if it needs
to be replaced

24.18 Replace the rubber interconnect
tube (arrow) with a new one whenever
the case halves are separated

12   Pull the retention pins out of the balance shafts.

**Caution: If you're using the Harley-
Davidson or JIMS tool, check each pin to
make sure the ball in the end of it hasn't
come loose. If it has, make sure you find
it, so it doesn't accidentally get left inside
the engine.**

Inspection

13   Rotate the bearings with fingers and
check for roughness, looseness or noise
(see illustration). Replace the bearings if
problems are found.
14   Measure flatness of the sprockets with
a straightedge and feeler gauge. If you find
any warpage, compare it to the limit listed in
this Chapter's Specifications. Check the
sprockets for worn or damaged teeth. If
problems are found, replace all three sprockets including the crankshaft sprocket. Check
the chain as well and replace it with the
sprockets if problems are found.
15   Check the chain tensioner pistons for
wear or pitted ends. Replace them if problems are found. **Note:** If you're in doubt
about the internal condition of the tensioner,
have a leakdown test done by a dealer service department or other qualified shop .
16   Measure free length of the tensioner
springs and compare it to the value listed in
this Chapter's Specifications. Replace the
springs if they're at less than the specified
limit.
17   Check the chain contact surfaces on
the tensioner guides for wear or damage. If
grooves are visible, measure their depth and
replace the guides if the depth is more than
the limit listed in this Chapter's Specifications.
18   Replace the rubber interconnect tube
with a new one whenever the crankcase is
disassembled **(see illustration)**.

Bearing replacement

In crankcase

19   With the balancers removed, pull the
left balancer bearings from the crankcase

with a blind hole puller. Press new bearings
into the crankcase, making sure the bearing
driver presses against the bearing outer race.
Pressing against the inner race will damage
the bearing.

In bearing housings

20   Place the bearing housing over a hollow
support with the dowel side up. Press the
bearing out of the bearing housing into the
support. Discard the bearing and retaining
ring.
21   Turn the housing over and position it on
a press plate. Press in a new bearing and
retaining ring until the retaining ring stops
against the housing.

Installation

22   Turn the crankshaft so its balance
weight is toward the top of the engine.
23   Install the balancers in the crankcase
bearings. The balancers are interchangeable
between front and rear positions, but the balancer housings and sprockets are not.
24   Make sure the dowels are installed in
the front balancer housing, then install it in
the crankcase. The front housing can be

24.24 The front and rear balancer
housings are identified by F and
R marks (arrow, front shown)

identified by its F mark **(see illustration)**.
25   Install the rear balancer housing in the
same manner.
26   Install the tensioners in the chain guide
bracket. Compress them and hold them in
the compressed position with the tools
described in Step 3.
27   Install the chain guide bracket over the
balancer housings. Apply non-permanent
thread locking agent (Loctite 262 red or
equivalent) to the threads of the bracket's
Torx bolts, then install them. Tighten the
bolts in the proper sequence to the torque
listed in this Chapter's Specifications.
28   Turn the crankshaft so its balancer
alignment mark is in the 6 o'clock position.
29   Turn the balancers so their retention pin
notches align with the holes in the housings,
then insert the pins **(see illustration 24.2b)**.
This positions the balancers in proper alignment.
30   Install the spacer on the front balancer
shaft. Install both sprockets (without the
chain), with the sprocket marked F on the
front balancer and the sprocket marked R on
the rear balancer. The sprocket marks face
away from the engine.

24.32 A special tool is needed to
measure sprocket alignment
(JIMS tool shown)

24.34 Be sure to align the timing marks on chain and sprockets correctly (arrows)

31   Install the sprocket nuts and washer, but don't tighten them.
32   Install a sprocket alignment tool (HD-44064 or JIMS) on the crankshaft and tighten it until it bottoms against the sprocket shoulder **(see illustration)**. Swing the tool's measuring arm over each sprocket to check the alignment. **Note:** *If you don't have the special tool, use a precision straightedge.* If the sprocket alignment is not within the limit listed in this Chapter's Specifications, install a thicker or thinner spacer under the front sprocket.
33   Remove the nuts, washers and sprockets.
34   Coat the chain with a thin film of clean engine oil. Install it on the sprockets so all three sprocket timing marks will line up when the chain is installed **(see illustration)**.
35   Install the rear sprocket, then engage the chain with the crankshaft sprocket, then install the front sprocket, making sure the timing marks stay in alignment.
36   Install washers and new nuts on the balance shafts. If you can't get new ones, clean the threads of the old nuts and apply thread locking agent (Loctite 262 red or equivalent) to the threads of the nuts. Tighten the nuts to the torque listed in this Chapter's Specifications.
37   Install the chain tensioner guides on their posts, making sure the guide labeled F goes on the front post and the guide labeled R on the rear post. Push both guides onto their posts until they snap into place, then slide the retaining clips into position.
38   Compress one of the tensioners with the compression tool and remove the retaining clip. Release the tool and let the tensioner expand against the chain. Do this with the other tensioner.
39   Remove the retaining pins from the balance shafts. Again, if you're using the Harley tool or equivalent, check to make sure the ball hasn't fallen out of the hole in the end of

each pin. If it has, locate it before continuing with engine assembly. Severe engine damage may occur if the engine is run with the ball inside it.
40   The remainder of installation is the reverse of the removal steps.

25 Crankshaft and connecting rods - inspection

1   The crankshaft and connecting rods are replaced as an assembly, even by dealer service departments. Removing the crankshaft from the left case half for crankshaft or bearing replacement requires a press and several special tools and should be done by a dealer service department or other qualified shop.
2   Remove the engine and separate the crankcase halves (see Sections 6 and 22).
3   Measure side clearance of the connecting rods with a feeler gauge. If it's not within the limits listed in this Chapter's Specifications, replace the crankshaft and connecting rods as an assembly.
4   While an assistant supports the connecting rods, spin the crankshaft and check for roughness, looseness or noise in the Timken bearings that support the left side. If problems are found, have the bearings replaced by a dealer service department or other qualified shop.
5   Installation is the reverse of the removal steps.

26 Initial start-up after overhaul

1   Make sure the engine oil level is correct, then remove the spark plugs from the engine. Place the engine STOP switch in the

Off position and disconnect the primary wires from the ignition coil.
2   Turn on the key switch and crank the engine over with the starter until the oil pressure indicator light goes off (which indicates that oil pressure exists). Reinstall the spark plugs, connect the wires and turn the switch to On. **Note:** *If the oil pressure light won't go out, remove the oil filter* (see Chapter 1). *Hold the filter with the open end upright and pour oil into the center hole until the filter is full. Let the oil settle, then top it off again (you may need to do this twice). Reinstall the filter (a small amount of oil may leak out when you install it).*
3   Make sure there is fuel in the tank, then turn the fuel tap to the On position and operate the choke (carbureted models).
4   Start the engine and allow it to run at a moderately fast idle until it reaches operating temperature.

Caution: If the oil pressure indicator light doesn't go off, or it comes on while the engine is running, stop the engine immediately.

5   Check carefully for oil leaks and make sure the transmission and controls, especially the brakes, function properly before road testing the machine. Refer to Section 27 for the recommended break-in procedure.

27 Recommended break-in procedure

1   Any rebuilt engine needs time to break-in, even if parts have been installed in their original locations. For this reason, treat the machine gently for the first few miles to make sure oil has circulated throughout the engine and any new parts installed have started to seat.
2   Even greater care is necessary if the engine has been rebored or a new crankshaft has been installed. In the case of a rebore, the engine will have to be broken in as if the machine were new. This means greater use of the transmission and a restraining hand on the throttle until at least 500 miles (800 km) have been covered. There's no point in keeping to any set speed limit - the main idea is to keep from lugging the engine and to gradually increase performance until the 500 mile (800 km) mark is reached. These recommendations can be lessened to an extent when only a new crankshaft is installed. Experience is the best guide, since it's easy to tell when an engine is running freely.
3   If a lubrication failure is suspected, stop the engine immediately and try to find the cause. If an engine is run without oil, even for a short period of time, severe damage will occur.

2A

Notes

Chapter 2 Part B
Clutch, primary drive and transmission

Contents

Degrees of difficulty

Easy, suitable for novice with little experience	**Fairly easy,** suitable for beginner with some experience 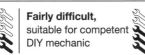	**Fairly difficult,** suitable for competent DIY mechanic	**Difficult,** suitable for experienced DIY mechanic	**Very difficult,** suitable for expert DIY or professional

Specifications

Clutch

Friction plate thickness limit	0.143 inch (3.62 mm)
Friction and steel plate warpage limit......................................	0.006 inch (0.15 mm)

Primary chain

Sprocket alignment limit..	0.030 inch (0.76 mm)

Transmission

Shift fork finger thickness	0.165 inch (4.19 mm)

Tightening torques

Clutch cable fitting..	36 to 60 inch-lbs (4.1 to 6.8 Nm)
Clutch release cover bolts	
Softail and Dyna	84 to 108 inch-lbs (9.5 to 12.2 Nm)
Touring models	
1999 through 2001..	84 to 108 inch-lbs (9.5 to 12.2 Nm)
2002 and later	120 to 180 inch-lbs (14 to 16 Nm)
Clutch spring retainer bolts	90 to 110 inch-lbs (10 to 12 Nm)
Clutch hub nut...	70 to 80 ft-lbs (95 to 108 Nm)
Primary chain tensioner nut...	21 to 29 ft-lbs (29 to 39 Nm)
Compensating sprocket nut..	150 to 165 ft-lbs (203 to 223 Nm)
Primary chaincase cover bolts	108 to 120 inch-lbs (12 to 13 Nm)
Primary chaincase inspection cover bolts..................................	84 to 108 inch-lbs (9.5 to 12 Nm)
Primary chaincase bolts	18 to 21 ft-lbs (24 to 28 Nm)
Transmission side door bolts	
1/4- inch	84 to 108 inch-lbs (9.5 to 12 Nm)
5/16-inch	13 to 16 ft-lbs (18 to 22 Nm)
Transmission top cover bolts	84 to 108 inch-lbs (9.5 to 12 Nm)
Shifter cam support block bolts	84 to 108 inch-lbs (9.5 to 12 Nm)
Shifter cam detent pivot bolt (later models)	84 to 108 inch-lbs (9.5 to 12 Nm)
Transmission shaft nuts...	45 to 55 ft-lbs (61 to 75 Nm)

2B

2.3 Loosen the bolts (arrows) in sequence, then remove them and take the clutch release cover off the transmission

2.4a Note the position of the retaining ring gap (arrow) . . .

1 General information

Power from the engine crankshaft is transmitted to the clutch, through the primary chain and compensating sprocket to the transmission. The clutch, primary chain, its tensioner and the compensating sprocket are located in the primary drive housing, which is a removable unit located on the left side of the engine.

The transmission is a separate unit located behind the engine and bolted to the back of it. The gears are mounted on a mainshaft (input shaft) and countershaft (output shaft). The mainshaft is driven by the primary drive chain through the compensating sprocket, while the countershaft operates the rear wheel drivebelt through the belt sprocket.

The gears consist of five pairs, one pair for each transmission ratio. Each pair is in constant mesh with its mating gear. When a particular ratio is selected, both gears for that ratio are locked to their shaft. One gear for each of the other four ratios spins freely on its shaft, so that only one ratio is engaged at a time.

Shifting is accomplished by three shift forks, which are moved by a shifter cam mounted in the transmission case.

2.4b . . . then remove the retaining ring . . .

2 Clutch cable - replacement

1   Loosen the midline cable adjuster to provide as much slack as possible in the cable (see Chapter 1).
2   Remove the snap-ring from the underside of the cable retaining pin at the handlebar lever, then pull out the pin and disconnect the upper end of the clutch cable from the lever.
3   Remove the transmission dipstick and drain the transmission oil (see Chapter 1). Remove the clutch release cover from the transmission **(see illustration)**.
4   Note the location of the gap in the retaining ring so it can be reinstalled in the same location, then remove the retaining ring **(see illustrations)**. Take the inner ramp and coupling out of the transmission cover **(see illustrations)**. Hold them together as you remove them so the coupling balls don't fall out.
5   Turn the inner ramp and disconnect the coupling from it, then detach the end of the

2.4c . . . remove the coupling and take the three steel balls out of their slots (arrow) . . .

2.4d . . . and take the inner ramp out of the cover

2.5 Unscrew the clutch cable fitting from the transmission cover and remove its O-ring

3.4a Loosen the pressure plate bolts (arrows) in a criss-cross pattern

3.4b Remove the pressure plate bolts (clutch assembly removed for clarity) . . .

3.4c . . . lift off the spring retainer . . .

3.4d . . . the diaphragm spring . . .

3.4e . . . and the spring seat

3.5a Remove the first friction plate . . .

cable from the coupling. Unscrew the cable fitting from the transmission cover and remove its O-ring **(see illustration)**.

6   Before removing the cable from the bike, tape the lower end of the new cable to the upper end of the old cable. Slowly pull the lower end of the old cable out, guiding the new cable down into position. Using this method will ensure the cable is routed correctly.

7   Installation is the reverse of the removal

steps, with the following additions:
a) *Use a new O-ring on the clutch cable threaded fitting.*
b) *Position the retaining ring gap as noted during removal.*
c) *Use a new gasket on the clutch release cover and tighten its bolts to the torque listed in this Chapter's Specifications.*
d) *Lubricate and adjust the clutch cable (see Chapter 1).*

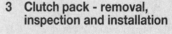

3   Clutch pack - removal, inspection and installation

Removal

1   The clutch plates and discs can be removed without removing the clutch housing from the motorcycle, but removal of the clutch housing requires removal of the primary chain and compensating sprocket. Unless you're sure there's a problem with the clutch housing, it's a good idea to start the procedure by removing just the clutch plates, which will allow you to inspect the clutch housing to see if needs to be removed.

2   Prop the bike securely upright.

3   Remove the primary chaincase cover (see Section 5).

4   Remove the retaining ring and the release plate together with the adjusting screw. Loosen the pressure plate bolts in a criss-cross pattern **(see illustration)**. Remove the spring retainer, diaphragm spring and pressure plate **(see illustrations)**.

5   Pull off the friction and metal plates, then remove the damper spring and seat from the clutch housing **(see illustrations)**.

2B

3.5b . . . to expose the first metal plate . . .

3.5c . . . then lift out the metal plate and the remaining plates . . .

3.5d . . . then remove the damper spring and spring seat

6   Inspect the plates and the clutch housing as described below to decide whether you need to remove the clutch housing (which means removing the primary chain and compensating sprocket from the motorcycle).

Inspection

7   If you're planning to remove the clutch housing, remove it together with the primary chain and compensating sprocket (see Section 5).

8   Examine the splines on the outside of the clutch center **(see illustration)**. (If the clutch housing has been removed, also examine the splines on the inside of the clutch center.) If any wear is evident, replace the hub with a new one.

9   Check the diaphragm spring for cracked, bent or worn spring fingers. If any problems are found, replace the spring.

10   If the lining material of the friction plates smells burnt or if it is glazed, new parts are required. If the metal clutch plates are scored or discolored, they must be replaced with new ones. Measure the thickness of each friction plate **(see illustration)** and compare the results to this Chapter's Specifications. Replace the friction plates as a set

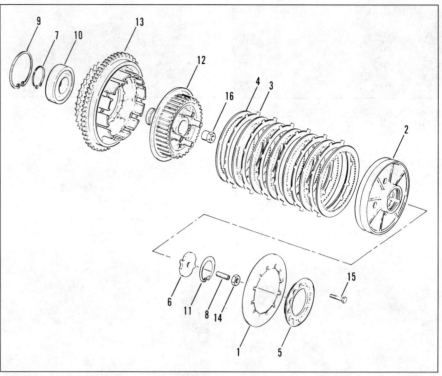

3.8 Clutch components - exploded view

1	Diaphragm spring	5	Adjuster plate
2	Pressure plate	6	Release plate
3	Friction plates (9) - install narrow plate first	7	Circlip - external
4	Metal plates (8) - install between friction plates	8	Adjuster screw
		9	Circlip - internal
		10	Pilot bearing
		11	Retaining ring

12	Clutch center
13	Clutch housing
14	Locknut
15	Bolt (6)
16	Transmission mainshaft nut (LH thread)

if they are near the wear limit.

11   Lay all metal plates, one at a time, on a perfectly flat surface (such as a piece of plate glass) and check for warpage by trying to slip a 0.006-inch (0.15 mm) feeler gauge between the flat surface and the plate **(see illustration)**. Do this at several places around the plate's circumference. If the feeler gauge can be slipped under the plate, it is warped and should be replaced with a new one.

12   Check the tabs on the friction plates for excessive wear and mushroomed edges. They can be cleaned up with a file if the deformation is not severe.

13   Check the edges of the slots in the clutch housing for indentations made by the friction plate tabs **(see illustration)**. If the indentations are deep they can prevent clutch release, so the housing should be replaced with a new one. If the indentations

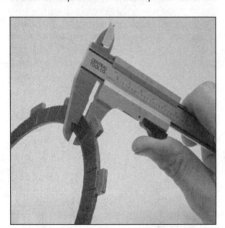

3.10 Measure the thickness of the friction plates

3.11 Check all plates for warpage

3.13 Check the clutch housing slots for wear or damage

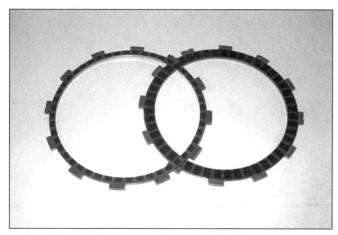

3.15 The narrow friction plate goes on first; it's narrower to accommodate the damper spring seat

4.4 If you want to replace the bearing, remove the snap-ring (lower arrow); otherwise, pull the oil slinger (upper arrow) out as an assembly

can be removed easily with a file, the life of the housing can be prolonged to an extent.

14 Check the damper spring and seat for wear and damage and replace them if problems are found.

Clutch installation

15 Soak the clutch friction plates in primary chaincase lubricant for at least 30 minutes before installation. Install the narrow friction plate on the clutch housing (see illustration), then install the damper spring seat, making sure it fits inside the friction plate. Install the damper spring with its concave side facing away from the spring seat.

16 Install a steel plate against the friction plate with its rounded edge facing away from the engine.

17 Install another friction plate, then install the remaining friction and steel plates, alternating them and placing the rounded edges of the steel plates away from the engine.

18 Install the pressure plate on top of the last friction plate, aligning its holes with the bolt towers on the clutch center.

19 Install the diaphragm spring in the pressure plate groove with the spring's concave side facing the engine.

20 Place the diaphragm spring retainer over the pressure plate, aligning the spring retainer's tabs with the flats on the bolt towers.

21 Install the bolts and tighten them evenly, in a criss-cross pattern, to the torque listed in this Chapter's Specifications.

22 The remainder of installation is the reverse of the removal steps.

23 Fill the primary chaincase with lubricant (see Chapter 1).

4 Clutch release mechanism - removal, inspection and installation

Removal

1 These models use a long pushrod, located inside the transmission output shaft, that transfers release lever motion through the transmission output shaft to the clutch. The pushrod is actuated by a ball-and-ramp mechanism located in the clutch release cover.

2 Remove the clutch release cover (see Section 2). Disconnect the clutch cable and remove the ball-and-ramp mechanism from the cover.

3 Separate the inner and outer ramp and remove the balls (see Section 2). Place them in a container so they won't be lost.

4 Remove the oil slinger and release bearing from the transmission mainshaft (see illustration). Use a pencil magnet to remove the clutch pushrod.

5 On the other side of the motorcycle, hold the adjusting screw with an Allen wrench and unscrew the locknut (see illustration). Remove the plate snap-ring and then the release plate (see illustrations).

Inspection

6 Check the balls and ramps for wear or damage. Replace them if any problems are found. Check the ramp contact area in the clutch release cover. Replace the cover if any wear can be seen.

7 Remove the snap-ring from the oil slinger and take off the washer, bearing and second washer. Check all parts for wear or damage, paying special attention to the bearing. Replace them if any problems are found.

4.5b Remove the snap-ring . . .

4.5c . . . then remove the plate; its OUT mark faces away from the engine

4.5a Hold the adjusting screw with an Allen wrench and remove the locknut

2B

5.2a Primary chaincase cover bolt LOOSENING sequence

5.2b Remove the cover . . .

5.2c . . . locate the dowels (arrows) and remove the gasket

5.4a Loosen the chain tensioner nut (arrow) . . .

Installation

8   Installation is the reverse of the removal steps, with the following additions:

   a) *Install the release plate with the word OUT facing away from the engine. Use a new release plate snap-ring.*
   b) *Use a new gasket on the clutch release cover and tighten the screws to the torque listed in this Chapter's Specifications.*
   c) *Check the transmission oil level and top it up if necessary (see Chapter 1).*
   d) *Adjust the clutch cable freeplay (see Chapter 1).*

5 Primary chain and sprockets - removal, inspection and installation

Removal

1   Disconnect the negative cable from the battery, drain the lubricant from the primary chaincase and remove the primary chaincase inspection cover (see Chapter 1).
2   Remove the primary chaincase cover bolts and take the cover off **(see illustrations)**.

Caution: Be sure to remove the top and rear bolts inside the inspection cover hole or the cover will be damaged during removal.

3   Check the alignment of the primary chain sprockets. To do this, tighten the primary chain adjuster until the chain is snug, then push the sprockets and chain toward the engine as far as they will go. Lay a straightedge across the chain, then measure the distance from the chain to the primary chaincase gasket surface with a vernier caliper. Take two measurements, one as near as possible to the compensating sprocket and one as near as possible to the clutch sprocket. If there's a difference between the two measurements that's greater than the value listed in this Chapter's Specifications, you'll need to change the thickness of the spacer on the engine sprocket shaft behind the alternator rotor (see Chapter 8).
4   Loosen the top center nut on the primary chain tensioner **(see illustration)**. Pull the tensioner outward, then down, until it rests on the primary chaincase **(see illustration)**.

5   Loosen the clutch release plate locknut, then remove the retaining ring and clutch release plate (see Section 4). If you're planning to inspect the clutch, remove the plates, diaphragm spring and damper spring now (see Section 3).
6   Prevent the clutch from turning by inserting a locking tool (HD-41214 or JIMS equivalent) between the upper side of the chain and the clutch hub sprocket **(see illus-**

5.4b . . . then lower the tensioner pad until it rests on the chaincase

5.6 This is the JIMS tool used to lock the primary chain sprockets

5.7 Wedge the tool into the upper chain run (arrow) and turn the clutch hub nut clockwise to loosen it

5.8 Wedge the tool into the upper chain run (arrow) and turn the compensating sprocket nut counterclockwise to loosen it

5.9 Compensating sprocket details

1	Sprocket shaft spacer	4	Sliding cam
2	Shaft extension	5	Cover
3	Compensating sprocket	6	Nut

5.10 Remove the chain, clutch hub and compensating sprocket as an assembly

tration). Use a wooden wedge if you don't have the special tool.

7 Loosen the clutch hub nut that's threaded onto the mainshaft (see illustration). The nut has left-hand threads, so turn it counterclockwise to loosen. The nut is also secured with Loctite, which will make it difficult to remove. If you can't get it loose, heat it with a hair dryer or use an impact wrench just to loosen the nut, then unscrew it with a socket and breaker bar.

8 Remove the locking tool and insert it between the upper side of the primary chain and the compensating sprocket (see illustration). Unscrew the sprocket locknut, this time turning it counterclockwise to loosen it. If it's difficult to remove, use the same methods as for the clutch locknut. Again, be sure to use an impact wrench only to loosen the nut and finish removal with a socket and breaker bar.

9 Remove the cover and sliding cam from the compensating sprocket (see illustration).

10 Pull the chain off, together with the clutch hub and compensating sprocket (see illustration).

Inspection

11 Spin the clutch hub while holding the clutch housing. Listen and feel for roughness, looseness or noise in the clutch hub bearing. If problems are found, disassemble the hub to replace the bearing; otherwise leave it assembled. The bearing must be replaced whenever the clutch hub and center are separated.

12 To replace the bearing, remove the snap-ring (see illustration). Place the clutch shell on a press plate and press the clutch hub out.

13 Turn the clutch shell over and remove the snap-ring that secures the bearing (see illustration 3.8). Place the clutch shell on a press plate, sprocket side up, and press the bearing out.

14 Reverse the removal procedure to install the new bearing. Install the bearing snap-ring with its flat side against the bearing.

15 Check the primary chain and sprockets for wear and damage. Replace them as a set if problems are found.

16 Check the tensioner pad for deep wear

5.12 Remove the snap-ring (arrow) to replace the bearing

or grooves. If it was so worn that chain tension couldn't be adjusted within the Chapter 1 Specifications, replace it. Remove the snap-ring that secures the tensioner pad to its post and slide it off.

2B

5.17 Check the compensating sprocket splines (arrow) and their matching splines on the shaft extension for wear or damage

6.4a Wrap the splines with tape to protect the seal

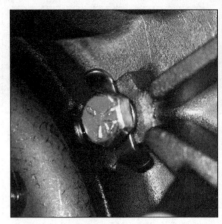

6.4b Bend back the lockplates on bolts so equipped . . .

17   Check the splines in the compensating sprocket and the matching splines on the shaft extension for wear and damage **(see illustration)**. Replace them both if problems are found.

18   Check the contact surfaces of the compensating sprocket and its sliding cam for excessive wear and replace them if worn.

Installation

19   If you remove the chain tensioner, position it so its pad rests on the bottom of the primary chaincase. Install the top center nut, leaving it loose.

20   Assemble the primary chain onto the clutch sprocket and compensating sprocket. Slide the sprockets into their shafts, rotating them slightly to align the splines.

21   Install the sliding cam and cover on the compensating sprocket.

22   Clean the threads of the compensating sprocket nut. Apply two drops of thread locking agent (Loctite 262 red or equivalent) to the threads of the nut, then install it, but don't torque it yet.

23   Clean the threads of the clutch hub

mainshaft nut. Apply two drops of thread locking agent (Loctite 262 red or equivalent) to the threads of the nut, then install it, but don't torque it yet.

24   Using the same chain locking tool used for removal, prevent the compensating sprocket from rotating while its nut is tightened. Since you'll be turning the nut clockwise, insert the locking tool between the upper chain run and the clutch sprocket. Tighten the compensating sprocket nut to the torque listed in this Chapter's Specifications, then remove the locking tool.

25   Insert the locking tool between the upper chain run and the compensating sprocket, then tighten the clutch mainshaft nut to the torque listed in this Chapter's Specifications. The nut has left-hand threads, so turn it counterclockwise to tighten it.

26   Installation is the reverse of the removal steps, with the following additions:

a) *Use a new primary chaincase gasket.*
b) *Tighten the primary chaincase screws evenly, in the proper sequence, to the torque listed in this Chapter's Specifications.*
c) *Fill the primary chaincase lubricant (see Chapter 1).*

6   Primary chaincase - removal and installation

Removal

1   Disconnect the negative cable from the battery.

2   Remove the primary chain, clutch housing and compensating sprocket (see Section 5).

3   Remove the starter jackshaft and two of the starter mounting bolts (see Chapter 8).

4   Wrap the end of the crankshaft with tape to protect the chaincase seal **(see illustration)**. Bend back the locktabs on the bolts so equipped and remove all of the bolts securing the chaincase to the engine and transmission **(see illustrations)**. Take the chaincase off the bike.

5   Replace the lip seal and inspect the bearing (see Section 7).

Installation

6   Apply a thin bead of silicone sealant to the mating surface of the primary chaincase and crankshaft. Make sure the O-ring is in

6.4c . . . remove the chaincase bolts at the clutch end (arrows) . . .

6.4d . . . and at the compensating sprocket end (arrows), then take the chaincase off

8.2a If the bike has fore-and-aft shift pedals, remove both pinch bolts (arrows)

8.2b Single shift pedals have only one pinch bolt (arrow)

8.3 Mark the shaft next to the split in the shift arm, then remove the bolt (arrow) and take off the arm

place around the alternator, then lubricate the seal lips with clean engine oil and install the primary chaincase on the engine.

7   Install the primary chaincase to engine bolts. Tighten them to the torque listed in this Chapter's Specifications and bend up the locktabs on the bolts so equipped.

8   Install the primary chaincase to transmission bolts. Tighten them to the torque listed in this Chapter's Specifications and bend up the locktabs on the bolts so equipped.

9   The remainder of installation is the reverse of the removal steps.

10   Fill the primary chaincase lubricant (see Chapter 1).

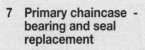

7 Primary chaincase - bearing and seal replacement

1   Remove the primary chaincase from the engine (see Section 6).

2   Pry out the crankcase lip seal.

3   Spin the primary chaincase bearing with fingers and check for roughness, looseness or noise. If any problems are found, remove the snap-rings. Place the primary chaincase on a press plate with the clutch side supported, then press out the bearing from the pulley side. Make sure the driver bears against the bearing outer race.

4   Install a new snap-ring on the pulley side. Place the primary chaincase on a press plate with the clutch side upward and support the area around the retaining ring.

Caution: If the retaining ring area isn't supported, the chaincase may damaged when the bearing is pressed in.

5   Press the new bearing in with its lettered side upward until it seats solidly against the snap-ring.

6   Install the second snap-ring and make sure it seats securely in its groove.

7   Drive in a new lip seal with its open side

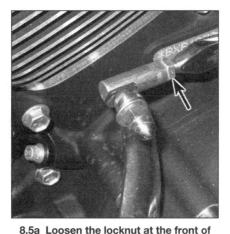

8.5a Loosen the locknut at the front of the shifter rod (arrow) . . .

toward the bearing. Make sure the seal seats securely in the bore.

8   Lubricate the bearing and the lip of the seal with clean engine oil or multi-purpose grease.

9   Check the primary chaincase bushings for wear and damage and replace them if problems are found.

10   Check the jackshaft oil seal for leakage. It's a good idea to replace it whenever the primary chaincase is removed from the engine. Pry the old seal out and drive a new one in from the inner side of the primary chaincase, making sure the seal seats securely against the shoulder in its bore.

8 External shift mechanism - removal, inspection and installation

Removal

1   Prop the bike securely upright.

2   Mark the shift pedal shaft next to the

8.5b . . . and at the rear (arrow), then turn the rod to make adjustments

split in the pedal, then remove the shift pedal bolt **(see illustrations)**. Take the shift pedal off the shaft and remove the shaft from its pivot bore. On fore-and-aft models, remove both shift pedals.

3   Mark the shift shaft next to the split in the linkage lever, then remove the shift linkage arm pinch bolt **(see illustration)**.

Installation

4   Installation is the reverse of removal.

Adjustment

5   Adjustment shouldn't be necessary unless shifting becomes difficult. To make the adjustment, disconnect one end of the shift rod **(see illustrations)**. Loosen the locknuts on the shift rod ends and turn the adjusters as needed to change shift rod length. Tighten the locknuts and reconnect the linkage. **Note:** *On Touring models, be sure the linkage doesn't contact the floorboard during shifting. There must be at least 3/8-inch clearance between the shifter and floorboard so they don't hit each other as the engine moves.*

2B

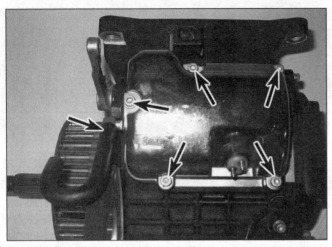

9.4 Remove the vent hose from the shifter cover and unscrew the Allen bolts (arrows)

9.6a Remove the support block bolts (arrows)

9 Shifter cam and forks - removal, inspection and installation

Removal

1   Prop the bike securely upright.
2   Disconnect the negative cable from the battery. Remove the battery and starter and disconnect the neutral switch (see Chapter 8).
3   Remove the oil tank (see Chapter 2A).
4   Disconnect the vent hose from the shifter cover (see illustration).
5   Remove the cover Allen bolts, then lift off the cover and remove the gasket. If the cover is difficult to remove, tap it gently with a rubber mallet to free it. Don't pry between the gasket surfaces or they'll be damaged.
6   Unscrew the support block bolts (see illustration). Pull back the shifter cam pawl so it clears the pins (see illustration), then lift the shifter cam out of the case. Note the locations of the support block dowels (see illustration).
7   Remove the transmission side cover

9.6b Pull the shifter cam pawl (arrow) up to clear the pins

(see Section 10).
8   Push on one end of the fork shaft to free it and pull it out of the case (see illustrations). Lift out the shifter forks, then immediately put them back on the shaft in the correct order so you remember how they go (see illustration).

9.6c Lift the shifter cam out of the case . . .

Inspection

9   Check the edges of the grooves in the shifter cam for signs of excessive wear (see illustration). Also check the pins on the forks. Replace the shifter cam and forks if wear can be seen. Replace the shifter cam if the pawl pins are worn or damaged (see illustration).
10   Check the shift forks for distortion and

9.6d . . . and note the locations of the support block dowels (arrows)

9.8a Push on one end of the fork shaft (arrow) . . .

9.8b . . . pull it out of the case and remove the shift forks . . .

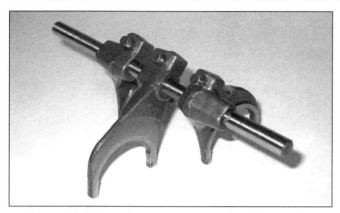

9.8c ... then immediately put the forks on the shaft in the correct order so you'll remember how they go

9.9a Check the shifter cam grooves, especially at the corners, and the shift fork pins (arrows)

wear, especially at the fork fingers. If they are discolored or severely worn they are probably bent. If damage or wear is evident, check the shift fork groove in the corresponding gear as well. Check the forks for bending with a square **(see illustration)**. Replace them if they're bent at all. Measure the thickness of the fork fingers and replace them if they're worn to less than the limit listed in this Chapter's Specifications.

11   Rotate the shift cam in the support block bearings with fingers and check the bearings for roughness, looseness or noise. If there's any doubt about the condition of

the bearings, replace them as described below.

Early models

12   Early models have needle roller shifter

cam bearings and a plunger-type cam follower.

13   Slip a feeler gauge between the outer thrust washer (on the cam follower end of the shift cam) and the right support block **(see**

9.9b Check the pawl pins for wear and damage

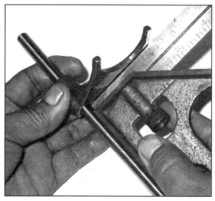

9.10 Check the shift forks for bending with a square

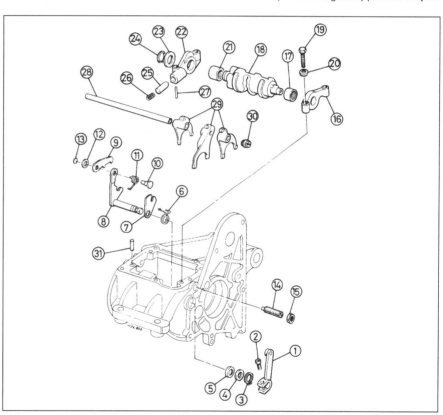

9.13 Shift mechanism components - exploded view

1	Shifter arm	13	Retaining ring	22	Right support block
2	Screw	14	Gear engagement	23	Thrust washer
3	Snap-ring		adjuster	24	Snap-ring
4	Washer	15	Locknut	25	Cam follower (early
5	Oil seal	16	Left support block		models)
6	Return spring	17	Left shifter cam	26	Spring (early models)
7	Plate		bearing	27	Roll pin (early models)
8	Shifter rod	18	Shifter cam	28	Shift fork shaft
9	Shifter pawl	19	Bolts	29	Shift forks
10	Spring post	20	Washers	30	Set screw
11	return spring	21	Right shifter cam	31	Support block dowels
12	Washer		bearing		

2B

9.18a Remove the snap-ring from the support block
(right side shown)

9.18b In the left support block, position the snap-ring with its
gap downward and its large tab to the right

illustration). Clearance should be 0.001 to 0.004 inch (0.025 to 0.100 mm). If not, replace the thrust washer with a thicker or thinner one. If the correct thrust washer is installed, there should be enough clearance so the thrust washer can be turned easily.

14 Remove the bearing snap-rings. On the cam follower end of the shift cam, remove the thrust washer. Slide the bearings off the shift cam.

15 Lubricate new bearings and install them with the lettered sides facing out (away from the shifter cam). Press on the lettered side to position the bearings on the shift cam. Install the thrust washer and snap-rings.

16 Check the cam follower plunger and its contact surfaces on the shifter cam for wear or damage. If problems are found, drive out the roll pin and remove the spring and plunger. Install new parts as needed. Always use a new roll pin.

Later models

17 Later models have ball shifter cam bearings and a roller arm-type shifter cam follower.

18 Remove the bearing snap-rings **(see illustration)** and remove the support blocks from the shifter cam (if not already done). Drive the bearings out of the support blocks. Drive new ones in using a bearing driver that bears against the outer race of the bearings. The driver should contact the lettered side of the bearing; the lettered side of each bearing should face outward when the bearings and support blocks are installed on the shifter cam. Install the large retaining rings with their beveled sides facing out. On the left support block, position the large tab of the snap-ring to the right and the snap-ring gap so it will be downward when the shifter cam is installed on the vehicle **(see illustration)**. Install the small snap-ring to secure the bearing to the left end of the shifter cam.

19 Move the detent follower against its spring and check for a broken or weak spring and loose movement on the follower bushing. Also check the end of the follower that contacts the shifter cam for wear or damage.

If problems are found, remove the detent pivot screw, spring and bushing and replace the defective parts **(see illustration)**.

All models

20 Check the shift fork rod for wear, galling or other damage. Make sure the shift forks move smoothly on the rod. If the rod is worn or bent, replace it with a new one.

Installation

21 Make sure the dowel pins are in position in the case.

22 Pull back the shifter cam pawl and lay the shifter cam in position, engaging the shift forks with the gear grooves. Release the pawl.

23 Install the support block bolts and tighten them evenly, in a criss-cross pattern, to the torque listed in this Chapter's Specifications.

24 Operate the shifter through all of the gear positions. If you can't engage all of the gears, stop and find out why before continuing.

25 If the neutral switch was removed from the cover, make sure the gears are in the neutral position before installing the cover.

9.19 If the detent follower or spring (later models) is worn or damaged, remove the bolt and collar (arrows), then remove the spring and detent follower

26 Install the cover, using a new gasket. Place the long cover screw next to the vent hose and tighten all of the screws to the torque listed in this Chapter's Specifications.

27 The remainder of installation is the reverse of the removal steps.

---

10 Transmission shafts and gears - removal and installation

Removal

1 Remove the exhaust system (see Chapter 3).

2 Remove the clutch, primary chain and compensating sprocket (see Section 6).

3 Remove the primary chaincase (see Section 7).

4 Remove the shifter cam and forks (see Section 9).

5 Remove the transmission mainshaft bearing inner race with a puller.

6 Drain the transmission oil (see Chapter 1).

7 Remove the clutch release cover (see Section 2).

8 Slide two of the sliding gears along their shafts so the dogs engage the slots on the gears next to them. This engages two gears at the same time, locking the transmission.

9 Remove the clutch release components from the mainshaft (see Section 4).

10 If you're planning to disassemble the transmission shafts, unscrew the locknuts and remove the spacers from both shafts.

11 If you're planning to remove the main drive gear, unscrew the transmission sprocket nut now, while the transmission is still locked (see Chapter 5).

12 Unbolt the transmission side door from the case and carefully pry it loose, taking care not to damage the gasket surfaces **(see illustration)**. Pull out the side door, together with the transmission shafts.

13 Refer to Section 11 for information pertaining to transmission shaft service.

10.12 Remove the side door mounting bolts (arrows) to separate the gears and shafts from the case; tighten the bolts in sequence

(2.54 to 3.81 mm) from the main drive gear.
18 The remainder of installation is the reverse of the removal steps.

11 Transmission shafts and gears - disassembly, inspection and reassembly

Note: *When disassembling the transmission shafts, place the parts on a long rod or thread a wire through them to keep them in order and facing the proper direction.*
1 Remove the transmission side door and shafts from the crankcase (see Section 10).

Disassembly

2 If you haven't already done so, remove the clutch pushrod and oil slinger from the mainshaft.
3 If you didn't do it during removal, lock the shafts by engaging two gears at once, unscrew the shaft locknuts and remove the spacers (see Section 10).
4 Place the transmission side door on a workbench with the shafts upward.
5 Remove the snap-ring from the countershaft and lift off countershaft fifth gear **(see illustration)**.

Installation

14 Place a new gasket on the side door, then install the side door and shafts in the transmission case.
15 Install the bolts, noting that there are two different sizes, which have different torque settings. In addition, on FLSTS and FLSTF models, the long 5/16-inch bolt goes in the forward hole. Tighten all of the bolts to the torque listed in this Chapter's Specifications.
16 If the shaft locknuts were loosened,

lock the transmission (see Step 8) and tighten them to the torque listed in this Chapter's Specifications.
17 Install the inner race on the mainshaft bearing, using a thread-type installation tool (HD-34902-B or equivalent). The bearing's chamfered end goes onto the mainshaft first. Before you start, measure the width of the bearing race; it must be 0.9950 to 1.000 inches (25.27 to 25.40 mm). Press the inner race onto the shaft, using the special tools, until its inner edge is 0.10 to 0.15 inches

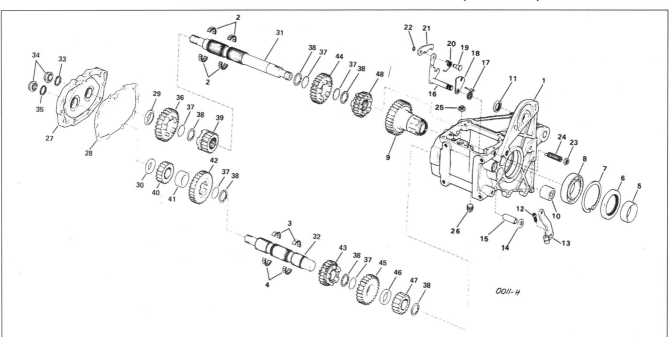

11.5 Transmission and main drive gear - exploded view

1	Transmission case	13	Shift lever	25	Relief valve	37	Thrust washer
2	Bearings	14	Oil seal	26	Drain plug	38	Retaining ring
3	Bearing halves	15	Spacer	27	Side door	39	Mainshaft 1st gear
4	Bearing halves	16	Shift arm	28	Gasket	40	Countershaft 4th gear
5	Spacer	17	Spring	29	Mainshaft spacer	41	Spacer
6	Oil seal	18	Centering plate	30	Countershaft spacer	42	Countershaft 1st gear
7	Retaining ring	19	Pin	31	Mainshaft	43	Countershaft 3rd gear
8	Bearing	20	Spring	32	Countershaft	44	Mainshaft 3rd gear
9	Main drive gear	21	Pawl	33	Spacer	45	Countershaft 2nd gear
10	Bearing	22	Retaining ring	34	Nuts	46	Spacer
11	Oil seal	23	Locknut	35	Spacer	47	Countershaft 5th gear
12	Screw	24	Adjusting screw	36	Mainshaft 4th gear	48	Mainshaft 2nd gear

2B

6   Lift off the countershaft second gear. This exposes a split needle roller bearing. Separate its halves and take it off the countershaft.

7   Remove the snap-ring from the countershaft and lift off countershaft third gear.

8   Lift off the mainshaft second gear.

9   Expand the snap-ring below the mainshaft third gear and slide it down the shaft. This allows mainshaft third gear to slide down the shaft so you can expand and remove the snap-ring above it. Once you've done this, remove the thrust washer, mainshaft third gear, its split needle roller bearing and the lower snap-ring.

Caution: Be sure to support the gears when pressing the countershaft in the next steps, or the countershaft may be damaged.

10   Turn the side door over so the shafts are facing downward. Support the countershaft first gear from below by placing the countershaft in a long hollow tube that contacts first gear. Press the countershaft out of the side door. Remove the first gear, fourth gear and spacer.

11   Remove first gear from the mainshaft.

12   Support the mainshaft fourth gear from below and press the mainshaft out of the side door. Remove the spacer, fourth gear, thrust washer and snap-ring from the mainshaft.

Inspection

13   Wash all of the components in clean solvent and dry them off.

14   Measure the shift fork grooves in the gears. If the groove width exceeds the figure listed in this Chapter's Specifications, replace the gear, and also check the shift fork (see Section 9).

15   Check the gear teeth for cracking and other obvious damage. Check the gear bushings for scoring or heat discoloration. If a gear or bushing is damaged, replace the gear. Also give a close look to its corresponding gear on the other shaft.

16   Inspect the dogs and the dog holes in the gears for excessive wear **(see illustration)**. Replace the paired gears as a set if necessary.

17   Spin the side door bearings with fingers and check them for roughness, looseness or noise. If any problems are found, remove their snap-rings, support the side door on a press plate and press the bearings out. Press new bearings in and secure them with new snap-rings. **Note:** *Some models are equipped with beveled snap-rings. These have a punch mark on the side door between the bearing bores. Install the snap-rings with their beveled sides facing away from the bearings.*

Reassembly

18   Assembly is the reverse of the disassembly steps, with the following additions:

a) *Always use new snap-rings. Snap-ring failure can allow two gears to engage at once, which will lockup the transmission and rear wheel, possibly leading to loss of control of the motorcycle.*

b) *Lubricate the needle roller bearings with clean transmission lubricant.*

c) *Check the gears to make sure the mesh correctly* **(see illustration)**.

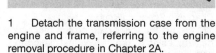

12 Transmission case - removal, inspection and installation

1   Detach the transmission case from the engine and frame, referring to the engine removal procedure in Chapter 2A.

2   Remove the swingarm pivot bolt (see Chapter 5).

2   Once the case has been detached from the frame and engine, lift it out from the right side of the motorcycle.

3   Installation is the reverse of the removal steps. Refer to Chapter 2A for tightening torques.

13 Shift pawl - removal, inspection and installation

Removal

1   Remove the transmission shafts (see Section 11).

2   Remove the pinch bolt and separate the shifter lever from the shaft **(see illustration 9.13)**.

3   If you're working on an early model, loosen the adjusting screw locknut and back the locknut out of the centering plate.

4   Remove the snap- ring and washer and pull off the shaft seal, then slide the shaft out of the transmission case.

Inspection

5   Check the shift mechanism arm for cracks, distortion and wear. Pay special attention to the tips of the pawl where they engage the shifter cam pegs. If any of these conditions are found, replace the shift mechanism.

6   Check the shaft for bending or wear and for step wear of the splines. If any of these conditions are found, replace the shaft.

7   Check the pawl spring for breakage or weakness and replace it of problems are found. If you're working on an early model, remove the snap-ring, washer and pawl to remove the spring. Use a new snap-ring on assembly. If you're working on a later model, pull off the spring.

8   Check the shaft spring for bending and breakage and replace it if problems are found.

Installation

9   Installation is the reverse of the removal steps. Use a new snap-ring on the shaft.

14 Main drive gear and bearing - removal, inspection and installation

Removal

1   Remove the transmission side door and shafts (see Section 10). It isn't necessary to remove the transmission case from the motorcycle.

2   Remove the drivebelt sprocket (see Chapter 5).

Inspection and bearing replacement

3   Check the gear for worn or damaged teeth and replace it if necessary **(see illustration 11.5)**. Removing the drive gear will damage the bearing, so it must be replaced whenever the drive gear is removed.

4   Spin the drive gear and check the bearing for roughness, looseness or noise. If problems are found, remove the drive gear and replace the bearing as described below.

5   Remove and discard the drive gear snap-ring.

6   Pull the main drive gear out of the transmission case with a puller.

7   Tap the bearing out of the case with a hammer and block of wood.

8   Install a new bearing in the case, using a new snap-ring. The flat side of the snap-ring faces the bearing. The gap in the snap-ring must be within a 90-degree range centered on the bolt hole nearest the swingarm pivot shaft bracket.

9   Install the gear from inside the transmission case, using a screw-type installation tool (HD 35316A or equivalent) so pressure won't be applied to the bearing inner race. Don't press on the inner race or the bearing will be damaged.

Installation

10   Installation is the reverse of the removal steps.

Chapter 3
Fuel and exhaust systems

Contents

Degrees of difficulty

Easy, suitable for novice with little experience	**Fairly easy,** suitable for beginner with some experience	**Fairly difficult,** suitable for competent DIY mechanic	**Difficult,** suitable for experienced DIY mechanic	**Very difficult,** suitable for expert DIY or professional 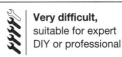

Specifications

General

Fuel tank capacity

Softail
- Main tank (all except FXSTD) .... 5 gallons (18.92 liters)
- Main tank (FXSTD) .... 4.9 gallons (18.55 liters)
- Reserve (all) .... 0.5 gallons (1.89 liters)

Dyna
- All except FXDWG
  - Main tank .... 4.9 gallons (18.5 liters)
  - Reserve .... 0.9 gallons (3.4 liters)
- FXDWG
  - Main tank .... 5.2 gallons (19.7 liters)
  - Reserve .... 1.1 gallons (4.2 liters)

Touring models
- Main tank (all except FXSTD) .... 5 gallons (18.92 liters)
- Reserve .... 0.9 gallons (3.4 liters)

Fuel grade .... Unleaded or low-lead (subject to local regulations), minimum octane rating 91 RON

Carburetor type .... Keihin CVH

Idle speed .... See Chapter 1

3

Fuel injection system pressure

Softail and 2002-on Touring models .... 55 to 62 psi (380 to 425 kPa)
1999 through 2001 Touring models .... 40 to 47 psi (280 to 325 kPa)

Carburetor jet sizes

Softail

Main jet 190
Slow jet 45

Dyna

1999
   Main jet
      US models 185
      All other models 195
   Slow jet.. 42
2000 and later
   Main jet 190
   Slow jet 45

Touring models

1999
   Main jet
      US models 185
      All other models 195
   Slow jet.. 42
2000 and later
   Main jet
      US models 190
      All other models 195
   Slow jet.. 45

Float level

All models .... 0.413 to 0.453 inch (10.49 to 11.51 mm)

Torque specifications

Softail models

Air cleaner cover screw .... 30 to 60 inch-lbs (4.1 to 6.8 Nm)
Air cleaner bracket screws .... 20 to 40 inch-lbs (2.3 to 4.5 Nm)
Air cleaner breather bolts .... 120 to 144 inch-lbs (13.6 to 16.3 Nm)
Fuel tank front mounting bolt .... 28 to 32 ft-lbs (38.0 to 43.4 Nm)
Fuel tank rear mounting bolt (all except FXSTD) .... 18 to 22 ft-lbs (24.4 to 29.8 Nm)
Fuel tank rear mounting nut (FXSTD)... 14 to 18 ft-lbs (19.0 to 24.4 Nm)
Fuel tank top plate screws
   Carbureted models .... 18 to 22 inch-lbs (2.0 to 2.7 Nm)
   Fuel injected models .... 18 to 24 inch-lbs (2.0 to 2.7 Nm)
Engine temperature sensor .... 120 to 180 inch-lbs (13.6 to 20.3 Nm)
Fuel rail screws... 18 inch-lbs (2.0 Nm)
Idle air control motor screws .... 25 inch-lbs (2.8 Nm)
Throttle body to intake manifold.. 27 to 33 inch-lbs (3.0 to 3.7 Nm)
Intake air temperature sensor screws .... 12 inch-lbs (1.4 Nm)
Throttle cable housing screw (horizontal) .... 18 inch-lbs (2.0 Nm)
Throttle position sensor screws.. 18 inch-lbs (2.0 Nm)
Carburetor top cover screws... 17 to 23 inch-lbs (1.9 to 2.6 Nm)*
Intake manifold screws/bolts... 96 to 144 inch-lbs (10.9 to 16.3 Nm)
Exhaust pipe to engine nuts
   First step (upper nut) .... Finger tight
   Second step (lower nut) .... 9 to 18 inch-lbs (1 to 2 Nm)
   Third step (upper nut) .... 60 to 80 inch-lbs (6.8 to 9.0 Nm)
   Fourth step (lower nut) .... 60 to 80 inch-lbs (6.8 to 9.0 Nm)
Exhaust interconnect tube locknuts... 30 to 33 ft-lbs (40.7 to 44.7 Nm)
Muffler clamp nuts.. 45 to 60 ft-lbs (61.0 to 81.3 Nm)
Muffler to interconnect bolts .... 96 to 120 inch-lbs (10.8 to 13.6 Nm)

Dyna models

Air cleaner cover screw	30 to 60 inch-lbs (4.1 to 6.8 Nm)
Air cleaner bracket screws	20 to 40 inch-lbs (2.3 to 4.5 Nm)
Fuel tank mounting bolts	120 to 216 inch-lbs (13.6 to 24.4 Nm)
Intake manifold screws/bolts	96 to 144 inch-lbs (10.9 to 16.3 Nm)
Exhaust pipe to engine nuts (front cylinder)	
First step (lower nut)	Finger tight
Second step (upper nut)	9 to 18 inch-lbs (1 to 2 Nm)
Third step (lower nut)	60 to 80 inch-lbs (6.8 to 9.0 Nm)
Fourth step (upper nut)	60 to 80 inch-lbs (6.8 to 9.0 Nm)
Exhaust pipe to engine nuts (rear cylinder)	
First step (upper nut)	Finger tight
Second step (lower nut)	9 to 18 inch-lbs (1 to 2 Nm)
Third step (upper nut)	60 to 80 inch-lbs (6.8 to 9.0 Nm)
Fourth step (lower nut)	60 to 80 inch-lbs (6.8 to 9.0 Nm)
Front exhaust bracket bolt	90 to 120 inch-lbs (10.2 to 13.5 Nm)
Muffler clamp nuts	45 to 60 ft-lbs (61.0 to 81.3 Nm)

1999 through 2001 Touring models

Air cleaner cover screw	30 to 60 inch-lbs (4.1 to 6.8 Nm)
Air cleaner breather bolts	120 to 144 inch-lbs (13.6 to 16.3 Nm)
Fuel tank front mounting bolts	15 to 18 ft-lbs (20 to 24 Nm)
Fuel tank top plate screws	15 to 20 inch-lbs (1.7 to 2.3 Nm)
Fuel tank rear mounting bolt	72 inch-lbs (8 Nm)
Engine temperature sensor	120 to 144 inch-lbs (13.6 to 16 Nm)
Fuel injector retaining plate screw	35 inch-lbs (3.9 Nm)
Intake air temperature sensor screws	6 inch-lbs (7 Nm)
Carburetor top cover screws	17 to 23 inch-lbs (1.9 to 2.6 Nm)
Intake manifold screws/bolts	72 to 120 inch-lbs (8 to 14 Nm)
Exhaust pipe to engine nuts	
First step (upper nut)	9 to 18 inch-lbs (1 to 2 Nm)
Second step (lower nut)	120 inch-lbs (14 Nm)
Third step (upper nut)	120 inch-lbs (14 Nm)
Muffler and pipe clamp nuts	45 to 60 ft-lbs (61.0 to 81.3 Nm)
Heat shield clamp nuts	20 to 40 inch-lbs (2.3 to 4.5 Nm)

2002-on Touring models

Air cleaner cover screw	30 to 60 inch-lbs (4.1 to 6.8 Nm)
Air cleaner bracket screws	20 to 40 inch-lbs (2.3 to 4.5 Nm)
Air cleaner breather bolts	120 to 144 inch-lbs (13.6 to 16.3 Nm)
Fuel tank front mounting bolt	28 to 32 ft-lbs (38.0 to 43.4 Nm)
Fuel tank rear mounting bolt (all except FXSTD)	18 to 22 ft-lbs (24.4 to 29.8 Nm)
Fuel tank rear mounting nut (FXSTD)	14 to 18 ft-lbs (19.0 to 24.4 Nm)
Fuel tank top plate screws	18 to 24 inch-lbs (2.0 to 2.7 Nm)
Engine temperature sensor	120 to 180 inch-lbs (13.6 to 20.3 Nm)
Fuel rail screws	18 inch-lbs (2.0 Nm)
Idle air control motor screws	25 inch-lbs (2.8 Nm)
Throttle body to intake manifold	27 to 33 inch-lbs (3.0 to 3.7 Nm)
Intake air temperature sensor screws	12 inch-lbs (1.4 Nm)
Throttle cable housing screw (horizontal)	18 inch-lbs (2.0 Nm)
Throttle position sensor screws	18 inch-lbs (2.0 Nm)
Carburetor top cover screws	17 to 23 inch-lbs (1.9 to 2.6 Nm)*
Intake manifold screws/bolts	96 to 144 inch-lbs (10.9 to 16.3 Nm)
Exhaust pipe to engine nuts (front cylinder)	
First step (lower nut)	Finger tight
Second step (upper nut)	9 to 18 inch-lbs (1 to 2 Nm)
Third step (lower nut)	60 to 80 inch-lbs (6.8 to 9.0 Nm)
Fourth step (upper nut)	60 to 80 inch-lbs (6.8 to 9.0 Nm)
Exhaust pipe to engine nuts (rear cylinder)	
First step (upper nut)	Finger tight
Second step (lower nut)	9 to 18 inch-lbs (1 to 2 Nm)
Third step (upper nut)	60 to 80 inch-lbs (6.8 to 9.0 Nm)
Fourth step (lower nut)	60 to 80 inch-lbs (6.8 to 9.0 Nm)
Heat shield clamps	20 to 40 inch-lbs (2.3 to 4.5 Nm)

3

3.2 Pull up on the sleeve (arrow) and down on the fuel line to disconnect it

1 General information

All Dyna models use a carburetor. Softail and Touring models may be equipped with a carburetor or sequential port fuel injection.

The fuel system on carbureted models consists of the fuel tank, the fuel tap and filter, the carburetor and the connecting lines, hoses and control cables.

The carburetor is a constant vacuum type with a butterfly-type throttle valve and accelerator pump. For cold starting, an enrichment circuit is actuated by a knob on the left side of the bike under the fuel tank.

The fuel system on fuel injected models consists of the fuel tank with in-tank fuel pump and filter, induction module, electronic control module, sensors, hoses, wiring harnesses and control cables. The sensors indicate supply the ECM with information on crankshaft position, manifold absolute pressure, intake air temperature, engine temperature, throttle position and vehicle speed. The induction module contains two fuel injectors and an idle air control motor.

The exhaust system uses separate pipes for each cylinder.

Many of the fuel system service procedures are considered routine maintenance items and for that reason are included in Chapter 1.

2 Relieving fuel injection system pressure

1   Remove the seat and fuse block cover (see Chapters 7 and 8).
2   Locate the fuel pump fuse and remove it from the wiring harness (see Chapter 8).
3   Start the engine and let it idle until it stalls. Once it stalls, crank the engine with the starter for three seconds to relieve any residual fuel pressure, then turn the key off.

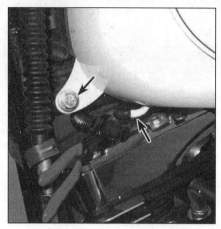

3.4a Disconnect and cap the crossover hose (lower arrow) and hold the fuel tank through-bolt (upper arrow) with a wrench . . .

3 Fuel tank - removal and installation

⚠ *Warning: Gasoline is extremely flammable, so take extra precautions when you work on any part of the fuel system. Don't smoke or allow open flames or bare light bulbs near the work area, and don't work in a garage where a natural gas-type appliance (such as a water heater or clothes dryer) is present. Since gasoline is carcinogenic, wear fuel-resistant gloves when there's a possibility of being exposed to fuel, and, if you spill any fuel on your skin, rinse it off immediately with soap and water. Mop up any spills immediately and do not store fuel-soaked rags where they could ignite. When you perform any kind of work on the fuel system, wear safety glasses and have a fire extinguisher suitable for a Class B type fire (flammable liquids) on hand.*

1   Relieve fuel system pressure (see Section 2). Disconnect the negative cable from

3.5a Disconnect the electrical connector from the top plate (fuel injected models)

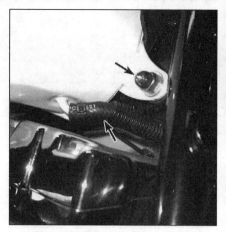

3.4b . . . and unscrew the acorn nut (arrow); the crossover hose and fitting (arrow) are below it

the battery.
2   If you're working on a fuel injected model, disconnect the fuel line from the tank. To do this, pull up on the fitting sleeve and down on the fuel line **(see illustration)**.
3   If you're working on a carbureted model, disconnect the fuel line from the fuel supply valve on the underside of the carburetor (see Chapter 1 if necessary).
4   The fuel tank on Softail and Dyna models is held in place by at the forward end by a through-bolt, which passes through bushings and mounting grommets **(see illustrations)**. The Touring model arrangement is similar, but uses two short bolts instead of a single through-bolt. At the rear, Softails and Touring models use a single vertical bolt, O-ring, grommet and T-nut to secure the tank to the frame. Dynas use a through-bolt similar to the front through-bolt.
5   Remove the instrument cluster from the top of the tank on models so equipped (see Chapter 8). On fuel-injected models, disconnect the electrical connector from the fuel tank top plate **(see illustration)**. Disconnect the vent line from the front of the tank (if equipped) **(see illustration)**.

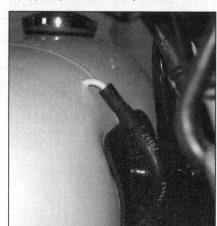

3.5b Disconnect the vent line (if equipped) from the front of the tank

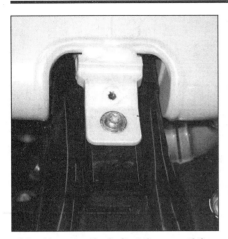

3.8a Unscrew the bolt at the rear of the tank (vertical bolt shown)

6   Make a cap for the crossover hose fitting out of a short piece of 5/16-inch hose, a bolt and a clamp. Push the bolt into the hose and secure it with the clamp. You can also use a rubber vacuum cap.

7   Place a fuel container below the tank and place the cap you made in Step 6 where it's easily reached. Cut the clamp at one end of the crossover hose **(see illustration 3.4a)**. Pull the crossover hose off the fitting, then quickly put the cap on the fitting. Lower the free end of the crossover hose so it can drain into the fuel container.

8   Remove the tank mounting bolts and nuts **(see illustrations 3.4a, 3.4b and the accompanying illustration)**. Disconnect the vent hose and free any remaining electrical harnesses, then remove the tank from the motorcycle **(see illustration)**. On some models, you'll need to remove the rubber trim at the front of the tank for access to the electrical connectors along the frame rail **(see illustration)**.

9   Before installing the tank, check the condition of the rubber mounting dampers and grommets and the hoses on the underside of the tank - if they're hardened, cracked, or show any other signs of deterio-ration, replace them **(see illustrations)**.

10   When installing the tank, reverse the above procedure. Make sure the tank seats properly and does not pinch any control cables or wires.

4 Fuel tank - cleaning and repair

1   All repairs to the fuel tank should be carried out by a professional who has experience in this critical and potentially dangerous work. Even after cleaning and flushing of the fuel system, explosive fumes can remain and ignite during repair of the tank.

2   If the fuel tank is removed from the vehicle, it should not be placed in an area where sparks or open flames could ignite the fumes coming out of the tank. Be especially careful inside garages where a natural gas-type appliance is located, because the pilot light could cause an explosion.

3.8b Lift the tank and disconnect the underside electrical connector(s)

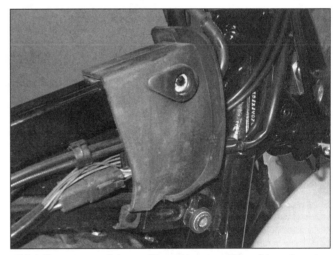

3.8c On some models, you'll need to move this rubber piece to get at the electrical connector underneath it

3.9a Thread a tap into the collar and remove it, then remove the rubber bushing

3.9b Models with a vertical rear tank bolt use a similar bushing arrangement at the rear

3

7.6a Loosen and tighten the mounting plate screws (arrows) in a criss-cross pattern

7.6b Lift the mounting plate to expose the hose clamp (arrow), then cut the clamp and disconnect the hose

5 Fuel injection system pressure test

1   Relieve fuel system pressure (see Section 2). Reinstall the fuel pump fuse.
2   Disconnect the fuel supply line fitting and attach a fuel pressure test fitting (Schrader valve) to the disconnected end of the line. Be sure to use two adapters to avoid twisting the line. Tug on the connections to make sure they're secure.
3   Start the engine and let it idle long enough to re-pressurize the fuel system, then bleed the gauge line of air, following the gauge manufacturer's instructions.
4   Rev the engine and note the fuel pressure reading. It should stabilize at a steady reading within the limits listed in this Chapter's Specifications.
5   Relieve fuel system pressure and remove the gauge. Reconnect the fuel supply line.
6   If the fuel pressure reading wasn't within the specified range, check the fuel filter and the pump inlet screen for clogging

and replace it as necessary.
7   If the pump inlet screen and filter are clear, check for an internal leak in the fuel tank. The easiest way to do this is to turn the key to On with a low fuel level in the tank. During the first two seconds of fuel pump operation, fuel from an internal leak may be heard spraying against the sides of the tank.
8   If the pump, inlet screen and fuel filter are good and there's no internal leak, the pressure regulator may be at fault. Have it tested by a dealer service department or other qualified shop, or substitute a regulator known to be good.

6 Fuel injection system relay test

1   Remove the seat and locate the fuel system relay on the fuse block (see Chapter 8 if necessary). Remove the relay.
2   Connect an ohmmeter between terminals 87 and 30 on the relay. The ohmmeter

should indicate infinite resistance (no continuity).
3   Connect a 12-volt battery to terminals 85 and 86 on the relay (the motorcycle's battery will work if it's fully charged). There should now be continuity (little or no resistance) between terminals 87 and 30.
4   If the relay doesn't perform as described, replace it.

7 Fuel pump and filter (2000-on) - removal and installation

1   This section applies to Softail models and 2000 and later Touring models equipped with electronic fuel injection. These models have the fuel pump and filter mounted on an assembly inside the fuel tank. On 1999 through 2001 Touring models, the pressure regulator is mounted on the induction module (see Section 19).

Pump assembly removal

2   Relieve fuel system pressure (see Section 2).
3   Remove the seat, disconnect the battery and remove the instrument console or pod from the top of the fuel tank (see Chapters 7 and 8).
4   Drain the fuel tank (see Section 3).
5   Disconnect the electrical connector for the fuel pump module on top of the tank **(see illustration 3.5a)**.
6   Remove the mounting plate screws **(see illustration)**. Lift the mounting plate off the tank far enough to expose the end of the fuel line **(see illustration)**. Cut the clamp, then disconnect the fuel line from the fitting.
7   Reach inside the fuel tank and push the pump housing free of the end cap. Lift the pump assembly out of the tank, taking care not to catch the float rod on the edge of the hole **(see illustration)**.

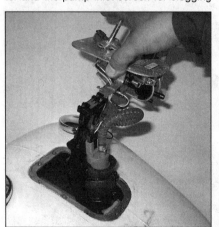

7.7 Lift the pump assembly out of the tank, taking care not to catch the float rod on the edge of the hole

7.9a Unhook the wire bail (arrow) from the bracket . . .

7.9b . . . then slide the bracket (left arrow) out of its slot (right arrow)

7.10 Fuel filter and pressure regulator components (Softail and 2002-on Touring models)

1	O-ring	4	O-ring
2	Fuel pressure regulator	5	Fuel filter
3	O-ring	6	Housing

Fuel filter replacement

Softail and 2002-on Touring models

8   Remove the pump assembly from the fuel tank as described above.
9   Unhook the wire bail from the filter bracket, then slide the bracket out of its slot in the fuel tank top plate **(see illustrations)**.
10   Cut the hose clamp and disconnect the hose from the filter. Detach the filter from the regulator and remove its O-ring **(see illustration)**.
11   Installation is the reverse of the removal steps, with the following additions:

 a)   *Replace the hose if it shows any signs of damage or wear at all. Even small leaks can reduce fuel pressure and degrade performance. Use denatured alcohol or glass cleaner to lubricate the hose for installation.*
 b)   *Be sure the inlet port of the filter is toward the fuel pump.*
 c)   *Use a new hose clamp and crimp it securely.*

2000 and 2001 FLHTCI, FLHTCUI, FLTRI

12   The fuel filter is secured to a bracket on the fuel pump housing by a retaining ring.
13   Remove the pump assembly from the fuel tank as described above.
14   Cut the clamp and disconnect the outlet hose from the filter. Remove the retaining ring and take the filter out of the bracket. Cut the clamp, disconnect the inlet hose and remove the filter.
15   Installation is the reverse of the removal steps. Use new hose clamps and a new retaining ring.

2000 and 2001 FLHRI, FLHRCI

16   The fuel filter is mounted in the fuel tank top plate.
17   Remove the pump assembly from the fuel tank as described above.
18   Cut the clamps and disconnect the

hoses from the filter. Carefully pry the slotted end of the filter bracket free of the filter groove, then lower the filter out of its bracket.
19   Installation is the reverse of the removal steps. Place the rounded end of the filter in the bracket, then push the neck of the filter into the V on the other side of the bracket until it engages securely. Use new hose clamps.

Fuel pump removal and installation

Softail and 2002-on Touring models

20   At the top of the fuel pump, cut the hose clamp and disconnect the hose from the pump **(see illustration)**. Disconnect the pump electrical connector.
21   On 2002 and later models, unhook the spring that attaches the fuel pump housing to the fuel tank top plate.
22   On 2000 and 2001 models, disengage the tab on the plastic cap from the arm on the fuel tank top plate.

7.20 Cut the clamp and disconnect the hose (left arrow) and the electrical connector (right arrow)

Caution: The plastic cap will have to be replaced with a new one if it's removed.
23   Insert a screwdriver into the webbing on top of the end cap and pry it open. Take the end cap off of the fuel tank top plate, then remove the fuel pump and bracket.

Caution: To remove the fuel pump from the support arm on 2002 and later models, you'll have to crack the plastic, which means you'll have to replace the complete fuel pump assembly with a new one. Don't do this unless you're absolutely sure the fuel pump needs to be replaced.
24   Check the insulation on the fuel pump wiring and replace it if it's cracked or deteriorated.

Caution: Don't use standard electrical wire for this harness. The fuel pump wires are Teflon-coated to resist fuel.
25   Install a new fuel pump end cap (all models) on the fuel tank top plate, engaging the top plate tab with the end cap.
26   Attach the spring (2002 and later) and fuel level sending unit to the fuel pump housing.
27   Connect the wiring harness and fuel hose to the fuel pump. Use a new clamp on the hose and crimp it securely.

2000 and 2001 Touring models

Caution: The fuel pump housing must be replaced with a new one once it has been removed, which also means installing a new fuel pump. Be absolutely sure the fuel pump needs to be replaced before removing it from the assembly.
28   At the top of the fuel pump, cut the hose clamp and disconnect the hose from the pump **(see illustration 7.20)**. Disconnect the pump electrical connector.
29   If you're working on an FLHRI or FLHRCI, remove the fuel filter retaining ring and pull the outlet port and hose out of the bracket on the fuel pump housing.
30   Drive the retaining pin out of the spring

3

stop and pump support rod.
31   Installation is the reverse of the removal steps. Use a new retaining pin and pump housing.

Pump assembly installation

32   Installation is the reverse of the removal steps, with the following additions:

a) *Use a new top plate gasket without sealant and new screws. The screws have a built-in sealant.*

b) *Hold the gauge float up, install the fuel pump assembly with its float in the left side of the tank, then release the float.*

c) *Make sure the end cap in the top plate engages the fuel pump housing.*

d) *Use a new clamp on the internal fuel hose.*

e) *Install the screws loosely in the left side of the top plate, then install the remaining screws loosely, then tighten all of the screws in a criss-cross pattern to the torque listed in this Chapter's Specifications* (see illustration 7.6a).

8   Fuel pressure regulator (late EFI) - removal and installation

1   This section applies to Softail models and 2002 and later Touring models equipped with electronic fuel injection. These models have he fuel pump, filter and pressure regulator mounted on an assembly inside the fuel tank.

2   Remove the fuel pump assembly and fuel filter as described in Section 7. Slide the regulator housing tabs out from under the tabs on the fuel tank top plate (see illustration).

3   Work the regulator back-and-forth while pulling on it to free its O-rings from the housing. Take the regulator out (see illustration 7.10).

4   Use new O-rings, whether you're installing a new regulator or the old one. Wipe them with a thin coat of engine oil.

8.2 With the filter removed, slide the regulator housing tabs out from under the top plate tabs (arrows)

Push the regulator into the housing, then slide the housing into the top plate.
5   The remainder of installation is the reverse of the removal steps.

9   Fuel pump and filter (1999 Touring models) - removal and installation

Fuel filter replacement

1   Relieve fuel system pressure (see Section 2).
2   Drain the fuel tank (see Section 3).
3   Remove the instrument panel or console from the top of the fuel tank (see Chapter 7 or 8). Remove the fuel tank top plate and gasket.
4   Reach inside the right side of the tank and cut the clamp on the short hose connected to the fuel filter.

⚠ *Warning: Don't cut yourself on the edges of the fuel tank opening while reaching inside.*

5   Remove the filter mounting nut, lockwasher, washer and bolt.
6   Detach the filter mounting bracket from the inside of the tank and lift it up for access to the remaining fuel line clamp. Cut the clamp and take the filter out.
7   Installation is the reverse of the removal steps. Use new hose clamps and crimp them securely. The hose that runs to the fuel pump (long hose) goes on the filter fitting farthest from the mounting bracket.

Fuel pump removal and installation

8   Reach inside the left side of the fuel tank and lift the pump off its mounting posts.
9   At the top of the fuel pump, cut the hose clamp and disconnect the hose from the pump. Disconnect the pump electrical connectors.
10   Connect the wires and fuel hose to the fuel pump. The black wire goes on the same side of the pump as the fuel inlet screen. Use a new clamp on the hose and crimp it securely.
11   The remainder of installation is the reverse of the removal steps.

10 Diagnostic trouble codes

1   These models have self-diagnostic capabilities. When the engine is running, the ECM monitors the system component circuits. If a malfunction occurs in one of these circuits, the module stores a diagnostic code and turns on the Check Engine lamp.
2   When the ignition key is turned to On (after it's been turned to Off for 10 or more seconds), and the engine kill switch is in the

Run position, the Check Engine lamp lights for about 4 seconds, then goes out.
3   If the Check Engine Lamp does not come on when the ignition key is
turned to ON, or if it fails to go out after four seconds, there is a malfunction in one or more of the monitored circuits in the ignition system.
4   There are three ways to output any diagnostic trouble code(s) stored in the ignition module. Harley-Davidson dealers use "Scanalyzer" or "Digital Technician" diagnostic equipment which interfaces directly with the ignition module through the Data Link Connector. This method is beyond the scope of the home mechanic. The other method, which can be done at home, requires no fancy tools. This method is simply a matter of determining the two-digit trouble code(s) by counting the number of flashes of the Check Engine lamp.
5   Fabricate a two-inch jumper wire from 18-gauge wire with the correct terminal (Harley part no. 72191-94) on each end.
6   Remove the seat (see Chapter 7) and locate the Data Link Connector. The Data Link Connector has four wires (light green/red, black, violet/red, white/black) on one side of the connector, and none on the other side. Bridge terminals 1 and 2 (light green/red and black wires) with the jumper wire. Disconnect the negative cable from the battery. Turn the ignition switch key to IGNITION and wait about eight seconds for the Check Engine Lamp to begin flashing.
7   Each stored code is preceded by a series of rapid flashes (about three per second), followed by a two-second pause (lamp is off), followed by the code. (If the lamp continues to flash at the faster rate, no codes are stored.)
8   The lamp indicates the first digit of the trouble code by flashing one or more times. Each flash is about one second in duration, followed by a one-second pause (lamp off). To determine the first digit, simply count the number of times the lamp flashes (it could be one, two, three, four or five flashes). Write down this number.
9   After the lamp has flashed the first digit of the code, there is another two-second pause (lamp off). The lamp then flashes one or more times to indicate the second digit of the code (two, four, five or six flashes).
10   After the lamp has flashed the second digit of the code, there is another two-second pause. Then, if there are no other codes stored, the lamp will repeat this trouble code again. If there is more than one code stored, the lamp will flash out the second stored code, in the same manner as the first. Again, jot down the code. This will be followed by another two-second pause, then the lamp will either repeat the first two codes again or, if there is a third code, it will display that code.
11   After the lamp has completed its output of all stored codes, it repeats, starting with the first code again. Once you note that the

lamp is repeating itself, there is no need for further observation. (You may wish to record them a second time just to be sure that you counted the correct number of flashes for each digit of each code the first time.)

12   Compare the displayed trouble codes to the following list. You now know which circuit(s) has/have a problem.

Note: *Some of the following components are used on fuel injected models and are covered in this Chapter. Others are part of the ignition system and are used on carbureted and fuel injected models. These are covered in Chapter 4.*

- *11   Throttle position sensor*
- *12   Barometric pressure or MAP sensor*
- *14   Engine temperature sensor*
- *15   Intake air temperature sensor*
- *16   Battery voltage (high or low)*
- *23   Front fuel injector*
- *24   Front ignition coil*
- *25   Rear ignition coil*
- *32   Rear fuel injector*
- *33   Fuel pump relay*
- *35   Tachometer*
- *41   Crankshaft position sensor*
- *42   Camshaft position sensor*
- *44   Bank angle sensor*
- *52   ECM RAM error*
- *53   ECM ROM error*
- *54   EEPROM error*
- *55   Microprocessor malfunction*
- *56   Crankshaft or camshaft position sensor signal error*

13   The first things to check in any circuit with an apparent problem are the connectors and the wires. Make sure that all connectors are clean, dry, corrosion-free and tight. Inspect each wire in the circuit and make sure that it's not grounded, open or shorted. If all the connectors and wires are in good shape, take the bike to a dealer service department or other qualified shop. No further diagnosis is possible at home.

14   To take the ignition module out of diagnostic mode, remove the jumper wire from the Data Link Connector and turn the ignition switch to OFF. Once any problems have been corrected, the trouble codes can be cleared in one of two ways. The convenient method requires the Scanalyzer. The other method is not convenient, but can be done at home if necessary. It requires 50 "start-and-run" cycles (each start-and-run cycle consists of starting the engine, allowing it to run for at least 30 seconds, then turning it off).

11 Fuel injection system - check

1   Check the ground wire connections for tightness, referring to the wiring diagrams at the end of this manual. Check all wiring and electrical connectors that are related to the system. Loose electrical connectors and poor grounds can cause many problems that

12.4 Pull back the wire bails (arrows) and disconnect the electrical connectors from the fuel injectors

resemble more serious malfunctions. A quick way to check for loose connections is to gently shake the wiring harness with fingers and note whether the symptom changes.

2   Check to see that the battery is fully charged, as the control unit and sensors depend on an accurate supply voltage in order to properly meter the fuel.

3   Check the air cleaner element - a dirt or partially blocked filter will severely reduce performance and economy (see Chapter 1).

4   If a blown fuse is found, replace it and see if it blows again. If it does, search for a grounded wire in the harness related t the system.

5   Check the intake manifold and induction module for leaks, which will result in an excessively lean mixture. Also check the condition of the vacuum hoses connected to the intake manifold. **Note:** *An easy way to check for vacuum leaks is to spray water on the induction module and vacuum hoses with the engine idling. If the engine runs better, there's a leak which is being temporarily sealed by the water.*

6   Remove the air cleaner housing and check the intake area of the induction unit for carbon and residue build-up. If it's dirty, Wipe it clean with a rag.

7   If the engine runs, start it and let it idle. Check the operation of each injector using a stethoscope or sounding rod; each injector will make a steady clicking noise if it's working (similar to a noisy valve lifter). If either injector is quiet, either the injector or its wiring harness is defective.

8   If the engine doesn't run, disconnect the electrical connector from each injector. Connect a fuel injector test lamp, sometimes called a "noid" light, to each connector in turn. Crank the engine with the starter and watch the test lamp. It should flash steadily if the injector is receiving current. If it doesn't flash, the wiring is probably at fault; if it does, the injector may be the problem, especially if there's a trouble code indicating a problem with the injector circuits.

9   If the injectors aren't sealing properly, they can leak fuel into the engine, which may cause erratic running and hard starting. To

check for this problem, remove the air cleaner housing (see Section 22). While holding the throttle wide open, turn the key to On for two seconds, then turn it to Off for two seconds. Do this on-off sequence a total of five times, then check for liquid gasoline in the intake tract (use a flashlight if necessary). If there is any, one or both injectors are leaking and should be replaced.

10   The remainder of the system checks should be left to a dealer service department or other qualified shop, as there is a chance the control unit may be damaged if the checks are not performed properly.

12 Induction module - removal and installation

Softail and 2002-on Touring models

1   The induction module consists of the throttle body, intake manifold, fuel injection system sensors, idle air control motor and fuel injectors. It's removed as an assembly, then if necessary the throttle body and intake manifold can be separated.

2   On Softail FXSTDI models, remove the fuel tank completely (see Section 3). On all others, remove the tank partway and prop it up.

3   Remove the air cleaner housing (see Section 22).

4   Disconnect the electrical connectors for the throttle position sensor, MAP sensor, intake air temperature sensor, idle air control motor and fuel injectors **(see illustration)**. **Note:** *To disconnect the fuel injector connectors, pull back the wire bail and rock the connector back-and-forth while pulling it free.*

5   Disconnect the throttle cables (see Section 21). If you're working on a bike equipped with cruise control, disconnect the cruise control cable as well.

6   If you're working on a California model, disconnect the evaporative emission hose

12.6 On California models, disconnect the EVAP hose (arrow)

12.7 Remove the intake manifold bolts (arrows) (left side bolts hidden)

from the throttle body (see illustration).

7 Remove two bolts on each side of the intake manifold to detach the manifold flanges from the cylinder heads (hex-head bolts on the left side; Allen-head bolts on the right side) (see illustration). Take the assembly off the engine and remove the sealing rings from the intake passages.

8 If you're planning to replace the fuel line, squeeze the tab and separate the tube from the line.

9 If necessary, remove the screws and separate the throttle body from the intake manifold. Remove the O-ring; it should be replaced with a new one whenever the throttle body is removed from the manifold.

10 If you separated the throttle body and manifold, wipe a new O-ring with a thin film of clean engine oil and position it in the passageway. Assemble the throttle body to the manifold. Apply Loctite Wicking Threadlock no. 290 (green) to the screws, then tighten the screws to the torque listed in this Chapter's Specifications.

11 Install new manifold seals in the passages with their tapered sides facing toward

13.2 Remove the clamp screw (arrow), but don't remove the clamp unless you plan to remove the tube

the manifold. Position the flanges (they're marked R and L for right and left sides of the engine) and manifold on the engine, then tighten the screws evenly until they're just snug.

12 Connect the cables, wires and hoses, then install the air cleaner housing (see Section 22).

13 Tighten the manifold screws to the torque listed in this Chapter's Specifications.

14 The remainder of installation is the reverse of the removal steps. Check the throttle cable adjustment (see Chapter 1).

1999 through 2001 Touring models

15 The induction module on these models consists of the throttle body, intake manifold, fuel injection system sensors, idle air control motor, fuel pressure regulator and fuel injectors. The throttle body and intake manifold are a single unit.

16 Remove the fuel tank partway and prop it up (see Section 3).

17 Remove the air cleaner housing (see Section 22).

18 Disconnect the electrical connectors for the throttle position sensor, intake air temperature sensor, idle air control motor and fuel injectors. Note: To disconnect the fuel injector connectors, pull back the wire bail and rock the connector back-and-forth while pulling it free.

19 Disconnect the throttle cables (see Section 21). If you're working on a bike equipped with cruise control, disconnect the cruise control cable as well.

20 If you're working on a California model, disconnect the evaporative emission hose from the throttle body.

21 Disconnect the vacuum hose from the fuel pressure regulator on the underside of the induction module.

22 Remove two bolts on each side of the intake manifold to detach the manifold flanges from the cylinder heads (hex-head

bolts on the left side; Allen-head bolts on the right side). Take the assembly off the engine and remove the sealing rings from the intake passages.

23 If you're planning to replace the fuel lines, remove the external retaining rings and slip the lines off the fittings. Use new O-rings and retaining rings when you reinstall the lines.

24 Install new manifold seals in the passages with their tapered sides facing toward the manifold. Position the flanges (they're marked R and L for right and left sides of the engine) and manifold on the engine, then tighten the screws evenly until they're just snug.

25 Connect the cables, wires and hoses, then install the air cleaner housing (see Section 22).

26 Tighten the manifold screws to the torque listed in this Chapter's Specifications.

27 The remainder of installation is the reverse of the removal steps. Check the throttle cable adjustment (see Chapter 1).

13 Fuel injectors - replacement

Softail and 2002-on Touring models

1 Remove the induction module (see Section 12).

2 Remove the screw from the fuel supply tube clamp, but don't remove the tube unless you're planning to replace the tube or its O-ring (see illustration).

3 Pull the fuel injector clip out of the fuel rail (see illustration). Remove the fuel rail screws, then pull the fuel rail off (see illustration). If the injectors come with it, pull them out of the fuel rail; otherwise, pull them out of the intake manifold (see illustration). Using a back-and-forth rocking motion to

13.3a Remove the fuel injector clip (arrow)

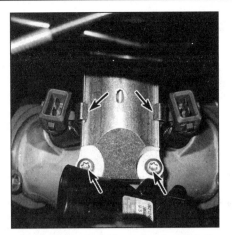

13.3b Noting how its ends grip the fuel rail (upper arrows) and remove the fuel rail screws (lower arrows)

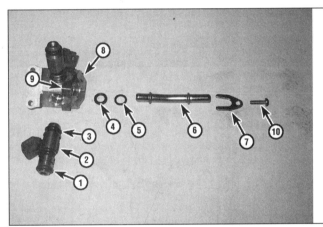

13.3c Fuel injector details

1   O-ring
2   Fuel injector
3   O-ring
4   O-ring
5   Washer
6   Fuel supply tube
7   Clamp
9   Fuel rail (shown with one injector removed)
9   Fuel injector clip
10 Screw

free the O-rings.

4   Remove the O-rings from the injectors.

5   Wipe new injector O-rings with a thin coat of clean engine oil and install them on the injectors.

6   Install the injectors in the intake manifold, with their electrical connectors pointing upward. Rotate the injectors so their electrical connectors point outward.

14.3 The engine temperature sensor is mounted in the back of the front cylinder head

7   Push the fuel rail onto the injectors as far as it will go **(see illustration 13.2)**. Install the fuel rail screws, but don't tighten them yet.

8   Install the injector clip and make sure it's securely fastened.

9   Tighten the fuel rail screws to the torque listed in this Chapter's Specifications.

10   The remainder of installation is the reverse of the removal steps.

1999 through 2001 Touring models

11   Remove the fuel tank partway and prop it up for access to the induction module (see Section 3).

12   Disconnect the fuel injector electrical connectors. **Note:** *To disconnect the fuel injector connectors, pull back the wire bail and rock the connector back-and-forth while pulling it free.*

13   Remove the Torx screw and retaining plate that secure the injectors to the induction module.

14   Free the injectors from the induction module. The ideal way to do this is with Harley tool HD-41320 or equivalent. This is a prying tool shaped to fit around the injectors. If you don't have the tool, work the injectors

back-and-forth to free them from the module, taking care not to crack the plastic.

15   Check the injector filter screens for clogging or damage. Clean the screens or replace the injectors as necessary.

16   Installation is the reverse of the removal steps, with the following additions:

a) *Wipe the injector O-rings with clean engine oil.*

b) *Set the injectors in their bores so they line up with the retaining plate. Place the retaining plate over the injectors to verify the alignment, then push the injectors into their bores until they seat.*

c) *Tighten the retaining plate Torx screw to the torque listed in this Chapter's Specifications.*

14 Engine temperature sensor - check, removal and installation

Check

1   If you're working on a Softail, relieve fuel system pressure (see Section 2). Disconnect the fuel line from under the fuel tank (this is part of the fuel tank removal procedure; see Section 3).

2   If you're working on a Touring model, remove the seat (see Chapter 7).

3   Locate the engine temperature sensor on the back of the front cylinder and disconnect its electrical connector **(see illustration)**.

4   Connect an ohmmeter between the terminals of the sensor. At low engine temperatures, sensor resistance should be very high, and at high temperatures it should be much lower.

5   If sensor readings are not as described, replace the sensor.

Replacement

6   If you haven't already done so, disconnect the electrical connector from the sensor.

7   Unscrew the sensor with a socket and take it off the cylinder head.

8   Installation is the reverse of the removal steps. Thread the sensor into the engine two or three turns, then tighten it to the torque listed in this Chapter's Specifications.

15 Throttle position sensor - check and replacement

Softail and 2002-on Touring models

Check

1   Locate the sensor on the induction module **(see illustration)**. Backprobe the sensor input and ground terminals with a

3

15.1 The throttle position sensor (Softail and 2002-on Touring models) is on the rear side of the induction module

15.6 Align the hole in the throttle position sensor with the shaft on the throttle body

voltmeter (for terminal identification, refer to the wiring diagrams at the end of this manual).

2   Turn the key to On, but don't start the engine.

3   Operate the throttle and watch the voltmeter. It should be low with the throttle closed - from 0.2 to 0.6 volts - and high with the throttle wide open - 4.6 to 4.9 volts.

4   If the voltmeter doesn't give the correct readings, disconnect the electrical connector from the sensor and connect a voltmeter between the sensor power and ground terminals. The voltmeter should indicate approximately 5 volts. If it doesn't, check the wiring back to the ECU. If the wiring is good, the ECU may be at fault. Have further testing done by a dealer service department or other qualified shop.

Replacement

5   Disconnect the sensor electrical connector (if you haven't already done so).

Remove the mounting screws and take the sensor off the induction module (see illustration 15.1).

6   Align the throttle shaft with the hole in the throttle position sensor and position the sensor in the induction module (see illustration). Install its screws and tighten them to the torque listed in this Chapter's Specifications.

7   Install all components removed for access. Adjustment isn't necessary.

1999 through 2001 Touring models

8   The throttle position sensor on these models requires a voltmeter that can read to three decimal places to check and adjust it, as well as a breakout box to connect test equipment into the wiring harness. Checking, adjustment and replacement should be done by a dealer service department or other qualified shop.

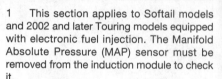

16 MAP sensor (late EFI) - check, removal and installation

1   This section applies to Softail models and 2002 and later Touring models equipped with electronic fuel injection. The Manifold Absolute Pressure (MAP) sensor must be removed from the induction module to check it.

2   Remove the air cleaner housing (see Section 22).

3   Carefully heat the idle air control motor front screw with a heat gun to loosen the thread locking agent that secures (see illustration). Don't apply too much heat or you'll damage the throttle housing. Remove the screw.

4   Remove the throttle cable housing horizontal screw, then remove the throttle cable housing (see illustration 16.3 and the accompanying illustration). Carefully work

16.3 Here are the Softail and 2002-on Touring model idle air control motor screws (arrows); the forward screw also secures the throttle cable housing

16.4a Remove the throttle cable housing horizontal screw (arrow) and take the housing off the throttle body

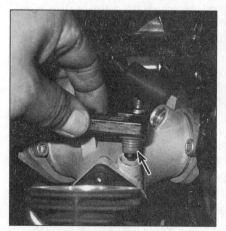

16.4b Work the MAP sensor grommet (arrow) free of its bore

16.7 Disconnect the MAP sensor electrical connector (arrow)

17.5 Lift the idle air control motor off the throttle body and remove its O-ring

the MAP sensor grommet out of the intake manifold **(see illustration)**.

6 Inspect the grommet and replace if it's deteriorated or damaged.

7 Connect a voltmeter between terminals B and C of the MAP sensor connector **(see illustration)**. Use the wiring diagrams at the end of this manual to identify the terminals.

8 Remove the grommet from the MAP sensor pressure port and connect a vacuum pump to the port.

9 Turn the key ON but don't start the engine. The MAP sensor should indicate a high voltage, which should drop as vacuum is applied to the port.

10 If the sensor doesn't perform as described, it's probably defective. Refer further service to a dealer service department or other qualified shop.

11 Install the MAP sensor and grommet on the intake manifold. Install the throttle housing and install a new front idle air control motor screw, but don't torque it yet.

12 Install the throttle housing screw and tighten it to the torque listed in this Chapter's Specifications.

13 Tighten the front idle air control motor screw to the torque listed in this Chapter's Specifications.

14 Install the air cleaner housing.

17 Idle air control (IAC) motor - check, removal and installation

Softail and 2002-on Touring models

Check

1 Remove the air cleaner housing (see Section 22).

2 Without cranking the engine, turn the ignition key to On, then Off, while you look at the IAC motor pintle inside the bore of the throttle body at the top. As the key is turned off, the pintle should extend, then retract

within 10 seconds. If it doesn't, the IAC motor may be defective. Refer further testing to a dealer service department or other qualified shop .

Replacement

3 Carefully heat the IAC motor screws with a heat gun to soften the thread locking agent that secures them.

4 Remove both IAC motor screws and the throttle housing screw **(see illustrations 16.3 and 16.4a)**.

5 Carefully work the IAC motor free of the throttle housing and remove the O-ring **(see illustration)**.

6 Installation is the reverse of the removal steps, with the following additions:

a) *Use a new O-ring and wipe it with a thin film of clean engine oil.*

b) *Use new IAC motor screws. Install them loosely, then install the throttle housing screw and tighten it to the torque listed in this Chapter's Specifications, then tighten the IAC motor screws to the torque listed in this Chapter's Specifications.*

1999 through 2001 Touring models

7 The idle air control motor on these models requires a voltmeter that can read to three decimal places to check and adjust it, as well as a breakout box to connect test equipment into the wiring harness. Checking, adjustment and replacement should be done by a dealer service department or other qualified shop.

18 Barometric pressure sensor (early EFI) - check and replacement

Check

1 This procedure applies to 1999 through

2001 Touring models.

2 Remove the right side cover (see Chapter 7). Locate the sensor on the electrical panel. Backprobe terminals B and C of the sensor with a voltmeter (for terminal identification, refer to the wiring diagrams at the end of this manual).

3 Remove the rubber seal from the pressure port and connect a vacuum pump to the port.

4 Turn the key to On but don't start the engine. The BARO sensor should indicate a high voltage (about 4.0 to 4.8 volts), which should drop (to about 3 volts) as vacuum is applied to the port.

5 If the sensor doesn't perform as described, it's probably defective. Refer further service to a dealer service department or other qualified shop.

Replacement

6 Disconnect the electrical connector from the sensor.

7 Work the sensor free of its rubber seal. The seal can be re-used if it's in good condition.

8 Install the new sensor in the seal and connect the connector.

9 Install the side cover.

19 Fuel pressure regulator (early EFI) - removal and installation

1 This procedure applies to 1999 through 2001 Touring models. The fuel pressure regulator on these models is mounted on the underside of the induction module, between the "V" of the intake manifold runners.

2 Remove the fuel tank (see Section 3).

3 From the upper side of the induction module, remove the Torx screw that secures the fuel injector retaining plate.

4 Reach under the induction module and work the fuel pressure regulator free (it's held in place by an O-ring).

20.1 The intake air temperature sensor (arrow) is on the induction module next to the throttle position sensor (Softail and 2002-on Touring design shown)

5   Installation is the reverse of the removal steps. Use a new O-ring, coated with a thin layer of clean engine oil. Position the vacuum port directly under the bracket bolt on the underside of the induction module.

20 Intake air temperature sensor - check and replacement

1   Locate the intake air temperature sensor on the induction module and disconnect its electrical connector (see illustration).
2   Connect an ohmmeter between the terminals of the sensor. At low engine temperatures, sensor resistance should be very high, and at high temperatures it should be much lower.
3   If sensor readings are not within the specified range, replace the sensor.

Replacement

4   If you haven't already done so, disconnect the electrical connector from the sensor.

21.5a Detach the cable ends from the pulley and remove the end plugs . . .

21.3a Remove the throttle housing upper screw (arrow) . . .

5   Remove the sensor mounting screws, then take the sensor and gasket off the throttle body.
6   Installation is the reverse of the removal steps. Use a new gasket.

21 Throttle cables - removal, installation and adjustment

Removal

1   Remove the fuel tank (see Section 3).
2   Loosen the locknuts on the pull cable and idle cable at the handlebar and screw the cable adjusters in to create as much slack as possible (see Chapter 1).
3   Remove the screws and separate the handlebar throttle housing halves (see illustrations).
4   Remove the air cleaner housing (see Section 22).
5   At the handlebar, lift each cable out of its grooves in the pulley, align the cables with the pulley slots and slip the cable ends out of

21.5b . . . then unscrew the outer cables from the housing and slip them out; remove the friction pad (arrow) if necessary

21.3b . . . and lower screw (arrow) and separate the housing halves

the pulley (see illustration). Take the end plug off each cable. Unscrew each cable fitting from the housing, then pull the cables out (see illustration). Inspect the friction adjuster pad and remove it if it's worn or damaged.
6   At the engine, lift each cable out of its grooves in the throttle pulley, align the cables with the pulley slots and slip the cable ends out of the throttle pulley (see illustration).
7   Slip the cable housings up out of the bracket, then slide the cables through the gaps in the bracket (see illustration).
8   Remove the cables, noting how they are routed.

Installation

9   Route the cables into place. Make sure they don't interfere with any other components and aren't kinked or bent sharply.
10   Lubricate the end of the pull cable with multi-purpose grease and connect it to the throttle pulley at the carburetor or throttle body. Pass the inner cable through the slot in the bracket, then seat the cable housing in the bracket.

21.6 Lift the cables out of the throttle pulley, then slip them out through the pulley slots (fuel injection shown)

21.7a Lift the outer cable out of the cable housing (arrow) . . .

21.7b . . . then slip it out of the housing slot (arrow)

22.5 Unscrew the backplate studs and screws (arrows)

11   Repeat the previous step to connect the idle cable.

12   Reinstall the air cleaner housing (see Section 22).

13   Connect the cables to the throttle grip pulley and position them in their slots.

14   Install the throttle cable housing and tighten its screws securely.

Adjustment

15   Follow the procedure outlined in Chapter 1, Throttle operation/grip freeplay - check and adjustment, to adjust the cables.

16   Turn the handlebars back and forth to make sure the cables don't cause the steering to bind.

17   Operate the throttle and check the cable action. The cables should move freely and the throttle pulley at the carburetor or throttle body should move back and forth in response to both acceleration and deceleration. If the cables don't operate properly, find and fix the problem before you operate the motorcycle.

18   Start the engine. With the engine idling, turn the handlebars all the way to left and right while listening for changes in idle speed. If idle speed increases as the handlebars turn, the cables are improperly routed. This is dangerous. Find the problem and fix it before riding the bike.

22 Air cleaner housing - removal and installation

1   Remove the air cleaner element (see Chapter 1).

Carbureted models

2   Disconnect the breather hoses from the fitting on the air cleaner housing.

3   Unscrew the breather bolts evenly, a few turns at a time, while pulling the housing free of the carburetor. Continue this until the housing is completely removed, then remove O-rings and gasket.

4   If you're working on a California model, disconnect the emission hose form the housing. Operate the EVAP system trap door and make sure it moves smoothly, without binding.

Fuel injected models

5   Unscrew the backplate studs and screws **(see illustrations)**.

6   Take the backplate off the throttle body and disconnect the vent hose (if equipped) **(see illustration)**.

7   Unbolt the backplate bracket and detach it from the engine **(see illustrations)**.

All models

8   Installation is the reverse of the removal steps. Use new gaskets.

23 Carburetor fuel mixture adjustment - general information

1   Due to the increased emphasis on controlling motorcycle exhaust emissions, certain governmental regulations have been formulated which directly affect the carburetion of this machine. In order to comply with the regulations, the carburetors on these models have a metal sealing plug pressed into the hole over the pilot screw (which controls the

22.6 Disconnect the vent hose from the rear side (if equipped)

22.7a Remove the bracket bolts (arrows) . . .

22.7b . . . noting how the bolt hardware is arranged

3

26.2a Remove the cover screws . . .

26.2b . . . lift off the cover and remove the spring and diaphragm

26.3 Lift the vacuum piston and jet needle from the carburetor

idle fuel/air mixture), so they can't be tampered with. These should not be removed.

2   If the engine runs extremely rough at idle or continually stalls, and if a carburetor overhaul does not cure the problem, take the motorcycle to a dealer service department or other repair shop equipped with an exhaust gas analyzer. They will be able to properly adjust the idle fuel/air mixture to achieve a smooth idle and restore low speed performance.

24 Carburetor overhaul - general information

1   Poor engine performance, hesitation, hard starting, stalling, flooding and backfiring are all signs that major carburetor maintenance may be required.

2   Keep in mind that many so-called carburetor problems are really not carburetor problems at all, but mechanical problems within the engine or malfunctions within the ignition system. Try to establish for certain that the carburetors are in need of a major overhaul before beginning.

3   Check the fuel tap filter, the fuel lines, the tank cap vent, the intake manifold hose clamps, the vacuum hoses, the air filter ele-

ment, the cylinder compression, the spark plugs and the ignition system before assuming that a carburetor overhaul is required.

4   Most carburetor problems are caused by dirt particles, varnish and other deposits which build up in and block the fuel and air passages. Also, in time, gaskets and O-rings shrink or deteriorate and cause fuel and air leaks which lead to poor performance.

5   When the carburetor is overhauled, it is generally disassembled completely and the parts are cleaned thoroughly with a carburetor cleaning solvent and dried with filtered, unlubricated compressed air. The fuel and air passages are also blown through with compressed air to force out any dirt that may have been loosened but not removed by the solvent. Once the cleaning process is complete, the carburetor is reassembled using new gaskets, O-rings and, generally, a new inlet needle valve and seat.

6   Before disassembling the carburetor(s), make sure you have a carburetor rebuild kit (which will include all necessary O-rings and other parts), some carburetor cleaner, a supply of rags, some means of blowing out the carburetor passages and a clean place to work. It is recommended that only one carburetor be overhauled at a time to avoid mixing up parts.

25 Carburetor - removal and installation

⚠ Warning: Gasoline is extremely flammable, so take extra precautions when you work on any part of the fuel system (see the Warning in Section 2).

Removal

1   Remove the seat (see Chapter 8).

2   Remove the fuel tank and air cleaner housing (see Sections 3 and 22).

3   Disconnect the vacuum hoses from the carburetor and loosen the intake manifold clamp screw.

4   Unbolt the carburetor bracket from the engine.

5   Pull the carburetor out of the intake duct so you can get at the throttle cables.

6   Disconnect the throttle cables from the carburetor and free the choke knob from its bracket (see Sections 21 and 28). Take the carburetor out.

7   If necessary, remove the intake manifold bolts and take the manifold off the engine.

Installation

8   Installation is the reverse of the removal steps, with the following additions:

a) Adjust the throttle grip freeplay (see Chapter 1).

b) Check for fuel leaks.

c) Check and, if necessary, adjust the idle speed (see Chapter 1).

26 Carburetor - disassembly, cleaning and inspection

⚠ Warning: Gasoline is extremely flammable, so take extra precautions when you work on any part of the fuel system (see the Warning in Section 2).

26.4a Remove the vacuum piston spring seat from the piston

26.4b Remove the needle from the piston

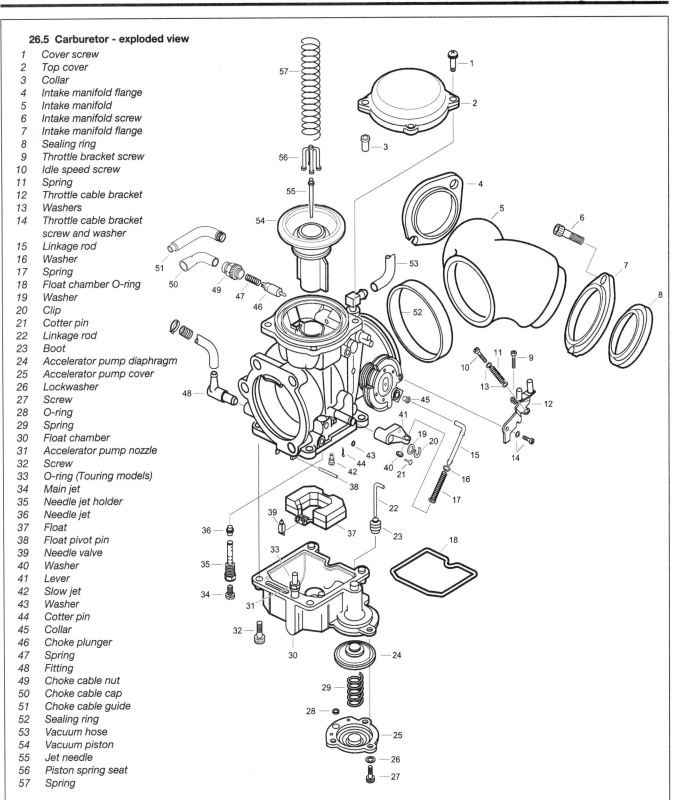

26.5 Carburetor - exploded view

1 Cover screw
2 Top cover
3 Collar
4 Intake manifold flange
5 Intake manifold
6 Intake manifold screw
7 Intake manifold flange
8 Sealing ring
9 Throttle bracket screw
10 Idle speed screw
11 Spring
12 Throttle cable bracket
13 Washers
14 Throttle cable bracket screw and washer
15 Linkage rod
16 Washer
17 Spring
18 Float chamber O-ring
19 Washer
20 Clip
21 Cotter pin
22 Linkage rod
23 Boot
24 Accelerator pump diaphragm
25 Accelerator pump cover
26 Lockwasher
27 Screw
28 O-ring
29 Spring
30 Float chamber
31 Accelerator pump nozzle
32 Screw
33 O-ring (Touring models)
34 Main jet
35 Needle jet holder
36 Needle jet
37 Float
38 Float pivot pin
39 Needle valve
40 Washer
41 Lever
42 Slow jet
43 Washer
44 Cotter pin
45 Collar
46 Choke plunger
47 Spring
48 Fitting
49 Choke cable nut
50 Choke cable cap
51 Choke cable guide
52 Sealing ring
53 Vacuum hose
54 Vacuum piston
55 Jet needle
56 Piston spring seat
57 Spring

3

Disassembly

1   Remove the carburetor from the machine as described in Section 25. Set the assembly on a clean working surface.
2   Remove the four screws securing the top cover to the carburetor body **(see illus-**

tration). Lift the cover off and remove the piston spring **(see illustration)**.
3   Peel the diaphragm away from its groove in the carburetor body, being careful not to tear it. Lift out the diaphragm/piston assembly **(see illustration)**.
4   Remove the piston spring seat and sep-

arate the needle from the piston **(see illustrations)**.
5   Refer to the accompanying illustration and note the following **(see illustration)**:
6   Make sure the screwdrivers fit their slots.
7   Remove the float chamber cover and O-

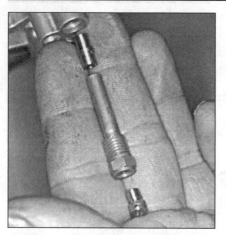

26.7 Here's how the needle jet, needle jet holder and main jet are arranged

26.10a Compress the spring . . .

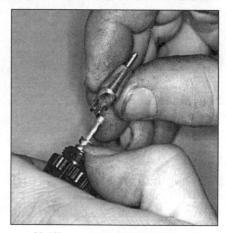

26.10b . . . and slip the cable end out of the plunger

ring for access to the jets and floats. Hold the needle jet holder with a wrench while you unscrew the main jet. Note which way the needle jet goes in the bore **(see illustration)**.

8   Push out the float pin to remove the floats.

9   When removing the diaphragm covers, do not lose the small O-ring in the passage next to the diaphragm.

10   The choke plunger is part of the choke cable **(see illustration)**. To remove it, unscrew it from the carburetor, then compress the spring and slip the cable end out of the plunger **(see illustration)**.

11   Remove the accelerator pump diaphragm screws **(see illustration 26.5)**. Take out the pump cover, noting the location of the O-ring. Take out the spring and diaphragm.

Cleaning

Caution: Use only a carburetor cleaning solution that is safe for use with plastic parts (be sure to read the label on the container).

12   Submerge the metal components in the carburetor cleaner for approximately thirty minutes (or longer, if the directions recommend it).

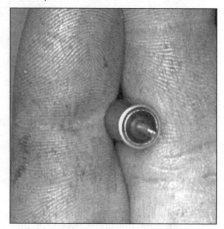

26.14 Check the plunger tip for wear

13   After the carburetor has soaked long enough for the cleaner to loosen and dissolve most of the varnish and other deposits, use a brush to remove the stubborn deposits. Rinse it again, then dry it with compressed air. Blow out all of the fuel and air passages in the main and upper body. **Caution:** *Never clean the jets or passages with a piece of wire or a drill bit, as they will be enlarged, causing the fuel and air metering rates to be upset.*

Inspection

14   Check the operation of the choke plunger. If it doesn't move smoothly, replace it, along with the return spring. Check the tapered end of plunger for wear and replace if it's worn **(see illustration)**.

15   Check the carburetor body, float bowl and top cover for cracks, distorted sealing surfaces and other damage. If any defects are found, replace the faulty component, although replacement of the entire carburetor will probably be necessary (check with your parts supplier for the availability of separate components).

16   Check the diaphragms for splits, holes and general deterioration. Holding them up to a light will help to reveal problems of this nature.

17   Insert the vacuum piston in the carburetor body and see that it moves up-and-down smoothly. Check the surface of the piston for

wear. If it's worn excessively or doesn't move smoothly in the bore, replace the carburetor.

18   Check the jet needle for straightness by rolling it on a flat surface (such as a piece of glass). Replace it if it's bent or if the tip is worn.

19   Check the tip of the fuel inlet valve needle. If it has grooves or scratches in it, it must be replaced. Push in on the rod in the other end of the needle, then release it - if it doesn't spring back, replace the valve needle **(see illustration)**.

20   Check the O-rings. Replace them if they're damaged.

21   Operate the throttle shaft to make sure the throttle butterfly valve opens and closes smoothly. If it doesn't, replace the carburetor.

22   Check the floats for damage. This will usually be apparent by the presence of fuel inside one of the floats. If the floats are damaged, they must be replaced.

27 Carburetor - reassembly and float level adjustment

Caution: When installing the jets, be careful not to over-tighten them - they're made of soft material and can strip or shear easily.

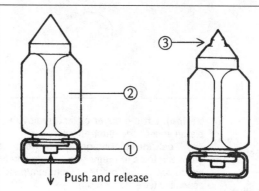

26.19 Check the tip of the fuel inlet valve needle for grooves or scratches - also make sure the rod in the end of the needle pops back out quickly after it's pushed in

1   Rod
2   Valve needle
3   Groove in tip

27.4 Don't let the jet needle retainer block the vacuum hole (arrow)

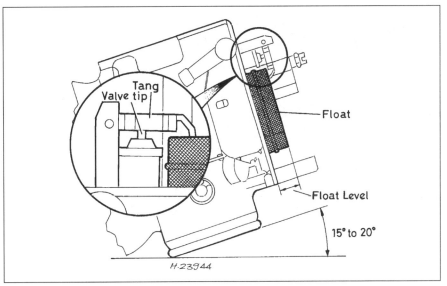

27.8 Checking the float level

Note: *When reassembling the carburetors, be sure to use the new O-rings, gaskets and other parts supplied in the rebuild kit.*

Reassembly

1   If the choke plunger was removed, install it in its bore, followed by its spring and nut. Tighten the nut securely and install the cap.
2   Install the pilot screw (if removed) along with its spring, washer and O-ring, turning it in until it seats lightly. Now, turn the screw out the number of turns that was previously recorded. Install a new metal plug in the hole over the screw. Apply a little bonding agent around the circumference of the plug after it has been seated.
3   Install the pilot jet, needle jet, needle jet holder/air bleed pipe and main jet.
4   Drop the jet needle down into its hole in the vacuum piston and install the spring seat over the needle. Make sure the spring seat doesn't cover the hole at the bottom of the vacuum piston - reposition it if necessary **(see illustration)**.
5   Install the diaphragm/vacuum piston assembly into the carburetor body. Lower the spring into the piston. Seat the bead of the diaphragm into the groove in the top of the carburetor body, making sure the diaphragm isn't distorted or kinked **(see illustration 26.2d)**. This isn't always an easy task. If the diaphragm seems too large in diameter and doesn't want to seat in the groove, place the top cover over the carburetor diaphragm, insert your finger into the throat of the carburetor and push up on the vacuum piston. Push down gently on the top cover - it should drop into place, indicating the diaphragm has seated in its groove.
6   Install the top cover, tightening the screws to the torque listed in this Chapter's Specifications. If you're working on a Softail FXSTD model, either use non-permanent thread locking agent on the threads of the screws or use new screws, which come with adhesive attached.
7   Install the accelerator pump diaphragm

and spring. Install the cover (don't forget the O-ring) and secure it with the screws.

Float level adjustment

8   Invert the carburetor. Attach the fuel inlet valve needle to the float. Set the float into position in the carburetor, making sure the valve needle seats correctly. Install the float pivot pin. To check the float level, hold the carburetor so the float hangs down, then tilt it back until the valve needle is just seated (the rod in the end of the valve shouldn't be compressed). Measure the distance from the carburetor body to the top of the float **(see illustration)** and compare your measurement to the float level listed in this Chapter's Specifications. If it isn't as specified, carefully bend the tang that contacts the valve needle up or down until the float height is correct.
9   Install the O-ring into the groove in the float bowl. Place the float bowl on the carburetor and install the screws, tightening them securely.

28.1 Loosen the hex nut (hidden behind the bracket, arrow) and separate the knob from the bracket

28 Choke knob - removal, installation and adjustment

Removal

1   Loosen the nut at the back of the choke knob bracket and slide the knob out of the bracket **(see illustration)**.
2   Unscrew the choke plunger from the carburetor **(see illustration 26.5)**. Remove the cable and choke plunger together.
3   If necessary, separate the choke plunger from the cable (see Section 26).

Installation

4   Installation is the reverse of the removal steps.

Adjustment

5   Refer to Chapter 1 for knob tension procedures.

29 Exhaust system - removal and installation

3

Note: *These motorcycles use special exhaust system clamps that eliminate the need for silicone or graphite tape. They should be replaced with new ones whenever they're removed.*

Softail models

FXST, FLSTC, FXSTS, FXSTB

1   Loosen the clamps and remove the heat shields.
2   Unscrew the exhaust pipe-to-cylinder head nuts.
3   Unbolt the mufflers from the crossover tube.

29.9 Remove the pipe-to-cylinder head nuts (arrows)

4 Remove the exhaust system as a unit, then disassemble it as needed.
5 Installation is the reverse of the removal steps. Use new muffler clamps and tighten all of the fasteners to the torque listed in this Chapter's Specifications.

FXSTD and FLSTF

6 To remove the mufflers, loosen their clamps. Remove the muffler support bolts and pull both mufflers free of the exhaust pipes, then separate them.
7 If you're working on an FLSTF, unbolt the right floorboard (see Chapter 7).
8 Remove the heat shields and muffler brackets.
9 Remove the nuts that secure the exhaust pipes to the manifold clamps, then remove the pipes (see illustration).
10 Installation is the reverse of the removal steps, with the following additions:

a) If the mufflers were separated from each other, use a new washer and seal at the crossover pipe.
b) Use new clamps at the muffler-to-exhaust pipe connections.
c) Use new gaskets at the cylinder heads, making sure the thin side of each gasket fits over its exhaust pipe. Replace the retaining rings at the cylinder head connections if they're damaged or deteriorated.
d) Tighten all of the nuts and bolts until they're snug, but don't torque them yet.
e) Tighten the exhaust pipe upper and lower nuts in sequence, following the steps listed in this Chapter's Specifications. Tighten all remaining fasteners to the torques listed in this Chapter's Specifications, working from front to rear of the bike.

FLSTS

11 Remove the saddlebags (see Chapter 7).
12 Label the heat shields so they don't get mixed up (there are five of them), then loosen the clamps and remove them from the bike.
13 Loosen one muffler clamp on the right side of the bike and two clamps on the right side.
14 Remove the muffler mounting bolts and remove the mufflers from the bike.
15 Unbolt the crossover pipe from the passenger footrest and take it off the motorcycle.
16 Unscrew the nuts at the rear exhaust pipe-to-cylinder head connection. Unbolt the rear exhaust pipe clamps and remove the pipe from the motorcycle.
17 Unscrew the nuts at the front exhaust pipe-to-cylinder head connection and remove the pipe from the motorcycle.
18 Installation is the reverse of the removal steps, with the following additions:

a) Use new gaskets at the pipe-to-cylinder head connections, with their tapered sides facing out of the engine.
b) Use new muffler clamps.
c) Use a new washer and gasket at the crossover pipe connection.
d) Tighten all of the nuts and bolts until they're snug, but don't torque them yet.
e) Tighten the exhaust pipe-to-engine upper and lower nuts in sequence, following the steps listed in this Chapter's Specifications. Tighten all remaining fasteners to the torques listed in this Chapter's Specifications, working from front to rear of the bike.

Dyna models

19 Loosen the clamps and remove the heat shields.
20 Unscrew the exhaust pipe-to-cylinder head nuts. Unbolt the front pipe clamp from the bracket at the gear cover.
21 Unbolt the rear exhaust pipe from the transmission side door bracket.
22 Remove the exhaust system as a unit, then separate the pieces as necessary.
23 Installation is the reverse of the removal steps, with the following additions:

a) Use new muffler clamps.
b) Install all of the fasteners loosely, then tighten to the torque listed in this Chapter's Specifications, working from front to back of the motorcycle.

Touring models

Removal

24 Remove the saddlebags (see Chapter 7).
25 Label the heat shields so they don't get mixed up (there are six of them), then loosen the clamps and remove them from the bike.
26 Hang the left muffler form the lower saddlebag rail with rope or a bungee cords.
27 Unscrew the nuts at both exhaust pipe-to-cylinder head connections. Unbolt the rear exhaust pipe clamps and remove the pipe from the motorcycle.
28 Loosen the four joint clamps (not the transmission clamp on the front header pipe).
29 Unbolt the mufflers from the saddlebag rails.
30 Remove the right muffler.
31 Detach the rear header pipe (on the left side of the motorcycle) from the rear cylinder head, crossover pipe (on the right side of the motorcycle) and front header pipe.
32 Remove the transmission clamp from the front header pipe, then remove the header pipe from the cylinder head.
33 Remove the crossover pipe and left muffler.

Installation

34 During installation, use new clamps at the connections between the front and rear header pipes, crossover pipe and rear header pipe, and pipes to mufflers. Also use new gaskets at the pipe-to-cylinder head connections, with the tapered side facing away from the engine.
35 Install the front header pipe in the cylinder head and transmission clamp, then place a new muffler clamp on its rear end. Don't tighten the nuts yet.
36 Install the rear header pipe, positioning it in the cylinder head and connecting it to the front header pipe. Slide the muffler clamp over the joint of the front and rear header pipes, but don't tighten it yet.
37 Install new clamps on the ends of the rear header pipe. The clamp that secures the rear header pipe to the crossover pipe has a slot for the bracket tab.
38 Install the right muffler, tightening its fasteners loosely. Slide the muffler clamp into position.
39 Connect the crossover pipe to the rear header pipe. Slide the clamp into position, engaging the bracket tab with the slot in the clamp. Install the bracket nut and tighten it loosely.
40 Slide the left muffler clamp onto the rear end of the crossover pipe. Install the muffler, support to from the saddlebag rail and install its fasteners loosely.
41 Tighten the exhaust pipe-to-engine upper and lower nuts in sequence, following the steps listed in this Chapter's Specifications.
42 Tighten the transmission clamp bolt, then the muffler mounting bolts, to the torque listed in this Chapter's Specifications.

30.1 On California models, the EVAP canister (arrow) stores fuel vapors (Dyna shown)

43   Check the exhaust pipes and mufflers for proper alignment and make sure no exhaust system parts touch the motorcycle.

44   Tighten the clamps in order:

a) *Crossover pipe-to-left muffler*
b) *Rear header pipe to right muffler*
c) *Front and rear header pipe connection*
d) *Crossover pipe and rear header pipe connection*

45   Tighten the nut on the exhaust support bracket (located at the joint between the rear header pipe and crossover pipe) to the torque listed in this Chapter's Specifications.

46   Install the heat shields, placing their clamp screws where they're accessible form the outside, and tighten the screws to the torque listed in this Chapter's Specifications.

47   Remove the support from the left muffler and reinstall the saddlebags (see Chapter 7).

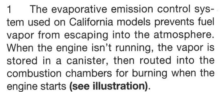

30 EVAP system (California models) - removal and installation

1   The evaporative emission control system used on California models prevents fuel vapor from escaping into the atmosphere. When the engine isn't running, the vapor is stored in a canister, then routed into the combustion chambers for burning when the engine starts **(see illustration)**.

2   The hoses should be checked periodically for loose connections, damage and deterioration. Tighten or replace the hoses as needed.

Canister removal

Softail models

3   The canister is mounted below the swingarm pivot shaft.

4   Loosen the drivebelt and slip it off the rear sprocket (see Chapter 1). Remove the rear splash guard.

5   If you're working on a carbureted model, disconnect the canister hose that runs to the air cleaner housing.

6   Carefully pry up the tang on the left side of the canister and slide it to the left. Label the two remaining hoses, disconnect them and take the canister out of the motorcycle.

Dyna models

7   The canister is located between the front frame tubes **(see illustration 30.1)**.

8   Disconnect the canister hose that runs to the air cleaner housing.

9   Carefully pry up the tang on the side of the canister and slide the canister out of the bracket. Label the two remaining hoses, disconnect them and take the canister out of the motorcycle.

Touring models

10   Remove the rear fender and the battery (see Chapters 7 and 8).

11   Pry the plastic retaining pin out of the hole in the left side of the battery box.

12   Disconnect the air inlet tube from the end of the canister (you can reach it between the right frame member and the battery box).

13   Label and disconnect the two hoses from the opposite end of the canister (again, reach between the frame and battery box).

14   Tap the canister toward the left side of the motorcycle until it frees itself from the underside of the battery box, then pull it out from the right side of the motorcycle.

Canister installation

15   Installation is the reverse of the removal steps.

3

Notes

Chapter 4
Ignition system

Contents

Degrees of difficulty

Easy, suitable for novice with little experience		Fairly easy, suitable for beginner with some experience	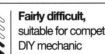	Fairly difficult, suitable for competent DIY mechanic		Difficult, suitable for experienced DIY mechanic		Very difficult, suitable for expert DIY or professional	

4

Specifications

Ignition coil
Primary resistance .... 0.5 to 0.7 ohms
Secondary resistance .... 5.5 to 7.5 k-ohms
Arcing distance .... 6 mm (1/4 in) or more

Ignition timing .... Not adjustable

1 General information

These motorcycles are equipped with a battery operated, fully transistorized, breakerless ignition system. The system consists of the following components:

Crankshaft position sensor
Camshaft position sensor (1999 and 2000 models only)
Bank angle sensor
Ignition module
Battery and fuse
Ignition coil
Spark plugs
Stop and main (key) switches
Primary and secondary circuit wiring

The transistorized ignition system functions on the same principle as a breaker point DC ignition system with the position sensor(s) and ignition module performing the tasks previously associated with the breaker points and mechanical advance system. As a result, adjustment and maintenance of ignition components is eliminated (with the exception of spark plug replacement).

Because of their nature, the individual ignition system components can be checked but not repaired. If ignition system troubles occur, and the faulty component can be isolated, the only cure for the problem is to replace the part with a new one. Keep in mind that most electrical parts, once purchased, can't be returned. To avoid unnecessary expense, make very sure the faulty component has been positively identified before buying a replacement part.

2 Ignition system - check

 Warning: Because of the very high voltage generated by the ignition system, extreme care should be taken to avoid electrical shock when these checks are performed.

1   If the ignition system is the suspected cause of poor engine performance or failure to start, a number of checks can be made to isolate the problem.

2   Make sure the ignition stop switch is in the Run or On position.

Engine will not start

3   Disconnect one of the spark plug wires, connect the wire to a spare spark plug and lay the plug on the engine with the threads contacting the engine. If it's necessary to hold the spark plug, use an insulated tool. Crank the engine over and make sure a well-defined, blue spark occurs between the spark plug electrodes.

 Warning: DO NOT remove one of the spark plugs from the engine to perform this check - atomized fuel being pumped out of the open spark plug hole could ignite, causing severe injury!

4   If no spark occurs, the following checks should be made:

5   Check the resistance of the spark plug wires with an ohmmeter. If the resistance is not within the range listed in this Chapter's Specifications, replace it with a new one. Repeat this check on the other plug wire.

6   Make sure all electrical connectors are clean and tight. Refer to the wiring diagrams at the end of this book and check all wires for shorts, opens and correct installation.

7   Check the battery voltage with a voltmeter. On 1999 Touring models, which were originally equipped with fillable batteries, check the specific gravity with a hydrometer (see Chapter 1). If the voltage is less than 12-volts or if the specific gravity is low, recharge the battery.

8   Check the ignition fuse and the fuse connections. If the fuse is blown, replace it with a new one; if the connections are loose or corroded, clean or repair them.

9   If the preceding checks produce positive results but there is still no spark at the plugs, check the remaining components as described elsewhere in this Chapter, using the trouble codes that can be produced by the ignition module. If the problem still hasn't been located, have the ignition module checked by a dealer service department or other qualified shop.

Engine starts but misfires

10   If the engine starts but misfires, make the following checks before deciding that the ignition system is at fault.

11   The ignition system must be able to produce a spark across a seven millimeter (1/4-inch) gap (minimum). A simple test fixture **(see illustration)** can be constructed to make sure the minimum spark gap can be jumped. Make sure the fixture electrodes are positioned seven millimeters apart.

12   Connect one of the spark plug wires to the protruding test fixture electrode, then attach the fixture's alligator clip to a good engine ground/earth.

13   Crank the engine over (it may start and run on the remaining cylinder) and see if well-defined, blue sparks occur between the test fixture electrodes. If the minimum spark gap test is positive, the ignition coil for that cylinder is functioning properly. Repeat the check on the spark plug wire that is connected to the other coil. If the spark will not jump the gap during either test, or if it is weak (orange colored), refer to Steps 5 through 9 of this Section and perform the component checks described.

Ignition system trouble codes

14   Ignition system problem areas can be located by using the diagnostic capability built into the system. These codes can be

2.11 A simple spark gap testing fixture can be made from a block of wood, a large alligator clip, two nails, a screw and a piece of wire

accessed using the Check Engine lamp and a simple jumper wire. The method is the same as for the fuel injection system used on some models. Refer to Chapter 3 for information on reading trouble codes.

3 Ignition coil - check, removal and installation

Check

1   In order to determine conclusively that the ignition coil is defective, it should be tested by a dealer service department or other qualified shop which is equipped with the special electrical tester required for this check.

2   However, the coil can be checked visually (for cracks and other damage) and the primary and secondary coil resistances can be measured with an ohmmeter. If the coil is undamaged, and if the resistances are as specified, it is probably capable of proper operation.

3   Depending on model, you may have to remove the coil to check it for physical damage or disconnect the primary electrical connector to check resistance (see Step 9).

4   To check the resistances, disconnect the primary circuit electrical connectors from the coil and remove the spark plug wires. Mark the locations of all wires before disconnecting them.

5   To check the coil primary resistance, place the ohmmeter selector switch in the Rx1 position. Attach one ohmmeter lead to the coil B+ terminal and the other ohmmeter lead to each of the other primary terminals in turn **(see illustration)**. Compare the measured resistance to the value listed in this Chapter's Specifications.

6   If the coil primary resistance is as specified, check the coil secondary resistance. Place the ohmmeter selector switch in the Rx100 position. Leave the ohmmeter connected to the primary B+ terminal and connect the other ohmmeter lead to each of the secondary (spark plug wire) terminals in turn

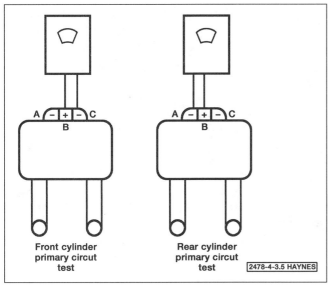

3.5 Ignition coil primary circuit test

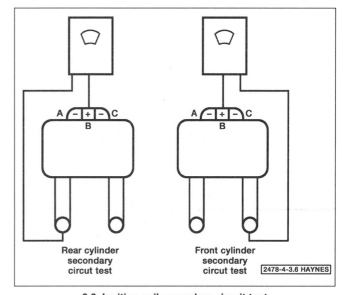

3.6 Ignition coil secondary circuit test

(see illustration). Compare the measured resistance to the values listed in this Chapter's Specifications.

7   If the resistances are not as specified, the coil is probably defective and should be replaced with a new one.

Removal and installation

8   On Touring models, partially remove the fuel tank and prop it up for access to the coil (see Chapter 3). The coil is mounted above the front cylinder.

9   Remove the coil cover (if equipped)

(see illustration).

10   Disconnect the spark plug wires from the coil after labeling them with tape to aid in reinstallation (see illustration).

11   If necessary for access to the primary terminal, remove the coil mounting bolts and lift it partway out (see illustration). Disconnect the coil primary circuit electrical connector (see illustration).

12   Remove the coil mounting bolts (if not already done), then remove the coil.

13   Installation is the reverse of removal. Make sure the spark plug wires are attached to the proper terminals.

 4   Crankshaft position sensor - check, removal and installation

Check

1   The crankshaft position sensor produces alternating current as the crankshaft rotates. To test it, you'll need a voltmeter that

3.9 Remove the ignition coil cover (if equipped)

3.10 Disconnect the plug wires from the coil

3.11a Remove the coil mounting bolts (arrows; Softail shown)

3.11b Disconnect the coil primary terminal (arrow)

 4

4.2 The crankshaft position sensor is mounted on the left front corner of the crankcase

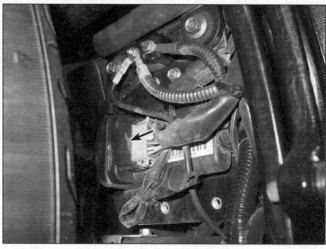

6.2 The bank angle sensor on 2001 and later models is part of the turn signal/security module (arrow)

measures AC (not DC) at low voltages.

2   Follow the sensor wiring harness from the point where it leaves the engine to the electrical connector, then disconnect the connector **(see illustration)**.

3   Connect an AC voltmeter to the side of the connector that leads back to the engine, then crank the engine with the starter. The voltmeter reading should fluctuate steadily between zero and one volt AC.

4   If the reading isn't correct, check the sensor mounting screw and make sure it's tight. If it is, thee sensor is probably defective and should be replaced.

Replacement

7   Disconnect the negative cable from the battery.

8   Disconnect the sensor electrical connector (if not already done). Free the wiring harness from its retainers.

9   Remove the sensor mounting screws and take the sensor and its O-ring out of the crankcase.

10   Installation is the reverse of the removal steps. Use a new O-ring and wipe it with a thin coat of clean engine oil. Tighten the sensor mounting bolt to the torque listed in this Chapter's Specifications.

<table>
<tr><td>5</td><td>Camshaft position sensor
(1999 and 2000 models) -
check and replacement</td><td></td></tr>
</table>

Check

1   The camshaft position sensor produces a fluctuating voltage signal as the camshaft rotates, using a Hall-effect sensor. A rotor mounted on the camshaft sprocket passes through a slot in the sensor as the camshaft turns.

2   Remove the inspection cover from the right side of the crankcase.

3   Remove the sensor mounting screws and take it off the engine, leaving the electrical connector connected.

4   Connect a voltmeter between terminal 1 of the sensor and chassis ground (refer to the wiring diagrams at the end of the manual for terminal identification). With the key on, the reading should be 5 volts. If not, check the wiring.

5   Backprobe connector terminals 2 and 3 with a voltmeter.

6   Pass a screwdriver tip in and out of the slot in the sensor. The voltmeter should indicate zero when the screwdriver blade is in the slot, and 5 volts when it isn't.

7   If the reading isn't correct, the sensor may be defective. Since the problem may also be in the ignition module, further checking should be done by a dealer service department or other qualified shop.

Replacement

8   Disconnect the negative cable from the battery.

9   If necessary for access, remove the seat (see Chapter 7).

10   Remove the inspection cover and disconnect the sensor electrical connector (if not already done). Free the wiring harness from its retainers.

11   Remove the sensor mounting screw and washer and take the sensor and its O-ring out of the crankcase. Guide the wiring harness through the hole in the cam cover.

12   Installation is the reverse of the removal steps, with the following additions:

a)   *Make sure the wires are connected to the proper terminal in the harness after you guide them through the cam cover hole.*

b)   *Use a new O-ring and wipe it with a thin coat of clean engine oil.*

c)   *Tighten the sensor mounting bolt to the torque listed in this Chapter's Specifications.*

<table>
<tr><td>6</td><td>Bank angle sensor - check
and replacement</td><td></td></tr>
</table>

1   The bank angle sensor consists of a disc-shaped magnet that moves in a V-shaped channel. If the bike leans more than 55 degrees to one side or the other, the magnet moves from its normal position, causing an open in the ignition module circuit. When the module detects this open, it shuts off the system. On 1999 and 2000 models, the bank angle sensor is a separate unit. On 2001 and later models, the bank angle sensor is an integral part of the turn signal/security module.

Check

2   Locate the bank angle sensor or turn signal/security model on the electrical panel **(see illustration)**. It can be identified by its wires colors (see the wiring diagrams at the end of this manual).

3   Start the engine.

4   Place a magnet on top of the bank angle sensor. If the sensor is operating correctly, the magnetic disc inside the sensor will move, causing the engine to stall. Remove the magnet and turn the engine off (this resets the bank angle sensor, unless it was defective).

Replacement

5   If you're working on a 1999 or 2000 model, remove the sensor mounting screw and disconnect the electrical connector. Reverse the removal procedure to install the sensor.

6   If you're working on a 2001 or later model, free the turn signal/security module from its clip and disconnect the electrical connector. Reverse the removal procedure to install the module.

8.3 Remove the ECU mounting screws (arrows) and disconnect the electrical connector (later Softail shown)

7 MAP sensor - check and replacement

Check

1   The Manifold Absolute Pressure sensor on carbureted models is tested in the same way as the MAP sensor on fuel injected models (see Chapter 3).

Replacement

2   The MAP sensor is mounted on the intake manifold. Disconnect its electrical connector, remove the bracket screw and take the sensor off.
3   Installation is the reverse of the removal steps.

8 Electronic control module - removal, check and installation

Check

1   Electronic control module failure may cause one of several trouble codes, as well as a no-spark condition or a failure of the Check Engine lamp to illuminate when the key is turned on. If a trouble code indicates a problem with the ignition module, have the results confirmed by a dealer service department or other qualified shop.

Replacement

Softail models

2   Remove the seat (see Chapter 7).
3   Remove the ECM mounting screws **(see illustration)**. Lift the unit up, disconnect its electrical connector and remove it.
4   Installation is the reverse of the removal steps.

Dyna models

5   The ECM is mounted on the back of the electrical panel, so you'll need to remove it partway to remove the ECM.
6   Remove the seat (see Chapter 7). Pull off the electrical panel cover. Remove the nuts and lift off the panel top plate. Remove the nut from the back right side of the panel and remove the screw from the front right side.
7   Remove two nuts (with captive washers) from the back side of the panel. On FXDL, FXDXT and FXDWG models, remove the ignition coil cover.
8   Disconnect the primary connector from the ignition coil. This will allow you to move the electrical panel out so you can get at the ECU.
9   Remove the ECU mounting screws, disconnect its electrical connector and take it out.
10   Installation is the reverse of the removal steps.

Touring models

11   Remove the right saddlebag and side cover (see Chapter 7).
15   Disconnect the electrical connector, remove the module mounting screws and take the module out.
16   Installation is the reverse of the removal steps.

4

Notes

Chapter 5
Steering, suspension and final drive

Contents

Degrees of difficulty

Easy, suitable for novice with little experience		Fairly easy, suitable for beginner with some experience		Fairly difficult, suitable for competent DIY mechanic		Difficult, suitable for experienced DIY mechanic		Very difficult, suitable for expert DIY or professional	

Specifications

Front suspension

Fork oil type and amount..	See Chapter 1
Front fork standard settings (Dyna FXDX and FXDXT)	
Rebound damping...	8
Compression damping	10
Fork air pressure (1999 through 2001 Touring models only)	
Standard...	0 to 15 psi (0 to 1.035 Bar)
For each additional 25 lbs rider weight add:.....................	1 psi (0.069 Bar)
For each additional 10 lbs luggage weight add:	1 psi (0.069 Bar)
Maximum..	25 psi (1.725 Bar)

Rear suspension and final drive

Rear shock absorber standard settings (Dyna FXDX and FXDXT)	
Rebound damping...	3
Spring preload..	Third step
Shock absorber air pressure	
1999 through 2001 Touring models	
Standard	0 to 10 psi (0 to 0.69 Bar)
For each additional 25 lbs rider weight add:	1 psi (0.069 Bar)
For each additional 50 lbs passenger weight add:.......	1.5 psi (0.1035 Bar)
For each additional 10 lbs luggage weight add:..........	3 psi (0.207 Bar)
Maximum	35 psi (2.415 Bar)

5

Rear suspension and final drive (continued)

2002 and later Touring models

Rider only, up to 150 lbs (68 kg)	0 psi (0 Bar)
Rider only, 150 to 200 lbs (68 to 91 kg)	0 to 10 psi (0 to 1.035 Bar)
Rider only, 200 to 250 lbs	5 to 15 psi (0.345 to 1.035 Bar)
Rider and passenger, each up to 150 lbs (68 kg)	10 to 15 psi (0.69 to 1.035 Bar)
Rider up to 150 lbs, passenger up to 200 lbs	20 to 25 psi (1.38 to 1.725 Bar)
At maximum gross vehicle weight rating	20 to 35 psi (1.38 to 2.415 Bar)
Maximum	35 psi (2.415 Bar)

Torque specifications

Softail models

Drivebelt sprocket bolts

2000 models, laced wheels	45 to 55 ft-lbs (61.0 to 74.6 Nm)
All others	55 to 65 ft-lbs (74.6 to 88.12 Nm)

Springer front suspension

Shock absorber acorn nuts	45 to 50 ft-lbs (61.0 to 67.8 Nm)
Fork leg bracket to fork (FLSTS)	35 to 40 ft-lbs (47.5 to 54.2 Nm)
Fork rocker bearing retainer locknut	95 to 105 ft-lbs (128.8 to 142.4 Nm)
Fork rocker nut	45 to 50 ft-lbs (61 to 68 Nm)
Rigid fork leg studs	60 to 65 ft-lbs (81.3 to 88.1 Nm)
Rocker pivot stud nut	45 to 50 ft-lbs (61.0 to 67.8 Nm)
Steering stem (upper triple clamp) pinch bolt	25 to 30 ft-lbs (33.9 to 47.0 Nm)

Steering stem nut

Springer models	30 to 35 inch-lbs (3.4 to 4.0 Nm)
All except Springer models	35 to 40 ft-lbs (47.5 to 54.2 Nm)
Fork caps	40 to 60 ft-lbs (54.2 to 81.3 Nm)
Upper triple clamp pinch bolts (FLSTC, FLSTF)	23 to 28 ft-lbs (31.2 to 38.0 Nm)

Lower triple clamp pinch bolt

FXSTD	35 to 40 ft-lbs (47.5 to 54.2 Nm)
All except FXSTD	30 to 35 ft-lbs (40.7 to 47.5 Nm)
Swingarm pivot shaft nut	90 to 110 ft-lbs (122 to 149 Nm)
Rear shock mounting bolts	115 to 130 ft-lbs (155.9 to 176.2 Nm)
Rear shock absorber locknuts	32 to 39 ft-lbs (43.4 to 52.9 Nm)

Dyna models

Drivebelt sprocket bolts

Laced wheels	45 to 55 ft-lbs (61.0 to 74.6 Nm)
Cast wheels	55 to 65 ft-lbs (74.6 to 88.12 Nm)
Fork cap (FXDX, FXDXT)	22 to 29 ft-lbs (29 to 39 Nm)
Fork damper rod bolt	22 to 29 ft-lbs (29 to 39 NM)
Fork tube caps (all except FXDX, FXDXT)	11 to 22 ft-lbs (14.9 to 29.8 Nm)
Triple clamp pinch bolts	30 to 35 ft-lbs (40.7 to 47.5 Nm)
Steering stem nut (all except FXDWG)	30 to 35 inch-lbs (3.4 to 4.0 Nm)
Steering stem pinch bolt (FXDWG)	21 to 27 ft-lbs (28.5 to 36.6 Nm)

Rear shock absorbers

Upper mounts, lower bolts	25 to 40 ft-lbs
Upper locknuts	60 to 80 ft-lbs (81.3 to108.5 Nm)
Swingarm pivot shaft bolt	45 to 50 ft-lbs (61.0 to 67.8 Nm)
Rear axle nut	60 to 65 ft-lbs (81.3 to 88.1 Nm)

Touring models

Drivebelt sprocket bolts	55 to 65 ft-lbs (74.6 to 88.12 Nm)
Fork tube plug	22 to 58 ft-lbs (30 to 79 Nm)
Fork cap	50 to 60 ft-lbs (68 to 81 Nm)
Fork damper rod bolt	132 to 216 inch-lbs (14.9 to 24.4 Nm)
Triple clamp pinch bolts	30 to 35 ft-lbs (40.7 to 47.5 Nm)
Steering stem nut	60 to 80 ft-lbs (81 to 109 Nm)

Rear shock absorbers

Upper bolts	33 to 35 ft-lbs (45 to 48 Nm)
Lower bolts	35 to 40 ft-lbs (47 to 54 Nm)
Swingarm pivot shaft nut	40 to 45 ft-lbs (54 to 61 Nm)
Rear axle nut	95 to 105 ft-lbs (128.8 to 142.4 Nm)

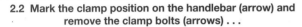
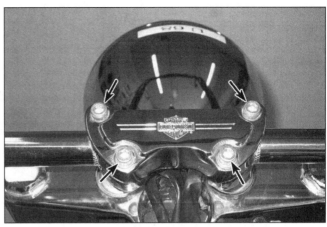

2.2 Mark the clamp position on the handlebar (arrow) and remove the clamp bolts (arrows) . . .

2.3 . . . some models use a one-piece clamp with four bolts (arrows)

1 General information

The front forks on all except Softail Springer models are of the conventional coil spring, hydraulically-damped telescopic type (damper rod design or cartridge design, depending on model). 1999 through 2001 Touring models include an air pressure adjustment mechanism. 2002 and later Touring models (except Road King) have a cartridge fork on the left side and a damper rod fork on the right side. 2002 and later Road King models use damper rod forks on both sides of the bike.

Softail Springer models have a unique, retro-look front suspension, consisting of a pair of front forks, a lever linkage, exposed springs and a single shock absorber. One fork (the fixed fork) is fixed to the frame through the steering head. The other fork (the spring fork) is free to move separately from the fixed fork, with its motion controlled by the springs and shock absorber. At the bottom, both forks are connected to the front axle through the lever linkage. As the wheel

moves up and down, the levers pivot on the bottom of the fixed fork, pushing and pulling the spring fork through its vertical travel. The movements of the spring fork are cushioned by the springs and damped by the shock absorber.

The steering head on all models uses tapered roller bearings.

The rear suspension on Dyna and Touring models consists of two coil spring/shock absorbers and a swingarm. All Touring models include an air pressure adjustment mechanism in the rear suspension.

The rear suspension on Softail models is a simulated rigid frame, consisting of a rocker-type swingarm with dual shock absorbers.

The final drive on all models consists of a cogged rubber belt and sprockets at the engine and rear wheel.

2 Handlebars - removal and installation

1   These motorcycles use a one-piece handlebar, clamped in risers that extend upward from the fork legs.

2   Before removing the handlebars, look for a punch mark indicating the position of the handlebar in the brackets **(see illustration)**. Make your own mark if you can't see one.

3   If the handlebars must be removed for access to other components, such as the forks or the steering head, simply remove the clamp bolts and lift the handlebar off **(see illustration 2.2 and the accompanying illustration)**. It's not necessary to disconnect the cables, wires or hoses, but it is a good idea to support the assembly with a piece of wire or rope, to avoid unnecessary strain on the cables, wires and (on the right side) the brake hose.

4   Check the handlebar for cracks and distortion and replace it if any undesirable conditions are found.

5   If the handlebar risers need to be

removed, unscrew their nuts from the underside of the upper triple clamp **(see illustration)**. Pull the riser out and immediately reinstall its hardware in the correct order so you don't forget how it goes.

6   Installation is the reverse of the removal steps. Tighten the clamp bolts to the torque listed in this Chapter's Specifications, but don't overtighten them or the brackets may break.

3 Forks (except Softail Springer models) - removal and installation

Removal

1   Support the bike securely upright with the front wheel off the ground.

2   Remove the front caliper(s) and the front wheel (see Chapter 6).

3   Remove the front fender (see Chapter 7).

Softail models

4   If you're working on an FLSTF or FLSTC, remove the front and rear trim panels from the upper fork legs **(see illustrations)**.

2.5 Remove the nuts (arrows), take the risers off the triple clamp, then immediately reassemble the risers and hardware

3.4a Remove the screws (arrows) from the right trim panel . . .

5

5 Remove the fork cap, spacer and oil seal from the top of the fork **(see illustration)**.

6 Loosen the pinch bolt that secures the fork leg in the triple clamp, then slide the fork leg downward out of the triple clamp.

Dyna models

7 Remove the headlamp bulb (see Chapter 8), then remove the headlamp assembly. The wires can be left attached if the assembly is supported so it doesn't hang by the wires.

8 Loosen the fork caps. If you're working on an FXDWG model, unscrew the fork caps and remove the spacers and oil seals. **Note:** *On all except FXDWG models, loosen the fork caps, but do not remove the fork cap or rebound adjuster from either fork leg.* Loosen the upper and lower triple clamp bolts. Slide the fork leg downward out of the triple clamps.

Touring models

9 If the bike has an air-adjustable front suspension, release the front fork air pressure. Unscrew the air hose banjo fitting bolts from the fork caps and remove the O-rings.

10 If you're working on an FLHT model, remove the outer fairing and radio or storage box (see Chapters 7 and 8).

11 If you're working on an FLHR model, remove the headlamp housing.

12 If you're working on an FLTR model, remove the instrument housing (see Chapter 8).

13 Remove any wiring harness clamps or straps from the fork tubes.

14 If you're working on a 1999 through 2001 model, loosen the fork cap bolt and upper triple clamp bolt. Slide the fork tube out of the triple clamps and remove it from the bike, then do the same with the other fork leg.

15 If you're working on a 2002 or later model, loosen the triple clamp bolt and fork cap bolt, but don't remove them. Spray the fork tube above the rubber stop with glass cleaner to lubricate it, then slide the rubber stop upward as far as it will go. Remove the fork cap bolt, slide the fork leg downward and remove it from the bike. Do the same with the other fork leg.

All models

16 If you removed the fork caps and don't plan to disassemble the forks immediately, put the fork caps back in the fork legs.

Installation

17 Slide each fork leg into the lower triple clamp.

18 Slide the fork legs up, installing the tops of the tubes into the upper triple clamp. On Dyna FXD and FXDL models, position the top of the fork cap 0.42 to 0.50 inches above the top of the fork leg.

19 On Dyna FXDWG models, make sure the flats of the fork tube plug face left and right, not to front and back of the motorcycle.

3.4b . . . and from the left trim panel (arrows), then take the panel pieces off

3.5 Unscrew the fork cap bolt (arrow)

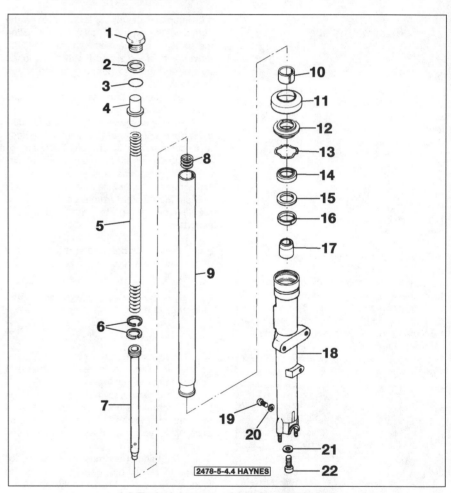

4.4 Typical damper rod fork (exploded view)

1	Fork top bolt	12	Dust seal
2	Washer (if equipped)	13	Retaining ring
3	O-ring	14	Oil seal
4	Top plug (if equipped)	15	Back-up ring
5	Fork spring	16	Slider bushing
6	Damper rod rings	17	Damper rod base
7	Damper rod	18	Fork slider
8	Rebound spring	19	Drain screw
9	Fork tube	20	Sealing washer
10	Fork tube bushing	21	Sealing washer
11	Dust seal cover (if equipped)	22	Damper rod bolt

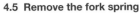

4.5 Remove the fork spring

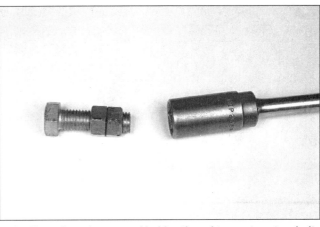

4.6a To make a damper rod holder, thread two nuts onto a bolt with a head that will wedge inside the damper rod and tighten the nuts against each other . . .

20 The remainder of installation is the reverse of the removal steps, with the following additions:

a) *Tighten all fasteners to the torques listed in the Specifications (Chapters 5, 6, 7 and 8).*

b) *Check the fork oil level (see Chapter 1). Check the fork air pressure (if applicable) (see Section 18).*

21 Pump the front brake lever several times to bring the pads into contact with the disc(s).

---

4 Forks (except Springer) - disassembly, inspection and reassembly

Damper rod forks

1 Damper rod forks are used on both sides of all non-Springer models except the 2000-on Dyna FXDX and FXDXT, as well as on the right fork leg of 2002 and later Touring models equipped with a fairing.

Disassembly

Note: *Work on one fork leg at a time to avoid mixing up the parts.*

2 Remove the forks following the procedure in Section 3. Work on one fork leg at a time to avoid mixing up the parts.

3 Place the fork leg in a bench vise (clamp the jaws onto the slider; do not clamp the friction surface of the fork tube itself).

4 Loosen (DO NOT remove) the damper rod bolt in the bottom of the fork leg **(see illustration)**. If the bolt just spins without loosening, continue with disassembly and remove it in Step 6.

5 Remove the top plug, washer and O-ring, spacer and spring seat (if equipped) and take out the fork spring **(see illustration 4.4 and the accompanying illustration)**.

6 Remove the fork leg from the vise. Invert the fork leg over a container and allow the oil to drain out.

7 Place the fork leg back in the vise again. To finish disassembly, you must remove the damper rod bolt from the bottom of the fork leg. This bolt is threaded into the damper rod inside the fork slider and secured with thread locking agent. If it came loose in Step 4, it

should be easy to unscrew. If not, the ideal way to unscrew it is with an air wrench. If you don't have one, you'll need to prevent the damper rod from turning with a piece of hardwood dowel cut to a taper or a holding tool. **Note:** *If you don't have a holding tool, you can fabricate your own using a bolt with a head that fits inside the damper rod, two nuts, a socket (to fit on the nuts), a long extension and a ratchet. Thread the two nuts onto the bolt and tighten them against each other* **(see illustration)**. *Insert the assembly into the socket and tape it into place* **(see illustration)**. *Now, insert the tool into the fork tube and engage the bolt head into the round hole in the damper rod. Unscrew the Allen bolt at the bottom of the outer tube and retrieve the copper washer* **(see illustration 4.3)**.

8 Pry the dust seal from the fork slider **(see illustration)**.

9 Slide the dust seal up the fork tube and pry out the retaining ring **(see illustration)**.

10 Hold the outer tube and yank the inner tube upward, repeatedly (like a slide hammer), until the seal, washer and outer tube guide bushing pop loose **(see illustration)**.

4.6b . . . then install the nut-end into a socket (connected to a long extension) and tape it into place

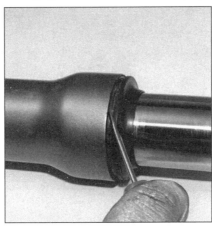

4.8 Pry the dust seal out of the fork slider with a small screwdriver

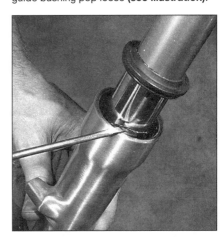

4.9 Pry the retaining ring out of its groove

5

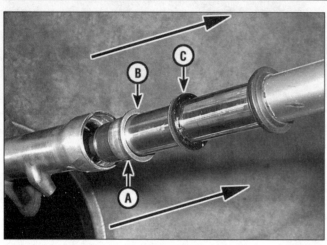

4.10 Yank the slider and tube apart until they separate; the slider bushing (A), back-up ring (B) and oil seal (C) will pop out of the slider

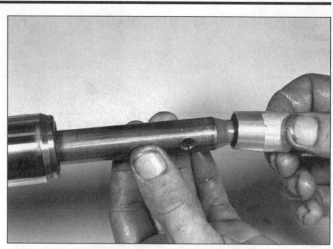

4.12 Remove the damper rod base from the damper rod (if it's not there, it's probably in the bottom of the slider) . . .

11   Slide the seal, washer and outer tube guide bushing from the inner tube.

12   Remove the oil lock piece from the bottom end of the damper rod (see illustration). (If it's not there, it's probably in the bottom of the slider).

4.13 . . . and remove the damper rod and rebound spring from the other (upper) end of the fork tube

13   Invert the outer tube and remove the damper rod and rebound spring (see illustration).

Inspection

14   Clean all parts in solvent and blow them dry with compressed air, if available. Check the inner and outer fork tubes and the damper rod for score marks, scratches, flaking of the chrome and excessive or abnormal wear. Look for dents in the tubes and replace them if any are found. Check the fork seal seat for nicks, gouges and scratches. If damage is evident, leaks will occur around the seal-to-outer tube junction. Replace worn or defective parts with new ones.

15   There are two bushings in the lower end of the inner fork tube, the smaller diameter fork tube bushing and the larger-diameter slider bushing (see illustration). The fork tube bushing fits tightly around the end of the tube and is seated against a shoulder on the endow the tube. The slider bushing slides freely up and down the fork tube and is seated against a shoulder inside the fork tube. You need not remove either bushing

unless it appears worn or scratched. If it's necessary to replace the fork tube bushing (the lower bushing on the tube, the one that doesn't slide up and down), pry it apart at the split and slide it off (see illustration). To remove the slider bushing, simply slide it off the fork tube (see illustration).

16   Have the fork inner tube checked for runout at a dealer service department or other repair shop.

⚠ **Warning: If it is bent, it should not be straightened; replace it with a new one.**

17   Check the fork spring for cracks and other damage. If it's defective or sagged, replace both fork springs with new ones. Never replace only one spring.

Reassembly

18   Lightly lubricate all parts with clean fork oil as they're reassembled.

19   Install the new fork tube bushing if the old one was removed. Do not pry open the bushing any more than necessary to reinstall it. Be sure the bushing is seated at the bot-

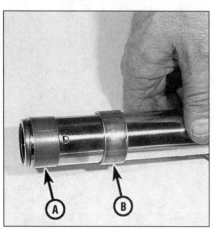

4.15a The fork tube bushing (A) and slider bushing (B) are on the bottom of the fork tube

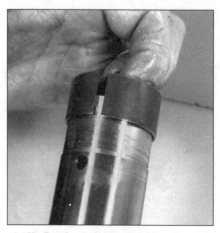

4.15b Pry the fork tube bushing apart at the slit just enough to slide it off . . .

4.15c . . . the slider bushing can now be slid off the fork tube

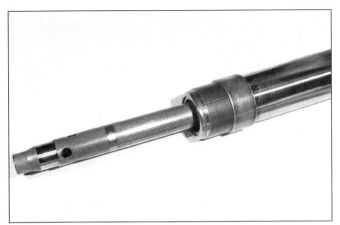

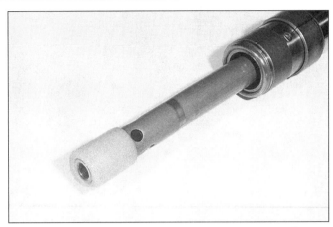

4.21 Put the rebound spring on the damper rod, then place it in the fork tube so it protrudes from the lower end like this

4.22 Install the damper rod base on the damper rod

4.24 The damper rod, base and damper rod bolt fit together like this in the lower end of the fork slider (slider removed for clarity)

4.25 Install the slider bushing and back-up ring on the fork tube

4.26a Using a seal driver or equivalent tool . . .

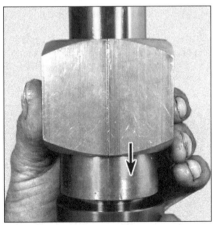

tom of the fork tube, against the shoulder.
20 Install the slider bushing on the fork tube.
21 Place the rebound spring over the damper rod and slide the rod into the inner fork tube until it protrudes from the lower end of the tube **(see illustration)**.
22 Install the damper rod base onto the end of the damper rod **(see illustration)**.
23 Holding the fork slider upside down (so the damper rod base doesn't fall off), insert the fork tube/damper rod assembly into the slider.
24 Apply non-permanent thread locking agent to the threads of the damper rod bolt, then install the bolt and a new sealing washer **(see illustration)**. Keep the two tubes fairly horizontal so the damper rod base doesn't fall off. Using the tool described in Step 6, hold the damper rod and tighten the Allen bolt to the torque listed in this Chapter's Specifications. **Note:** *If the bolt won't catch the damper rod threads, the damper rod isn't lined up correctly. Using a flashlight and a Phillips screwdriver with a taped tip, align the threaded bore in the lower end of the damper rod with the bore in the bottom of the slider.*

4.26b . . . tap down gently and repeatedly to seat the slider bushing firmly against the shoulder inside the slider

4.26cc If you don't have a bushing driver, you can use a section of pipe (be sure to tape the ends of the pipe so it doesn't scratch the fork tube)

5

25 Slide the back-up ring down the fork tube **(see illustration)**.
26 Using a special bushing driver or equivalent and a used guide bushing placed on top of the guide bushing being installed, drive the bushing into place until it is fully seated **(see illustration)**. If you don't have access to one of these tools, it is highly rec-

ommended that you take the assembly to a dealer service department or other motorcycle repair shop to have this done. It is possible, however, to drive the bushing into place using a section of pipe and an old guide bushing **(see illustration)**. Wrap tape around the ends of the tubing to prevent it from scratching the fork tube.

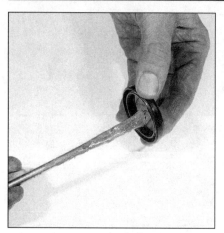

4.27a Coat the inner lip and the outer circumference of the new seal with fork oil . . .

4.27b . . . and install the seal on the fork tube; don't let the upper edge of the fork tube damage the seal lip

4.27c Tap the seal gently with a driver just until it's fully seated

27 Lubricate the lips and the outer diameter of the fork seal with the recommended fork oil (see Chapter 1) and slide it down the inner tube, with the lips facing down **(see illustration)**. Drive the seal into place with a special seal driver (or use the same tool used to drive in the slider bushing) **(see illustration)** or make something that will do the job **(see illustration)**. Again, if you don't have a suitable tool for the job, it is recommended that you take the assembly to a dealer service department or other motorcycle repair shop to have the seal driven in. If you are extremely careful, the seal can be driven in with a hammer and a drift punch. Work around the circumference of the seal, tapping gently on the outer edge of the seal until it's seated. Be careful - if you distort the seal, you'll have to disassemble the fork again and end up taking it to a dealer anyway!

28 Install the retaining ring, making sure the ring is completely seated in its groove **(see illustration)**.

29 Install the dust seal and drive it into place with the same tool used to install the

oil seal **(see illustration)**, or use the tool used to install the slider bushing. Make sure the dust seal is fully seated.

30 Install the drain screw and a new gasket, if it was removed.

31 Compress the fork fully and add the recommended type and quantity of fork oil (see Chapter 1).

32 Install the fork spring. The remainder of assembly is the reverse of the disassembly steps. Tighten the topbolt to the torque listed in this Chapter's Specifications.

33 Install the fork by following the procedure outlined in Section 3. If you won't be installing the fork right away, store it in an upright position to prevent leakage.

Cartridge forks

34 A cartridge design is used on both fork legs of the 2000 and later Dyna FXDX and FXDXT, as well as on the left fork leg of 2002 and later Touring models (except road King).

35 Disassembly of the cartridge fork legs is not possible without a special compression

4.27d This is the JIMS seal driver

tool, due to the very high strength of the spring. If the forks on one of these models need to be overhauled, take the job to a dealer service department or other qualified shop. You can save money by removing and installing the forks yourself.

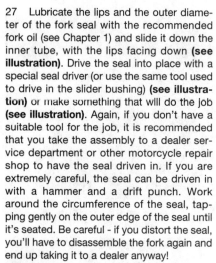

4.27e If you don't have a driver, you can use plastic plumbing fittings; place one piece on the seal and strike it with the other piece

4.28 Compress the stopper ring and fit it securely into its groove in the fork slider

4.29 Use any of the tools previously shown to drive the dust seal into place

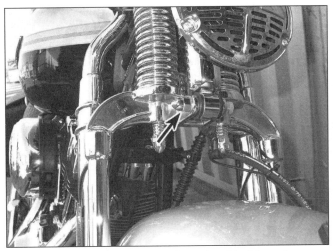

5.2a Remove the acorn nut (arrow) and bolt from the bottom of the shock absorber . . .

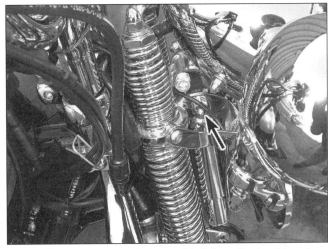

5.2b . . . then remove the nut and bolt from the top (arrow)

5 Front shock absorber (Softail Springer models) - removal and installation

1   Support the bike securely upright.
2   Remove the acorn nuts from the shock absorber bolts, then remove the bolts and take the shock off the motorcycle (see illustrations).
3   Installation is the reverse of the removal steps. Use non-permanent thread locking agent on the bolts and tighten them to the torque listed in this Chapter's Specifications.

6 Forks and steering stem (Softail Springer models) - removal and installation

Removal

1   Support the bike securely upright with the front wheel off the ground.

2   Remove the headlight and its mounting block (and the passing lights on FLSTS models). **Note:** *The headlight wires can be left connected, as long as the headlight is supported so it doesn't hang by the wires.*
3   Remove the handlebar and risers (see Section 2).
4   Remove the front brake caliper, wheel and fender (see Chapters 6 and 7).
5   Loosen the pinch bolt on the upper triple clamp (see illustration). Remove the acorn nut and washer and unscrew the fork studs, then lift up the upper triple clamp. Lower the steering stem enough to remove the fork lock (see Chapter 8 for details), then remove the steering stem and fork assembly from the frame (see illustration).

⚠️ *Warning: Do not attempt to disassemble the Springer fork assembly. If forks or springs need to be replaced, take the assembly to a dealer service department or other qualified shop .*

6   Refer to Section 11 for steering head bearing inspection and replacement.

Installation

7   Make sure the upper steering stem bearing is installed in the steering head and that both the upper and lower bearings are packed with grease.
8   Slip the steering stem (with lower bearing installed) into the steering head and install the fork lock.
9   Install the upper dust shield on top of the upper bearing, then install the retainer with its hex downward (toward the bearing).
10   Tighten the bearing retainer to 40 ft-lbs to seat the bearings. Loosen the retainer, then retighten it to 72 inch-lbs.
11   Lay the upper triple clamp on the fork legs and steering stem.
12   Thread the fork studs into the fork legs and tighten them slightly. Then tighten the studs to the torque listed in this Chapter's Specifications.
13   Tighten the upper triple clamp pinch

6.5a Loosen the clamp bolt (lower arrow) and remove the acorn nut and rubber washer (upper arrow)

6.5b Springer fork components (FLSTS shown)

1   Steering stem   3   Spring fork
2   Rigid fork   4   Rocker

5

bolt to the torque listed in this Chapter's Specifications. Install the rubber washer and acorn nut on the steering stem and tighten them to the torque listed in this Chapter's Specifications.

14 Adjust the steering head bearings (see Section 10).

7 Rocker bearings (Softail Springer models) - adjustment

1 Tie the spring fork legs to the rigid fork legs with heavy-duty cable ties (see illustration). The cable ties must be strong enough to contain the spring force, which would otherwise cause the spring fork legs to snap forward suddenly.

⚠ Warning: Don't skip this step or the spring legs may fly up suddenly and cause injury.
Place the ties securely so they can't slip out of position. Be aware throughout the procedure that if the ties slip or break, the spring fork legs may fly up suddenly and hit you.

2 Remove the front fender, wheel and brake caliper (see Chapters 6 and 7).

3 Loosen the bearing retainer locknuts and retainers, but don't remove them (see illustrations). Loosen the spring fork pivot studs and remove their nuts and washers, but don't remove the studs yet.

4 Tighten the bearing retainers to 25 to 35 inch-lbs, then hold each bearing retainer with an Allen wrench and tighten its locknut to 95 to 105 ft-lbs.

7.1 Tie the rigid fork legs to the spring fork legs with heavy-duty tie wraps at the point indicated (arrows)

7.3a Here's how the FLSTS rocker bearing adjuster is installed; on FXSTS models, the adjuster is to the inside and the nut is to the outside

1 *Bearing retainer locknut*   4 *Pivot stud*
2 *Bearing retainer*   5 *Nut*
3 *Nut*   6 *Rocker*

7.3b Here's a top view of the right side components (FLSTS shown)

1 *Bearing retainer*   5 *Nut*
2 *Bearing retainer locknut* 6 *Washer*
3 *Nut*   7 *Rocker*
4 *Pivot stud*

7.3c Here are the left side rocker components (FLSTS shown)

1 *Bearing retainer locknut*   3 *Pivot stud*
2 *Bearing retainer*   4 *Rocker*

7.6 With the axle and spring fork pivot removed from the rocker, rotate the rocker 180-degrees around the rigid fork pivot (arrow) and measure the turning torque

9.3 Remove the acorn locknuts, Allen screws and washers (arrows) to detach the reaction link from the brackets

5   Remove the pivot stud from each spring fork. At this point, the rockers should be attached to the rigid fork legs and detached from the spring fork legs.

6   Place an inch-pound torque wrench on the rocker nut and turn the rocker through a 180-degree arc **(see illustration)**. The torque wrench should indicate 25 to 35 inch-pounds. If it doesn't, loosen the bearing retainer locknut and readjust the bearing retainer to obtain the correct reading. Do the same thing with the other rocker.

7   Once the readings are correct, secure the bearing retainer with the locknut.

8   Reverse the disassembly procedure to reinstall the pivot studs. Tighten the fasteners to the torque listed in this Chapter's Specifications.

9   Install all parts removed for access.

8 Fork rockers (Springer) - removal, bearing replacement and installation

Removal

1   Support the bike securely upright with the front wheel off the ground.

2   Remove the front brake caliper and wheel. On FLSTS models, remove the fender (see Chapters 6 and 7).

3   Tie each spring fork leg to its rigid fork leg with heavy-duty cable ties **(see illustration 7.1)**. The cable ties must be strong enough to contain the spring force, which would otherwise cause the spring fork legs to snap forward suddenly.

 Warning: Don't skip this step or the spring legs may fly up suddenly and cause injury. Place the ties securely so they can't slip out of position. Be aware throughout the procedure that if the ties slip or break, the spring fork legs may fly up suddenly and hit you.

4   Remove the nuts, washers and studs from the spring fork rocker pivots **(see illustration 7.3a)**.

5   Loosen the bearing retainer locknuts and unscrew the bearing retainers **(see illustrations 7.3b and 7.3c)**.

6   Remove the nuts, washers and studs from the rigid fork and separate the rockers from the rigid fork legs.

7   Remove the bearings from the rockers, keeping them in order. Check the bearings for wear and damage and replace them if any problems are visible.

8   Install the bearing races in the rockers if they were removed.

9   Grease both halves of a rigid fork spherical bearing. Install one half on the pivot stud and the other half in the bearing race, so that the flat sides of the bearing halves will face each other when the rocker is assembled to the rigid fork. Do the same with the other rigid fork spherical bearing.

10   Align the holes in rocker and rigid fork leg, then install the pivot stud **(see illustration 7.3a)**. Note that the hex on FLSTS models faces outward and the hex on FXSTS models faces inward. Do the same with the other rocker and fork leg. Install the washer and nuts on the threaded end of each pivot stud, using non-permanent thread locking agent on the pivot stud threads. Tighten the nuts to the torque listed in this Chapter's Specifications.

11   Lubricate the bearing retainer threads with Loctite Anti-seize or equivalent. Lubricate the bearing race with a tablespoon or so of multipurpose grease, then install the bearing retainer and tighten it to the torque listed in this Chapter's Specifications. Install the bearing retainer locknut, hold the bearing retainer with an Allen bit and tighten the locknut to the torque listed in this Chapter's Specifications. Do the same with the other bearing retainer.

12   Installation is the reverse of the removal steps.

13   Adjust the rocker bearings (see Section 7).

9 Brake reaction link (Softail Springer models) - removal and installation

FLSTS models

1   Support the bike securely upright with its front wheel off the ground.

2   Remove the front brake caliper, wheel and fender (see Chapters 6 and 7).

3   Remove the long Allen screw, acorn locknut and washer and detach the reaction link from the caliper bracket **(see illustration)**. **Note:** *Replace the acorn locknut with a new one whenever it's removed.*

4   Detach the caliper bracket from the rocker.

5   Remove the Allen screw, acorn locknut and washer and detach the reaction link from

the fork leg bracket. **Note:** *Replace the acorn locknut with a new one whenever it's removed.*

6   If necessary, detach the fork leg bracket from the rigid fork leg.

7   Installation is the reverse of the removal steps, with the following additions:

a) *Tighten all fasteners to the torque listed in this Chapter's Specifications.*

b) *If the pivot sleeve and bushing were removed from the caliper bracket, replace them with new ones.*

c) *Install the washer in the lower end of the caliper bracket with its Teflon-coated side toward the bracket.*

FXSTS models

8   This is part of the caliper removal and installation procedure (see Chapter 6).

10 Steering head bearings - adjustment

1   Remove any aftermarket accessories, such as a non-stock windshield. Check to make sure the clutch and throttle cables don't cause pull or drag. If they do, reroute or disconnect the cables to correct the problem. It won't be possible to measure steering head adjustment accurately if a cable is affecting the adjustment.

2   Loosen the fork lower pinch bolts **(see illustration 2.5)**. This allows the necessary vertical movement of the steering stem in relation to the fork tubes. If you're working on a Touring model, push the rubber fork boots up away from the lower triple clamp.

Softail and Dyna models (except Springer)

3   You'll need a way to measure the side-to-side movement of the front wheel accurately. There are two ways to do this. One is to place a strip of masking tape across the leading edge of the front fender. And set up a pointer on the floor with its tip centered on the tape (you can make the pointer out of wood). Another is to hang a plumb bob from the rear edge of the fender and lay a ruler beneath it.

4   Center the pointer on the tape and center the wheel in the straight-ahead position. Slowly push the wheel to one side until it begins to move on its own. Note where the pointer is when the wheel starts to move and either mark it on the tape or write the measurement down.

5   Center the wheel again, then slowly push it in the other direction. Once again, note where the pointer is when the wheel starts to move on its own.

6   Measure the distance between the two marked points and compare it to the value listed in this Chapter's Specifications. If the measured distance is greater than specified, loosen the adjustment as described below. If

5

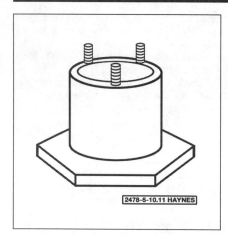

10.11 If you make a tool like this from an extra bearing retainer, you won't need to remove the handlebars and upper triple clamp

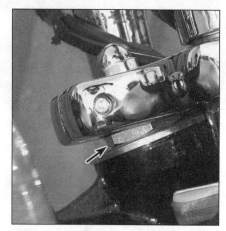

10.16 The Softail bearing retainer (arrow) is beneath the upper triple clamp

11.7 Lower the steering stem and bearing out of the steering head

it's less than specified, tighten the adjustment.

7 On models equipped with a steering head bolt, tighten or loosen the bolt to change the bearing adjustment. Turn the bolt only a little at a time, then recheck the adjustment.

8 On models equipped with a steering stem nut, bend back the lockwasher and loosen the nut, then make the adjustment with the adjusting nut below the upper triple clamp. Turn the adjusting nut by tapping it with a hammer and punch. Turn the nut a little at a time; even one notch can make a noticeable difference. Retighten the steering stem nut to the torque values listed in the Chapter 5 Specifications and secure it with the lockwasher.

9 Recheck the steering head bearings for play as described above. If necessary, repeat the adjustment procedure. Reinstall all parts previously removed.

Softail Springer models

10 To adjust the bearings, you'll either need to make a special tool or remove the handlebars, risers, rigid fork leg studs and upper triple clamp so you can use a socket. If you use the special tool, it will only be necessary to remove the upper triple clamp acorn nut and washer.

11 Make the tool from an extra bearing retainer (Harley part no. 48306-88) and three roll pins (Harley part no. 614). Secure a pin in each of the three holes in the retainer with non-permanent thread locking agent, then cut the pins so they extend 1/2-inch from the retainer (see illustration).

12 If you're using the special tool, remove the acorn nut and rubber washer from the upper triple clamp.

13 Turn the front wheel all the way to the left.

14 Set up a plumb bob and ruler as described in Step 8 above, but start the measurement with the front wheel turned all the way to the left, rather than centered.

15 Slowly turn the wheel to the right until it begins to move by itself. Note the distance the plumb bob travels along the ruler and compare it with the value listed in this Chapter's Specifications.

16 If the measured distance is greater than specified, loosen the bearing retainer (see illustration). If it's less, tighten the bearing retainer. If you don't have the special tool, use a socket.

17 Recheck the steering head bearings for play as described above. If necessary, repeat the adjustment procedure. Reinstall all parts previously removed and tighten the fasteners to the torques listed in the Chapter 5 Specifications.

Touring models

18 Make as special tool from a length of steel rod, 16 inches long and 1/4-inch in diameter. Grind the end into a 1/8-inch by 5/32-inch rectangle. If you're working on a Road Glide (FLTR), bend the end of the rod in a curve.

19 Bend back the tab on the lockwasher, then loosen the steering stem nut. Adjust the bearings by tapping the adjusting nut tabs with the special tool. Adjust only a little at a time; even one notch can make a noticeable difference in how tight or loose the bearings are.

20 Recheck the steering head bearings for play as described above. If necessary, repeat the adjustment procedure. Reinstall all parts previously removed and tighten the fasteners to the torques listed in the Chapter 5 Specifications. Bend the lockwasher against the steering stem nut.

11 Steering head bearings - removal, inspection and installation

1 If the steering head bearing check/adjustment (see Section 10) does not remedy excessive play or roughness in the steering head bearings, the entire front end must

be disassembled and the bearings and races replaced with new ones.

Removal

Softail models (except Springer)

2 Remove both fork legs (see Section 3).
3 Remove the headlight (see Chapter 8) and its mounting bracket.
4 Detach the brake hose bracket from the steering stem.
5 Remove the trim cap from the top of the fork stem.
6 If you're working on an FLSTC or FLSTS model, loosen the pinch bolt that secures the fork stem top bolt, then unscrew the top bolt. Remove the washer and upper triple clamp, together with the handlebar, and lower the steering stem out of the steering head.
7 If you're working on an FXST, FXSTB or FXSTD, bend the lockwasher down, away from the nut at the top of the steering stem. Remove the lockwasher and upper triple clamp, together with the handlebar. Unscrew the adjusting nut and lower the steering stem out of the steering head (see illustration).
8 Remove the washer and upper bearing from the steering head (see illustration).

11.8 Lift off the bearing cover and upper bearing

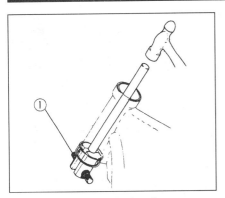

11.27a Drive out the bearing races with a driver like this or with a hammer and punch

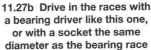

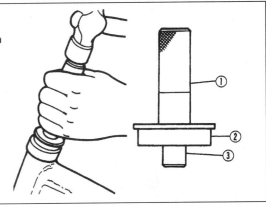

11.27b Drive in the races with a bearing driver like this one, or with a socket the same diameter as the bearing race
1   Bearing driver handle
2   Bearing driver
3   Bearing driver

Softail Springer models

9   Remove the fork assembly (see Section 6).

10   Lift the dust shield off the upper bearing and lift the upper bearing out of the steering head.

Dyna models (except FXDWG)

11   Remove both fork legs (see Section 3).

12   Loosen the pinch bolt that secures the fork stem top bolt, then unscrew the top bolt. Remove the washer and upper triple clamp, together with the handlebar.

13   Remove the washer and upper bearing from the steering head lower the steering stem out of the steering head.

Dyna FXDWG models

14   Remove both fork legs (see Section 3).

15   Remove the headlight and its mounting bracket (see Chapter 8).

16   Detach the brake hose bracket from the steering stem.

17   Remove the trim cap from the top of the fork stem.

18   Bend the lockwasher down, away from the nut at the top of the steering stem. Remove the lockwasher and upper triple clamp, together with the handlebar. Unscrew the adjusting nut and lower the steering stem out of the steering head.

19   Remove the washer and upper bearing from the steering head.

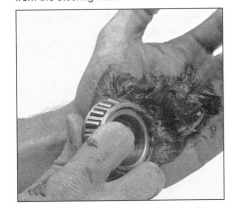

11.34 Work the grease completely into the rollers

Touring models

20   Remove both fork legs (see Section 3).

21   Remove the headlight and its mounting bracket (see Chapter 8).

22   Detach the brake hose bracket from the steering stem.

23   Bend the lockwasher down, away from the nut at the top of the steering stem. Remove the lockwasher and upper triple clamp, together with the handlebar. Unscrew the adjusting nut and lower the steering stem out of the steering head.

24   Remove the washer and upper bearing from the steering head.

Inspection

25   Clean all the parts with solvent and dry them thoroughly, using compressed air, if available. If you do use compressed air, don't let the bearings spin as they're dried - it could ruin them. Wipe the old grease out of the frame steering head and bearing races.

26   Examine the races in the steering head for cracks, dents, and pits. If even the slightest amount of wear or damage is evident, the races should be replaced with new ones.

27   To remove the races, drive them out of the steering head with a bearing driver (see illustration). A slide hammer with the proper internal-jaw puller will also work. Since the races are an interference fit in the frame, installation will be easier if the new races are left overnight in a refrigerator. This will cause them to contract and slip into place in the frame with very little effort. Before installing the races, coat the outsides of the races with clean engine oil. Tap them gently into place with a hammer and bearing driver or a large socket (see illustration). Do not strike the bearing surface or the race will be damaged.

28   Check the bearings for wear. Look for cracks, dents, and pits in the races and flat spots on the bearings. Replace any defective parts with new ones. If a new bearing is required, replace both of them as a set.

29   To remove the lower bearing from the steering stem on all except Softail Springer models, cut the roller retainer with a chisel. While holding the steering stem upside down, heat the inner race until the bearing expands and falls off the steering stem. Don't remove this bearing unless it, or the grease seal underneath, must be replaced.

30   To remove the lower bearing from the steering stem on Softail Springer models, pry it loose, using the notches in the steering stem. Don't remove this bearing unless it, or the grease seal underneath, must be replaced.

31   Check the grease seal under the lower bearing and replace it with a new one if necessary.

32   Inspect the steering stem/lower triple clamp for cracks and other damage. Do not attempt to repair any steering components. Replace them with new parts if defects are found.

33   Check the bearing cover - if it's worn or deteriorated, replace it.

Installation

34   Pack the bearings with high-quality grease (preferably a moly-based grease) (see illustration). Harley-Davidson recommends Harley-Davidson Special Purpose Grease, part no. 99857-97. Coat the outer races with grease also.

35   Install the grease seal and lower bearing onto the steering stem. Drive the lower bearing onto the steering stem using a section of pipe with a diameter the same as the inner race of the bearing (see illustration).

Caution: Don't use a piece of pipe bigger than the inner race, or the bearing cage will be damaged. Drive the bearing on until it is fully seated.

11.35 Drive the grease seal and bearing lower race on with a hollow driver (or equivalent piece of pipe) and a hammer

5

12.2 Remove the bolts and washers (arrows) to detach the shock absorbers from the swingarm

12.3 Remove the nut at the front of the shock (A) to detach it from the frame; the locknut (B) and holes (C) are used to set spring preload

36 Insert the steering stem/lower triple clamp into the frame head. Install the upper bearing and the race cover.

Softail FLSTC and FLSTF models

37 Install the upper triple clamp, using a new washer. Install the steering stem bolt and tighten it just enough so there's no looseness (shake) in the bearings. The steering stem must pivot freely from side to side.

Caution: Don't overtighten the stem bolt or the bearings will be damaged.

38 The remainder of installation is the reverse of the removal steps, with the following additions:

a) Fill the steering head with the same grease used to lubricate the bearings, using the grease nipple on the steering head.

b) Adjust the steering head bearings (see Section 10).

c) Use Loctite on the threads of the steering stem punch bolt and tighten it to the torque listed in this Chapter's Specifications.

Softail FLSTC and FLSTF models

39 Install the bearing adjusting nut and tighten it just enough so there's no looseness (shake) in the bearings. The steering stem must pivot freely from side to side.

Caution: Don't overtighten the adjusting nut or the bearings will be damaged.

40 Install the upper triple clamp, using a new lockwasher. Make sure the lockwasher tab engages the hole in the upper triple clamp. Install the steering stem nut, but don't tighten it yet.

41 The remainder of installation is the reverse of the removal steps, with the following additions:

a) Adjust the steering head bearings (see Section 10).

b) Tighten the steering stem nut to the torque listed in this Chapter's Specifications, then bend the lockwasher against the nut to secure it.

Softail Springer models

42 This procedure is part of rigid fork installation, described in Section 6.

Dyna models (except FXDWG)

43 Install the upper triple clamp, washer and steering stem bolt. Tighten the steering stem pinch bolt to the torque listed in this Chapter's Specifications. Tighten the steering stem bolt just enough so there's no looseness (shake) in the bearings. The steering stem must pivot freely from side to side.

Caution: Don't overtighten the stem bolt or the bearings will be damaged.

44 The remainder of installation is the reverse of the removal steps. Adjust the steering head bearings (see Section 10).

Dyna FXDWG models

45 Install the bearing adjusting nut and tighten it just enough so there's no looseness (shake) in the bearings. The steering stem must pivot freely from side to side.

Caution: Don't overtighten the adjusting nut or the bearings will be damaged.

46 Install the upper triple clamp, using a new lockwasher. Make sure the lockwasher tab engages the hole in the upper triple clamp. Install the steering stem nut, but don't tighten it yet.

47 Tighten the upper triple clamp pinch screws to the torque listed in this Chapter's Specifications.

48 The remainder of installation is the reverse of the removal steps, with the following additions:

a) Adjust the steering head bearings (see Section 10).

b) Tighten the steering stem nut to the torque listed in this Chapter's Specifications, then bend the lockwasher against the nut to secure it.

Touring models

49 Install the bearing adjusting nut and tighten it just enough so there's no looseness (shake) in the bearings. The steering

stem must pivot freely from side to side.

Caution: Don't overtighten the adjusting nut or the bearings will be damaged.

50 Install the upper triple clamp, lockplate and steering stem nut. Tighten the nut to the torque listed in this Chapter's Specifications and bend a lockplate tab against the nut to secure it.

51 The remainder of installation is the reverse of the removal steps. Check the steering head bearing play and adjust it if necessary (see Section 10).

12 Rear shock absorbers - removal and installation

Softail models

1 Securely support the motorcycle with the rear wheel off the ground.

2 Unscrew the bolt and remove the washer to detach the rear end of the shock absorber from the swingarm **(see illustration)**. This requires an adapter (Snap-On tool SRES24 or equivalent).

3 Remove the nut and washer at the front end of the shock and take it out from under the motorcycle **(see illustration)**.

4 Repeat Steps 2 and 3 to remove the other shock.

5 Install the bushing on the shock stud, then position it in the hole in the frame. Install the washer and nut, but don't tighten them yet.

6 Coat the shaft of the shock bolt with Loctite Anti-seize or equivalent. Coat the threads with non-permanent thread locking agent.

7 Tighten the bolt to the torque listed in this Chapter's Specifications. The special adapter required for access to the bolts will change the effective length of the torque wrench, so you'll need to calculate the torque based on the combined length of the torque wrench (measured from the head to the center

12.11 Dyna rear shocks are secured by upper and lower bolts (arrows)

14.7a On Softail models, unscrew the nut from the swingarm pivot bolt . . .

of the handle) and the adapter. For example, a torque wrench with a length of 1.5 feet (18 inches) will apply 15 foot-pounds of torque when 10 pounds of force is applied to the handle (10 pounds X 1.5 feet = 15 foot-pounds). If you increase the length to 2 feet by adding a 6-inch adapter, the torque wrench will apply 20 foot-pounds of torque when 10 pounds of force is applied to the handle (2 feet X 10 pounds = 20 foot-pounds).

8   Tighten the nut at the front of the shock to the torque listed in this Chapter's Specifications.

9   Install the other shock in the same manner.

Dyna models

10   Securely support the motorcycle with the rear wheel off the ground. **Note:** *This won't be necessary if you remove and install one shock at a time.*

11   Remove the shock absorber lower nut, washer and bolt **(see illustration)**.

12   Remove the upper nut (and the stud cover if equipped) and pull the shock off the upper stud **(see illustration 12.11)**. If necessary, remove the nut that secures the stud to the frame and pull it out.

13   Installation is the reverse of the removal steps, with the following additions:

a) Use non-permanent thread locking agent on the threads of the upper stud.
b) Tighten all fasteners to the torques listed in this Chapter's Specifications.

Touring models

14   Where necessary for access, remove the saddlebag (see Chapter 7).

15   Securely support the motorcycle with the rear wheel off the ground. **Note:** *This won't be necessary if you remove and install one shock at a time.*

16   On models so equipped, release air pressure from the rear suspension, then compress the compression fitting and disconnect the air tube from the shock.

17   Remove the shock absorber upper bolt

and washer, then unscrew the lower bolt. Take the shock off the motorcycle.

18   Installation is the reverse of the removal steps, with the following additions:

a) *If the compression fittings were removed from the shocks, lubricate their threads with pipe sealant containing Teflon.*
b) *Use non-permanent thread locking agent on the threads of the shock absorber bolts.*
c) *Tighten all fasteners to the torques listed in this Chapter's Specifications.*
d) *After connecting the air lines to the shocks, tug on them gently to make sure they're securely connected.*

13 Swingarm bearings - check

1   Refer to Chapter 7 and remove the rear wheel, then refer to Section 12 and remove the rear shock absorbers.

2   Grasp the rear of the swingarm with one hand and place your other hand at the junc-

14.7b . . . pull out the bolt and remove the spacer collars (arrow)

tion of the swingarm and the frame. Try to move the rear of the swingarm from side-to-side. Any wear (play) in the bearings should be felt as movement between the swingarm and the frame at the front. The swingarm will actually be felt to move forward and backward at the front (not from side-to-side). If any play is noted, the bearings should be replaced with new ones (see Section 15).

3   Next, move the swingarm up and down through its full travel. It should move freely, without any binding or rough spots. If it does not move freely, refer to Section 14 for servicing procedures.

14 Swingarm - removal and installation

Softail models

Removal

1   Support the bike securely upright with its rear wheel off the ground.

2   Remove the rear wheel, brake caliper and bracket (see Chapter 6).

3   Remove the drivebelt guard (see Section 16).

4   Unbolt the inner rear fender (see Chapter 7). Lift it from the bottom and tilt it out of the way.

5   Unbolt the rear ends of the shock absorbers (see Section 12).

6   If you're working on a California model, detach the evaporative emission canister.

7   Remove the nut from the swingarm pivot shaft **(see illustration)**. Support the swingarm, pull out the pivot shaft and remove the spacers **(see illustration)**. Remove the bushings from inside the swingarm bearings, then remove the swingarm from the frame.

8   Clean the pivot bearings in the swingarm with a cloth and check them for dryness or deterioration. If they're in need of lubrication or replacement, refer to Section 15.

5

14.17 On Dyna models, pry out the trim cap (arrow) for access to the pivot bolt nut

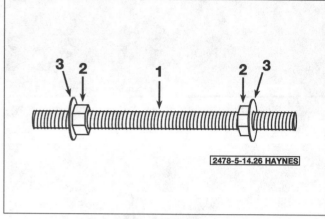

14.26 On 1999 through 2001 Touring models, spread the swingarm bushings using a tool made of threaded stock (1), nuts (2) and washers (3)

Installation

9   Support the swing arm so its pivot holes are aligned with the holes in the frame. Install the pivot bushings from the inside of the swingarm, with their collars facing inward.

10   Lubricate the pivot shaft with Loctite Anti-seize or equivalent and install it through the frame and spacers. The spacer collars face inward and rest against the transmission.

11   Apply semi-permanent thread locking agent (Loctite no. 262 red or equivalent) to the pivot shaft threads. Install the shaft nut and tighten it to the torque listed in this Chapter's Specifications, making sure the frame isn't distorted while you tighten.

12   Raise and lower the swingarm and make sure it moves freely, without binding.

13   The remainder of installation is the reverse of the removal steps.

Dyna models

Removal

14   Support the bike securely upright with its rear wheel off the ground.

15   Remove the rear wheel and brake caliper (see Chapter 6).

16   Remove the drivebelt guard, debris deflector and rear shock absorbers (see Sections 16 and 12).

17   Pry the trim cap out of the hole for access to the pivot shaft screw **(see illustration)**.

18   Unscrew the pivot shaft screw (hold the pivot shaft with a socket on its hex head if necessary). Remove the screw and lockwasher.

19   Support the swingarm and remove the pivot shaft. Take the swingarm out of the frame.

20   Installation is the reverse of the removal steps, with the following additions:

  a) *Tighten all fasteners to the torques listed in this Chapter's Specifications.*

  b) *Raise and lower the swingarm and make sure it moves freely, without binding.*

Touring models

Removal

21   Remove the saddlebags and rear footrests (see Chapter 7).

22   Remove the mufflers (see Chapter 3).

23   Remove the brake caliper and rear wheel (see Chapter 6).

24   Support the swingarm. Hold the pivot bolt head with a wrench and unscrew the pivot bolt nut with a deep socket. Remove the nut and cup washer. Remove the swingarm pivot bolt and nut and remove it from the frame.

Installation (1999 through 2001 models)

25   Place the swingarm in its installed position and align it with the frame holes and transmission mount.

26   If the swingarm won't fit onto the pivot on the back of the transmission, make a spreader tool from piece of threaded rod, two nuts and two washers **(see illustration)**. Place it between the swingarm bearings and turn the nuts away from each other to push the bearings apart to a distance of 4-9/16 inches, then remove the spreader tool.

27   Coat the pivot shaft with Loctite Anti-seize or equivalent, then slide the rubber mount onto the shaft, small diameter first. Slide the nylon spacer onto the shaft, small diameter last.

28   Install the pivot shaft from the right side of the bike, making sure the pin hole in the rubber mount will align with the footboard bracket. Insert the pivot shaft through the frame, swingarm and transmission.

29   Install the nylon spacer on the left end of the pivot shaft, small diameter first. Install the rubber mount, small diameter last. Make sure the pin hole in the rubber mount is in the 11 o'clock position to align with the footboard bracket. Install the cup washer and install the nut finger-tight.

30   If the chrome trim plugs are in the swingarm bracket, remove them. Install the swingarm brackets, noting that they're marked for left and right sides of the bike. Install the bracket bolts and tighten them to the torque listed in this Chapter's Specifications.

31   Hold the pivot shaft head with a wrench and tighten the nut to the torque listed in this Chapter's Specifications.

32   install the chrome plugs in the swingarm brackets. Install the footboard brackets, aligning them with the holes in the rubber mounts.

33   The remainder of installation is the reverse of the removal steps.

34   Adjust the drivebelt tension (see Chapter 1).

Installation (2002 and later models)

35   Place the rubber mount in the swingarm pivot hole on the right side of the bike. Position the rubber mount's pin hole so it will align with the floorboard bracket pin when it's installed, then install the outer spacer on the right side of the swingarm.

36   Position the swingarm in its installed position, making sure the drivebelt is within the left side of the swingarm. Tap the swingarm into the mounts if necessary, using a rubber mallet.

37   If the pivot shaft was disassembled, slide the outer spacer on, large diameter first, until it touches the shoulder on the pivot shaft. Install the rubber mount on the pivot shaft so its flat side will face the left side of the motorcycle when the shaft is installed. Install the cup washer in the rubber mount, concave side first, and secure it with the locknut. Tighten the locknut to the torque listed in this Chapter's Specifications.

38   Coat the pivot shaft with Loctite Anti-seize or equivalent. Push the assembled pivot shaft through the mounts from the left side of the motorcycle.

39   Install the cup washer on the right end of the pivot shaft, concave side first. Install the locknut.

40   Hold the locknut from turning with the pivot shaft nut and tighten the right side locknut to the torque listed in this Chapter's

16.6 Remove the belt/guard bolts (arrows) (Dyna shown)

Specifications. Hold the right side nut and tighten the left side locknut to the torque listed in this Chapter's Specifications.

41 Raise and lower the swingarm to make sure it moves freely, without binding.

42 Install the chrome trim plug in the right swingarm bracket.

43 Position the pin hole in the left side rubber mount so it aligns with the pin in the footboard bracket. Install the bracket and tighten its bolts to the torque listed in this Chapter's Specifications.

44 The remainder of installation is the reverse of the removal steps.

15 Swingarm bearings - replacement

1 Remove the swingarm (see Section 14).

Softail models

2 Pry out the bearing retainer rings and drive the old bearings out of the swingarm.

3 Drive in new bearings using a driver that presses against the bearing outer race, then secure them with new retainer rings.

Dyna models

4 Remove the bearing washer from the swingarm. Remove the spacer from each side, then remove the bearing cones and bearing spacer.

5 Use a hammer and pin punch to drive the bearing cups out of the swingarm.

6 Starting at the lock ring opening, mark the lock ring at 1/3 and 2/3 of the way around the lock ring circumference. Cut the lock ring at these points with a die grinder, then pry it out. Remove the bearing cones.

7 Press the pivot bushing and dust shield out of the swingarm.

8 Installation is the reverse of the removal steps, with the following additions:

a) *Both bearing cones and the lock ring, as well as the pivot bushing, must be replaced whenever they're removed.*

b) *The washer on the left side is installed with its small hole away from the bearing.*

c) *The thick wall of the spacer faces away from the bearing.*

d) *If the bushing is being replaced, press the new one into the bore so its final installed position ranges from 0.060-inch above the bore to flush with the bore.*

Touring models

9 Bearing replacement is a complicated procedure that requires a hydraulic press and special adapters. Have the job done by a dealer service department or other qualified shop.

16 Drivebelt - removal, inspection and installation

Caution: Once the drivebelt is removed, don't bend it into a circle smaller than five inches in diameter and don't bend it backwards. This will damage the belt, possibly causing it to fail during operation.

Removal

Softail and Dyna models

1 Remove the primary chaincase assembly, including the clutch, primary chain, chain adjuster, compensating sprocket and primary chaincase housing (see Chapter 2).

2 Remove the rear wheel (see Chapter 6).

3 Support the swingarm and remove the swingarm pivot shaft (see Section 14).

4 If you plan to reuse the drivebelt, mark an arrow indicating direction of rotation. A used belt must be installed so it rotates in the same direction as it did before removal.

5 Take the drivebelt off the engine sprocket and remove it from the bike.

6 Check the belt guard (and debris deflector on Softail models) for wear or damage and replace it as necessary **(see illustrations)**.

1999 through 2001 Touring models

7 Remove the saddlebags, left side footboard bracket and left side exhaust system (see Chapters 7 and 4).

8 Remove the spring clip from the left end of the axle and loosen the axle nut. Release belt tension, using the tension adjusters (see Chapter 1).

9 Remove the primary chaincase assembly, including the clutch, primary chain, chain adjuster, compensating sprocket and primary chaincase housing (see Chapter 2).

10 Remove the chrome trim plug from the right side of the swingarm bracket (which also functions as the passenger footboard bracket).

11 Insert an 11/16-inch socket through the right side swingarm bracket hole and hold the right side nut so it won't turn. Unscrew the left side nut with a 3/4-inch wrench and remove the cup washer from the pivot shaft.

12 Tap the left end of the swingarm pivot shaft into its bore far enough to create a gap for drivebelt removal.

13 Remove the rubber mount, nylon washer and shock absorber lower bolt.

14 Take the drivebelt off the sprockets and remove it from the bike.

15 Check the belt guard for wear or damage and replace it as necessary.

2002 and later Touring models

16 Remove the rear wheel and swingarm (see Chapter 6 and Section 14).

17 Remove the primary chaincase assembly, including the clutch, primary chain, chain adjuster, compensating sprocket and primary chaincase housing (see Chapter 2).

18 Take the drivebelt off the sprockets and remove it from the bike.

19 Check the belt guard for wear or damage and replace it as necessary.

Inspection

20 Spray the belt with soapy water to clean it. Do not dip it in water and do not use solvents.

21 Check the belt for wear and damage (see Chapter 1).

Installation

22 Installation is the reverse of the removal steps. Refer to Chapter 1 and adjust the belt tension.

17 Sprockets - check and replacement

1 Remove the drivebelt (see Section 16).

2 Whenever the sprockets are inspected, the belt should be inspected also and replaced if it's worn.

3 Check the sprockets for wear and damage as described in Chapter 1. If the sprockets are worn, remove the rear wheel (if not already done during belt removal) (see Chapter 6).

5

17.4 Hold the drivebelt sprocket with a special tool like JIMS 2260 (shown) or a strap wrench

17.5 Remove the locking plate bolts (arrows), then unscrew the nut and remove the sprocket

17.6 Unbolt the rear sprocket from the wheel (arrows) (FLSTF shown)

4   To remove the transmission sprocket, lock it using a locking tool (Harley-Davidson HD-41184 or JIMS 2260) **(see illustration)**. You can also use a strap wrench.

5   Unbolt the lockplate, remove the nut and detach the sprocket from the transmission shaft **(see illustration)**.

6   Unbolt the sprocket from the rear wheel **(see illustration)**.

7   Installation is the reverse of the removal steps, with the following additions:

a) *Tighten the sprocket nut and bolts at the engine and wheel to the torques listed in this Chapter's Specifications.*

b) *Refer to Chapter 1 and adjust the chain.*

 18 Suspension adjustments

Softail models

1   The rear shock absorber spring preload is adjustable.

2   Loosen the locknut on the stud at the front of each shock **(see illustration 12.3)**.

3   Use the spanner wrench provided in the bike's tool kit to rotate the shock body, engaging the spanner wrench pins with the holes in the front of the shock. When the correct setting is reached, tighten the locknut.

4   Set the other shock absorber to the same setting.

⚠ *Warning: Be sure to set both shocks to the same preload setting. Uneven settings may cause unstable handling, leading to loss of control of the motorcycle.*

Dyna models (except FXDX and FXDXT)

5   The rear shock absorber spring preload can be adjusted by turning the ring at the bot-

tom of each shock, using a spanner wrench. There are five settings, from hard to soft.

⚠ *Warning: Be sure to set both shocks to the same preload setting. Uneven settings may cause unstable handling, leading to loss of control of the motorcycle.*

Dyna FXDX and FXDXT

6   Sit on the seat and bounce up and down a few times to seat the suspension.

7   Hold the bike upright with no one on the seat. Measure the distance between the centers of the upper and lower rear shock absorber bolts and write it down. Now measure the distance from the enter of the front axle to the bottom of the lower triple clamp and write this down.

8   Have someone hold the bike upright while you sit on the seat with your feet on the pegs (the idea is to place the normal load on the bike). Repeat the measurements in Step 7. The difference between the measurements (squat) must be 1/2-inch to one inch (12.7 to 25.4 mm). If it's not within the specified range, adjust the front or rear suspension to compensate.

9   The rear shock absorber spring preload can be adjusted by turning the ring at the bottom of each shock, using a spanner wrench. There are five settings, from hard to soft.

⚠ *Warning: Be sure to set both shocks to the same preload setting. Uneven settings may cause unstable handling, leading to loss of control of the motorcycle.*

10   To adjust front spring preload, turn the hex at the top of each fork leg with a 7/8-inch wrench. Look at the grooves around each fork leg below the hex; these are measuring lines. The same number of lines must be exposed on each fork leg.

⚠ *Warning: Be sure to set both fork legs to the same preload setting. Uneven settings may cause unstable handling, leading to loss of control of the motorcycle.*

11   Once the squat is set correctly, you can make the following adjustments.

12   At the rear, rebound damping can be adjusted by turning the adjuster at the top rear of each shock, using a standard screwdriver. Turning the adjuster clockwise increases the damping; turning it counterclockwise decreases it.

13   At the front, rebound damping is adjusted by turning the knurled knob at the top of each fork. There are 17 adjuster positions. To set the adjusters, turn them all the way clockwise (maximum damping), then turn them back and count the clicks.

14   Also at the front, compression damping is set by turning the knuckled knob at the bottom rear of each fork leg. There are 14 adjuster positions. To set the adjusters, turn them all the way clockwise (maximum damping), then turn them back and count the clicks.

Touring models (air suspension)

15   The front forks on some Touring models and the rear shocks on all are equipped with air pressure valves. The recommended air pressure setting is listed in this Chapter's Specifications.

⚠ *Warning: Never exceed the maximum pressure listed in this Chapter's Specifications. Never remove the fork springs and rely on air pressure alone to support the forks or unstable handling may occur. Ensure that the pressure is equal in both legs.*

Chapter 6
Brakes, wheels and tires

Contents

Degrees of difficulty

Easy, suitable for novice with little experience		Fairly easy, suitable for beginner with some experience		Fairly difficult, suitable for competent DIY mechanic		Difficult, suitable for experienced DIY mechanic	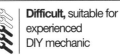	Very difficult, suitable for expert DIY or professional	

Specifications

Brakes

Brake fluid type..	DOT 5 only
Brake pad minimum thickness	See Chapter 1
Disc thickness..	Stamped in disc
Disc runout (maximum)...	0.008-inch (0.2 mm)
Brake pedal position and freeplay	See Chapter 1

Wheels and tires

Wheel runout limit	
Laced wheels (radial runout; up-and-down)	0.031 inch (0.79 mm)
Cast wheels	
Radial runout (up-and-down)...	0.030 inch (0.76 mm)
Axial runout (side-to-side)..	0.040-inch (1.02 mm)
Tire pressures	See Chapter 1

Torque specifications

Softail models

Caliper mounting bolts (all except FLSTS, FXSTS)	28 to 38 ft-lbs (38.0 to 51.5 Nm)
Caliper lower mounting bolt (FLSTS, FXSTS)	25 to 30 ft-lbs (33.9 to 47.0 Nm)
Caliper upper mounting bolt (FLSTS, FXSTS)	28 to 30 ft-lbs (38.0 to 40.7 Nm)
Caliper bleed valves	80 to 100 inch-lbs (9.0 to 11.3 Nm)
Caliper bridge bolts	28 to 38 ft-lbs (38.0 to 51.1 Nm)

Torque specifications

Softail models (continued)

Disc-to-hub bolts	
Front	16 to 24 ft-lbs (21.7 to 32.5 Nm)
Rear	30 to 45 ft-lbs (40.7 to 61.0 Nm)
Pad pins	180 to 200 inch-lbs (20.3 to 22.6 Nm)
Single-piston front caliper pad retaining screw	40 to 50 inch-lbs (4.5 to 5.6 Nm)
Brake reaction link acorn nuts (Softail FXSTS)	35 to 40 ft-lbs (37.5 to 54.2 Nm)
Brake reaction link-to-rigid fork locknut (Softail FXSTS)	14 to 18 ft-lbs (19.0 to 24.4 Nm)
Brake reaction link nut (Softail FXSTS)	10 to 20 ft-lbs (13.6 to 27.1 Nm)
Master cylinder banjo fitting bolt	17 to 22 ft-lbs (23.0 to 29.8 Nm)
Front master cylinder clamp bolts	70 to 80 inch-lbs (7.9 to 9.0 Nm)
Rear master cylinder mounting nut	50 ft-lbs (67.8 Nm)
Front axle nut	
All except FLSTS, FXSTS	50 to 55 ft-lbs (61.0 to 74.6 Nm)
FLSTS, FXSTS	60 to 65 ft-lbs (81.3 to 88.1 Nm)
Front axle clamp nuts (all except FXSTD)	123 to 180 inch-lbs (14.9 to 20.3 Nm)
Front axle clamp bolts (FXSTD)	15 to 21 ft-lbs (20.3 to 28.5 Nm)*
Rear axle nut	60 to 65 ft-lbs (81.3 to 88.1 Nm)

Tighten front bolt first, then tighten rear bolt.

Dyna models

Caliper mounting bolts	
Single-piston front caliper	25 to 30 ft-lbs (34 to 41 Nm)
Single-piston rear caliper	15 to 20 ft-lbs (20 to 27 Nm)
Four-piston front caliper	28 to 38 ft-lbs (38.0 to 51.5 Nm)
Caliper bleed valves	80 to 100 inch-lbs (9.0 to 11.3 Nm)
Caliper bridge bolts	28 to 38 ft-lbs 38.0 to 51.1 Nm)
Disc-to-hub bolts	
Front	16 to 24 ft-lbs (21.7 to 32.5 Nm)
Rear	
T45 Torx bolts	30 to 45 ft-lbs (40.7 to 61.0 Nm)
Allen bolts	23 to 27 ft-lbs (31 to 37 Nm)
Pad pins	180 to 200 inch-lbs (20.3 to 22.6 Nm)
Single-piston front caliper pad retaining screw	40 to 50 inch-lbs (4.5 to 5.6 Nm)
Master cylinder banjo fitting bolt	17 to 22 ft-lbs (23.0 to 29.8 Nm)
Front master cylinder clamp bolts	70 to 80 inch-lbs (7.9 to 9.0 Nm)
Rear master cylinder mounting nut	45 to 50 ft-lbs (61.0 to 67.8 Nm)
Front axle nut	50 to 55 ft-lbs (61.0 to 74.6 Nm)
Rear axle nut	60 to 65 ft-lbs (81.3 to 88.1 Nm)
Front axle pinch bolt nut (all except FXDWG)	25 to 30 ft-lbs (33.9 to 44.7 Nm)
Front axle clamp nuts (FXDWG)	60 to 132 inch-lbs (6.8 to 14.9 Nm)

Touring models

Caliper mounting bolts	
Single-piston front caliper	25 to 30 ft-lbs (34 to 41 Nm)
Single-piston rear caliper	15 to 20 ft-lbs (20 to 27 Nm)
Four-piston front caliper	28 to 38 ft-lbs (38.0 to 51.5 Nm)
Caliper bleed valves	80 to 100 inch-lbs (9.0 to 11.3 Nm)
Caliper bridge bolts	28 to 38 ft-lbs 38.0 to 51.1 Nm)
Disc-to-hub bolts	
Front	16 to 24 ft-lbs (21.7 to 32.5 Nm)
Rear	30 to 45 ft-lbs (40.7 to 61.0 Nm)
Pad pins	180 to 200 inch-lbs (20.3 to 22.6 Nm)
Single-piston front caliper pad retaining screw	40 to 50 inch-lbs (4.5 to 5.6 Nm)
Master cylinder banjo fitting bolt	17 to 22 ft-lbs (23.0 to 29.8 Nm)
Front master cylinder clamp bolts	70 to 80 inch-lbs (7.9 to 9.0 Nm)*
Rear master cylinder front nut	30 to 40 ft-lbs (41 to 54 Nm)
Rear brake pedal locknut	15 to 20 ft-lbs 20 to 27 Nm)
Front axle nut	50 to 55 ft-lbs (61.0 to 74.6 Nm)
Front axle clamp nuts	
1999 through 2001	108 to 156 inch-lbs (12 to 18 Nm)
2002 and later	132 to 180 inch-lbs (14.9 to 20.3 Nm)
Rear axle nut	
1999 through 2001	60 to 65 ft-lbs (81.3 to 88.1 Nm)
2002 and later	95 to 105 ft-lbs (129 to 142 Nm)

1 General information

The motorcycles covered by this manual are equipped with hydraulic disc brakes on the front and rear wheels. Four basic caliper designs are used: Front single-piston, rear single-piston, front four-piston and rear four-piston. Depending on model, the bike may be equipped with one or two front calipers. All models use a single caliper at the rear.

Some models are equipped with cast aluminum wheels, which require very little maintenance and allow tubeless tires to be used. Other models use wire wheels at the front and/or rear of the bike.

Caution: Disc brake components rarely require disassembly. Do not disassemble components unless absolutely necessary. If any hydraulic brake line connection in the system is loosened, the entire system should be disassembled, drained, cleaned and then properly filled and bled upon reassembly. Do not use solvents on internal brake components. Solvents will cause seals to swell and distort. Use only clean brake fluid or alcohol for cleaning. Use care when working with brake fluid as it can injure your eyes and it will damage painted surfaces and plastic parts

 Warning: All of the motorcycles covered in this manual use DOT 5 brake fluid. Do not use DOT 3, DOT 4 or DOT 5.1 fluid; they are incompatible with DOT 5 and may lead to loss of brake effectiveness when mixed with DOT 5.

2 Brake pads - replacement

 Warning: The dust created by the brake system may contain asbestos, which is harmful to your health. Never blow it out with compressed air and don't inhale any of it. An approved filtering mask should be worn when working on the brakes.

1   Support the bike securely upright.

Single-piston front calipers

2   Remove the pad retainer screw, then remove the pad retainer and inner pad **(see illustration)**.
3   Remove the caliper from the bike (see Section 3). **Note:** *If you're removing the caliper only to replace the pads, you can leave the brake hose connected to the caliper.*
4   Support the caliper with rope or wire so it doesn't hang by the brake hose. It's a good idea to wrap the caliper with rags and tape to protect the caliper and wheel from scratches.

2.2 Loosen the pad retainer screw on the back of the caliper (caliper removed for clarity)

5   Remove the outer brake pad from the caliper, together with the mounting bracket and spring clip **(see illustration)**. Separate the pad from the spring clip.

 Warning: The spring clip can fly out fast enough to cause injury. Wear eye protection when removing and installing it.

6   Remove the spring clip. If it appears damaged, replace it.
7   Check the condition of the brake disc (see Section 7). If it is in need of machining or replacement, follow the procedure in that Section to remove it. If it is okay, de-glaze it with sandpaper or emery cloth, using a swirling motion.
8   Remove the cap from the master cylinder reservoir and siphon out some fluid. Push the piston into the caliper as far as possible, while checking the master cylinder reservoir to make sure it doesn't overflow. If you can't depress the piston with thumb pressure, try using a C-clamp. If the piston sticks, remove the caliper and overhaul it as described in Section 3.
9   Install the spring clip and outer pad (without insulation material on the back side) on the mounting bracket **(see illustration 2.5)**. Note the location of the lips on the

2.5 Here's how the outer brake pad and clip should be installed in the pad holder

clip, and note also that the loop of the clip faces in the opposite direction from the insulation material on the back of the pad.
10   Install the assembled mounting bracket, pad and clip in the caliper.
11   Install the inner pad, retainer and retainer screw in the caliper.
12   Install the caliper (see Section 3).
13   Refill the master cylinder reservoir (see Chapter 1) and install the diaphragm and cap.
14   Operate the brake lever several times to bring the pads into contact with the disc. Check the operation of the brakes carefully before riding the motorcycle.
15   If you're working on a dual-caliper model, repeat the procedure to replace the pads in the other caliper.

Single-piston rear caliper

16   Where necessary for access, remove the right saddlebag and right side cover (see Chapter 7).
17   Remove the caliper, leaving the brake hose connected (see Section 4).
18   Carefully note how the wire retainer clip is installed, then remove it from the back side of the bracket **(see illustration)**. Slide the outer brake pad off the bracket.

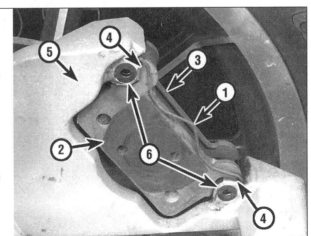

2.18 Brake pad details (single-piston rear caliper)

1   Wire retainer clip
2   Outer brake pad
3   Inner brake pad
4   Pad shim (2)
5   Bracket
6   Rubber bushing (2)

6

2.23 Position the pad shims (arrow) with the looped ends outward

19 Slide the inner pad off toward the wheel.
20 Detach the pad shims from the bracket.
21 Check the condition of the brake disc (see Section 7). If it is in need of machining or

replacement, follow the procedure in that Section to remove it. If it is okay, de-glaze it with sandpaper or emery cloth, using a swirling motion.
22 Remove the cap from the master cylinder reservoir and siphon out some fluid. Push the piston into the caliper as far as possible, while checking the master cylinder reservoir to make sure it doesn't overflow. If you can't depress the piston with thumb pressure, try using a C-clamp. If the piston sticks, remove the caliper and overhaul it as described in Section 4.
23 Install new pad shims so that their looped ends are positioned outwards (towards the piston) and hold them in place while the pads and wire retainer are installed **(see illustration)**.
24 Slide the inner pad onto the shims from the wheel side. Slide the outer pad on from the outside.
25 Insert the wire retainer clip ends into the mounting bracket holes and position the clip over the outer brake pad **(see illustration 2.18)**.

Caution: Make sure the pads are still riding on the shims after the retainer clip is installed.
26 Make sure the mounting (pin) bolts are clean so the caliper can move freely. Carefully lower the caliper over the pads and disc and align the holes, then install the mounting bolts.
27 Tighten the mounting bolts to the torque listed in this Chapter's Specifications

Four-piston front calipers

28 Loosen the pad pins but don't remove them yet **(see illustrations)**. Remove the caliper mounting bolts. Slide the caliper and pads off the disc. **Note:** If you're removing the caliper only to replace the pads, you can leave the brake hose connected to the caliper.
29 Support the caliper with rope or wire so it doesn't hang by the brake hose. It's a good idea to wrap the caliper with rags and tape to protect the caliper and wheel from scratches.
30 Remove the pad pins, then remove the

2.28a Four-piston caliper mounting details (front caliper, left side)

1 Mounting bolts
2 Pad pins
3 Brake hose banjo fitting bolt

2.28b Four-piston caliper mounting details (front caliper, right side)

1 Mounting bolts
2 Pad pins
3 Brake hose banjo fitting bolt

2.30a Unscrew the pad pins (arrows) ...

2.30b ... then remove the pads (arrows)

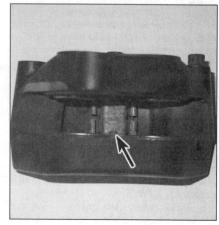

2.31 Remove the anti-rattle spring (arrow) from the caliper cavity

2.34a Install the inner pad, then the outer pad . . .

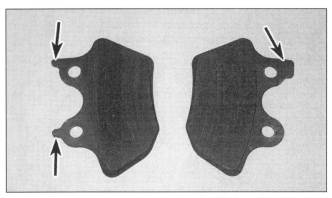

2.34b . . . the number of tabs (arrows) determines which pad
goes in the inner or outer position (see text)

brake pads **(see illustrations)**. If the pad pins are visibly worn, replace them.

31   Remove the anti-rattle spring **(see illustration)**. If it appears damaged, replace it.

32   Check the condition of the brake disc (see Section 7). If it is in need of machining or replacement, follow the procedure in that Section to remove it. If it is okay, de-glaze it with sandpaper or emery cloth, using a swirling motion.

2.35 Install the pad pins until they click,
but don't screw them in yet (arrows)

33   Remove the cap from the master cylinder reservoir and siphon out some fluid. Push the pistons into the caliper as far as possible, while checking the master cylinder reservoir to make sure it doesn't overflow. If you can't depress the pistons with thumb pressure, try using a C-clamp. If the pistons stick, remove the caliper and overhaul it as described in Section 3.

34   Install the new inner pad in the caliper with the curved portion toward the rear of the motorcycle **(see illustration)**, then install the outer pad. The inner and outer pads are different shapes **(see illustration)**. On the left side of the bike, the pad with two tabs is installed in the outer position and the pad with one tab is installed in the inner position. On the right side of the bike, it's the opposite; the pad with two tabs is installed in the inner position and the pad with one tab is installed in the outer position. **Note:** *The pads on four-piston front calipers are interchangeable with the pads on rear calipers, except on Softail FXSTD models. The rear pads on FXSTD models have vertical slots in the friction material and must be used only on the rear caliper.*

35   Install the pad pins until you hear them click, but don't tighten them yet **(see illus-**

tration). **Note:** *If the pins won't go in, push the pads firmly against the anti-rattle clip and try again. If that doesn't work, make sure the anti-rattle clip is installed correctly (see Section 5).*

36   Install the caliper on the fork leg (see Section 5). If you're working on a bike with dual four-pin calipers at the front, align the calipers after installation (see Section 5). Once the calipers are installed, tighten the pad pins to the torque listed in this Chapter's Specifications.

37   Refill the master cylinder reservoir (see Chapter 1) and install the diaphragm and cap.

38   Operate the brake lever several times to bring the pads into contact with the disc. Check the operation of the brakes carefully before riding the motorcycle.

Four-piston rear caliper

Note: *This procedure should be done in the exact order described or it will be difficult to line up the pin holes in the pads. Obtain the new pads ahead of time*

39   Where necessary for access, remove the right saddlebag (see Chapter 7).

40   Loosen the pad pins but don't remove them yet **(see illustrations)**.

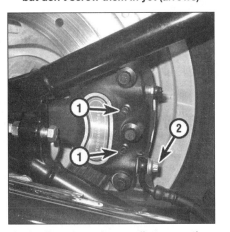

2.40a Rear four-piston caliper mounting
details (Softail)

1   Pad pins
2   Brake hose banjo fitting

2.40b Rear four-piston caliper mounting
details (Dyna)

1   Pad pins
2   Brake hose banjo fitting

2.40c Loosen the pad pins (arrows),
but don't remove them yet

6

2.41 Pry between the brake disc and inner pad to push the inner pistons into the caliper

2.42 Remove the inner pad, noting which way it faces

2.45 Pry between the outer pad and caliper to push the outer pistons all the way into the caliper

41   Remove the cap from the master cylinder reservoir and siphon out some fluid. Using a padded pry bar or screwdriver, pry between the brake disc and the inner pad to push the inner pistons all the way into the caliper **(see illustration)**. While you pry, check the master cylinder reservoir to make sure it doesn't overflow.

Caution: Don't use excessive force against the brake disc while prying the pistons. If they're stuck, remove and overhaul the caliper (see Section 4).

42   Pull the pad pins out just far enough so the inner pad drops out of the caliper **(see illustration 2.40c)**. Don't pull them out far enough for the outer pad to drop out. Remove the inner pad, noting which side goes upward **(see illustration)**.

43   Install the new inner pad. The curved side of the pad faces upward (Softail) or to the rear of the motorcycle (Dyna and Touring models). Install the pad pins until you hear them click, indicating that the inner pad is being held in position, but don't tighten the pad pins yet.

44   Operate the rear brake pedal several times, so the pistons push the inner pad firmly against the disc. This is necessary to

hold the inner pad in position while the pins are removed.

45   Using the padded pry bar or screwdriver, pry between the brake disc and the outer pad to push the outer pistons all the way into the caliper **(see illustration)**.

Caution: Don't use excessive force against the brake disc while prying the pistons. If they're stuck, remove and overhaul the caliper (see Section 6).

46   Remove the pad pins completely and pull out the outer pad **(see illustrations)**. The inner pad should be held in position by the pistons and brake disc, but if it moves, realign its pin holes before trying to reinstall the pins.

47   Install the new outer pad with its curved side upward, aligning the pin holes.

48   Install the pins through both pads, then tighten them to the torque listed in this Chapter's Specifications.

49   Refill the master cylinder reservoir (see Chapter 1) and install the diaphragm and cap.

50   Operate the brake pedal several times to bring the pads into contact with the disc. Check the operation of the brakes carefully before riding the motorcycle.

3   Single-piston front brake calipers - removal, overhaul and installation

⚠️ *Warning: If a caliper indicates the need for an overhaul (usually due to leaking fluid or sticky operation), all old brake fluid should be flushed from the system. Also, the dust created by the brake system may contain asbestos, which is harmful to your health. Never blow it out with compressed air and don't inhale any of it. An approved filtering mask should be worn when working on the brakes. Do not, under any circumstances, use petroleum-based solvents to clean brake parts. Use clean brake fluid, brake cleaner or denatured alcohol only!*

Note: *If you are removing the caliper only to replace or inspect the brake pads, don't disconnect the hose from the caliper.*

Removal

1   **Note:** *If you're planning to overhaul the caliper and don't have a source of compressed air to blow out the piston, leave the brake hose connected and use the bike's hydraulic system instead as described in Step 7.* Remove the brake hose banjo fitting bolt and separate the hose from the caliper **(see illustration 3.2 or 3.3)**. Discard the sealing washers. Plug the end of the hose or wrap a plastic bag tightly around it and secure the bag with a rubber band to prevent excessive fluid loss and contamination.

1999 Touring models

2   Remove the caliper mounting bolts and take the caliper off the fork leg **(see illustration)**.

Softail FLSTS models

3   Remove the clip from the upper caliper mounting bolt, then unscrew both mounting bolts and take the caliper off the fork leg **(see illustration)**.

2.46a Remove the pad pins completely . . .

2.46b . . . then remove the outer pad, noting which way it faces

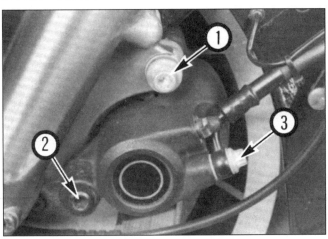

3.2 Single-piston front caliper mounting details (1999 Touring models)

| 1 | Caliper mounting bolt | 3 | Brake hose banjo fitting |
| 2 | Caliper mounting pin | | bolt |

3.3 Single-piston front caliper mounting details (Softail FLSTS)

| 1 | Upper mounting bolt | 3 | Brake hose banjo fitting |
| 2 | Lower mounting bolt | | bolt |

Softail FXSTS models

4   Remove the cotter pins from the reaction link stud on the right fork leg and from the reaction link screw.

5   Remove the nuts, washers and screw and remove the reaction link.

6   Remove the cotter pin and washer that secure the upper mounting bolt, then unscrew the bolt. Unscrew the lower mounting bolt, rock the caliper to move the pads away from the disc, then lift the caliper off.

All single-piston front calipers

7   If you're planning to overhaul the caliper and don't have a source of compressed air to blow out the piston, use the bike's hydraulic system instead. To do this, remove the pads and caliper as described in this Section and Section 2, leaving the brake hose connected. Operate the brake lever to force the piston out of the cylinder.

Caution: Brake fluid will run out of the caliper if you remove the piston(s) in this manner. Try to keep it off of the bike by holding the caliper over a pan. Be sure to

3.14 Clean and lubricate the pin and bushing surfaces (arrows)

wipe any spilled fluid off painted or plastic surfaces immediately and clean the area with soap and water.

Overhaul

8   Remove the brake pads from the caliper (see Section 2, if necessary).

9   Clean the exterior of the caliper with denatured alcohol or brake system cleaner.

10   If you didn't force out the piston with the bike's hydraulic system in Step 7, place a few rags between the piston and the caliper frame to act as a cushion, then use compressed air, directed into the fluid inlet, to remove the piston. Use only enough air pressure to ease the piston out of the bore. If a piston is blown out, even with the cushion in place, it may be damaged.

⚠️ *Warning: Never place your fingers in front of the piston in an attempt to catch or protect it when applying compressed air, as serious injury could occur.*

11   Using a wood or plastic tool, remove the dust seal. Metal tools may cause bore damage.

12   Using a wood or plastic tool, remove the piston seal from the groove in the caliper bore.

13   Clean the piston and the bore with denatured alcohol or brake system cleaner and blow dry them with filtered, unlubricated compressed air. Inspect the surface of the piston for nicks and burrs and loss of plating. Check the caliper bore, too. If surface defects are present, the caliper must be replaced. If the caliper is in bad shape, the master cylinder should also be checked.

14   Check the guide pin and lower mounting pin for burrs or excessive wear **(see illustration)**. Also check the pin bores in the caliper for wear and scoring. Replace the caliper bracket, caliper or pins if necessary.

15   **Note:** *Harley caliper kits come with the correct lubricants for assembling the caliper,*

moly-based grease for the pin and bushing and silicone grease for the caliper bore.

16   Coat new O-rings with the moly grease from the repair kit (Dow Corning 44 or equivalent). Install one O-ring in the guide pin bore and two O-rings in the lower pin bore. Seat the O-rings in their grooves.

17   Lubricate the inside of the guide pin boot with moly grease, then install the flanged end of the boot in its groove in the caliper guide pin bore.

18   Install the new piston seal in its groove in the caliper bore (don't lubricate it yet). Make sure it seats completely and isn't twisted.

19   Install the dust boot on the piston so its concave side will face the caliper when the piston is installed. Seat the dust boot securely in the piston groove.

20   Lightly coat the outside of the piston with silicone grease (GE Versilube G322L, supplied in the Harley overhaul kit, or the equivalent). Lightly coat the caliper bore and piston seal with the same grease. Push the piston all the way into the caliper bore, using a C-clamp if necessary. Once the piston is fully seated, install the outer edge of the dust boot in its groove in the caliper. Secure the dust boot with the wire retainer ring, positioning the gap of the retainer ring towards the top of the caliper.

21   Lubricate the guide pin bore and lower mounting pin bore in the caliper with moly grease. Lubricate the outside of the guide pin with moly grease, then push it into the boot and the pin bore in the caliper. Push the guide pin in until its boot seats in the groove of the guide pin located next to the guide pin flange.

22   Refer to Section 2 and install the pads in the caliper.

Installation

23   Lubricate the outside of the lower mounting pin with moly grease.

6

3.25 Single-piston upper mounting bolt bushing flanged head (A) and rivet (B)

4.2 The rear brake caliper is attached to the bracket and slides on two mounting (pin) bolts (arrows)

1999 Touring models

24   Make sure the caliper mounting bushings are in position in the fork leg.

25   Place the caliper and pads in position over the brake disc. Make sure the guide pin flange fits under the head of the rivet in the brake pad holder, with one of the cutouts in the flange aligned with the body of the rivet (see illustration).

26   Align the lower mounting pin holes, install the pin and tighten it to the torque listed in this Chapter's Specifications.

27   Align the upper mounting screw holes, install the upper mounting screw and tighten to the torque listed in this Chapter's Specifications.

28   Connect the brake hose to the caliper (if it was disconnected), using new sealing washers.

29   Install the bleed valve (if it was removed).

30   Refer to Section 11 and bleed the brakes.

31   Before riding the motorcycle, operate the front brake lever several times to seat the pads and position the caliper.

4   **Single-piston rear brake calipers - removal, overhaul and installation**

⚠ *Warning: If a caliper indicates the need for an overhaul (usually due to leaking fluid or sticky operation), all old brake fluid should be flushed from the system. Also, the dust created by the brake system may contain asbestos, which is harmful to your health. Never blow it out with compressed air and don't inhale any of it. An approved filtering mask should be worn when working on the brakes. Do not, under any circumstances, use petroleum-based solvents to clean brake parts. Use clean brake fluid, brake cleaner or denatured alcohol only!*

Note: *If you are removing the caliper only to*

replace or inspect the brake pads, don't disconnect the hose from the caliper.

Removal

1   Remove the right saddlebag (see Chapter 7).

2   **Note:** *If you're planning to overhaul the caliper and don't have a source of compressed air to blow out the piston, leave the brake hose connected and use the bike's hydraulic system instead as described in Step 4.* Remove the brake hose banjo fitting bolt and separate the hose from the caliper (see illustration). Discard the sealing washers. Plug the end of the hose or wrap a plastic bag tightly around it and secure the bag with a rubber band to prevent excessive fluid loss and contamination.

3   Remove the caliper mounting bolts and take the caliper off the fork leg (see illustration 4.2).

4   If you're planning to overhaul the caliper and don't have a source of compressed air to blow out the piston, use the bike's hydraulic system instead. To do this, remove the caliper and pads as described in this Section and Section 2, leaving the brake hose connected. Operate the brake lever to force the piston out of the cylinder.

Caution: Brake fluid will run out of the caliper if you remove the piston in this manner. Try to keep it off of the bike by holding the caliper over a pan. Be sure to wipe any spilled fluid off painted or plastic surfaces immediately and clean the area with soap and water.

Overhaul

5   Clean the exterior of the caliper with denatured alcohol or brake system cleaner.

6   Remove the wire retainer ring from the caliper bore.

7   If you didn't force out the piston with the bike's hydraulic system in Step 7, place a few rags or a block of wood on the ground to act as a cushion, then use compressed air, directed into the fluid inlet, to remove the piston. Use only enough air pressure to ease

the piston out of the bore. If a piston is blown out, even with the cushion in place, it may be damaged.

⚠ *Warning: Never place your fingers in front of the piston in an attempt to catch or protect it when applying compressed air, as serious injury could occur.*

8   Using a wood or plastic tool, remove the dust seal. Metal tools may cause bore damage.

9   Using a wood or plastic tool, remove the piston seal from the groove in the caliper bore.

10   Clean the piston and the bore with denatured alcohol or brake system cleaner and blow dry them with filtered, unlubricated compressed air. Inspect the surface of the piston for nicks and burrs and loss of plating. Check the caliper bore, too. If surface defects are present, the caliper must be replaced. If the caliper is in bad shape, the master cylinder should also be checked.

11   **Note:** *Harley caliper kits come with the correct lubricants for assembling the caliper, moly-based grease for the pin and bushing and silicone grease for the caliper bore.*

12   Install the new piston seal in its groove in the caliper bore (don't lubricate it yet). Make sure it seats completely and isn't twisted.

13   Install the dust boot on the piston so its concave side will face the caliper when the piston is installed. Seat the dust boot securely in the piston groove.

14   Lightly coat the outside of the piston with silicone grease (GE Versilube G322L, supplied in the Harley overhaul kit, or the equivalent). Lightly coat the caliper bore and piston seal with the same grease. Push the piston all the way into the caliper bore, using a C-clamp if necessary. Once the piston is fully seated, install the outer edge of the dust boot in its groove in the caliper. Secure the dust boot with the wire retainer ring, positioning the gap of the retainer ring towards the top of the caliper.

Installation

15   Place the caliper in position over the pads and brake disc. Align the mounting holes, install the pins and tighten them to the torque listed in this Chapter's Specifications.

16   Connect the brake hose to the caliper (if it was disconnected), using new sealing washers.

17   Install the bleed valve (if it was removed).

18   Refer to Section 11 and bleed the brakes.

19   Before riding the motorcycle, operate the rear brake pedal several times to seat the pads and position the caliper.

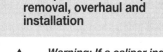

5   Four-piston front calipers - removal, overhaul and installation

5.1 Remove the banjo fitting bolt; use new sealing washers (arrows) on installation

5.3 This is the JIMS special tool used for caliper piston removal

Warning: If a caliper indicates the need for an overhaul (usually due to leaking fluid or sticky operation), all old brake fluid should be flushed from the system. Also, the dust created by the brake system may contain asbestos, which is harmful to your health. Never blow it out with compressed air and don't inhale any of it. An approved filtering mask should be worn when working on the brakes. Do not, under any circumstances, use petroleum-based solvents to clean brake parts. Use clean brake fluid, brake cleaner or denatured alcohol only!

Note: *If you are removing the caliper only to replace or inspect the brake pads, don't disconnect the hose from the caliper.*

Removal

1   **Note:** *If you're planning to overhaul the caliper and don't have a source of compressed air to blow out the piston, leave the brake hose connected and use the bike's hydraulic system instead as described in Step 3. Remove the brake hose banjo fitting bolt and separate the hose from the caliper* **(see illustration)**. Discard the sealing wash-

ers. Plug the end of the hose or wrap a plastic bag tightly around it and secure the bag with a rubber band to prevent excessive fluid loss and contamination.

2   Remove the caliper mounting bolts and take the caliper off the fork leg **(see illustration 2.28a or 2.28b)**.

3   If you're planning to overhaul the caliper and don't have a source of compressed air to blow out the piston, use the bike's hydraulic system instead. To do this, remove the pads and caliper as described in this Section and Section 2, leaving the brake hose connected. Operate the brake lever to force the pistons out of the cylinder. Block two pistons in the brake pad cavity, then push the remaining pistons almost all the way out. There's a special JIMS tool designed for this purpose **(see illustration)**. You can also place a block of wood in the brake pad cavity between two opposing pistons, then push the remaining pistons almost all the way out. Use a C-clamp to retain the piston that starts out first while you pop out the other one, then switch the block of wood to the other two pistons and remove them in the same manner. Remove the wood, then operate the brake lever to push the other pistons all the way out.

Caution: Brake fluid will run out of the caliper if you remove the pistons in this manner. Try to keep it off of the bike by holding the caliper over a pan. Be sure to wipe any spilled fluid off painted or plastic surfaces immediately and clean the area with soap and water.

Overhaul

4   Remove the brake pads from the caliper (see Section 2, if necessary).

5   Clean the exterior of the caliper with denatured alcohol or brake system cleaner.

6   If you didn't force out the piston with the bike's hydraulic system in Step 7, place a block of wood between the pistons to act as a cushion, then use compressed air, directed into the fluid inlet, to remove the pistons **(see illustration)**. Use only enough air pressure to ease the pistons out of the bore. If a piston is blown out, even with the wood in place, it may be damaged.

Warning: Never place your fingers in front of a piston in an attempt to catch or protect it when applying compressed air, as serious injury could occur.

7   Remove the caliper bridge bolts and separate the caliper halves **(see illustrations)**.

5.6 Gently blow low-pressure compressed air into the fluid outlet to push the pistons out

5.7a Remove the caliper bridge bolts (arrows) . . .

6

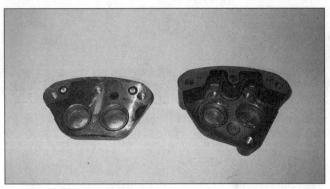

5.7b . . . and separate the caliper halves

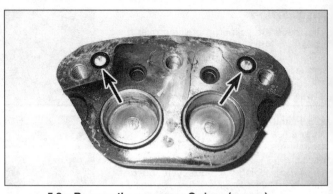

5.8a Remove the crossover O-rings (arrows) . . .

8   Using a wood or plastic tool, remove the crossover O-rings, dust seals and piston seals from the caliper bores **(see illustrations)**. Metal tools may cause bore damage.

9   Clean the pistons and bores with denatured alcohol or brake system cleaner and blow dry them with filtered, unlubricated compressed air. Inspect the surface of the piston for nicks and burrs and loss of plating. Check the caliper bore, too. If surface defects are present, the caliper must be replaced. If the caliper is in bad shape, the master cylinder should also be checked.

10   **Note:** *Harley caliper kits come with the correct lubricant for assembling the caliper,*

silicone grease for the piston. Apply it to the piston during assembly. Assemble all other parts without lubricant. Install the new piston seals in their grooves in the caliper bores (don't lubricate them). Make sure they seat completely and aren't twisted.

11   Install the dust boots, again without lubrication, in the grooves in the caliper bores.

12   Lightly coat the outside of the piston with silicone grease (GE Versilube G322L, supplied in the Harley-Davidson overhaul kit, or the equivalent). Lightly coat the caliper bore and seals with the same grease **(see illustration)**. Start the pistons into their

bores, making sure they're not tilted **(see illustration)**. Push each piston all the way into the caliper bore, using a C-clamp if necessary **(see illustrations)**. **Note:** *If the pistons are difficult to install, make sure the seals haven't slipped out of their bores.*

13   If the bleed valve was removed, install it **(see illustration)**. Install the anti-rattle clip in the outer caliper housing **(see illustration 5.12d)**.

14   Install two new crossover O-rings in their grooves in the caliper housing **(see illustration 5.12c)**.

15   Assemble the caliper halves, installing the bridge bolts loosely. Verify that the anti-rattle clip is still in position, then tighten the bridge bolts to the torque listed in this Chapter's Specifications.

16   Refer to Section 2 and install the pads in the caliper.

Installation

17   If you're working on a dual-caliper Dyna model, align the calipers. Start by making sure the axle nut is tightened to the torque listed in this Chapter's Specifications, then loosen the axle pinch bolts and nuts. Insert the shank end of a 7/16-inch drill bit as far as it will go into the axle hole. While holding the edge of the fork leg against the drill bit, tighten the pinch bolts and nuts to the torque listed in this Chapter's Specifications.

18   Place the caliper and pads in position over the brake disc, with the bleed valve upward. Loosely install the upper (long) mounting bolt. Install the bottom (short)

5.8b . . . and remove the piston and dust seals from their grooves

5.12a Lubricate the bores with the specified grease AFTER installing the seals without lubrication

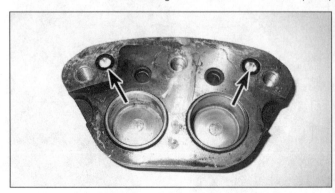

5.12b Make sure the pistons are squarely aligned with their bores . . .

5.12c . . . then push them all the way into the inner half and install the crossover O-rings (arrows) . . .

5.12d . . . and the outer half, then install the anti-rattle clip (arrow)

5.13 If the bleed valve was removed (arrow), install it

mounting bolt and tighten it to the torque listed in this Chapter's Specifications. Tighten the upper mounting bolt to the torque listed in this Chapter's Specifications.

19   Connect the brake hose to the caliper (if it was disconnected), using new sealing washers.

20   Install the bleed valve (if not already done).

21   Refer to Section 11 and bleed the brakes.

22   Before riding the motorcycle, operate the front brake lever several times to seat the pads and position the caliper.

6   Four-piston rear caliper - removal, overhaul and installation

⚠️ *Warning: If a caliper indicates the need for an overhaul (usually due to leaking fluid or sticky operation), all old brake fluid should be flushed from the system. Also, the dust created by the brake system may contain asbestos, which is harmful to your health. Never blow it out with compressed air and don't inhale any of it. An approved filtering mask should be worn when working on the brakes. Do not, under any circumstances, use petroleum-based solvents to clean brake parts. Use clean brake fluid, brake cleaner or denatured alcohol only!*

Note: *If you are removing the caliper only to replace or inspect the brake pads, don't disconnect the hose from the caliper.*

Removal

1   **Note:** *If you're planning to overhaul the caliper and don't have a source of compressed air to blow out the piston, leave the brake hose connected and use the bike's hydraulic system instead as described in Step 4.* Remove the brake hose banjo fitting bolt and separate the hose from the caliper **(see illustrations 2.40a, 2.40b and the accompanying illustration)**. Discard the sealing washers. Plug the end of the hose or wrap a plastic bag tightly around it and secure the bag with a rubber band to prevent excessive fluid loss and contamination.

2   If you're working on a Touring model, support the rear of the bike securely with the rear wheel off the ground. Remove the saddlebags and the right muffler (see Chapters 7 and 3).

3   On Softail and Dyna models equipped with saddlebags, remove the right saddlebag (see Chapter 7).

4   If you're working on a Softail or Dyna, remove the rear axle far enough to clear the caliper **(see illustration)**. Lift the caliper off the bike.

5   If you're working on a Touring model, remove the rear axle. Roll out the wheel to slide the brake disc out from between the pads. Remove the caliper mounting bolts and take the caliper off the bike.

6   If you're planning to overhaul the caliper and don't have a source of compressed air to blow out the piston, use the bike's hydraulic system instead. To do this, remove the pads and caliper as described in this Section and Section 2, leaving the brake hose connected. Operate the brake lever to force the pistons out of the cylinder. Block two pistons in the brake pad cavity, then push the remaining pistons almost all the way out. There's a special JIMS tool designed for this purpose **(see illustration 5.3)**. You can also place a block of wood between two opposing pistons, use a C-clamp to retain the piston that starts out first while you pop out the other one, then switch the block of wood to the other two pistons and remove them in the same manner. Remove the wood, then operate the brake lever to push the other pistons all the way out.

Caution: Brake fluid will run out of the caliper if you remove the pistons in this manner. Try to keep it off the bike by holding the caliper over a pan. Be sure to wipe any spilled fluid off painted or plastic surfaces immediately and clean the area with soap and water.

Overhaul

7   Remove the brake pads from the caliper (see Section 2, if necessary).

8   Clean the exterior of the caliper with denatured alcohol or brake system cleaner.

9   If you didn't force out the piston with the bike's hydraulic system in Step 7, place a block of wood between the pistons to act as

6.1 Remove the banjo fitting bolt; use new sealing washers (arrows) on installation

6.4 Pull the rear axle out far enough to clear the caliper bracket (arrow)

6

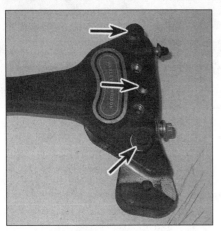

6.10 Remove the caliper bridge bolts (arrows)

6.12 On Softail and Dyna models, be sure the caliper notch is over the tab (arrow) on the swingarm

7.4 The minimum thickness is stamped in the disc (left arrow); on dual-disc models, the word LEFT or RIGHT is stamped below the patent number (right arrow)

a cushion, then use compressed air, directed into the fluid inlet, to remove the pistons **(see illustration 5.6)**. Use only enough air pressure to ease the pistons out of the bore. If a piston is blown out, even with the wood in place, it may be damaged.

 Warning: Never place your fingers in front of a piston in an attempt to catch or protect it when applying compressed air, as serious injury could occur.

10   Remove the caliper bridge bolts and separate the caliper halves **(see illustration)**.
11   Refer to Steps 7 through 16 in Section 5 to complete overhaul and assembly of the caliper.

Installation

12   Installation is the reverse of the removal steps, with the following additions:

a) *If you're working on a Softail or Dyna, be sure the caliper notch is inside the tab on the swingarm* **(see illustration)**.
b) *If you're working on a Touring model, position the caliper on the swingarm pad.*

13   Connect the brake hose to the caliper (if it was disconnected), using new sealing washers.
14   Install the bleed valve (if it was removed).
15   Refer to Section 11 and bleed the brakes.
16   Before riding the motorcycle, operate the brake pedal several times to seat the pads and position the caliper.

7   Brake disc(s) - inspection, removal and installation

Inspection

1   Prop the bike securely with the front or rear wheel off the ground.

2   Visually inspect the surface of the disc for score marks and other damage. Light scratches are normal after use and won't affect brake operation, but deep grooves and heavy score marks will reduce braking efficiency and accelerate pad wear. If the disc is badly grooved it must be machined or replaced.
3   To check disc runout, mount a dial indicator to a fork leg (front disc) or frame (rear disc) with the plunger on the indicator touching the surface of the disc about 1/2-inch from the outer edge. **Note:** *You may have to remove the muffler or saddlebag to check the rear disc* (see Chapter 3). Slowly turn the wheel and watch the indicator needle, comparing your reading with the limit listed in this Chapter's Specifications. If the runout is greater than allowed, check the hub bearings for play (see Chapter 1). If the bearings are worn, replace them and repeat this check. If the disc runout is still excessive, it will have to be replaced.
4   The disc must not be machined or allowed to wear down to a thickness less than the minimum allowable thickness listed in this Chapter's Specifications. The thickness of the disc can be checked with a micrometer. If the thickness of the disc is less than the minimum allowable, it must be replaced. The minimum thickness is also stamped into the disc **(see illustration)**. On dual-disc models, the word RIGHT or LEFT is stamped below the patent number.

Removal

5   Remove the wheel (see Section 14 or 15).

Caution: Don't lay the wheel down and allow it to rest on the disc - the disc could become warped.

6   Mark the relationship of the disc to the wheel, so it can be installed in the same position. Also make an arrow on the disc indicating the forward rotating direction. Remove the Allen bolts that retain the disc to the wheel **(see illustration)**. Loosen the bolts

a little at a time, in a criss-cross pattern, to avoid distorting the disc.

Installation

7   Position the disc on the wheel, aligning the previously applied matchmarks (if you're reinstalling the original disc). Also make sure the arrow mark is pointing in the forward rotating direction. If you're working on a dual-disc model, make sure the discs marked LEFT and RIGHT are installed on the correct sides of the bike **(see illustration 7.4)**.
8   Apply a non-hardening thread locking compound to the threads of the bolts. Install the bolts, tightening them a little at a time, in a criss-cross pattern, until the torque listed in this Chapter's Specifications is reached. Clean off all grease from the brake disc using acetone or brake system cleaner.
9   Install the wheel and brake caliper(s).
10   Operate the brake lever several times to bring the pads into contact with the disc. Check the operation of the brakes carefully before riding the motorcycle.

7.6 Remove the Allen bolts (arrows) and separate the disc from the hub

8.2 Place a wedge between the handle and bracket (arrow)

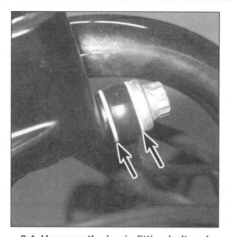

8.4 Unscrew the banjo fitting bolt and remove the sealing washers (arrows)

8.6 Remove the mounting bolts (arrows) and take the master cylinder off the handlebar

8 Front master cylinder - removal and installation

1   If the master cylinder is leaking fluid, or if the lever does not produce a firm feel when the brake is applied, and bleeding the brakes does not help, the master cylinder should be overhauled or replaced with a new one.

Caution: To prevent damage to the paint from spilled brake fluid, always cover the fuel tank when working on the master cylinder.

Removal

2   Before you start, obtain a piece of cardboard 5/32-inch thick and make a shim to go between the brake lever and master cylinder body **(see illustration)**. This is necessary to protect the brake light switch.
3   Loosen, but do not remove, the screws holding the reservoir cap in place.
4   Pull back the rubber boot (if equipped), loosen the banjo fitting bolt **(see illustration)** and separate the brake hose from the master cylinder. Wrap the end of the hose in a clean

rag and suspend the hose in an upright position or bend it down carefully and place the open end in a clean container. The objective is to prevent excess loss of brake fluid, fluid spills and system contamination.
5   Place the cardboard shim in position between the brake lever and master cylinder **(see illustration 8.2)**.
6   Remove the master cylinder mounting bolts **(see illustration)** and separate the master cylinder from the handlebar.

Caution: Do not tip the master cylinder upside down or brake fluid will run out.

7   Disconnect the electrical connectors from the brake light switch.

Installation

8   Installation is the reverse of the removal steps, with the following additions:
a) *Align the notch in the brake lever bracket with the tab on the handlebar switch housing* **(see illustration)**.
b) *Position the brake lever for rider preference, then install the retaining bolts and tighten them to the torque listed in this Chapter's Specifications.*
c) *Connect the brake hose to the master*

cylinder, using new sealing washers. Tighten the banjo fitting bolt to the torque listed in this Chapter's Specifications.
d) *Fill the master cylinder reservoir with fluid and bleed the brake as described in Section 11.*

9 Rear master cylinder - removal and installation

Removal

Softail models

1   Unscrew the banjo fitting bolt **(see illustration)** and separate the brake hose from the master cylinder. Wrap the end of the hose in a clean rag and suspend the hose in an upright position or bend it down carefully and place the open end in a clean container. The objective is to prevent excess loss of brake fluid, fluid spills and system contamination.
2   Unscrew the master cylinder mounting nut **(see illustration)**.

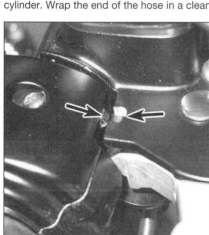

8.8 Align the notch in the bracket with the tab on the throttle housing (arrows)

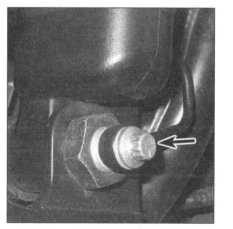

9.1 Unscrew the banjo fitting bolt (arrow) and remove the hose and washers

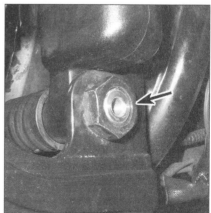

9.2 Unscrew the mounting nut (arrow)

6

9.3 Remove the cotter pin and washer (left arrows), then pull out the clevis pin (right arrow)

9.4 Here's the Dyna rear master cylinder

1	Brake hose banjo fitting bolt	3	Brake rod adjuster
2	Mounting nut	4	Locknut
		5	Brake rod

3   At the front end of the master cylinder, remove the cotter pin, clip and clevis pin **(see illustration)**. Separate the master cylinder from the pedal and take it off the bike.

Dyna models

4   Unscrew the banjo fitting bolt **(see illustration)** and separate the brake hose from the master cylinder. Wrap the end of the hose in a clean rag and suspend the hose in an upright position or bend it down carefully and place the open end in a clean container. The objective is to prevent excess loss of brake fluid, fluid spills and system contamination.
5   Unscrew the master cylinder mounting nut **(see illustration 9.4)**.
6   At the front end of the master cylinder, loosen the locknut on the brake rod **(see illustration 9.4)**. Using the flats on the master cylinder pushrod, unscrew it from the brake rod. Lift the pedal to separate the brake rod from the pushrod, then pull the master cylinder out of the bracket and take it off the bike.

Touring models

7   Remove the lower fairing (if equipped), right front footboard, right saddlebag and right lower cover (see Chapter 7).
8   Unscrew the banjo fitting bolt **(see illustration)** and separate the brake hose from the master cylinder. Wrap the end of the hose in a clean rag and suspend the hose in an upright position or bend it down carefully and place the open end in a clean container. The objective is to prevent excess loss of brake fluid, fluid spills and system contamination.
9   Free the brake line from the frame, cutting tie wraps as necessary, then move the brake line forward so you can get at the large nut that secures the pedal assembly. Unscrew the nut with a 1-1/8-inch socket, remove the locknut and washer and take the pedal/master cylinder assembly off the bike.

10   Remove the O-rings from the pedal bore.
11   Remove the cotter pin, washer and clevis pin and separate the master cylinder from the pedal.

Installation

12   Installation is the reverse of the removal steps, with the following additions:

a)   On Touring models, use a new brake pedal locknut, tightened to the torque listed in this Chapter's Specifications.
b)   Use non-permanent thread locking agent on the threads of the cartridge body nut and tighten it to the torque listed in this Chapter's Specifications.
c)   Use new sealing washers on the brake hose banjo fitting. Tighten the banjo fitting bolt to the torque listed in this Chapter's Specifications.
d)   Lubricate the brake pedal shift with multipurpose grease.

13   Refer to Section 11 and bleed the air from the system.
14   Operate the brake pedal and make sure the brake works correctly before riding the motorcycle.

9.8 Here's the Touring model rear master cylinder (arrow)

10 Brake hoses and lines - inspection and replacement

Inspection

1   Once a week, or if the motorcycle is used less frequently, before every ride, check the condition of the brake hose.
2   Twist and flex the rubber hose while looking for cracks, bulges and seeping fluid. Check extra carefully around the areas where the hose connects to the banjo fittings, as these are common areas for hose failure.

Replacement

3   Each brake hose has banjo fittings on each end. Cover the surrounding area with plenty of rags and unscrew the banjo bolts on either end of the hose. Remove any retainers that secure the hose to other components, detach the hose from the clips and remove the hose.
4   Position the new hose, making sure it isn't twisted or otherwise strained, between the two components. Install the banjo bolts, using new sealing washers on both sides of the fittings, and tighten them to the torque listed in this Chapter's Specifications.
5   Flush the old brake fluid from the system, refill the system with the recommended fluid (see Chapter 1) and bleed the air from the system (see Section 11). Check the operation of the brakes carefully before riding the motorcycle.

11 Brake system bleeding

1   Bleeding the brake is simply the process of removing all the air bubbles from the brake fluid reservoir, the hose and the brake

caliper. Bleeding is necessary whenever a brake system hydraulic connection is loosened, when a component or hose is replaced, or when the master cylinder or caliper is overhauled. Leaks in the system may also allow air to enter, but leaking brake fluid will reveal their presence and warn you of the need for repair.

2   To bleed the brake, you will need some new, clean brake fluid of the recommended type (see Chapter 1), a length of clear vinyl or plastic tubing, a small container partially filled with clean brake fluid, some rags and a wrench to fit the brake caliper bleed valve.

3   Cover the fuel tank and other painted components to prevent damage in the event that brake fluid is spilled.

4   Remove the reservoir cap and slowly pump the brake lever a few times, until no air bubbles can be seen floating up from the holes at the bottom of the reservoir. Doing this bleeds the air from the master cylinder end of the line. Reinstall the reservoir cap.

5   Attach one end of the clear vinyl or plastic tubing to the brake caliper bleeder valve and submerge the other end in the brake fluid in the container **(see illustrations)**.

6   Remove the reservoir cap and check the fluid level. Do not allow the fluid level to drop below the lower mark during the bleeding process.

7   Carefully pump the brake lever three or four times and hold it while opening the caliper bleeder valve. When the valve is opened, brake fluid will flow out of the caliper into the clear tubing and the lever will move toward the handlebar.

8   Retighten the bleeder valve, then release the brake lever gradually. Repeat the process until no air bubbles are visible in the brake fluid leaving the caliper and the lever is firm when applied. Remember to add fluid to the reservoir as the level drops. Use only new, clean brake fluid of the recommended type. Never reuse the fluid lost during bleeding; it absorbs moisture from the air, which

11.5a Here's the bleed valve (arrow) on a four-piston front caliper (rear caliper similar)

can lead to brake failure.

9   Replace the reservoir cap, wipe up any spilled brake fluid and check the entire system for leaks. **Note:** *If bleeding is difficult, it may be necessary to let the brake fluid in the system stabilize for a few hours (it may be aerated). Repeat the bleeding procedure when the tiny bubbles in the system have settled out.*

10   If you're working on a rear caliper, repeat the procedure for the other bleed valve.

12 Brake pedal (Softail and Dyna models) - removal and installation

Note: *The brake pedal on Touring models is removed together with the master cylinder (see Section 10).*

1   Place the motorcycle on its sidestand. Remove exhaust system and body components as necessary for access (see Chapters 3 and 7).

11.5b Here's the bleed valve (arrow) on a single-piston front caliper (rear caliper similar)

Softail models

2   Remove the right footboard (see Chapter 7).

3   Remove the cotter pin, washer and clevis pin and detach the brake rod from the pedal **(see illustration 9.3)**.

4   Remove the pedal bolt, washer and O-ring **(see illustration)**.

5   Slip the pedal off the shaft. Remove the bushings and inner O-ring.

6   Installation is the reverse of the removal steps. On 2000 and 2001 models, lubricate the bushings with multi-purpose grease through the grease nipple. On 2002 and later models, the bushings are permanently lubricated. Replace them if they're worn or damaged.

Dyna models

7   Remove the cotter pin, washer and clevis pin and detach the brake rod from the pedal **(see illustration)**.

8   If you're working on a 1999 through 2002 FXDWG, remove the pedal nut and outer washer. Sip the pedal off the shaft and

12.4 On Softail models, remove the pedal bolt and washer (arrow), then slip the pedal off

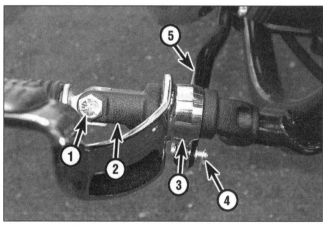

12.7 Rear brake pedal details (2003 Dyna FXDWG models)

1   Footpeg pivot bolt
2   Footpeg bracket
3   Pedal
4   Cotter pin
5   Brake rod

6

remove the inner washer.

9   If you're working on a 2003 FXDWG, remove the footpeg pivot bolt and take off the footpeg (see illustration 12.7). Insert a socket into the footpeg bracket and unscrew the footpeg bracket bolt. Pull off the footpeg bracket and pedal.

10   If you're working on any Dyna model except FXDWG, remove the snap-ring that retains the pedal. Slip the pedal off the shaft and remove the wave washer.

11   Installation is the reverse of the removal steps, with the following additions:

   a) Lubricate the pedal shaft with multi-pur-pose grease.
   b) Tighten the pedal nut (if equipped) to the torque listed in this Chapter's Spec-ifications.
   c) If the bike uses a snap-ring to retain the pedal, install a new one.
   d) Check brake pedal height and adjust if desired (see Chapter 1).

13 Wheels - inspection, repair and alignment check

Inspection and repair

1   Clean the wheels thoroughly to remove mud and dirt that may interfere with the inspection procedure or mask defects. Make a general check of the wheels and tires as described in Chapter 1.

2   Jack the bike up and support it so the wheel you're inspecting is off the ground. With the wheel in the air, attach a dial indica-tor to the fork slider or the swingarm and position the pointer against the side of the rim. Spin the wheel slowly and check the side-to-side (axial) runout of the rim, then compare your readings with the value listed in this Chapter's Specifications. In order to accurately check radial runout with the dial indicator, the wheel would have to be removed from the machine and the tire removed from the wheel. With the axle clamped in a vise, the wheel can be rotated to check the runout.

3   An easier, though slightly less accurate, method is to attach a stiff wire pointer to the fork slider or the swingarm and position the end a fraction of an inch from the wheel (where the wheel and tire join). If the wheel is true, the distance from the pointer to the rim will be constant as the wheel is rotated. Repeat the procedure to check the runout of the rear wheel. Note: If wheel runout is excessive, refer to the appropriate Section in this Chapter and check the wheel bearings very carefully before replacing the wheel. If you're checking a wire wheel, it may be pos-sible to true it by adjusting spoke tension. This is a job for a dealer service department or other qualified shop.

4   The wheels should also be visually inspected for cracks, flat spots on the rim and other damage. Since cast wheels use

tubeless tires, look very closely for dents in the area where the tire bead contacts the rim. Dents in this area may prevent complete sealing of the tire against the rim, which leads to deflation of the tire over a period of time.

5   If damage is evident, or if runout in either direction is excessive, the wheel will have to be replaced with a new one. Never attempt to repair a damaged wheel.

Alignment check

6   Misalignment of the wheels, which may be due to a cocked rear wheel or a bent frame or triple clamps, can cause strange and possibly serious handling problems. If the frame or triple clamps are at fault, repair by a frame specialist or replacement with new parts are the only alternatives.

7   To check the alignment you will need an assistant, a length of string or a perfectly straight piece of wood and a ruler graduated in 1/64 inch increments. A plumb bob or other suitable weight will also be required.

8   Prop the motorcycle straight upright, then measure the width of both tires at their widest points. Subtract the smaller measure-ment from the larger measurement, then divide the difference by two. The result is the amount of offset that should exist between the front and rear tires on both sides.

9   If a string is used, have your assistant hold one end of it about half way between the floor and the rear axle, touching the rear sidewall of the tire.

10   Run the other end of the string forward and pull it tight so that it is roughly parallel to the floor. Slowly bring the string into contact with the front sidewall of the rear tire, then turn the front wheel until it is parallel with the string. Measure the distance from the front tire sidewall to the string.

11   Repeat the procedure on the other side of the motorcycle. The distance from the front tire sidewall to the string should be equal on both sides.

12   As was previously pointed out, a per-fectly straight length of wood may be substi-tuted for the string. The procedure is the same.

13   If the distance between the string and tire is greater on one side, or if the rear wheel appears to be cocked, refer to Chapter 6, Swingarm bearings - check, and make sure the swingarm is tight. Also refer to the chain adjustment procedure in Chapter 1 and make sure the adjusters are set evenly.

14   If the front-to-back alignment is correct, the wheels still may be out of alignment verti-cally.

15   Using the plumb bob, or other suitable weight, and a length of string, check the rear wheel to make sure it is vertical. To do this, hold the string against the tire upper sidewall and allow the weight to settle just off the floor. When the string touches both the upper and lower tire sidewalls and is per-fectly straight, the wheel is vertical. If it is not, place thin spacers under one leg of the cen-

14.3a Insert a punch or screwdriver into the hole (arrow) and use it to keep the axle from turning . . .

terstand.

16   Once the rear wheel is vertical, check the front wheel in the same manner. If both wheels are not perfectly vertical, the frame and/or major suspension components are bent.

14 Front wheel - removal, inspection and installation

Removal

1   Support the bike securely so it can't be knocked over during this procedure. Raise the front wheel off the ground by jacking up the frame.

All except Softail Springer models

2   Remove the front brake caliper(s) (see Section 3 or 5).

3   Slip a punch or screwdriver shaft into the hole in the axle (see illustration). Use this to keep the axle from turning while you unscrew the nut from the other end (see illus-tration).

4   Loosen the axle pinch bolt or clamp nuts (see illustration).

5   Support the wheel, then use the punch or similar tool in the axle hole as a handle to pull the axle out. Remove the spacers (and the speedometer drive unit on 1999 Touring models).

6   Carefully lower the wheel away from the bike.

Caution: Don't lay the wheel down and allow it to rest on a disc - the disc could become warped. Set the wheel on wood blocks so the disc doesn't support the weight of the wheel. If the axle is corroded, remove the corrosion with fine emery cloth.

Note: Do not operate the front brake lever with the wheel removed. To prevent acciden-tal operation of the brake, slip a piece of wood between the brake pads.

14.3b . . . while you unscrew the nut on the other end

1   Nut   3   Bearing spacer
2   Washer

14.4 Unscrew the clamp nuts (shown) or pinch bolt, then pull the axle out

Softail Springer models

7   Carefully remove the hub caps and their seals **(see illustrations)**.

8   Remove the clip from the left end of the axle.

9   Hold the axle bolt (on the right side of the bike) with a wrench and unscrew the axle nut from the left side.

9   Support the wheel, then use the punch or similar tool in the axle hole as a handle to pull the axle out. Remove the spacers.

10   Carefully lower the wheel away from the bike.

Caution: Don't lay the wheel down and allow it to rest on a disc - the disc could become warped. Set the wheel on wood blocks so the disc doesn't support the weight of the wheel. If the axle is corroded, remove the corrosion with fine emery cloth.

Note: *Do not operate the front brake lever with the wheel removed. To prevent accidental operation of the brake, slip a piece of wood between the brake pads.*

Inspection

11   Check the axle for straightness by rolling it on a flat surface such as a piece of glass. If it's bent, replace it (do not try to straighten a bent axle).

12   Check the condition of the wheel bearings (see Section 16).

Installation

13   Installation is the reverse of removal, with the following additions:

a)   *Apply a thin coat of grease (Loctite anti-seize or equivalent) to the axle.*

b)   *Make sure the spacers are in the correct positions on either side of the hub.*

c)   *If you're working on a 1999 Touring model with a mechanical speedometer, position the speedometer drive unit and felt seal in place in the left side of the hub. Make sure the notches in the speedometer drive assembly in the wheel line up with the lugs in the drive unit (see Chapter 8).*

d)   *Slip the axle into place, then tighten the axle nut to the torque listed in this Chapter's Specifications.*

e)   *If you're working on a motorcycle with dual front brake calipers, align the calipers to the brake discs. To do this, loosen the axle clamp nuts and slip the shank end of a 7/16-inch drill bit into the axle removal hole. Pull the fork leg against the drill bit.*

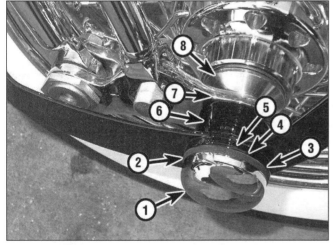

14.7a Springer FLSTS right side axle details

1   Hub cap   5   O-ring
2   Seal   6   Fender support
3   Spacer   7   Rocker
4   Nylon insert   8   Bearing spacer

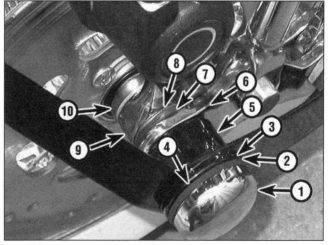

14.7b Springer FLSTS left side axle details

1   Hub cap (clip, castle nut   6   Rocker
     and spacer inside)   7   Rubber spacer
2   Seal   8   Washer
3   Nylon insert   9   Caliper support bracket
4   O-ring   and bushing
5   Fender support   10   Bearing spacer

6

14.13 Keep the clamp gap even on both sides (arrows) and don't try to close it by overtightening the nuts

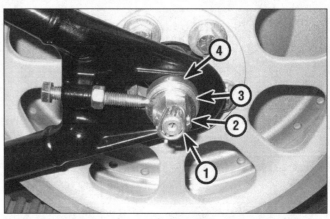

15.6a On Softail models, remove the spring clip from the end of the axle and back the drivebelt adjuster out of the collar notch

1	Spring clip	3	Washer
2	Nut	4	Adjuster collar

f) *Tighten the right side axle clamp bolts or nut to the torque listed in this Chapter's Specifications. Don't try to close the axle clamp gap* **(see illustration)**. *The gap should be even on both sides of the axle. If you're working on a dual-caliper model, pull out the drill bit used to align the calipers.*

g) *On Softail Springer models, use a new clip in the end of the axle.*

14 Apply the front brake, pump the forks up and down several times and check for binding and proper brake operation.

15 Rear wheel - removal, inspection and installation

Removal

1 If you're working on a Touring model, remove the right muffler (see Chapter 3).
2 If necessary for access, remove the right saddlebag (see Chapter 7).
3 If you're working on a Softail, remove the rear brake pads (see Section 2).
4 If you're working on a Dyna, loosen the upper shock absorber bolts, remove the lower shock absorber bolts and pivot the shocks out of the way (see Chapter 5).
5 Loosen the drivebelt and remove the drivebelt guard (see Chapters 1 and 5).
6 Remove the spring clip from the axle nut and loosen the nut **(see illustrations)**.
7 Support the bike securely so it can't be knocked over during this procedure. Raise the rear wheel off the ground by placing a floor jack, with a wood block on the jack head, under the frame.
8 Remove the axle nut and the washer **(see illustration 15.6a or 15.6b)**.
9 Support the wheel and slide the axle out **(see illustrations)**. Lower the wheel and remove it from the motorcycle, being careful not to lose the spacers on either side of the hub.

Caution: Don't lay the wheel down and allow it to rest on the brake disc - it could

15.6b On Dyna models, remove the spring clip (arrow) from the end of the axle

become warped. Set the wheel on wood blocks so the disc doesn't support the weight of the wheel.

15.9a On Softail models, back the drivebelt adjuster out of the collar notch and hold the axle (arrow) while you unscrew the nut on the other end . . .

15.9b . . . then slide the axle out and remove the spacer from each side

1	Adjuster collar	3	Brake caliper bracket
2	Swingarm	4	Spacer

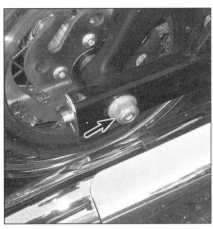

15.9c On Dyna models, hold the axle (arrow) while you unscrew the nut from the other end

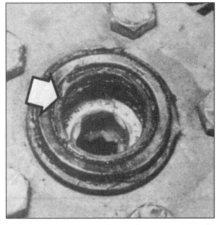

16.6a Pry the wheel bearing grease seal (arrow) out of the hub . . .

16.6b . . . take out the bearing cone from each side (1999 models, tapered roller bearings) . . .

16.6c . . . and remove the inner race

Inspection

10 Before installing the wheel, check the axle for straightness. If the axle is corroded, first remove the corrosion with fine emery cloth. Set the axle on V-blocks and check it for runout using a dial indicator. If the axle exceeds the maximum allowable runout limit listed in this Chapter's Specifications, it must be replaced.
11 Check the condition of the wheel bearings (see Section 16).

Installation

12 Installation is the reverse of the removal steps, with the following additions:
a) *Lightly grease the axle with Loctite Anti-Seize or equivalent.*
b) *Position the wheel with the brake disc in the caliper, then drape the drivebelt over the sprocket.*
c) *Install the axle from the right side, making sure the spacers are in position.*
d) *Tighten all fasteners to the torque listed in this Chapter's Specifications and the Chapter 5 Specifications. If necessary, tighten the axle nut further to align the spring clip holes. Don't loosen the axle nut to align the holes.*
e) *Adjust the drivebelt tension (see Chapter 1).*
f) *Operate the rear brake pedal several times to seat the pads against the disc.*
13 Check the operation of the brakes carefully before riding the motorcycle. It shouldn't be necessary to bleed the rear brake if the hose wasn't disconnected, but verify that the rear brake works and bleed it if necessary.

16 Wheel bearings - inspection and maintenance

1 The front and rear wheels on all except 1999 models use two ball bearings, which are permanently lubricated and sealed on both sides. 1999 models use two tapered roller bearings.
2 Support the bike securely so it can't be knocked over during this procedure. Remove the wheel (see Section 14 or 15).
3 Set the wheel on blocks so as not to allow the weight of the wheel to rest on the brake disc or drive chain sprocket.

Tapered roller bearings (1999 models)

4 If you haven't already done so, remove the speedometer gear housing and collar from models with a mechanical speedometer.
5 Remove the brake disc(s) (see Section 7).
6 Pry out the grease seal from the valve stem side of the wheel and remove the bearing inner race and spacer sleeve **(see illustrations)**.
7 On the opposite side of the wheel, pry out the grease seal and remove the bearing inner race and shim pack. Remove the bearing spacer from the hub.
8 Thoroughly clean the outer races and the inside of the hub with high-flash point solvent and blow them dry with compressed air, if available.
9 Thoroughly clean the bearings with high-flash point solvent and blow them dry with compressed air, if available.

⚠ *Warning: Do not spin the bearings with compressed air. They may fly apart and cause injury.*

10 Check the bearing rollers and outer races for scoring, flaking, pitting, chips, rust and the bluish tint that indicates overheating. Replace the bearings as a set (both bearings, including rollers and outer races) if any of these conditions is found.
11 If the bearing outer races need to be replaced, insert a soft metal drift through the hub and position it against the outer race of the opposite bearing. Tap on the drift with a hammer to drive the outer race out, working around the outer race in a circle as you tap. Insert the drift from the opposite side and drive out the remaining outer race in the same manner.
12 Lubricate new outer races with clean engine oil and drive them into position in the hub.
13 Coat the outer races with high quality wheel bearing grease. Pack the inner races with the same grease, making sure to work the grease into the spaces between the rollers. A bearing packer and grease gun, available from many auto parts stores, will make the job easier.
14 On the side of the wheel opposite the valve stem, install the shim pack, then install the shoulder washer with its shoulder facing outward. Install the bearing inner race against the shoulder washer, then drive in a new grease seal with its open side facing into the hub. The grease seal should be flush with the hub to as much as 0.040-inch recessed when installed. Pack the space between the grease seal and bearing inner race with wheel bearing grease.
15 On the valve stem side of the wheel, install the spacer in the hub, seating it in the bore on the opposite side of the hub. Be sure

6

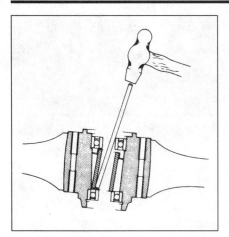

16.17a If there's enough room to tilt a metal rod so it will catch the bearing inner races, drive the bearings from the hub with a metal rod and hammer

16.17b The slotted end of the remover head fits inside the bearing; the wedge end of the remover shaft spreads the head and locks it to the bearing

16.17c Tap the slotted end of the remover head into the bearing

the spacer goes straight in and is not cocked in the bore. Install the bearing inner race against the spacer, then drive in a new grease seal with its open side facing into the hub. The grease seal should be flush with the hub to as much as 0.040-inch recessed when installed. Pack the space between the grease seal and bearing inner race with wheel bearing grease.

16 Insert the hub spacer into the grease seal on the side opposite the valve stem, with its chamfer facing into the hub. If the bike has an electronic speedometer, install the external spacer in the other side, also with its chamfer facing into the hub (models with mechanical speedometers have the speedo drive unit in this space).

Sealed ball bearings (2000 and later models)

17 Insert a brass drift from the right side of the hub and tap evenly around the inner race of the opposite bearing to remove it (see illustration). Remove the bearing spacer, then remove the remaining bearing in the same way. If there isn't room to insert a drift into the hub and push the spacer out of the way so you can catch the edge of the bearing with the drift, use a bearing remover tool. These can be ordered from aftermarket tool suppliers such as K and L supply, or fabricated from readily available hardware (a large bolt and a length of steel rod) (see illustrations). Note: *Bearing removal requires applying force to the unsupported inner race, which may damage the bearings. For this reason, the wheel bearings must be replaced with new ones whenever they're removed.*

18 Thoroughly clean the inside of the hub with high-flash point solvent and blow it out with compressed air, if available.

19 Drive in the new bearings with a bearing driver or a socket the same diameter as the bearing outer race. Don't forget to install the spacer after you've installed the first bearing.

20 The remainder of installation is the

reverse of the removal steps. Install new snap-rings and make sure they seat securely in their grooves.

17 Tubeless tires - general information

1 Tubeless tires are generally safer than tube-type tires but if problems do occur they require special repair techniques.

2 The force required to break the seal between the rim and the bead of the tire is substantial, and is usually beyond the capabilities of an individual working with normal tire irons.

3 Also, repair of the punctured tire and replacement on the wheel rim requires special tools, skills and experience that the average do-it-yourselfer lacks.

4 For these reasons, if a puncture or flat occurs with a tubeless tire, the wheel should be removed from the motorcycle and taken to a dealer service department or a motorcycle repair shop for repair or replacement of the tire.

18 Tube tires - removal and installation

1 To properly remove and install tires, you will need at least two motorcycle tire irons, some water and a tire pressure gauge.

2 Begin by removing the wheel from the motorcycle. If the tire is going to be re-used, mark it next to the valve stem, wheel balance weight or rim lock.

3 Deflate the tire by removing the valve stem core. When it is fully deflated, push the bead of the tire away from the rim on both sides. In some extreme cases, this can only be accomplished with a bead breaking tool, but most often it can be carried out with tire

irons. Riding on a deflated tire to break the bead is not recommended, as damage to the rim and tire will occur.

4 Dismounting a tire is easier when the tire is warm, so an indoor tire change is recommended in cold climates. The rubber gets very stiff and is difficult to manipulate when cold.

5 Place the wheel on a thick pad or old blanket. This will help keep the wheel and tire from slipping around.

6 Once the bead is completely free of the rim, lubricate the inside edge of the rim and the tire bead with soap and water or rubber lubricant (do not use any type of petroleum-based lubricant, as it will cause the tire to deteriorate). Remove the locknut and push the tire valve through the rim.

7 Insert one of the tire irons under the bead of the tire at the valve stem and lift the bead up over the rim. This should be fairly easy. Take care not to pinch the tube as this is done. If it is difficult to pry the bead up, make sure that the rest of the bead opposite the valve stem is in the dropped center section of the rim.

8 Hold the tire iron down with the bead over the rim, then move about 1 or 2 inches to either side and insert the second tire iron. Be careful not to cut or slice the bead or the tire may split when inflated. Also, take care not to catch or pinch the inner tube as the second tire iron is levered over. For this reason, tire irons are recommended over screwdrivers or other implements.

9 With a small section of the bead up over the rim, one of the levers can be removed and reinserted 1 or 2 inches farther around the rim until about 1/4 of the tire bead is above the rim edge. Make sure that the rest of the bead is in the dropped center of the rim. At this point, the bead can usually be pulled up over the rim by hand.

10 Once all of the first bead is over the rim, the inner tube can be withdrawn from the tire and rim. Push in on the valve stem, lift up on the tire next to the stem, reach inside the tire and carefully pull out the tube. It is usually not necessary to completely remove the tire

from the rim to repair the inner tube. It is sometimes recommended though, because checking for foreign objects in the tire is difficult while it is still mounted on the rim.

11   To remove the tire completely, make sure the bead is broken all the way around on the remaining edge, then stand the tire and wheel up on the tread and grab the wheel with one hand. Push the tire down over the same edge of the rim while pulling the rim away from the tire. If the bead is correctly positioned in the dropped center of the rim, the tire should roll off and separate from the rim very easily. If tire irons are used to work this last bead over the rim, the outer edge of the rim may be marred. If a tire iron is necessary, be sure to pad the rim as described earlier.

12   Refer to Section 19 for inner tube repair procedures.

13   Mounting a tire is basically the reverse of removal. Some tires have a balance mark and/or directional arrows molded into the tire sidewall. Look for these marks so that the tire can be installed properly. The dot should be aligned with the valve stem.

14   If the tire was not removed completely to repair or replace the inner tube, the tube should be inflated just enough to make it round. Sprinkle it with talcum powder, which acts as a dry lubricant, then carefully lift up the tire edge and install the tube with the valve stem next to the hole in the rim. Once the tube is in place, push the valve stem through the rim and start the locknut on the stem.

15   Lubricate the tire bead, then push it

over the rim edge and into the dropped center section opposite the inner tube valve stem. Work around each side of the rim, carefully pushing the bead over the rim. The last section may have to be levered on with tire irons. If so, take care not to pinch the inner tube as this is done.

16   Once the bead is over the rim edge, check to see that the inner tube valve stem is pointing to the center of the hub. If it's angled slightly in either direction, rotate the tire on the rim to straighten it out. Run the locknut the rest of the way onto the stem but don't tighten it completely.

17   Inflate the tube to approximately 1-1/2 times the pressure listed in the Chapter 1 Specifications and check to make sure the guidelines on the tire sidewalls are the same distance from the rim around the circumference of the tire.

⚠ **Warning: Do not over inflate the tube or the tire may burst, causing serious injury.**

18   After the tire bead is correctly seated on the rim, allow the tire to deflate. Replace the valve core and inflate the tube to the recommended pressure, then tighten the valve stem locknut securely and tighten the cap.

19 Tubes - repair

1   Tire tube repair requires a patching kit that's usually available from motorcycle

dealers, accessory stores or auto parts stores. Be sure to follow the directions supplied with the kit to ensure a safe repair. Patching should be done only when a new tube is unavailable. Replace the tube as soon as possible. Sudden deflation can cause loss of control and an accident.

2   To repair a tube, remove it from the tire, inflate and immerse it in a sink or tub full of water to pinpoint the leak. Mark the position of the leak, then deflate the tube. Dry it off and thoroughly clean the area around the puncture.

3   Most tire patching kits have a buffer to rough up the area around the hole for proper adhesion of the patch. Roughen an area slightly larger than the patch, then apply a thin coat of the patching cement to the roughened area. Allow the cement to dry until tacky, then apply the patch.

4   It may be necessary to remove a protective covering from the top surface of the patch after it has been attached to the tube. Keep in mind that tubes made from synthetic rubber may require a special patch and adhesive if a satisfactory bond is to be achieved.

5   Before replacing the tube, check the inside of the tire to make sure the object that caused the puncture is not still inside. Also check the outside of the tire, particularly the tread area, to make sure nothing is projecting through the tire that may cause another puncture. Check the rim for sharp edges or damage. Make sure the rubber trim band is in good condition and properly installed before inserting the tube.

6

TIRE CHANGING SEQUENCE - TUBED TIRES

 Deflate tire. After pushing tire beads away from rim flanges push tire bead into well of rim at point opposite valve. Insert tire lever next to valve and work bead over edge of rim.

Use two levers to work bead over edge of rim. Note use of rim protectors

 Remove inner tube from tire

When first bead is clear, remove tire as shown

 To install, partially inflate inner tube and insert in tire

Work first bead over rim and feed valve through hole in rim. Partially screw on retaining nut to hold valve in place.

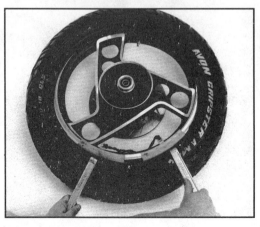

 Check that inner tube is positioned correctly and work second bead over rim using tire levers. Start at a point opposite valve.

Work final area of bead over rim while pushing valve inwards to ensure that inner tube is not trapped.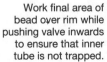

Chapter 7
Frame and bodywork

Contents

Degrees of difficulty

Easy, suitable for novice with little experience		**Fairly easy,** suitable for beginner with some experience		**Fairly difficult,** suitable for competent DIY mechanic		**Difficult,** suitable for experienced DIY mechanic		**Very difficult,** suitable for expert DIY or professional	

Specifications

Jiffy stand (sidestand) pivot bolt
    Softail .... 144 to 180 inch-lbs (16.3 to 20.3 Nm)
    Dyna .... 19 ft-lbs (25.8 Nm)
Jiffy stand (sidestand) pivot nut (Touring models)................................. 43 to 53 ft-lbs (58 to 72 Nm)
Jiffy stand (sidestand) bracket bolts
    Softail .... 25 to 30 ft-lbs (33.9 to 40.7 Nm)
    Dyna and Touring models .... Not specified

7

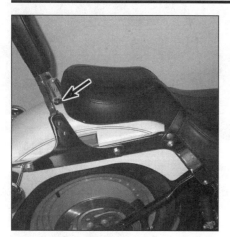

3.1a Remove the thumbscrew at the rear of the seat (arrow) . . .

3.1b . . . disengage the seat strap . . .

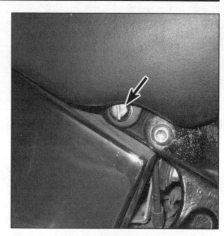

3.1c . . . and remove the screw on each side of the front seat

1 General information

The machines covered by this manual use a backbone frame made of steel tubing. This Chapter covers the procedures necessary to remove and install the saddlebags, windshield, fairing, side covers and other body parts. Since many service and repair operations on these motorcycles require removal of the side covers and/or other body parts, the procedures are grouped here and referred to from other Chapters.

2 Frame - inspection and repair

1   The frame should not require attention unless accident damage has occurred. In most cases, frame replacement is the only satisfactory remedy for such damage. A few frame specialists have the jigs and other equipment necessary for straightening the frame to the required standard of accuracy,

3.3 On some models, you'll need to lift the seat flaps for access to the side screws

but even then there is no simple way of assessing to what extent the frame may have been over stressed.
2   After the machine has accumulated a lot of miles, the frame should be examined closely for signs of cracking or splitting at the welded joints. Rust can also cause weakness at these joints. Loose engine mount bolts can cause ovaling or fracturing of the mounting tabs. Minor damage can often be repaired by welding, depending on the extent and nature of the damage.
3   Remember that a frame which is out of alignment will cause handling problems. If misalignment is suspected as the result of an accident, it will be necessary to strip the machine completely so the frame can be thoroughly checked.

3 Seat - removal and installation

Softail models
FLSTF, FLSTC
1   Remove the thumbscrew at the rear of the passenger seat (see illustration). Disengage the seat strap (see illustration). Unscrew one thumbscrew from each side of the front seat (see illustration). Disengage the tang at the front end of the seat from the slot in the frame and lift the seat off.
2   Installation is the reverse of the removal steps. Install the rear thumbscrew first, then the two side thumbscrews.

FLSTS
3   Remove the thumbscrew at the rear of the passenger seat and pull the seat rearward off of the two mounting nuts that secure the rear edge of the front seat. If necessary for access, lift the saddle flap (see illustration). Remove the mounting nuts at the rear edge of the front seat, disengage the tang at the front end of the seat from the slot in the frame and lift the seat off.

4   Installation is the reverse of the removal steps.

FXSTD
5   Remove the thumbscrew at the rear of the seat. Disengage the tang at the front end of the seat from the slot in the frame and lift the seat off.
6   Installation is the reverse of the removal steps.

Dyna models
7   Remove the thumbscrew at the rear of the seat. Disengage the tang at the front end of the seat from the welded bracket on the frame.
8   Work the seat forward out of the strap and lift it off.
9   Installation is the reverse of the removal steps. Be sure to reinstall the nylon clip in the rear bolt hole, between the fender and the seat bracket.

Touring models
FLHT
10   Remove the screw at the rear of the seat. Disengage the tang at the front end of the seat from the slot in the frame and lift the seat off.
11   Installation is the reverse of the removal steps.

FLHTC and FLHTC/U
12   Open the rear luggage compartment and move the rear seatback for access. If the luggage compartment is installed in the forward position, you'll need to move it to the rear.
13   Remove the screw at the rear of the seat. Cover the rear seat bracket with your hand to protect the luggage compartment and lift the rear of the seat up until it clears the luggage compartment.
14   Pull the seat rearward to disengage the tang at the front end of the seat from the slot in the frame and lift the seat off.
15   Installation is the reverse of the removal steps.

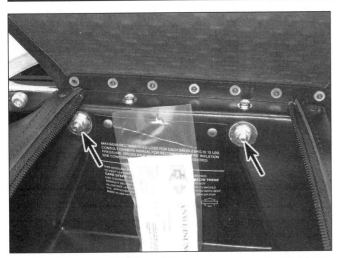

4.2 Saddlebags on FLSTS models are secured a nut at the front and two nuts inside (arrows)

6.1a Typical floorboard mounting pivots (arrows) (FXSTF shown)

FLHR

16 Remove the thumbscrew at the rear of the passenger seat and pull the seat rearward off of the two mounting nuts that secure the rear edge of the front seat. Remove the mounting nuts at the rear edge of the front seat, disengage the tang at the front end of the seat from the slot in the frame and lift the seat off.

17 Installation is the reverse of the removal steps.

FLHRC and FLTR

18 Remove the right saddlebag (see Section 4).

19 Unbolt the seat strap and saddlebag mounting bracket from the frame tube cover.

20 If you're working on an FLHRC, pull the seat strap up through the slots in the seat, taking care not to damage the seat or strap.

21 Remove the screw at the rear of the seat. Disengage the tang at the front end of the seat from the slot in the frame and lift the seat off.

22 Installation is the reverse of the removal steps.

4 Saddlebags - removal and installation

Softail models

1 Remove the acorn nut from the lower saddlebag support bracket, forward of the saddlebag.

2 Open the saddlebag and unscrew the mounting nuts (see illustration). Slip the saddlebag off the studs and remove it from the motorcycle.

3 Installation is the reverse of the removal steps.

Dyna models

4 Hold the saddlebag by the handle and push the pin on the lower end of the saddlebag release.

5 Pull the lower edge of the saddlebag clear of the frame, then slide the saddlebag frame forward off the mounting pins. Lift the saddlebag off the motorcycle.

6 To install, position the saddlebag over the mounting pins, then slide it down and to the rear until the retaining pin locks into position. Tug on the saddlebag top make sure it's securely attached.

Touring models

7 Open the saddlebag.

8 If the quick-release retainers have wire bails, flip them out and use them to twist the quick-release retainers 1/4-turn counterclockwise. If the retainers are not equipped with wire bails, use a screwdriver. Remove the retainers and pull the saddlebag off the mounting studs.

9 Installation is the reverse of the removal steps. Start the quick-release fasteners with their slots vertical, then twist them 1/4-turn clockwise until they snap into place.

10 Make sure the bottom of the saddlebag rests firmly on the support rail. If not, adjust the brackets so it does.

5 Rear luggage compartment (Touring models) - removal and installation

1 Open the luggage compartment. Remove the rubber mat (FLHTC) or map pocket (FLHTCU).

2 Disconnect the radio antenna cable and electrical connectors. Push the grommet into the compartment and remove it from the wires, then slip the wires out of the compartment through the grommet hole. If you're working on an FLHTCU, disconnect the headset and CB antenna cables and remove them from the compartment.

3 Hold the mounting nuts from underneath the compartment and unscrew the mounting bolts from within it. Be careful not to drop the compartment as the last bolt is removed. Once the compartment is unbolted, lift it off the rack and locate the bolt spacers.

4 Installation is the reverse of the removal steps. Position the concave end of the spacers to align with the rails of the luggage rack.

6 Footpegs, floorboards and brackets - removal and installation

1 If it's only necessary to detach the footpeg or floorboard from the bracket, remove the nut and pivot pin, slide out the pin(s) and detach the footpeg or floorboard from the bracket (see illustrations). Installation is the reverse of removal.

2 If it's necessary to remove the entire bracket from the frame, remove the bolts that secure the bracket to the frame.

3 Installation is the reverse of removal.

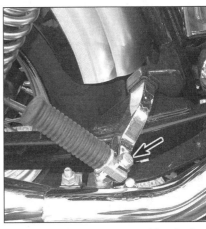

6.1b Footpegs are secured by pivot bolts (arrow) (FXDWG shown)

7.2 Make sure the sidestand spring is securely hooked

7.3 The sidestand is secured to the bracket by a pivot bolt (shown) or nut

7 Jiffy stand (sidestand) - maintenance

1   The sidestand pivots in a bracket bolted to the frame. An extension spring ensures that the stand is held in the retracted position.
2   Make sure the pivot bolt is securely fastened and the extension spring is in good condition and not over stretched (see illustration). An accident is almost certain to occur if the stand extends while the machine is in motion.
3   To remove the stand on Softail and Dyna models, unhook its spring and remove the pivot bolt, lockwasher and washer (see illustration). Slide the stand down out of the bracket.
4   To remove the stand on Touring models, unhook its spring and remove the pivot nut and stop. Slide the stand down out of the bracket.
5   If necessary, detach the bracket from the frame. On Softail and Touring models, the bracket is secured by bolts (see illustration). On Dyna models, the bracket is

secured by a bolt and a pin. The pin is secured by a washer and cotter pin.
6   Installation is the reverse of the removal steps, with the following additions:

a) *If you removed the bracket bolts, apply non-permanent thread locking agent (Loctite Threadlocker 243 (blue) or equivalent) to the threads of the bolts.*
b) *Be sure the side of the stop labeled DOWN goes downward. Tighten the bracket bolts and pivot bolt or nut to the torque listed in this Chapter's Specifications.*
c) *On Dyna models, use a new cotter pin if you removed the old one.*

8 Rear view mirrors - removal and installation

1   To remove a mirror, unscrew its mounting nut from below (see illustration). Lift the mirror from the bracket on the handlebar and remove the spacer (if equipped).
2   Installation is the reverse of removal. Position the mirror.

9 Side covers (Touring models) - removal and installation

1   The side covers are secured by pegs that fit into rubber grommets. To remove a cover, gently pull on the corners of the cover to free the pegs from the grommets, then lift the cover off (see illustration).
2   Installation is the reverse of the removal steps.

10 Front fender - removal and installation

Softail (except Springer) and Dyna models

1   If you're working on an FLSTC or FLSTF model, remove the front wheel (see Chapter 6).
2   If you're working on an FLSTC, disconnect the electrical connector for the fender tip light.

7.4 The Softail and Touring sidestand bracket is bolted to the frame from the side (Softail shown)

7.5 The Softail and Touring model bracket is secured by bolts (Softail shown)

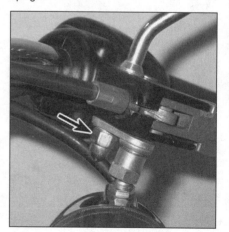

8.1 Unscrew the acorn nut (arrow) and lift the mirror off

9.1 Gently pull the side cover off, disengaging the posts (arrows) (posts hidden inside cover)

10.3 On Softail models (except FLSTS and FXSTS), the fender bolts are exposed on the outside of the fork legs (arrows)

3   Unbolt the fender from the fork legs and take it off (see illustration).

4   Installation is the reverse of the removal steps. Tighten the fender mounting bolts to the torque listed in this Chapter's Specifications.

Softail Springer FLSTS

5   Remove the brake caliper and front wheel (see Chapter 6).

6   Disconnect the electrical connector for the fender lamp.

7   Pull the clip out of the Allen bolt and unscrew the nut (see illustration).

8   Slip the axle into the fender to use as a handle. Hold the fender up with the axle and remove the Allen bolt and washer. Hold the fender at the rear to support it, then pull the axle out.

9   Working on the right side of the bike, lower the fender between the fork legs until its mounting bracket is slightly forward of the rigid fork leg on the left side of the bike. Turn the top of the fender away from you, keeping it between the fork legs. This will cause the fender struts to rotate toward you, so the bottom of the right fork leg is between the fender and the struts. At this point, lower the fender straight down untie it clears the fork legs, then remove it.

10   Inspect the front fender bearings. If they're worn or damaged, have them pressed out and new ones pressed in by a dealer service department or other qualified shop.

11   Installation is the reverse of the removal steps, with the following addition: Use a new nut on the bracket bolt, tighten it to the torque listed in this Chapter's Specifications and secure it with the clip.

Softail Springer FXSTS

12   Remove the cotter pin from the Allen bolt that attaches the brake reaction link to the caliper mounting bracket. Unscrew the locknut and shaft nut from the bolt, then

remove the washer and remove the bolt from the reaction link and caliper bracket.

13   Repeat Step 12 on the other side of the bike.

14   Place a spacer (Harley part no. HD-39754 or equivalent) between the fender pivot links to keep the correct spacing between them while the fender is removed.

15   Working inside the fender, unscrew the pivot link nut on each side. Remove the pivot link shoulder bolts. Note: The bolt bushings are loose in the fender. Locate them if they fall out.

16   Carefully lift the fender out from between the fork legs.

17   If necessary, remove the spacer tool from between the pivot links, then remove the pivot links, washers and rubber spacers from their shafts. The shafts are secured with thread locking agent, so don't remove them unless necessary.

18   Installation is the reverse of the removal steps. If the pivot link shafts were removed, apply thread locking agent (Loctite Thread-

10.7 On Softail FLSTS models, remove the clip (left arrow) and nut, then unscrew the Allen bolt (right arrow) to separate the caliper bracket from the fender

locker 262 (red) or equivalent) to the threads and tighten the shafts to the torque listed in this Chapter's Specifications.

Touring models

19   If you're working on an FLHR, remove the headlight housing (see Chapter 8).

20   If you're working on an FLHT, remove the outer fairing (see Section 16).

21   Disconnect the electrical connector for the fender tip lamp. Free the wiring harness from the brake hose and pass it between the fender and fork bracket.

22   Remove the front wheel (see Chapter 6).

23   Bend the lockwasher tabs away from the fender mounting bolts (see illustration). Unscrew the bolts and lift the fender out from between the fork legs.

24   Installation is the reverse of the removal steps. Tighten the fender mounting bolts to the torque listed in this Chapter's Specifications and bend the lockwasher tabs against the flats to secure the bolts.

10.23 On Touring models, the fender bolts thread into the mounting bosses (arrows) from inside the fender

11.4a Unscrew the rear support bolt (arrow) and center support bolt . . .

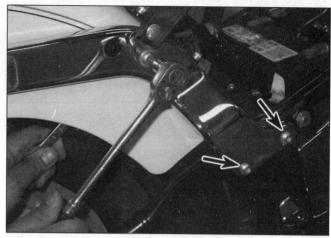

11.4b . . . the forward bolts and the bracket bolts (arrows) if equipped

11 Rear fender - removal and installation

Softail models (except FXSTD)

1 Remove the seat and saddlebags (if equipped) (see Sections 3 and 4).
2 Disconnect the negative cable from the battery. Disconnect the electrical connectors for the brake/taillight and rear turn signals. On all models, there's a connector under the seat. On FLSTS models, the turn signal connectors are under the fender. On all others, the turn signal connectors are inside the tail lamp housing.
3 Remove the ignition module and its tray (see Chapter 4).
4 Remove the fender mounting bolts and nuts and lift the fender out (see illustrations). On some models, the saddlebag studs also serve as fender mounting bolts.
5 Installation is the reverse of the removal steps.

Softail FXSTD

6 Support the motorcycle securely upright with the rear wheel off the ground. Remove the seat (see Section 3).
7 Unbolt both fender supports from the bike and from the fender, then remove all of the bolts, washers and nuts. Don't remove the fender yet.
8 Remove the taillight and rear turn signals. Disconnect the rear wiring harness and both of the ignition module connectors (see Chapter 4 if necessary).
9 Working inside the fender, unscrew the nuts that secure the fender to the mounting brackets. Lift the fender off, taking care not to scratch the paint.
10 Installation is the reverse of the removal steps.

Dyna models

11 Remove the seat (see Section 3).
12 Disconnect the negative cable from the

battery, then disconnect the positive cable.
13 Disconnect the electrical connector for the taillight and rear turn signal harness located under the seat.
14 Separate the turn signal and taillight wires from the connector. Cut the tie-wrap that secures the harness to the frame and pull it through the hole in the fender.
15 If you're working on an FXDWG, remove the license plate bracket.
16 If you're working on an FXDXT, remove the saddlebags (see Section 4).
17 On all except the FXDXT, remove the rear turn signals.
18 Working beneath the fender at the front, remove the screw that secures the fender to the caged nut on the frame.
19 Remove the fender and side plate mounting bolts. Lift the fender off.
20 Installation is the reverse of the removal steps. Use non-permanent thread locking agent on the threads of the side plate screws (all except FXDXT) or saddlebag mounting screws (FXDXT).

Touring models

21 Remove the seat (see Section 3).
22 Remove the rear wheel (see Chapter 6).
23 Disconnect the electrical connector for the rear wiring harness and free the harness from the retainer.
24 Free the retainer or the shock absorber air hose T-fitting from the hole in the rear fender.
25 Remove the side covers (see Section 9).
26 Remove the license plate bracket.
27 Reach inside the fender and unbolt the front of the fender from the battery box.
28 Unbolt the rear bumper from the saddlebag supports and take it off the motorcycle.
29 Remove the mounting bolts at the sides of the fender.
30 Support the fender and unbolt it from the saddlebag bracket on each side. Roll the fender to the rear and take it off the motorcycle.
31 Installation is the reverse of the removal steps.

12 Windshield (Softail FLSTC) - removal and installation

1 Unhook the wire spring latch on each side of the windshield.
2 Stand in front of the motorcycle and straddle the front wheel. Pull up on the top of the windshield to disengage the upper hooks from their grommets.
3 Shift your grip on the windshield as necessary and pull the lower hooks out of the mounting grommets. Lift the windshield off the motorcycle.
4 Installation is the reverse of the removal steps. Make sure the spring latches hook over the grommets. If they don't, loosen the mounting bolts, rotate them until they do and tighten the mounting bolts.

13 Windshield and fairing (Dyna FXDXT models) - removal and installation

1 Remove the headlight.
2 Loosen the upper fairing-to-bracket screws, but don't remove them.
3 Remove the lower fairing-to-bracket screws.
4 Stand in front of the motorcycle and straddle the front wheel. Pull the windshield and fairing slightly forward, then lift them up to disengage the support bracket from the screws. Take the fairing off.
5 Installation is the reverse of the removal steps.

14 Windshield and headlight nacelle (FLHR, FLHRC) - removal and installation

Windshield

1 Unhook the wire spring latch on each

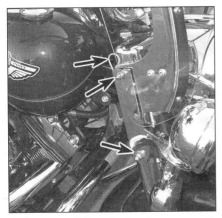

14.1 Lift the spring latches (upper arrow), pull the upper hooks off of the grommets (center arrow) and pull the lower hooks off the grommets (lower arrow)

side of the windshield (see illustration).
2   Stand in front of the motorcycle and straddle the front wheel. Pull up on the top of the windshield to disengage the upper hooks form their grommets.
3   Shift your grip on the windshield as necessary and pull the lower hooks out of the mounting grommets. Lift the windshield off the motorcycle.
4   Installation is the reverse of the removal steps. Make sure the spring latches hook over the grommets. If they don't, loosen the mounting bolts, rotate them until they do and tighten the mounting bolts.

Headlight nacelle

5   Remove the windshield as described above.
6   Remove the screw from the underside of the headlight trim ring and remove the ring.
7   Remove the headlight housing screws to detach it from the nacelle. Disconnect the headlight electrical connector and remove the headlight housing from the nacelle.
8   Unscrew the nut that holds the chrome strip to the top of the nacelle. Remove the wire clip (if equipped) that holds the bottom of the nacelle halves together.
9   Pry up the trim plate that surrounds the fork lock, taking care not to damage the handlebar cover. Remove the two Phillips screws beneath the plate, then loosen (but don't remove) the Phillips screw at the front of the handlebar cover.
10   Pad the front fender so it won't be scratched during the next step.
11   Remove two acorn nuts on each side that secure the passing lamp bracket to the fork studs. Lift the bracket off and lay it on the fender. Now remove the rubber grommets and clutch cable retainer form the fork studs.
12   Lift the handlebar cover, separate the halves of the headlamp nacelle, then remove the handlebar cover form the motorcycle.
13   Pull each half of the headlamp nacelle off its fork stud, separating the electrical

connectors for the passing lamp switch and accessory switch as you do this.
14   Installation is the reverse of the removal steps.

15 Windshield and outer fairing (FLTR) - removal and installation

Windshield

Note: *If you're planning to remove the outer fairing, remove the windshield and outer fairing together as described below.*
1   Loosen the five Phillips screws align the lower edge of the windshield, starting with the center screw and working outward. Once the screws are all loose, lift the windshield off the fairing.
2   Remove the nuts from the holes, taking care not to push them into the fairing. If the nuts are damaged or deteriorated, replace them.
3   Installation is the reverse of the removal steps.

Outer fairing

4   Pad the top of the fender so it won't be scratched when you remove the fairing. You'll need to set the fairing on top of the fender while it's being removed.
5   Sitting on the seat, locate the outer fairing Torx screws. There are three on each side of the fairing, one at the bottom, one just outboard of the speaker and one just outboard of the upper gauge (voltmeter and fuel gauge).
6   Unscrew the bottom left screw, then the center left screw. Loosen the two upper screws (don't remove them), then remove the center right and bottom right screws.
7   Above each turn signal lamp, remove the acorn nuts and plate washer from the studs on the turn signal lamp bracket. Push the studs out of the fairing and remove the stud plate.
8   **Note:** *The next steps will be easier with an assistant.* Remove the two top screws loosened earlier. Lift the fairing and lower it to the pad on the front fender.
9   Disconnect the electrical connector for the headlight wiring harness and take the fairing off the motorcycle.
10   Installation is the reverse of the removal steps. Install the stud plates with their shorter studs toward the front of the motorcycle. Tighten the four upper fairing screws evenly to the torque listed in this Chapter's Specifications, then tighten the two lower screws.

Inner fairing

11   Remove the instrument bezel (see Chapter 8).
12   Unscrew the odometer reset switch's rubber boot to detach the switch from the instrument nacelle, then pull the switch out of its hole.
13   Remove the outer fairing as described

above.
14   Pull the wiring harnesses, including the speedometer and tachometer harness, forward and straighten them out.
15   Disconnect the jumper harness and main harness connectors from the interconnect harness connectors (refer to wiring diagrams at the end of the book if necessary). Disconnect the ignition switch harness from the main harness.
16   Disconnect the handlebar switch electrical connectors.
17   Free the wiring harnesses from any retainers, then pull all of the harnesses to the front of the motorcycle and straighten them out. Wrap the harnesses with towels or a blanket to protect the fender, then lay them on the fender.
18   Remove the radio bracket nuts to detach the radio bracket and inner fairing from the fairing bracket. Lift the inner fairing and radio bracket off the fairing bracket.
19   Installation is the reverse of the removal steps. Tighten the radio bracket locknuts to the torque listed in this Chapter's Specifications.

16 Windshield and upper fairing (FLHT, FLHTC, FLHTU) - removal and installation

1   Remove the seat (see Section 3). Disconnect the negative cable from the battery.
2   From the front side of the fairing, remove the three Torx screws from the fairing below the windshield.
3   From the rear side of the fairing, remove the two outer screws, one on each side outboard and below the radio speakers.
4   Reach under the fairing cap and remove the two remaining screws (you'll need to turn the handlebars back-and-forth to reach the screws).
5   **Note:** *This step will be easier with an assistant.* Tilt the top of the fairing forward and disconnect the headlight electrical connectors. Lift the fairing off the motorcycle.
6   Installation is the reverse of the removal steps.

17 Fairing cap (FLHT, FLHTC, FLHTU) - removal and installation

1   Remove the ignition switch knob (see Chapter 8).
2   Remove the Torx screw from each end of the fairing cap.
3   Lift the fairing cap slightly and free the trim plate tabs from the fairing cap slots.
4   Turn the handlebars all the way to the left and disconnect the electrical connector for the fairing cap switches.
5   Lift the fairing cap off.
6   Installation is the reverse of the removal steps.

7

Notes

Chapter 8
Electrical system

Contents

Degrees of difficulty

| **Easy,** suitable for novice with little experience | | **Fairly easy,** suitable for beginner with some experience | | **Fairly difficult,** suitable for competent DIY mechanic | | **Difficult,** suitable for experienced DIY mechanic | | **Very difficult,** suitable for expert DIY or professional | |

Specifications

Battery

Type and rating

Softail and Dyna .... 12 volt, 19 Ah (amp-hours), maintenance free
1999 Touring models
Type.. 12 volt, 30 Ah (amp hours), fillable
Specific gravity... See Chapter 1
2000 and later Touring models.. 12 volt, 28 Ah (amp-hours), maintenance free

Open circuit voltage and state of charge (maintenance free batteries)

12.8 volts .... 100 per cent
12.6 volts .... 75 per cent
12.3 volts .... 50 per cent
12.0 volts .... 25 per cent
11.8 volts .... Zero per cent

8

Voltage reading and charge times (maintenance free batteries)

Softail and Dyna

12.6 volts

3 amp charger	1.75 hours
6 amp charger	50 minutes
10 amp charger	30 minutes
20 amp charger	15 minutes

12.3 volts

3 amp charger	3.5 hours
6 amp charger	1.75 hours
10 amp charger	1 hour
20 amp charger	30 minutes

12.0 volts

3 amp charger	5 hours
6 amp charger	2.5 hours
10 amp charger	1.5 hours
20 amp charger	45 minutes

11.8 volts

3 amp charger	6 hours, 40 minutes
6 amp charger	3 hours, 20 minutes
10 amp charger	2 hours
20 amp charger	1 hour

Touring models (2000 on)

12.6 volts

3 amp charger	2.5 hours
6 amp charger	1.25 hours
10 amp charger	45 minutes
20 amp charger	25 minutes

12.3 volts

3 amp charger	5 hours
6 amp charger	2.5 hours
10 amp charger	1.5 hours
20 amp charger	50 minutes

12.0 volts

3 amp charger	7.5 hours
6 amp charger	3.75 hours
10 amp charger	2.25 hours
20 amp charger	70 minutes

11.8 volts

3 amp charger	10 hours
6 amp charger	5 hours
10 amp charger	3 hours
20 amp charger	1.5 hours

Charging system

AC output	32 to 40 volts at 2000 rpm

Circuit fuse ratings

All except Touring model radio and P&A fuses	15 amps
Touring model P&A fuses	10 amps

Circuit breaker ratings

Softail and Dyna	30 amps
Touring models	40 amps

Bulb wattage

Softail

Headlight

FLSTC, FLSTS, FLSTS	40/60
FXSTS, FXSTB, FXSTD	60/55
Position lamp (non-US models)	4

Front turn signals

Turn signal/running lights (US)	27/7
Turn signals (except US)	21

Rear turn signals

US	27
Except US	21
Passing lamps	30

Taillights (US)	7
Taillights (except US)	7
2000 through early 2003 (bayonet type)	5
Late 2003 (wedge type)	7
Brake lights (US)	
2000 through early 2003 (bayonet type)	27
Late 2003 (wedge type)	25
Brake lights (except US)	
2000 through early 2003 (bayonet type)	21
Late 2003 (wedge type)	25
Fog lamp (non-US models)	35
License plate lights	
FLSTS	
US	4.2
Except US	5
FXSTD	5
Fender tip lamps	
FLSTC	1
FLSTS	4.2
Instrument and indicator lights	LED

Dyna

Headlight	60/55
Position lamp (non-US models)	3.9
Front turn signals	
Turn signal/running lights (US)	27/7
Turn signals (except US)	21
Rear turn signals	
US	27
Except US	21
Taillights (US)	7
Taillights (except US)	7
2000 through early 2003 (bayonet type)	5
Late 2003 (wedge type)	7
Brake lights (US)	
2000 through early 2003 (bayonet type)	27
Late 2003 (wedge type)	25
Brake lights (except US)	
2000 through early 2003 (bayonet type)	21
Late 2003 (wedge type)	25
Speedometer and tachometer lights	LED
Instrument and indicator lights	
All except FXDL and FXDWG	2.1
FXDL	1.1
FXDWG	LED

Touring models

Headlight	60/55
Position lamp (non-US models)	3.9
Front turn signals	
Turn signal/running lights (US)	27/7
Turn signals (except US)	21
Rear turn signals	
US	27
Except US	21
Passing lamps	
US	30
Except US	35
Taillights (US)	
2000 through early 2003 (bayonet type)	7
Late 2003 (wedge type)	6
Taillights (except US)	
2000 through early 2003 (bayonet type)	5
Late 2003 (wedge type)	6
Brake lights (US)	
2000 through early 2003 (bayonet type)	27
Late 2003 (wedge type)	24
Brake lights (except US)	
2000 through early 2003 (bayonet type)	21
Late 2003 (wedge type)	24

Touring models(continued)

License plate lights (non-US models)	5.2
Fender tip lamps (US only)	3.7
Speedometer light	
1999	1.7
2000 and later	LED
Tachometer light	
1999	3.4
2000 and later	LED
Gauge lights	3.4
Tour-Pak side marker lamps (US only)	3.7
Tour-Pak tail/brake lights (US FLHTCU only)	7
Instrument and indicator lights	
All except 1999 fuel gauge	LED
1999 fuel gauge	2.7

Torque specifications

Alternator stator screws	55 to 75 inch-lbs (6.2 to 8.5 Nm)
Starter mounting bolts	13 to 20 ft-lbs (18 to 27 Nm)
Starter jackshaft bolt	84 to 108 inch-lbs (9.5 to 12.2 Nm)
Starter cover screw	90 to 110 inch-lbs 10.2 to 12.4 Nm)
Radio bolts	35 to 45 inch-lbs (4.0 to 5.1 Nm)

1 General information

The machines covered by this manual are equipped with a 12-volt electrical system. The components include a crankshaft mounted permanent magnet alternator and a solid state voltage regulator/rectifier unit.

The regulator maintains the charging system output within the specified range to prevent overcharging. The rectifier converts the AC (alternating current) output of the alternator to DC (direct current) to power the lights and other components and to charge the battery.

The alternator consists of a multi-coil stator (mounted on the left end of the crankshaft, inside the primary chaincase) and a permanent magnet rotor mounted on the crankshaft.

An electric starter mounted to the engine case is standard equipment. The starting system includes the motor, the battery, the solenoid and the various wires and switches. If the engine stop switch and the main key switch are both in the On position, the circuit relay allows the starter motor to operate only if the transmission is in Neutral (Neutral switch on) or the clutch lever is pulled to the handlebar (clutch switch on) and the sidestand is up (sidestand switch on). **Note:** *Keep in mind that electrical parts, once purchased, can't be returned. To avoid unnecessary expense, make very sure the faulty component has been positively identified before buying a replacement part.*

2 Electrical troubleshooting

A typical electrical circuit consists of an electrical component, the switches, relays, etc. related to that component and the wiring and connectors that hook the component to both the battery and the frame. To aid in locating a problem in any electrical circuit, complete wiring diagrams of each model are included at the end of this Chapter.

Before tackling any troublesome electrical circuit, first study the appropriate diagrams thoroughly to get a complete picture of what makes up that individual circuit. Trouble spots, for instance, can often be narrowed down by noting if other components related to that circuit are operating properly or not. If several components or circuits fail at one time, chances are the fault lies in the fuse or ground connection, as several circuits often are routed through the same fuse and ground connections.

Electrical problems often stem from simple causes, such as loose or corroded connections or a blown fuse. Prior to any electrical troubleshooting, always visually check the condition of the fuse, wires and connections in the problem circuit.

If testing instruments are going to be utilized, use the diagrams to plan where you will make the necessary connections in order to accurately pinpoint the trouble spot.

The basic tools needed for electrical troubleshooting include a test light or voltmeter, a continuity tester (which includes a bulb, battery and set of test leads) and a jumper wire, preferably with a circuit breaker incorporated, which can be used to bypass electrical components. Specific checks described later in this Chapter may also require an ohmmeter.

Voltage checks should be performed if a circuit is not functioning properly. Connect one lead of a test light or voltmeter to either the negative battery terminal or a known good ground. Connect the other lead to a connector in the circuit being tested, preferably nearest to the battery or fuse. If the bulb lights, voltage is reaching that point, which means the part of the circuit between that connector and the battery is problem-free. Continue checking the remainder of the circuit in the same manner. When you reach a point where no voltage is present, the problem lies between there and the last good test point. Most of the time the problem is due to a loose connection. Keep in mind that some circuits only receive voltage when the ignition key is in the On position.

One method of finding short circuits is to remove the fuse and connect a test light or voltmeter in its place to the fuse terminals. There should be no load in the circuit. Move the wiring harness from side-to-side while watching the test light. If the bulb lights, there is a short to ground somewhere in that area, probably where insulation has rubbed off a wire. The same test can be performed on other components in the circuit, including the switch.

A ground check should be done to see if a component is grounded properly. Disconnect the battery and connect one lead of a self-powered test light (continuity tester) to a known good ground. Connect the other lead to the wire or ground connection being tested. If the bulb lights, the ground is good. If the bulb does not light, the ground is not good.

A continuity check is performed to see if a circuit, section of circuit or individual component is capable of passing electricity through it. Disconnect the battery and connect one lead of a self-powered test light (continuity tester) to one end of the circuit being tested and the other lead to the other end of the circuit. If the bulb lights, there is continuity, which means the circuit is passing electricity through it properly. Switches can be checked in the same way.

Remember that all electrical circuits are designed to conduct electricity from the battery, through the wires, switches, relays, etc. to the electrical component (light bulb, motor, etc.). From there it is directed to the frame (ground) where it is passed back to the battery. Electrical problems are basically an interruption in the flow of electricity from the battery or back to it.

3 Battery - inspection and maintenance

1   Most battery damage is caused by heat, vibration, and/or low electrolyte levels, so keep the battery securely mounted, check the electrolyte level frequently and make sure the charging system is functioning properly.
2   Refer to Chapter 1 for electrolyte level and specific gravity checking procedures for fillable batteries, which were original equipment on 1999 Touring models.
3   Remove the seat (see Chapter 7). Check around the base inside of the battery for sediment, which is the result of sulfation caused by low electrolyte levels. These deposits will cause internal short circuits, which can quickly discharge the battery. Look for cracks in the case and replace the battery if either of these conditions is found.
4   Check the battery terminals and cable ends for tightness and corrosion. If corrosion is evident, remove the cables from the battery and clean the terminals and cable ends with a wire brush or knife and emery paper. Reconnect the cables and apply a thin coat of petroleum jelly to the connections to slow further corrosion.
5   The battery case should be kept clean to prevent current leakage, which can discharge the battery over a period of time (especially when it sits unused). Wash the outside of the case with a solution of baking soda and water. Do not get any baking soda solution in the battery cells. Rinse the battery thoroughly, then dry it.
6   If acid has been spilled on the frame or

battery box, neutralize it with the baking soda and water solution, dry it thoroughly, then touch up any damaged paint.
7   If the motorcycle sits unused for long periods of time, disconnect the cables from the battery terminals. Refer to Section 4 and charge the battery approximately once every month.

4 Battery - charging

1   If the machine sits idle for extended periods or if the charging system malfunctions, the battery can be charged from an external source.

Maintenance-free battery

2   Charging the maintenance-free battery used on all except 1999 Touring models requires a standard battery charger. Do not use a constant-current type charger.
3   When charging the battery, always remove it from the machine and be sure to check the electrolyte level by looking through the translucent battery case before hooking up the charger. If the electrolyte level is low, the battery must be discarded; never remove the sealing plug to add water.
4   Disconnect the battery cables (negative cable first), then connect a digital voltmeter between the battery terminals and measure the voltage.
5   If terminal voltage is 12.8 volts or higher, the battery is fully charged. If it's lower, recharge the battery. Refer to this Chapter's Specifications for charging rate and time.
6   A quick charge can be used in an emergency, provided the maximum charge rates and times are not exceeded (exceeding the maximum rate or time may ruin the battery). A quick charge should always be followed as soon as possible by a charge at the specified rate and time.
7   Hook up the battery charger leads (positive lead to battery positive terminal and negative lead to battery negative terminal, then, and only then, plug in the battery charger.

⚠ *Warning: The gas escaping from a charging battery is explosive, so keep open flames and sparks well away from the area. Also, the electrolyte is extremely corrosive and will damage anything it comes in contact with.*

8   Allow the battery to charge for the specified time listed in this Chapter's Specifications. If the battery overheats or gases excessively, the charging rate is too high. Either disconnect the charger or lower the charging rate to prevent damage to the battery.

9   After the specified time, unplug the charger first, then disconnect the leads from the battery.
10   Wait 30 minutes, then measure voltage between the battery terminals. If it's 12.8 volts or higher, the battery is fully charged. If it's between 12.0 and 12.6 volts, charge the battery again (refer to this Chapter's Specifications for charge rate and time).

Fillable battery

11   To properly charge the battery, you will need a charger of the correct rating, a hydrometer, a clean rag and a syringe for adding distilled water to the battery cells.
12   The maximum charging rate for any battery is 1/10 of the rated amp/hour capacity. As an example, the maximum charging rate for a 14 amp/hour battery would be 1.4 amps. If the battery is charged at a higher rate, it could be damaged.
13   Do not allow the battery to be subjected to a so-called quick charge (high rate of charge over a short period of time) unless you are prepared to buy a new battery. The heat will warp the plates inside the battery until they touch each other, causing a short circuit.
14   When charging the battery, always remove it from the machine and be sure to check the electrolyte level before hooking up the charger. Add distilled water to any cells that are low.
15   Loosen the cell caps, hook up the battery charger leads (red to positive, black to negative), cover the top of the battery with a clean rag, then, and only then, plug in the battery charger.

⚠ *Warning: Remember, the gas escaping from a charging battery is explosive, so keep open flames and sparks well away from the area. If the gas ignites, the entire battery can explode and spray acid. Also, the electrolyte is extremely corrosive and will damage anything it comes in contact with.*

16   Allow the battery to charge until the specific gravity is as specified (refer to Chapter 1 for specific gravity checking procedures). The charger must be unplugged and disconnected from the battery when making specific gravity checks. If the battery overheats or gases excessively, the charging rate is too high. Either disconnect the charger or lower the charging rate to prevent damage to the battery.
17   If one or more of the cells do not show an increase in specific gravity after a long slow charge, or if the battery as a whole does not seem to want to take a charge, it is time for a new battery.
18   When the battery is fully charged, unplug the charger first, then disconnect the leads from the battery. Install the cell caps and wipe any electrolyte off the outside of the battery case.

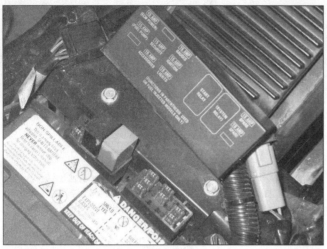

5.1 Remove the seat and fuse box cover for access to the fuses

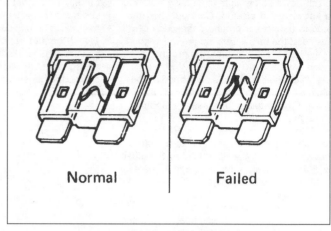

5.3 A blown "plug-in" type fuse can be identified by a break in the element - be sure to replace a blown fuse with one of the same amperage rating

5 Fuses - check and replacement

1   The fuses are located under the seat, on the fuse block **(see illustration)**. This block contains fuses (and spares) which protect the circuit wiring and components from damage caused by short circuits.

2   If you have a test light, the fuses can be checked without removing them. Turn the ignition to the On position, connect one end of the test light to a good ground, then probe each terminal on top of the fuse. If the fuse is good, there will be voltage available at both terminals. If the fuse is blown, there will only be voltage present at one of the terminals.

3   The "plug-in" type fuses can be pulled from position. If you can't pull the fuse out with your fingertips, use a pair of needle-nose pliers. A blown fuse is easily identified by a break in the element **(see illustration)**.

4   If a fuse blows, be sure to check the wiring harnesses very carefully for evidence of a short circuit. Look for bare wires and chafed, melted or burned insulation. If a fuse

6.1 The main circuit breaker (arrow) is located on the electrical panel

is replaced before the cause is located, the new fuse will blow immediately.

5   Never, under any circumstances, use a higher rated fuse or bridge the fuse block terminals, as damage to the electrical system - including melted wires, ruined components, and fire - could result.

6   Occasionally a fuse will blow or cause an open circuit for no obvious reason. Corrosion of the fuse ends and fuse block terminals may occur and cause poor fuse contact. If this happens, remove the corrosion with a wire brush or emery paper, then spray the fuse end and terminals with electrical contact cleaner.

6 Main circuit breaker - replacement

1   The main circuit breaker opens in response to an electrical overload, then resets itself as it cools down. If the condition that caused the overload still exists, the circuit breaker will open again. The circuit breaker is mounted on the electrical panel **(see illustration)**.

2   Remove the seat and disconnect the negative cable from the battery.

3   Disconnect the cables from the circuit breaker, then free it from its tabs and remove it from the motorcycle.

4   Installation is the reverse of the removal steps.

7 Lighting system - check

1   The battery provides power for operation of the headlight, taillight, brake light, license plate light and instrument cluster lights. If none of the lights operate, always check battery voltage before proceeding.

Low battery voltage indicates either a faulty battery or a defective charging system. Refer to Chapter 1 for battery checks and Sections 26 through 31 for charging system tests. Also, check the condition of the fuses and replace any blown fuses with new ones.

Headlight

2   If the headlight won't come on, check the fuse first with the key On (see Section 5), then unplug the electrical connector for the headlight and use jumper wires to connect the bulb directly to the battery terminals. If the light comes on, the problem lies in the wiring or one of the switches in the circuit. Refer to Sections 20 and 21 for the switch testing procedures, and also the wiring diagrams at the end of this Chapter. Also check the main circuit breaker (see Section 6).

Taillight/license plate light

3   If the taillight fails to work, check the bulbs and the bulb terminals first, then check for battery voltage at the red wire in the taillight. If voltage is present, check the ground circuit for an open or poor connection.

4   If no voltage is indicated, check the wiring between the taillight and the main (key) switch, then check the switch.

Brake light

5   See Section 14 for the brake light circuit checking procedure.

Indicator lights

6   The indicator lights (oil pressure, neutral, high/low beam and turn signals) consist of a light emitting diode (LED) assembly **(see illustration)** or individual bulbs, depending on model. If any of the LEDs are defective, the entire assembly must be replaced. Blown bulbs can be replaced individually.

7   If an indicator light doesn't work, locate the LED assembly electrical connector or bulb connector. On motorcycles equipped with a fuel tank instrument cluster, remove

7.6 An LED unit (arrow) houses the indicator lights on most models (FXSTD shown)

8.1a Remove or loosen the trim ring screw (retaining screw shown) . . .

8.1b . . . and take the trim ring off

the acorn nut that secures the instrument console to the top of the fuel tank and lift it up (see Section 14). On other models, the connector is located in the instrument cluster (see Section 15).

Oil pressure and neutral lights

8   Turn the key to ON and check for battery voltage at the indicator light connector's orange wire terminal (this is the power wire for the oil pressure and neutral lights). If there's no voltage, follow the orange wire back to the fuse, checking for a break, poor connection or blown fuse.

9   If there's battery voltage, check for continuity between chassis ground and the tan wire terminal (neutral light) or green/yellow wire terminal (oil pressure light). If there is continuity, the indicator has a good ground. The LED assembly is probably defective or the bulb is blown.

10   If there's no continuity, check the switch as described in Section 18 or 22. The switch connects the light to chassis ground, so the lack of ground may indicate the switch is defective.

11   If the switch is good and there's no ground, check the wiring from the light connector to the switch for a break or bad connection.

High beam or turn signal indicator lights

12   Check for ground at the black wire terminal of the light connector. If there isn't any, check the wire for a break or bad connection.

13   If the high beam indicator isn't working, turn the key to ON, switch on the high beams and check for battery voltage at the indicator light connector's white wire terminal. If there's no voltage, follow the white wire back to the fuse, checking for a break, poor connection or blown fuse.

14   If the right turn indicator isn't working, turn the turn signal switch to the right turn position and check for battery voltage at the indicator light connector's brown wire termi-

nal. If there's no voltage, follow the brown wire back to the fuse, checking for a break, poor connection or blown fuse.

15   If the left turn indicator isn't working, turn the turn signal switch to the left turn position and check for battery voltage at the indicator light connector's violet wire terminal. If there's no voltage, follow the violet wire back to the fuse, checking for a break, poor connection or blown fuse.

16   If there's battery voltage, the LED assembly or bulb is probably defective.

8   Headlight bulb - replacement

All except FLTR

1   Locate the trim ring screw at the bottom of the trim ring (see illustration). This is a retaining screw or clamp screw, depending on model. Remove the retaining screw or loosen the clamp screw and remove the trim ring (see illustration).

2   Remove the retaining ring screws and take off the retaining ring (see illustration).

8.2a Remove the retaining ring screws (arrows) and take off the retaining ring . . .

Pull out the headlight and disconnect the electrical connector (see illustration).

3   On Softail FLSTC and FLSTD models, the bulb is a sealed beam unit; simply replace it.

4   On all others, the bulb is a quartz halogen type held in the headlight assembly by a clip. Release the clip and swing it out of the way.

⚠️ *Warning: If the headlight has just been on, let the bulb cool before you continue. It will be hot to enough to cause burns.* Remove the bulb holder. When installing the new bulb, reverse the removal procedure. Be sure not to touch the bulb with your fingers - oil from your skin will cause the bulb to overheat and fail prematurely. If you do touch the bulb, wipe it off with a clean rag dampened with rubbing alcohol. Make sure the clip is securely seated (see illustration).

FLTR

5   Remove the outer fairing (see Chapter 7).

6   Disconnect the electrical connector from the bulb.

8.2b . . . then pull out the headlight and disconnect the connector

9.4 Horizontal adjusting bolt
(Dyna except FXDXT)

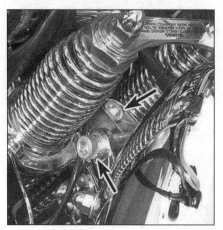

9.6 Here are the Springer's horizontal
adjusting bolt (right arrow) and vertical
adjusting bolt (left arrow)

10.1 Remove the lens screws (arrows)
and take off the lens

7   Remove the rubber dust cover from the back of the bulb.

 Warning: If the headlight has just been on, let the bulb cool before you continue. It will be hot to enough to cause burns. Turn the bulb retainer counterclockwise to free it from the housing, then pull out the retainer and bulb.

8   When installing the new bulb, reverse the removal procedure. Be sure not to touch the bulb with your fingers - oil from your skin will cause the bulb to overheat and fail prematurely. If you do touch the bulb, wipe it off with a clean rag dampened with rubbing alcohol. Make sure the retainer is securely seated.

9   Headlight aim - check and adjustment

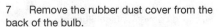

1   An improperly adjusted headlight may cause problems for oncoming traffic or provide poor, unsafe illumination of the road ahead. Before adjusting the headlight, be sure to consult with local traffic laws and regulations.
2   The headlight beam can be adjusted both vertically and horizontally. Before performing the adjustment, make sure the fuel tank has at least a half tank of fuel, and have an assistant sit on the seat.

Softail (except Springer) and Dyna FXDWG, FXDXT

3   The horizontal position of the beam is not adjustable on Dyna FXDXT models.
4   To adjust the horizontal position of the beam on all except Dyna FXDXT models, loosen the bolt on the underside of the lower triple clamp **(see illustration)**. Turn the headlight housing to adjust it and tighten the bolt.
5   To adjust the vertical position of the

beam, loosen the vertical adjusting bolt (below the headlight housing). Adjust the position of the headlight and tighten the bolt.

Softail Springer

6   To adjust the horizontal position of the beam, loosen the Allen bolt behind the headlight housing **(see illustration)**. Turn the headlight housing to adjust it and tighten the bolt.
7   To adjust the vertical position of the beam, loosen the vertical adjusting bolt (the Allen bolt below and behind the headlight housing) **(see illustration 9.6)**. Adjust the position of the headlight and tighten the bolt.

Dyna (except FXDWG)

8   Carefully pry the trim cap from the top of the headlight housing to expose the adjusting nut.
9   Loosen the nut, adjust the headlight housing and tighten the nut. Reinstall the trim cap.

Touring models (except FLTR)

10   The adjusting screws are accessible through notches in the headlight trim ring (it need not be removed to make the adjustment).
11   To adjust the horizontal position of the beam, insert a screwdriver into the hole in the left side of the headlight rim (viewed from the front of the motorcycle) and turn the adjuster.
12   Insert the screwdriver into the vertical adjuster screw hole (at the top of the headlight rim) and turn the adjuster screw as necessary to raise or lower the beam.

FLTR models

13   The adjustment is made with two hex screws in the back of the fairing, one on each side below the small gauges. To turn the adjusters, you'll need a 4.5 mm socket and flexible driver.
14   To adjust the horizontal position of either headlight, turn its adjuster clockwise

or counterclockwise.
15   To adjust the vertical position of the headlights, turn both adjusters simultaneously to raise or lower the headlights together.

10   Turn signal bulbs - replacement

1   Remove the lens securing screws and take off the lens **(see illustration)**.
2   Push the bulb in and turn it counterclockwise to remove it **(see illustration)**. Check the socket terminals for corrosion and clean them if necessary. Line up the pins on the new bulb with the slots in the socket, push in and turn the bulb clockwise until it locks in place. It is a good idea to use a paper towel or dry cloth when handling the new bulb to prevent injury if the bulb should break and to increase bulb life.
3   Position the lens on the reflector and install the screws. Be careful not to overtighten them.

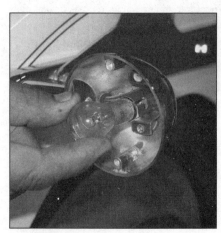

10.2 Push the bulb into its socket and
turn it counterclockwise to remove

11 Tail/brake light bulbs - replacement

1   Remove the lens and housing securing screws **(see illustration)**.
2   Pull the housing off the fender and pull the taillight bulb socket out **(see illustration)**.
3   On 1999 through early 2003 models, press the bulb into its socket and turn it counterclockwise to remove. On late 2003 models, the bulb is a wedge type - pull it out to remove.
4   Installation is the reverse of the removal steps.

12 Instrument and warning light bulbs - replacement

1   To replace a bulb, pull the appropriate rubber socket out of the back of the instrument housing, then pull the bulb out of the socket. If the socket contacts are dirty or corroded, they should be scraped clean and sprayed with electrical contact cleaner before new bulbs are installed.
2   Carefully push the new bulb into position, then push the socket into the instrument housing.

13 Turn signal circuit - check

1   The battery provides power for operation of the signal lights, so if they do not operate, always check the battery voltage and specific gravity first. Low battery voltage indicates either a faulty battery, low electrolyte level or a defective charging system. Refer to Chapter 1 for battery checks and Sections 26 through 31 for charging system

tests. Also, check the fuses (see Section 5).
2   Most turn signal problems are the result of a burned out bulb or corroded socket. This is especially true when the turn signals function properly in one direction, but fail to flash in the other direction. Check the bulbs and the sockets (see Section 10).
3   If the bulbs and sockets check out okay, refer to the wiring diagrams at the end of this manual and check for power at the turn signal module with the ignition On. If there's no power at the module, check the switch (see Sections 20 and 21).
4   If the junction box and switch are okay, check the wiring between the turn signal module and the turn signal lights (see the wiring diagrams at the end of this manual).
5   If the wiring checks out okay, the turn signal module may be at fault. The module, which also controls the anti-theft system on some models, should be tested by a dealer service department or other qualified shop.

14 Brake light switches - check and replacement

Circuit check

1   Before checking any electrical circuit, check the fuses (see Section 5).
2   Using a test light (or voltmeter) connected to a good ground, check for voltage at the power wire terminal in the electrical connector at the brake light switch. If there's no voltage present, check the wire between the switch and the fuse (see the wiring diagrams at the end of this manual).
3   If voltage is available, touch the probe of the test light to the other terminal of the switch, then pull the brake lever or depress the brake pedal - if the test light doesn't light up, replace the switch.
4   If the test light does light, check the wiring between the switch and the brake lights (see the wiring diagrams at the end of this manual).

11.1 Remove the screws (arrows) . . .

Switch replacement
Brake lever switch

5   Separate the right handlebar switch housings (see Section 21).
6   Working in the lower half of the switch housing, remove the wedge that holds the brake light switch in place. Push the switch plunger in, turn the switch up and rock it to free it from the housing.
7   Cut the switch wires 1 inch (25.4 mm) from the switch. Strip 1/2-inch (13 mm) of insulation from the ends of the wires in the harness.
8   Slip lengths of heat shrink tubing over the switch wires. Solder the wires, slide the tubing over the splices and shrink it with a heat gun or similar tool.

Caution: Don't use a flame to shrink the tubing.
9   Assemble the switch housings.

Brake pedal switch

10   Locate the switch at the brake pedal and disconnect its wires **(see illustration)**.
11   Unscrew the switch from the brake line bracket.
12   Screw in a new switch and tighten it securely.
13   Bleed the brakes.

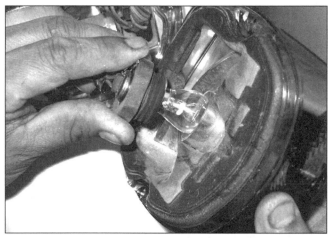

11.2 . . . take the housing off the fender and remove the bulb (see text)

14.10 Here's the rear brake light switch (Softail shown)

15.1a Unscrew the acorn nut (arrow) . . .

15.1b . . . and lift off the bezel

15 Instrument and warning light housings (tank mounted) - removal and installation

1   Unscrew the acorn nut from the gauge bezel and lift the bezel up (see illustrations).
2   Follow the wiring harnesses form the speedometer, ignition switch and LED warning light housing (if equipped) to their connectors and disconnect them.
3   Installation is the reverse of the removal steps.

16 Instrument bezel (FLTR) - removal and installation

1   Remove the Torx screws from each side of the bezel. Push the rear edge of the bezel toward the front of the motorcycle to disengage the bezel tabs from their slots.
2   Lift the front edge of the bezel out of the slots and disconnect the instrument electrical connectors. Free the harnesses from any retainers, then lift the bezel off.
3   Installation is the reverse of the removal steps. If you cut a tie-wrap to free the harness, replace it with a new one.

17 Meters and gauges - check and replacement

Check

Speedometer and tachometer

1   Special instruments are required to properly check the operation of these meters. Take the instrument cluster to a dealer service department or other qualified repair shop for diagnosis.

Oil pressure gauge

2   Refer to Section 18 for gauge and sending unit test procedures.

Voltmeter

3   Connect a test voltmeter between the positive terminal of the motorcycle's voltmeter and ground. With the key On and engine not running, there should be 12 volts. If not, check the fuse and wiring to the gauge.
4   If there is voltage to the gauge, connect an ohmmeter between the voltmeter negative terminal and ground (key Off). There should be little or no resistance (zero ohms). If not, check the wiring from the gauge negative terminal to chassis ground and repair or replace it as needed.

Fuel gauge (Softail and Dyna)

5   Locate the fuel gauge connector under the tank (see the wiring diagrams at the end of this manual). Disconnect the connector.
6   Turn the key to On. Ground the black wire in the tank side of the connector by connecting it to a frame ground with a length of wire. The fuel gauge should indicate Full. If so, the gauge is good and the problem is in the sender or wiring. If not, check the gauge as described in Step 7.
7   With the key On, connect a voltmeter between the pink wire's terminal in the tank side of the connector. It should indicate 2 to 7 volts. If not, check the wiring for a break or bad connection. If the wiring is good, the other likely cause is an open winding in the gauge, in which case the gauge must be replaced.
8   If the gauge indicated Full in Step 6, disconnect the ground wire from the black wire's terminal and connect an ohmmeter in its place. With the fuel tank full, the ohmmeter should indicate approximately 40 ohms. With it empty, the ohmmeter should indicate approximately 250 ohms.
9   If the ohmmeter is very high (or infinity), check the sender ground. Connect the ohmmeter between the sender flange on the fuel tank and a good chassis ground. If the reading is one ohm or less, the sender has a good ground and should be replaced. If the reading is above one ohm, check the sender ground wire for breaks or bad connections.

Fuel gauge (Touring models)

10   Locate the fuel gauge connector under the seat (see the wiring diagrams at the end of this manual). Disconnect the connector.
11   Turn the key to On. Ground the yellow/white wire in the tank side of the connector by connecting it to a frame ground with a length of wire. The fuel gauge should indicate Full. If so, the gauge is good and the problem is in the sender or wiring. If not, check the gauge as described in Step 7.
12   With the key On, connect a voltmeter between the power wire's terminal in the tank side of the connector. It should indicate 2 to 7 volts. If not, check the wiring for a break or bad connection. If the wiring is good, the other likely cause is an open winding in the gauge, in which case the gauge must be replaced.
13   If the gauge indicated Full in Step 6, disconnect the ground wire from the connector terminal and connect an ohmmeter in its place. With the fuel tank full, the ohmmeter should indicate approximately 7 to 14 ohms on FLHT, FLHTC and FLHTCU models, or 7 to 40 ohms on FLHR or FLHRC models. With it empty, the ohmmeter should indicate approximately 7 to 95 ohms on FLHT, FLHTC and FLHTCU models, or 27 to 260 ohms on FLHR or FLHRC models.
14   If the ohmmeter is very high (or infinity), check the sender ground. Connect the ohmmeter between the sender flange on the fuel tank and a good chassis ground. If the reading is one ohm or less, the sender has a good ground and should be replaced. If the reading is above one ohm, check the sender ground wire for breaks or bad connections.

Gauge replacement

Speedometer and tachometer (except FXDXT)

15   If you're working on an FLHR, FLHRC or FLTR, remove the instrument bezel (see Section 16).
16   If you're working on an FLHT, FLHTC, or FLHTCU, remove the outer fairing (see Chapter 7).

17.38 The speed sensor (arrow) is mounted near the starter motor

17 On models with an odometer reset knob on the left side of the instrument bezel, unscrew the knob and push the odometer reset switch into the bezel.

18 Disconnect the speedometer wiring connector and free the harness from any retainers.

19 If the speedometer is secured by a bracket and two Allen screws, undo the screws and remove the bracket.

20 If the speedometer is secured by a plastic lock ring, carefully pry its three latches up to free the ring, then turn the ring and detach it from the speedometer.

21 On 1999 Touring models with a mechanical speedometer, unscrew the cable nut from the back of the speedometer. Take the speedometer out of the bezel or fairing.

22 Installation is the reverse of the removal steps.

Speedometer and tachometer (FXDXT)

23 If you're working on an FXDXT, remove the fairing (see Chapter 7).

24 Working behind the speedometer or tachometer, remove two screws that secure

the backplate. Disconnect the speedometer or tachometer electrical connector and push the speedometer through the front of the gauge housing.

25 If necessary, remove the speedometer gasket.

26 Installation is the reverse of the removal steps. If necessary, lubricate the gasket with glass cleaner or alcohol to ease installation.

Oil pressure gauge, voltmeter

27 Remove the outer fairing (see Chapter 7).

28 Disconnect the gauge wiring connector(s). Remove the mounting nuts and take the gauge out of the inner fairing.

29 Installation is the reverse of the removal steps.

Fuel gauge

30 If the gauge is mounted in the left side of the fuel tank, carefully work it free of the tank without twisting it. Disconnect the electrical connector and remove the gauge. Installation is the reverse of the removal steps.

31 If the gauge is mounted in the fairing, it's removed in the same manner as the oil pressure gauge and voltmeter (Steps 27 through 29 above).

Speedometer cable replacement (1999 Touring models)

32 Remove the outer fairing for access to the back of the speedometer.

33 Unscrew the speedometer cable knurled nut from the speedometer.

34 Unscrew the knurled nut for the cable at the drive unit on the left fork leg.

35 Tape a piece of string to the cable so you can trace its routing, then pull the cable out, pulling the string into its place.

36 Tape the string to the new cable, then guide the cable into position, using the string to route it correctly.

37 Connect the ends of the cable to the

drive unit and speedometer, then install the outer fairing.

Speed sensor replacement (electronic speedometer)

38 The speed sensor is mounted on top of the engine to the right of the starter motor **(see illustration)**.

39 Follow the wiring harness from the speed sensor to the connector and disconnect it. Remove the seat if necessary for access (see Chapter 7).

40 Installation is the reverse of the removal steps.

Fuel gauge sender replacement

41 If the motorcycle has a tank-mounted fuel gauge, remove it as described above. Remove the screws that secure the sending unit plate to the tank and lift it out. Installation is the reverse of the removal steps.

42 If the fuel gauge is mounted in the instrument bezel, remove it for access to the fuel tank top plate (see Section 16).

43 Remove the top plate (see Chapter 3).

44 Lift out the fuel level sender or (carbureted models) or fuel pump assembly (fuel injected models).

45 On fuel injected models, detach the sending unit from the assembly and disconnect the electrical connectors **(see illustrations)**.

46 Installation is the reverse of the removal steps. Use a new top plate gasket and tighten it in the proper sequence (see Chapter 3).

---

18 Oil pressure switch/sending unit - check and replacement

1 If the oil pressure warning light fails to operate properly, check the oil level and make sure it is correct.

17.45a Disconnect the electrical connector at the sending unit . . .

17.45b . . . and at the tank top plate (arrow) . . .

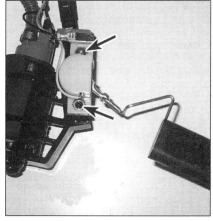

17.45c . . . and remove the screws (arrows) to detach the sender from the fuel pump assembly

18.2 The oil pressure switch or sending unit is mounted near the oil filter base

19.3 Disconnect the electrical connector from the switch (arrow)

Oil pressure switch (warning light)

2 If the oil level is correct, disconnect the wire from the oil pressure switch, which is located on the right side of the crankcase near the oil filter mounting base **(see illustration)**. Turn the ignition switch On and ground the end of the wire. If the light comes on, the oil pressure switch is defective and must be replaced with a new one.

3 If the light does not come on, check the oil pressure warning light LED or bulb, the wiring between the oil pressure switch and the light, and between the light and the fuse (see the wiring diagrams at the end of this manual).

4 To replace the switch, unscrew the switch from the crankcase. Coat the threads of the new switch with electrically conductive sealant, then screw the unit into its hole and tighten it securely.

5 Run the engine and check for leaks.

Oil pressure switch/sending unit (gauge and light)

6 If the pressure gauge indicates oil pressure but the warning light comes on, disconnect the electrical connector from the sending unit **(see illustration 18.2)**. Connect an ohmmeter between the sender's warning lamp terminal (closest to the connector latch) and ground (bare metal on the engine). With the engine off, the ohmmeter should indicate zero ohms; with the engine running at a fast idle, the ohmmeter should indicate infinity. If not, replace the sender as described in Step 4.

7 If the warning light works but the pressure gauge doesn't, disconnect the electrical connector from the sending unit **(see illustration 18.2)**. Turn the key to On, but don't start the engine. The gauge should read zero. Connect a jumper wire between the brown/green wire's terminal in the wiring harness and ground (bare metal on the engine). The gauge should now read 70 psi.

8 If the gauge operates correctly in Step 7, replace the sending unit as described in Step 4.

9 If the gauge does not operate correctly in Step 7, check for power at the gauge positive terminal with a voltmeter (key ON, engine not running). If voltage is reaching the gauge and it doesn't work, replace the gauge.

19 Ignition main (key) switch - removal, installation and check

Removal and installation

1 Remove the seat (see Chapter 7). Disconnect the negative cable from the battery.

Softail and Dyna FXDWG models

2 Remove the acorn nut that secures the instrument bezel and lift it up **(see illustration 15.1a)**.

3 Disconnect the switch electrical connector **(see illustration)**. Remove the switch mounting screws and take it out.

4 Installation is the reverse of the removal steps.

Dyna models (except FXDWG)

5 Remove the seat (see Chapter 7).

6 Unscrew the ignition switch retaining nut and push the switch through the bracket.

7 The wires can't be disconnected; you'll need to cut them about 3 inches (75 mm) from the switch.

8 Connect the wires to the new switch, using butt connectors and a crimping tool.

9 The remainder of installation is the reverse of the removal steps.

Touring models (US)

10 For removal access, you'll need to remove the outer fairing (see Chapter 7).

11 Place the ignition key in the Unlock position and turn the ignition switch knob clockwise to the Access position. Leave the key in. Reach under the knob on the left side, straight back from the Unlock indicator, and find the release button. Push the key straight down, lift the release button (you'll probably need the tip of a key or a similar tool to do this), and turn the knob 1/6-turn (60-degrees) counterclockwise.

12 Lift off the switch knob, unscrew the nut, then lift off the collar and spacer.

13 Remove the fairing cap Torx screws, one on the left and one on the right. Remove the decal plate from the fairing cap, lifting the fairing cap slightly if necessary.

14 Turn the handlebars to full left lock and disconnect the fairing switch electrical connector behind the fairing cap (not the ignition switch connector).

15 Disconnect the ignition switch electrical connector. Remove the switch mounting screws, disengage the switch harness from the inner fairing and remove the switch.

16 Installation is the reverse of the removal steps.

Touring models (all except US)

17 The switch is secured by four screws, covered by plugs meant to prevent tampering. It should be possible to remove the plugs, but if not, you can drill them out with a 3/8-inch drill bit.

Caution: If you use a drill bit, be careful not to damage the screws under the plugs.

Note: *It's probably not possible to peel off the switch knob decal without ruining it.*

18 Remove the outer fairing (see Chapter 7).

19 Peel off the switch knob decal and discard it.

20 Remove the tamper-resistant plugs from over the screws, using a stud extractor or screw extractor. Drill out the plugs if necessary.

21 Remove the four switch knob screws.

21.1a Remove the switch housing screws from the bottom (arrow) . . .

21.1b . . . and from the top (arrow)

21.2 Remove the mounting screw and cut the wires to remove individual switches

22 Lift off the knob and remove the gasket (if equipped).

23 Remove the plate from the fairing cap, raising the fairing cap slightly if necessary.

24 Turn the handlebars to full left lock and disconnect the fairing switch electrical connector behind the fairing cap (not the ignition switch connector).

25 Remove the fairing cap.

26 Disconnect the ignition switch electrical connector.

27 Center-punch the two breakaway screws on the ignition switch base. Drill out the screws with a 3/16-inch bit, then remove them with pliers.

28 Disengage the switch harness from the inner fairing and remove the switch.

29 Installation is the reverse of the removal steps.

Check

30 Checking requires partial removal of the switch for access to the electrical connector.

31 Disconnect the ignition switch electrical connector.

32 Using an ohmmeter, check the continuity of the terminal pairs indicated in the wiring diagrams at the end of this manual. Continuity should exist between the terminals connected by a solid line when the switch is in the indicated position.

33 If the switch fails any of the tests, replace it.

20 Handlebar switches - check

1 Generally speaking, the switches are reliable and trouble-free. Most troubles, when they do occur, are caused by dirty or corroded contacts, but wear and breakage of internal parts is a possibility that should not be overlooked. If breakage does occur, the switches can be replaced individually.

2 The switches can be checked for continuity with an ohmmeter or a continuity test

light. Always disconnect the battery ground cable, which will prevent the possibility of a short circuit, before making the checks.

3 Trace the wiring harness of the switch in question and disconnect the electrical connectors.

4 Using the ohmmeter or test light, check for continuity between the terminals of the switch harness with the switch in the On and Off positions. Continuity should exist between the terminals connected by a solid line when the switch is in the On position, but not in the Off position.

5 If the continuity check indicates a problem exists, refer to Section 21, disassemble the switch and spray the switch contacts with electrical contact cleaner. If they are accessible, the contacts can be scraped clean with a knife or polished with crocus cloth. If switch components are damaged or broken, it will be obvious when the switch is disassembled.

21 Handlebar switches - removal and installation

1 The handlebar switches are composed of two halves that clamp around the bars.

22.1 The neutral switch is on top of the transmission case

They are easily removed for cleaning or inspection by taking out the clamp screws and pulling the switch halves away from the handlebars (see illustrations).

2 To completely remove the switches, the mounting screws should be removed (see illustration) and the switch wires should be cut about one inch from the old switch. Replacement switches come with wires attached and already stripped.

3 When installing the new switch, use heat shrink tubing and solder the wires.

22 Neutral switch - check and replacement

Check

1 Locate the neutral switch on top of the transmission case (see illustration).

2 Disconnect the wires from the neutral switch. Connect an ohmmeter between the posts on the switch.

3 When the transmission is in neutral, the ohmmeter should read 0 ohms - in any other gear, the meter should read infinite resistance.

4 If the switch doesn't check out as described, replace it.

Replacement

5 Unscrew the neutral switch from the case.

6 Wrap the switch threads with Teflon tape. Install the switch and tighten it securely.

23 Horn - check and replacement

Check

1 Remove the horn mounting nut and take it off the bracket (see illustrations).

8

23.1a On all except Springers, the horn is mounted on the side of the engine . . .

23.1b . . . the Springer horn is at the front, secured by a screw (arrow)

2   Disconnect the electrical connectors from the horn **(see illustration)**. Using two jumper wires, apply battery voltage directly to the terminals on the horn. If the horn sounds, check the switch (see Section 20) and the wiring between the switch and the

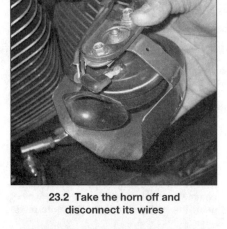

23.2 Take the horn off and disconnect its wires

24.2 The starter relay is mounted on the fuse block (arrow)

horn (see the wiring diagrams at the end of this manual).
3   If the horn doesn't sound, replace it.

Replacement

4   If you haven't already done so, remove the horn and disconnect its wires (see Steps 1 and 2).
5   Installation is the reverse of removal.

24 Starter relay - check and replacement

Starter relay

Check

1   Remove the seat (see Chapter 7).
2   Pull the starter relay off the fuse block **(see illustration)**.
3   Connect an ohmmeter between terminals 87 and 30 on the relay. The ohmmeter should indicate infinite resistance (no continuity).

25.3 Bend back the lockplate tab (arrow) and remove the jackshaft bolt

4   Connect a 12-volt battery to terminals 85 and 86 on the relay (the motorcycle's battery will work if it's fully charged). There should now be continuity (little or no resistance) between terminals 87 and 30.
5   If the relay doesn't perform as described, replace it.

Replacement

6   Remove the relay as described in Steps 1 and 2.
7   Installation is the reverse of removal.

25 Starter motor - removal and installation

Removal

1   Disconnect the cable from the negative terminal of the battery.
2   Remove the primary chaincase cover (see Chapter 2B). If you're working on a Softail, remove the oil tank (see Chapter 2A). Where necessary for access, remove the exhaust pipe(s) (see Chapter 3).
3   Bend back the tab on the starter jackshaft lockplate **(see illustration)**. Unscrew the bolt from the starter jackshaft.
4   Remove the starter cover screw **(see illustration)**. Pull back the rubber cover and, remove the terminal nut and disconnect the starter cable and circuit breaker cable from the starter. Disconnect the solenoid wire. Remove the starter mounting bolts and pull the starter out of the engine. The jackshaft coupling will stay on the starter shaft.
5   If necessary, remove the jackshaft from the other side of the engine.

Installation

6   Install the starter by reversing the removal procedure. Use a new lockplate on the jackshaft. Tighten the mounting bolts, jackshaft bolt and terminal nut to the torques listed in this Chapter's Specifications.

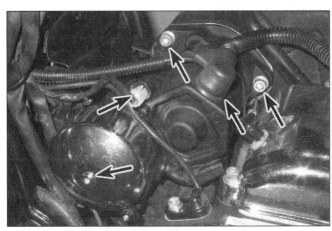

25.4 Remove the cover screw, terminal nut and cables, solenoid wires and mounting bolts (arrows)

28.2a The regulator ground wire on Softails is secured by the left bracket bolt (arrow)

26 Charging system testing - general information and precautions

1   If the performance of the charging system is suspect, the system as a whole should be checked first, followed by testing of the individual components (the alternator and the voltage regulator/rectifier). **Note:** *Before beginning the checks, make sure the battery is fully charged and that all system connections are clean and tight.*

2   Checking the output of the charging system and the performance of the various components within the charging system requires the use of special electrical test equipment. A voltmeter or a multimeter is the absolute minimum equipment required. In addition, an ohmmeter is generally required for checking the remainder of the system. Some test procedures require the use of a load tester with induction pickup.

3   When making the checks, follow the procedures carefully to prevent incorrect connections or short circuits, as irreparable damage

to electrical system components may result if short circuits occur. Because of the special tools and expertise required, it is recommended that the job of checking the charging system be left to a dealer service department or a reputable motorcycle repair shop.

27 Current draw test

1   This test requires an ammeter that can read milliamps.
2   Remove the seat (see Chapter 7).
3   Disconnect the negative cable from the battery. With the ignition off, connect the ammeter between terminal and the disconnected end of the cable.
4   If there is any current draw, it will show on the ammeter. Normal current draws are as follows:

   a) *Electronic control module - 1 milliamp*
   b) *Voltage regulator - 2 milliamps*
   c) *Radio - 4 milliamps*

5   If there is a total draw more than 7 mil-

liamps, the cause may be an aftermarket accessory (alarm or radio), defective voltage regulator, defective radio or a short in the wiring harness.

28 Voltage regulator - test

Ground test

1   The voltage regulator requires a good ground connection to the frame to work properly.
2   To check, connect one terminal of an ohmmeter to the motorcycle's frame and the other to the regulator ground terminal. On Softail and Dyna models, the ground terminal is secured by the left-hand regulator mounting bolt **(see illustrations)**. On Touring models, the ground terminal is at the left side frame ground stud, forward of the battery box. To find it, follow the wire from the regulator **(see illustration)** back to the stud. The ohmmeter should read zero ohms.

28.2b Here's the Dyna installation

1	*Ground wire and*	2 *Mounting bolt*
	mounting bolt	3 *Connector*

28.2c Here's the Touring model installation

28.4a The Softail connector is to the right of the regulator (arrow)

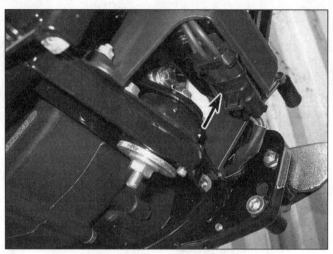

28.4b The Touring model connector is above the front engine mount (arrow)

3   If the ohmmeter reads higher than zero, clean and tighten the ground connection. If that doesn't help, replace the regulator.

Bleed test

4   Disconnect the two-pin regulator connector **(see illustration 28.2b or the accompanying illustrations)**.
5   Make sure the regulator power wire is still connected to the battery.
6   Connect one lead of a 12-volt test light to a good ground on the frame. Connect the other lead to each of the connector terminals in turn (on the voltmeter side). If the test light illuminates in either case, replace the regulator.

29 Voltage regulator - replacement

1   The voltage regulator is mounted at the front of the motorcycle between the frame downtubes.
2   Disconnect the regulator electrical connector(s) **(see illustration 28.2b, 28.4a or 28.4b)**.
3   Remove the regulator mounting bolts **(see illustration 28.2b, 28.2c or the accompanying illustration)**.
4   Installation is the reverse of the removal steps. On Softail and Dyna models, secure the ground wire terminal with the left-hand mounting bolt.

30 Charging system - output test

Caution: Never disconnect the battery cables from the battery while the engine is running. If the battery is disconnected, the alternator and regulator/rectifier will be damaged.

DC voltage check

1   This is a quick and easy test, requiring only a simple DC voltmeter, that will tell you if the charging system is working properly. If a problem is found, other more specific tests will locate the cause.
2   The battery must be fully charged (charge it from an external source if necessary) and the engine must be at normal operating temperature to obtain an accurate reading.
3   Remove the seat (see Chapter 7).
4   Attach the positive voltmeter lead to the battery positive terminal and the negative lead to the battery negative terminal. The voltmeter selector switch (if so equipped) must be in a DC volt range greater than 15 volts.
5   Start the engine. Run it at varying speeds up to 3,000 rpm, with headlight off and with it on.
6   The voltage should be within an approximate range of 14.3 to 14.7 volts.
7   If the output is as specified, the alternator is functioning properly. If the charging system as a whole is not performing as it should, refer to Section 28 and check the voltage regulator.
8   Low voltage - little or no higher than the reading obtained by connecting a voltmeter between the battery terminals with the engine off - may be the result of damaged windings in the alternator stator coils, loss of magnetism in the alternator rotor or wiring problems. Make sure all electrical connections are clean and tight, then refer to the following Steps and Section 31 for specific alternator tests.
9   High voltage output, above 15 volts, may indicate a defective regulator or bad regulator wiring connections.

Total current draw check

10   This test requires a load tester with an inductive pickup. It will tell you whether the charging system is producing enough current for the load being placed on it.
11   Connect the load tester between the battery terminals and connect the inductive pickup to the battery negative cable.
12   Disconnect the electrical connector from the voltage regulator **(see illustration 28.2b, 28.4a or 28.4b)**.
13   If the bike doesn't have a tachometer, connect a tune-up tachometer.
14   Start the engine and run it at 3000 rpm. Switch on all electrical accessories and lights and switch the headlight to high beam.
15   Note the current output. Write this reading down and shut off the engine.
16   Reconnect the electrical connector to the voltage regulator. Place the load tester inductive pickup over the regulator positive wire (the one that runs to the circuit breaker).
17   Again, run the engine at 3000 rpm. Adjust the load to obtain a steady 13.0 volts.

Caution: Do not leave the load switch on for more than 20 seconds.

18   With the voltage at 13.0 volts, note the current output. It should exceed the amount written down in Step 6 by at least 3.5 amps. If it doesn't, the problem may be that the current draw from aftermarket accessories is more than the capacity of the charging system.
19   If the charging system voltage exceeded 15 volts during the test, the regulator either has bad wiring connections or is defective.

AC voltage check

20   This test requires a voltmeter that will read alternating current (AC). It will tell you if a problem exists in the stator coils or rotor.
21   Follow the wiring harness from the voltage regulator to the connector, then disconnect the connector.
22   Connect a voltmeter with an AC scale to the side of the connector that runs back to the stator on the left side of the engine (at this point, you're measuring the alternator output before it has been rectified from alter-

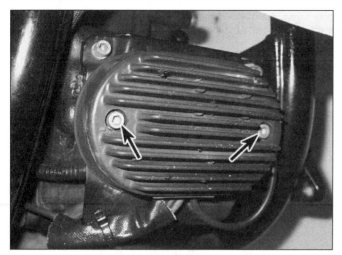

29.3 Remove the mounting bolts (arrows)

32.4 The rotor on all except 45-amp Touring models can be removed by threading bolts or inserting screwdrivers into the removal holes to act as handles

nating current to direct current, so the voltmeter must be able to measure AC).

23　Run the engine at 2,000 rpm and note the voltage reading. Compare it to the value listed in this Chapter's Specifications.

  a) *If the voltage reading is correct, the regulator is probably defective. Refer to Section 28 for test procedures.*

  b) *If the voltage reading is low, the alternator may be defective. Test the stator coils as described in Section 31. If the stator coils test out OK, the rotor magnets have probably lost magnetism. This can be caused by dropping or hitting the alternator, by leaving the alternator near another source of magnetism, or by age.*

31 Alternator stator coils - continuity test

1　If charging system output is low or non-existent, the alternator stator coil windings and leads should be checked for proper continuity. The test can be made with the stator in place on the machine.

2　Using an ohmmeter (preferred) or a continuity test light, check for continuity between the terminals in the stator side of the regulator connector **(see illustration 28.2b, 28.4a or 28.4b)**. Continuity should exist between the wires.

3　Check for continuity between each of the wires and the engine. No continuity should exist between either wire and the engine.

4　If there is no continuity between the wires, or if there is continuity between either wire and an engine ground, an open circuit or a short exists within the stator coils. Since repair of the stator is not feasible, it must be replaced with a new one. **Note:** *An open or shorted stator coil will cause low output or no*

output. Weak or damaged rotor magnets will cause low output.

32 Alternator - rotor removal and installation

Removal

1　Remove the seat (see Chapter 7).

2　Disconnect the cable from the negative terminal of the battery.

3　Remove the primary chaincase cover, then remove the clutch, primary chain and compensating sprocket (see Chapter 2B). The inner chaincase cover does not need to be removed, but the shaft extension and outer spacer do need to be removed from the crankshaft.

4　Pull the rotor off. The rotor magnets will hold it on, so you'll need to overcome their resistance. On all except Touring models with a 45-amp alternator, you can do this with a pair of bolts or screwdrivers inserted into the removal holes **(see illustration)**. The stronger magnets of the 45-amp alternator may require that you use a removal tool (HD-41771 or equivalent). The tool consists of a protective sleeve for the crankshaft, a housing that fits over the crankshaft and attaches to the rotor with two thumbscrews, and a forcing screw that threads into the housing to push against the crankshaft and pull the housing off together with the rotor.

Installation

5　Clean all dirt from the crankshaft and the inside of the rotor with high flash point solvent. Before you install the rotor, make sure the rotor magnets haven't picked up any pieces of metal that could damage the alternator.

6　Position the rotor on the crankshaft.

7　The remainder of installation is the reverse of the removal steps.

33 Alternator - stator coil replacement

1　Remove the alternator rotor (see Section 32).

2　Disconnect the regulator electrical connector **(see illustration 27.2b, 27.4a or 27.4b)**.

3　Remove the stator screws, free the wiring harness from the crankcase and lift the stator coils out of the alternator housing. **Note:** *To ease removal of the wiring harness grommet from the crankcase hole, wet it with glass cleaner, alcohol or electrical contact cleaner.*

4　Installation is the reverse of the removal steps. Tighten the stator screws to the torque listed in this Chapter's Specifications.

34 Radio - removal and installation

1　Remove the seat (see Chapter 7).

2　Disconnect the negative cable from the battery.

3　Remove the outer fairing (see Chapter 7).

4　Disconnect the radio electrical connector (two connectors on Ultra models). Disconnect the antenna cable (and CB cable on Ultra models).

5　Locate the main harness to interconnect harness connectors (one gray, one black). The gray connector is at the T-stud forward of the right fairing bracket. The black connector is at the T-stud for the right radio support bracket.

6　Remove two Allen screws on each side of the radio. The screws are accessible through holes in the fairing brackets. To reach them, you'll need an Allen bolt bit (ideally, a ball-end bit) on a long extension.

7   Work the radio out of its bracket, rocking it if necessary to free it from the nose seal.

8   Place the radio in its brackets, aligning the top of the nose seal with the top of the brackets. If this is difficult, lubricate the nose seal with alcohol, glass cleaner or electrical contact cleaner.

9   Lift the back end of the radio at a 45-degree angle and line up the bolt holes. Install the bolts, rear bolts first, and tighten them to the torque listed in this Chapter's Specifications.

10   The remainder of installation is the reverse of the removal steps.

35 Cruise control - description and check

1   The cruise control system maintains vehicle speed with a stepper motor located in the cruise control module under the left side cover, which is connected to the throttle linkage by a cable. The system consists of the stepper motor, brake switches, control switch, idle cable roll-off switch, module and fuse. Some features of the system require special testers and diagnostic procedures that are beyond the scope the home mechanic. Listed below are some general procedures that may be used to locate common problems.

2   Check the fuse (see Section 5).

3   The brake light switches deactivate the cruise control system. With the key On, operate the front and rear brakes and check brake light operation.

4   If the brake light does not operate properly, correct the problem and retest the cruise control.

5   Check the control cable between the module and carburetor for wear or damage and have it replaced by a dealer service department or other qualified shop if necessary.

6   The cruise control module reads the speed signal from the speedometer and uses this to control the stepper motor.

7   The module senses the engine speed signal from the tachometer and uses this to shut off the cruise control system if the engine over-revs (for example, if the clutch is disengaged without letting off the throttle). It also uses the tachometer signal to detect that the engine stop switch has been activated, and shuts off the cruise control system.

8   The idle cable roll-off switch causes the system to disengage whenever the throttle is closed.

9   The system will also shut off if speed drops below 30mph (48 kph) while the Set switch is being held on.

36 Wiring diagrams

Prior to troubleshooting a circuit, check the fuses to make sure they're in good condition. Make sure the battery is fully charged and check the cable connections.

When checking a circuit, make sure all connectors are clean, with no broken or loose terminals or wires. When disconnecting a connector, don't pull on the wires - pull only on the connector housings themselves.

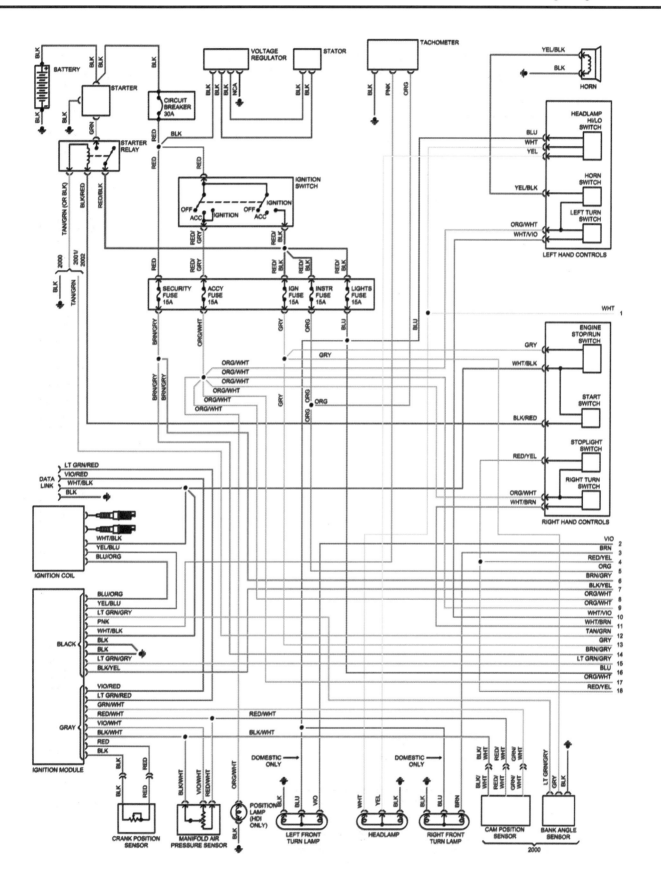

Wiring diagram - Dyna models (page 1 of 2)

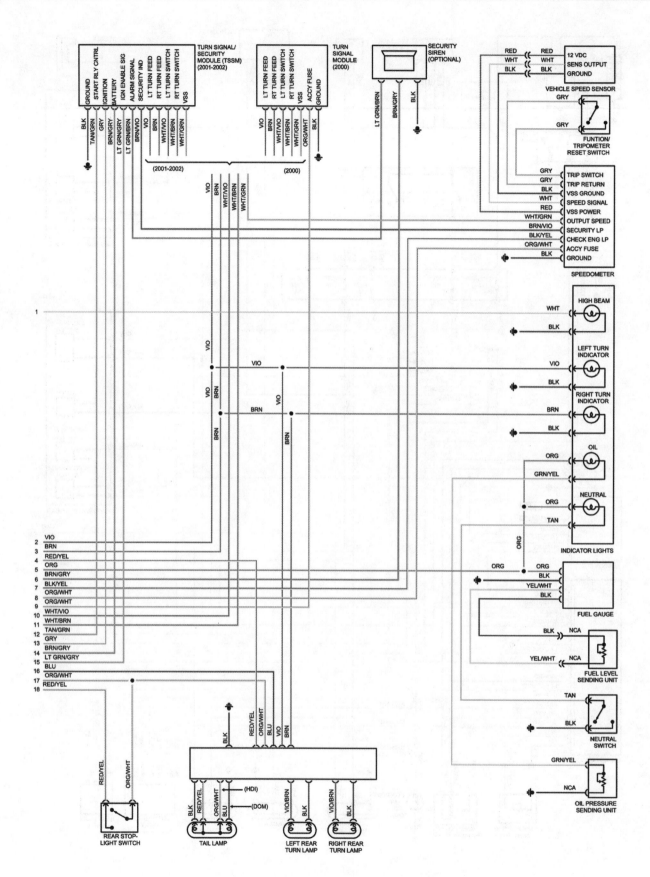

Wiring diagram - Dyna models (page 2 of 2)

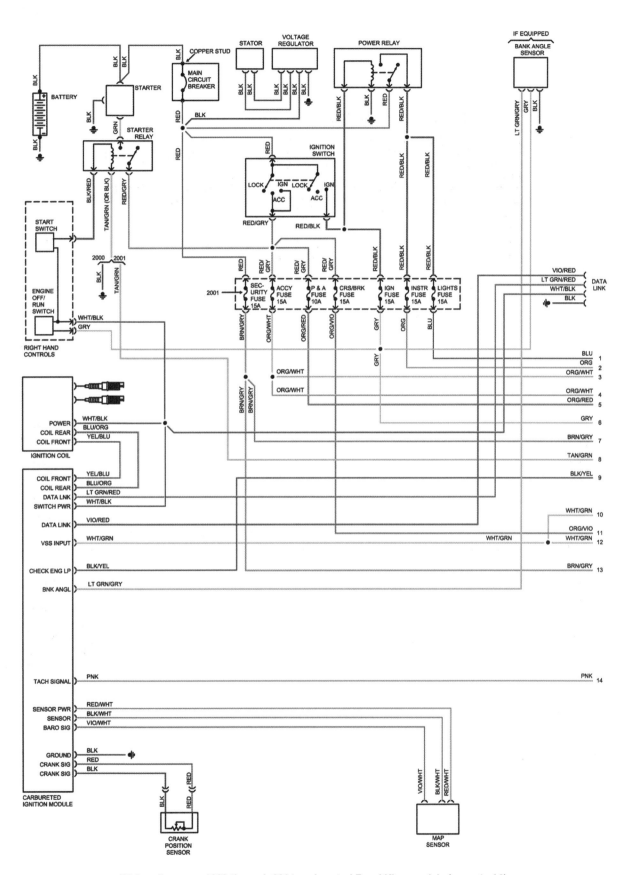

Wiring diagram - 1999 through 2001 carbureted Road King models (page 1 of 3)

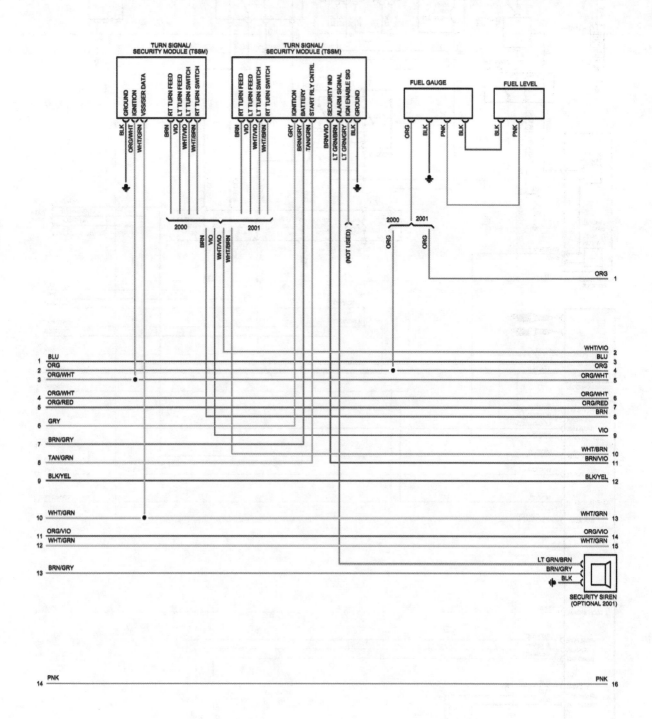

Wiring diagram - 1999 through 2001 carbureted Road King models (page 2 of 3)

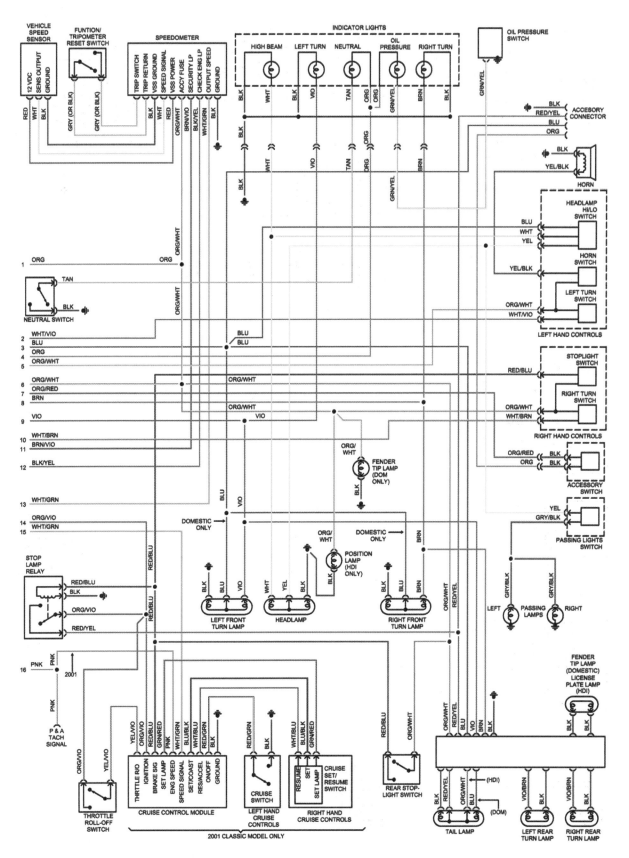

Wiring diagram - 1999 through 2001 carbureted Road King models (page 3 of 3)

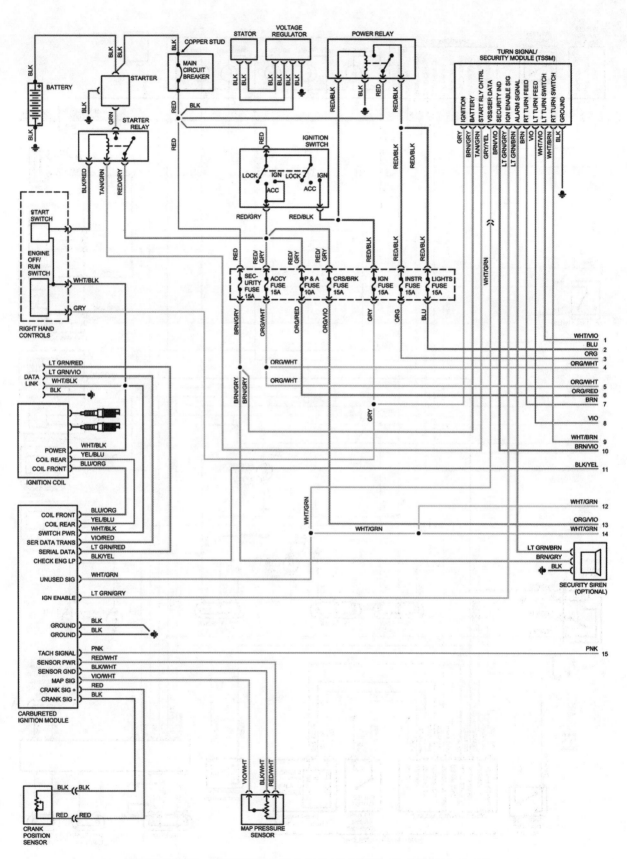

Wiring diagram - 2002 and later carbureted Road King models (page 1 of 2)

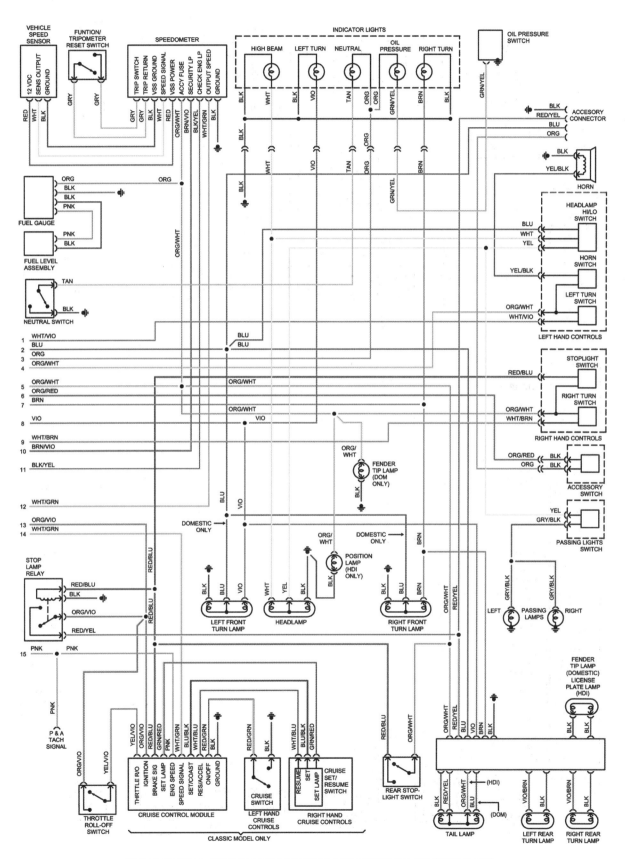

Wiring diagram - 2002 and later carbureted Road King models (page 2 of 2)

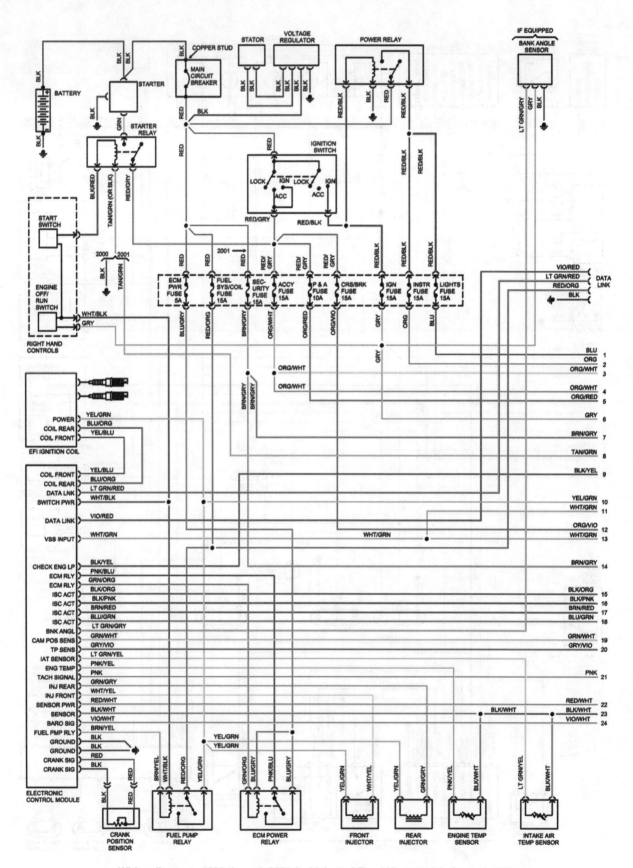

Wiring diagram - 1999 through 2001 fuel injected Road King models (page 1 of 3)

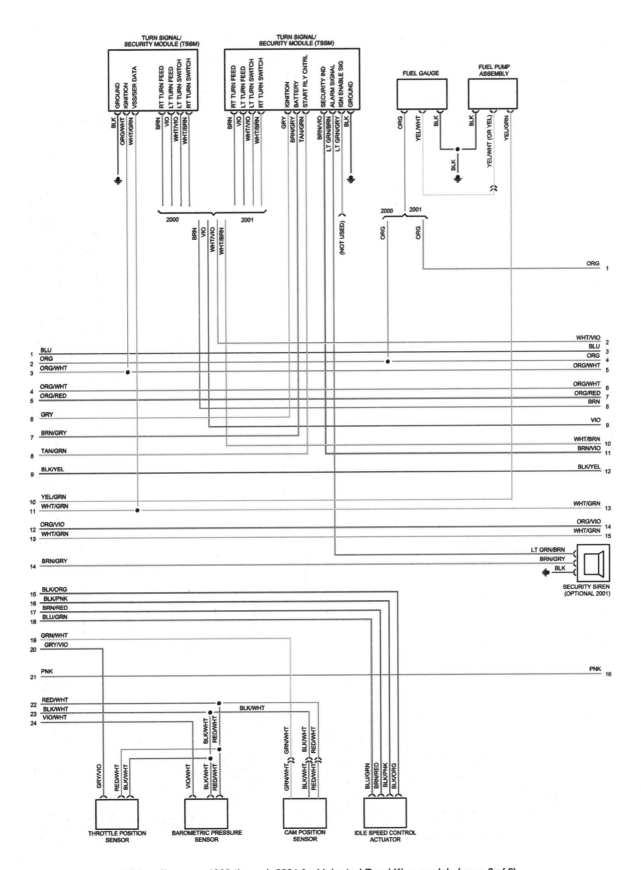

Wiring diagram - 1999 through 2001 fuel injected Road King models (page 2 of 3)

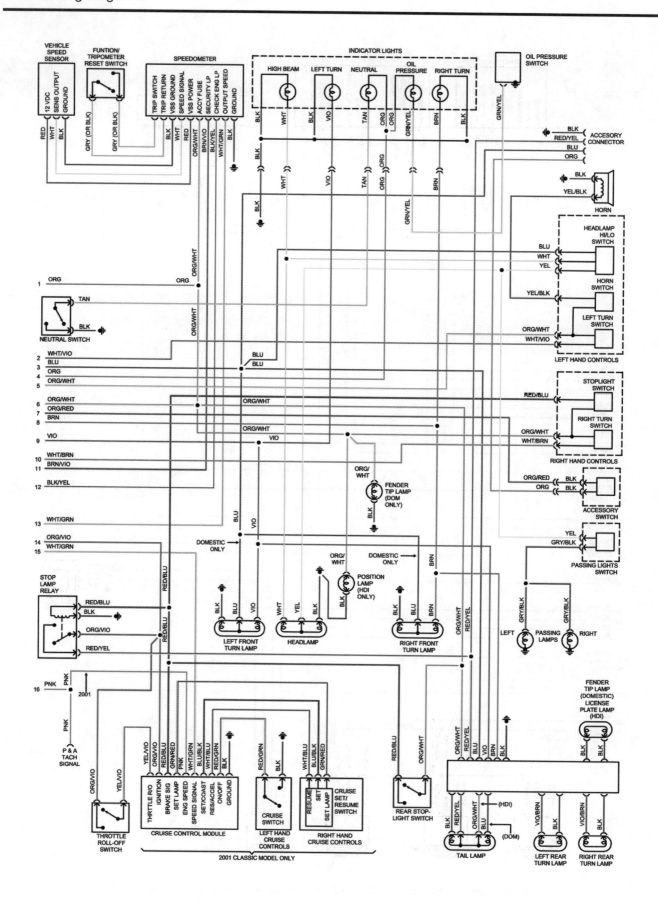

Wiring diagram - 1999 through 2001 fuel injected Road King models (page 3 of 3)

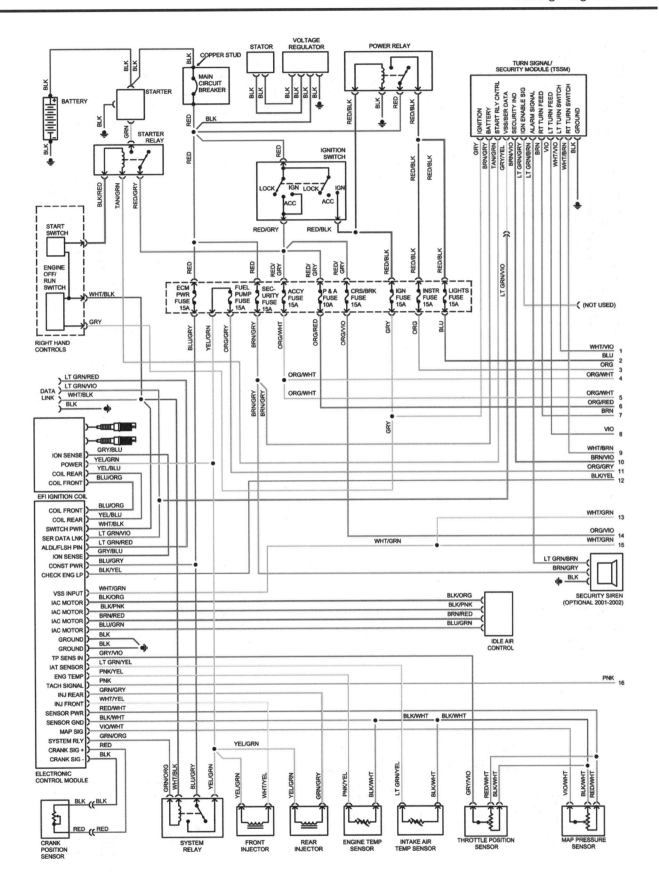

Wiring diagram - 2002 and later fuel injected Road King models (page 1 of 2)

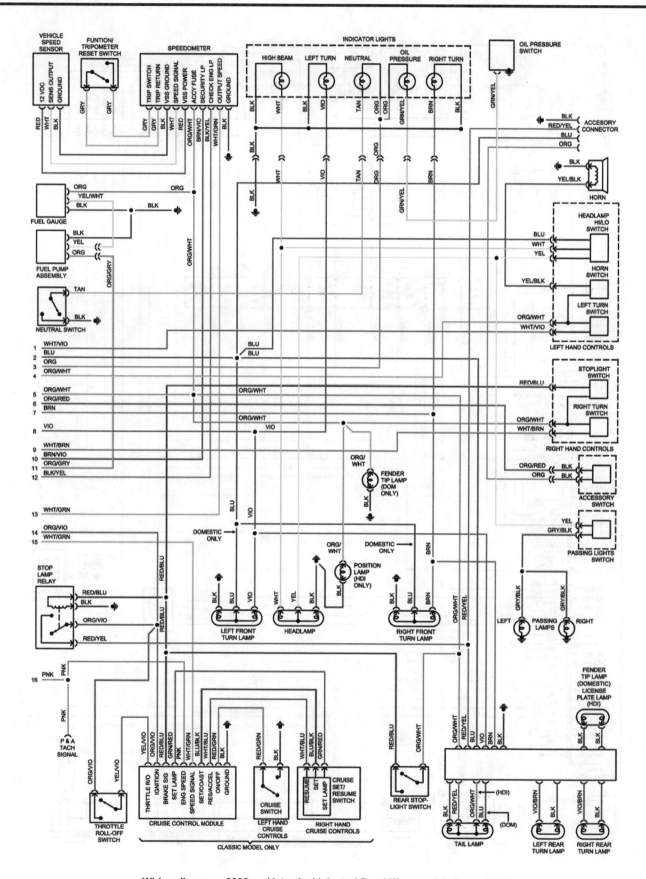

Wiring diagram - 2002 and later fuel injected Road King models (page 2 of 2)

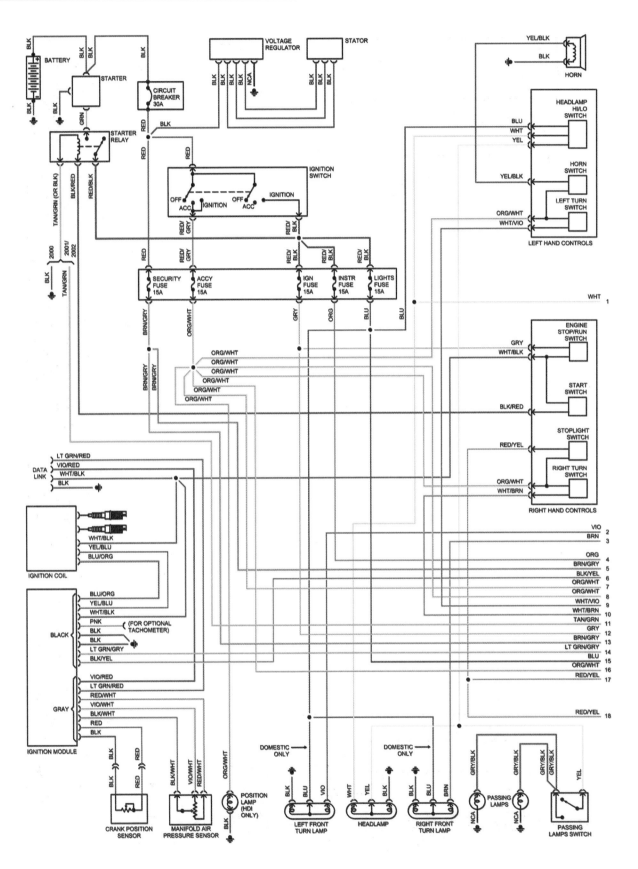

Wiring diagram - carbureted Softail models (page 1 of 2)

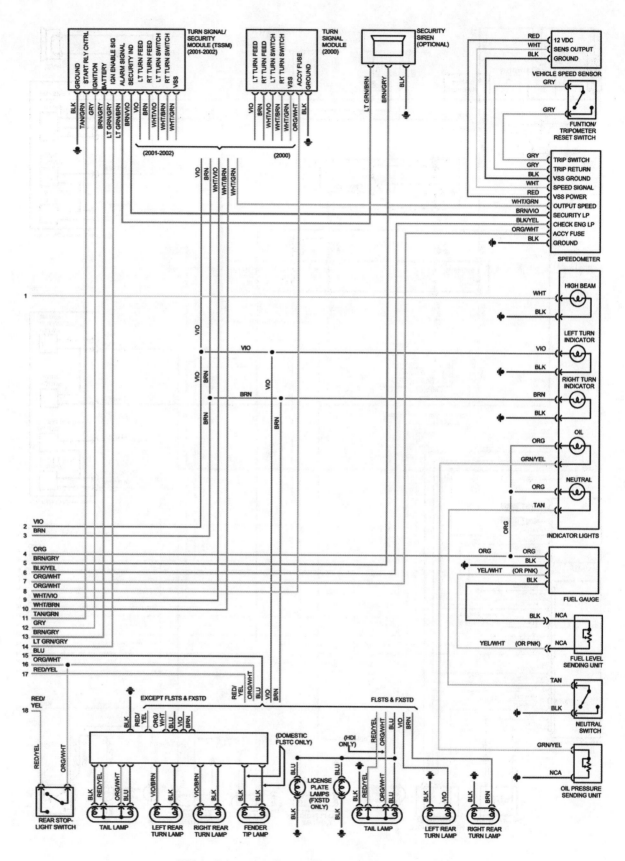

Wiring diagram - carbureted Softail models (page 2 of 2)

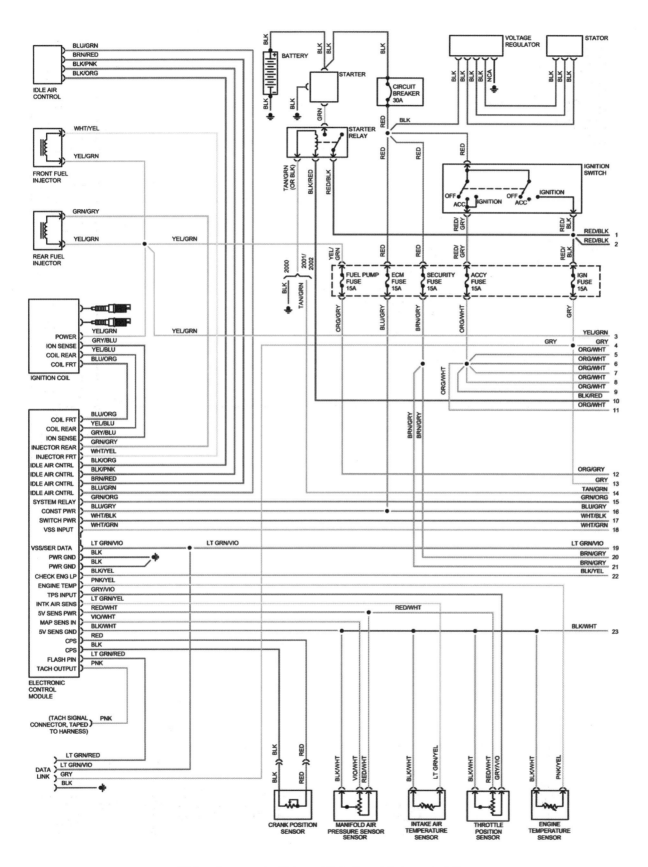

Wiring diagram - fuel injected Softail models (page 1 of 3)

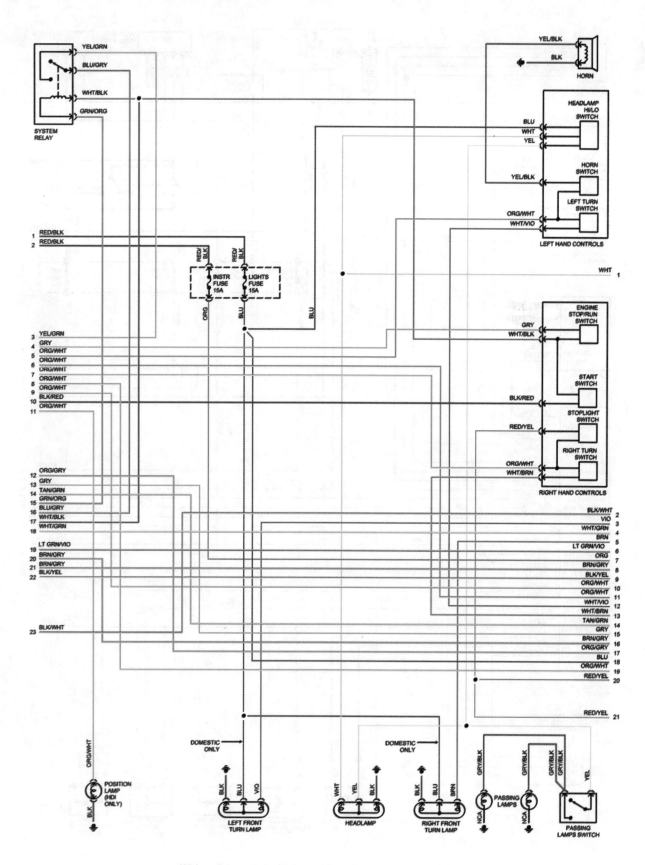

Wiring diagram - fuel injected Softail models (page 2 of 3)

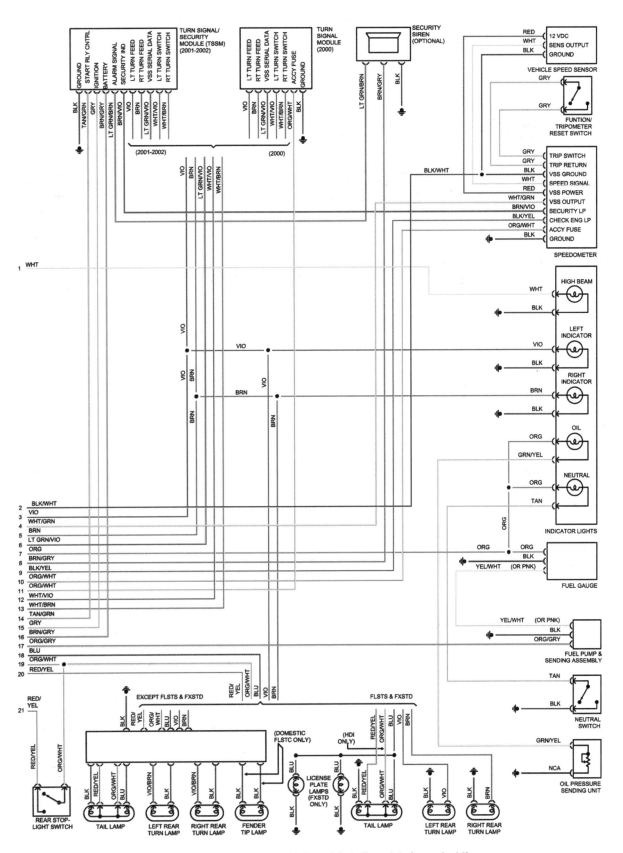

Wiring diagram - fuel injected Softail models (page 3 of 3)

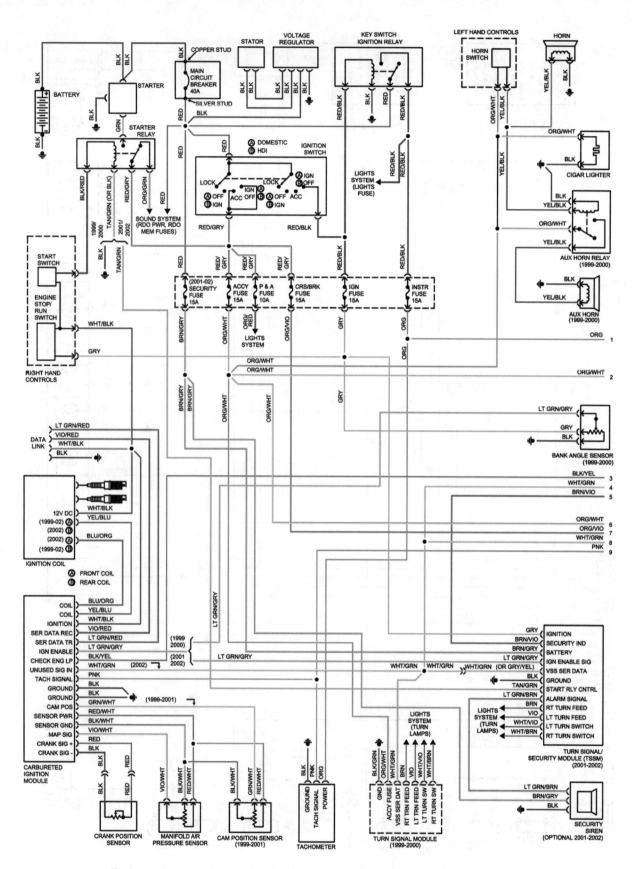

Engine and accessories - carbureted Touring models except Road King (page 1 of 2)

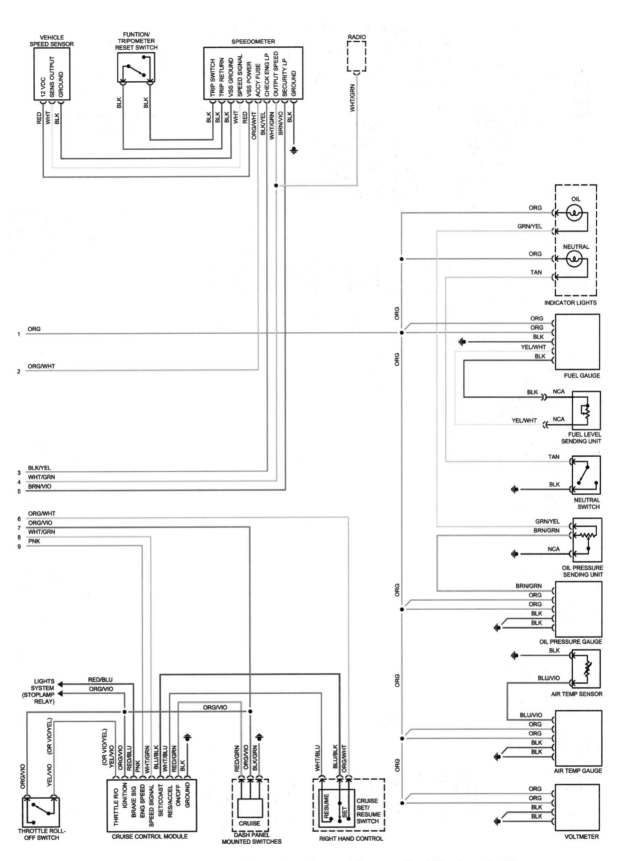

Engine and accessories - carbureted Touring models except Road King (page 2 of 2)

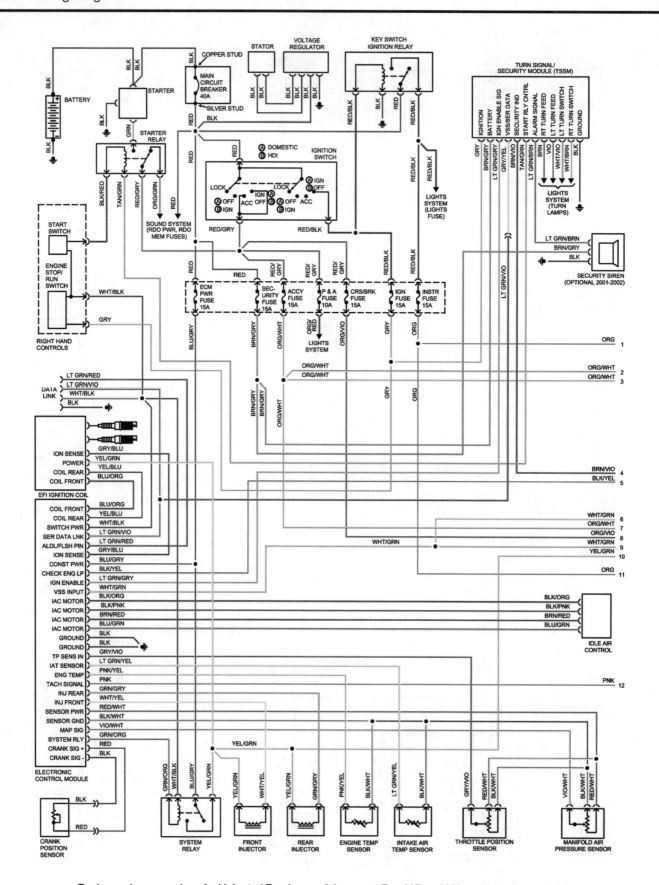

Engine and accessories - fuel injected Touring models except Road King, 2002 and later (page 1 of 2)

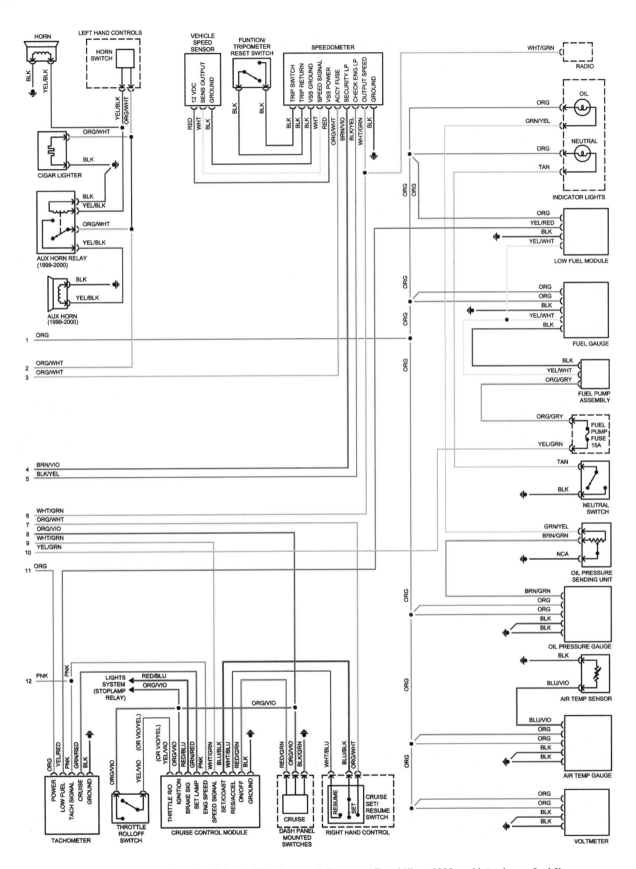

Engine and accessories - fuel injected Touring models except Road King, 2002 and later (page 2 of 2)

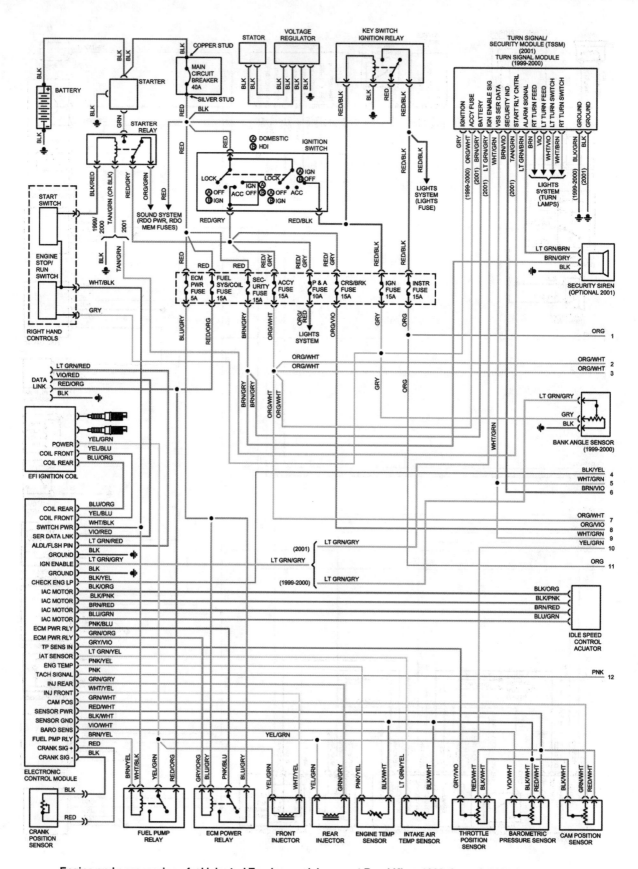

Engine and accessories - fuel injected Touring models except Road King, 1999 through 2001 (page 1 of 2)

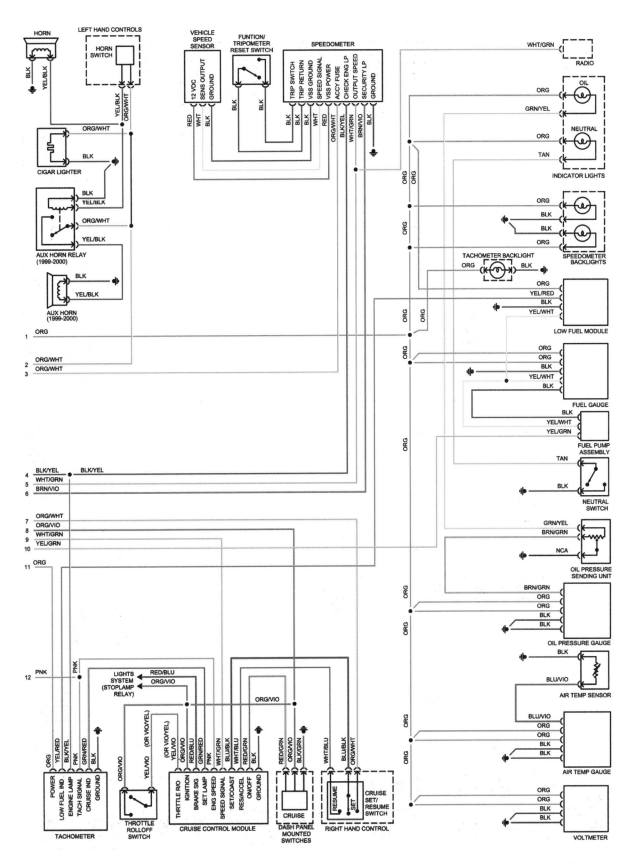

Engine and accessories - fuel injected Touring models except Road King, 1999 through 2001 (page 2 of 2)

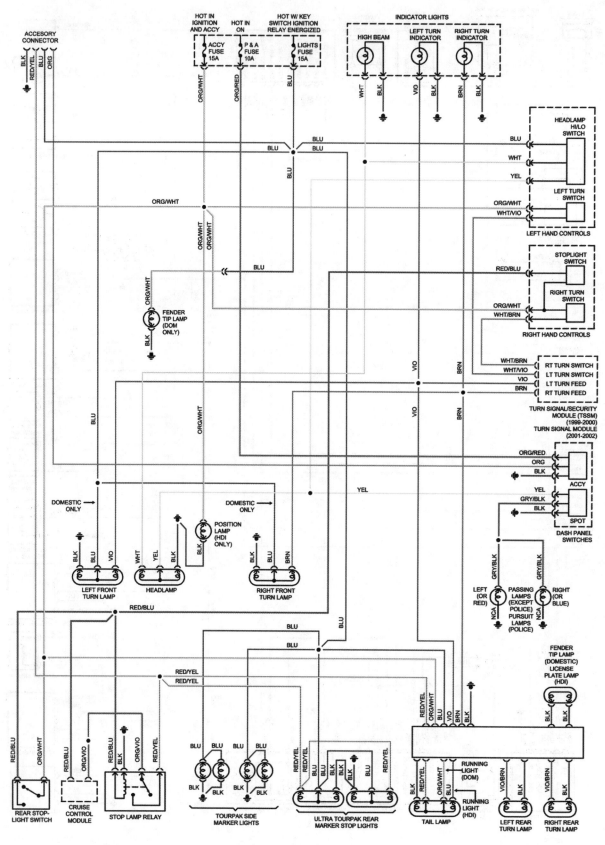

Lighting system - Touring models except Road King

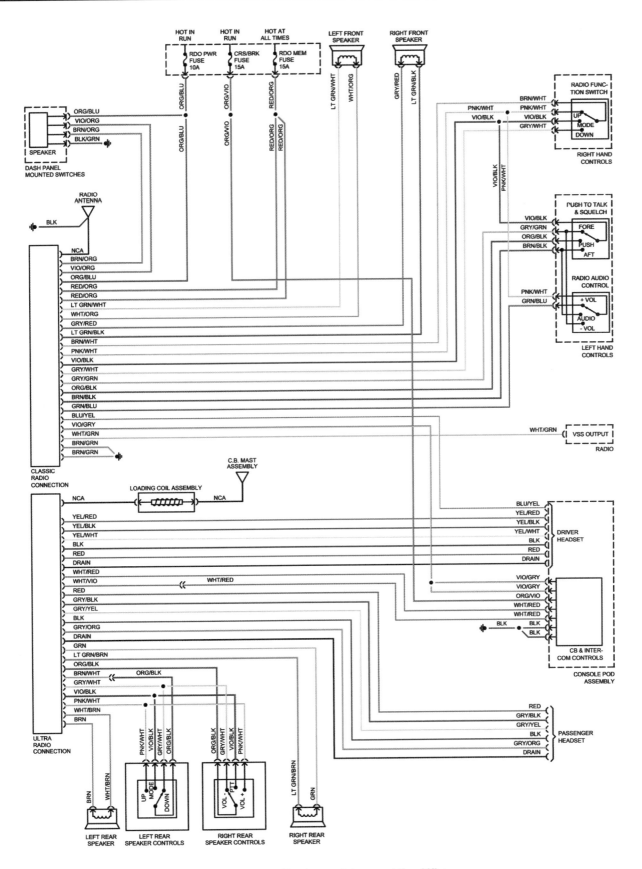

Sound system - Touring models except Road King

Notes

Dimensions and weights

Softail models

Wheelbase
FLSTC, FLSTF	64.5 inches (1638.3 mm)
FLSTS	64.2 inches (1680.7 mm)
FXST, FXSTB	66.9 inches (1699.2 mm)
FXSTS	
2000 through 2002	65.4 inches (1661.2 mm)
2003	66.9 inches (1699.2 mm)
FXSTD	66.6 inches (1691.6 mm)

Overall length
FLSTC	94.5 inches (2400.3 mm)
FLSTF	94.3 inches (2395.2 mm)
FLSTS	94.1 inches (2390.1 mm)
FXST, FXSTB	95.0 inches (2413.0 mm)
FXSTS	93.5 inches (2374.9 mm)
FXSTD	95.4 inches (2423.2 mm)

Overall width
FLSTC	37.5 inches (952.5 mm)
FLSTF	40.2 inches (1021.1 mm)
FLSTS	35.0 inches (889.0 mm)
FXST	37.9 inches (961.9 mm)
FXSTB	30.9 inches (784.9 mm)
FXSTS	32.6 inches (828.0 mm)
FXSTD	35.9 inches (911.9 mm)

Overall height
FLSTC	57.8 inches (1468.1 mm)
FLSTF	44.5 inches (1130.3 mm)
FLSTS	46.0 inches (1168.4 mm)
FXST	46.4 inches (1178.0 mm)
FXSTB	44.9 inches (1140.0 mm)
FXSTS	47.3 inches (1201.4 mm)
FXSTD	46.4 inches (1178.6 mm)

Minimum ground clearance
FLSTC, FLSTF	5.1 inches (129.5 mm)
FLSTS	4.9 inches (124.5 mm)
FXST, FXSTB, FXSTD	5.6 inches (142.2 mm)
FXSTS	5.4 inches (137.2 mm)

Dry weight
FLSTC	
2000 through 2002	695.6 lbs (315.5 kg)
2003	699 lbs (317 kg)
FLSTF	
2000 and 2001	665 lbs (301.6 kg)
2002	665.6 lbs (301.9 kg)
2003	699 lbs (317 kg)
FLSTS	
2000 through 2002	716.6 lbs (325 kg)
2003	721 lbs (327 kg)
FXST	
2000 through 2002	626.6 lbs (285.1 kg)
2003	632 lbs (287 kg)
FXSTB	
2000 through 2002	629.6 lbs (285.6 kg)
2003	633 lbs (288 kg)

FXSTS
2000	625.6 lbs (296 kg)
2003	656 lbs (298 kg)

FXSTD
2001 and 2002	644.6 lbs (292.4 kg)
2003	645 lbs (293 kg)

Seat height
FLSTC	25.4 inches (645.2 mm)
FLSTF	25.5 inches (647.7 mm)
FLSTS	25.9 inches (657.86 mm)
FXST	26.1 inches (662.9 mm)
FXSTB	25.2 inches (640.1 mm)
FXSTS	25.8 inches (655.3 mm)
FXSTD	26.0 inches (660.4 mm)

Dyna models

Wheelbase
FXD	62.5 inches (1587.5 mm)
FXDL	65.5 inches (1663.7 mm)
FXDX	
1999	63.88 inches (1625.5 mm)
2000 and later	63.9 inches (1623.1 mm)
FXDS-CONV	63.88 inches (1625.5 mm)
FXDXT	63.9 inches (1623.1 mm)
FXDWG	66.1 inches (1678.9 mm)

Overall length
FXD	91.0 inches (2311.4 mm)
FXDL	94.0 inches (2387.6 mm)
FXDX, FXDXT, FXDS-CONV	92.9 inches (2359.7 mm)
FXDWG	94.5 inches (2400.3 mm)

Overall width
FXD, FXDL	28.5 inches (723.9 mm)
FXDX, FXDXT	33.0 inches (838.2 mm)
FXDS-CONV	28.95 inches (735.33 mm)
FXDWG	33.5 inches (850.9 mm)

Overall height
FXD, FXDL, FXDWG	47.5 inches (1206.5 mm)
FXDX, FXDXT	51.25 inches (1301.8 mm)
FXDS-CONV	59.25 inches (1504.95 mm)

Minimum ground clearance
FXD, FXDWG	
1999	Not specified
2000	
FXD	5.38 inches (138.65 mm)
FXDWG	5.62 inches (142.75 mm)
2001 and later	5.4 inches (137.2 mm)
FXDL	4.6 inches (116.8 mm)
FXDX, FXDXT	5.9 inches (149.7 mm)
FXDS-CONV	5.75 inches (146.05 mm)

Dyna models (continued)

Dry weight
  FXD
    1999 through 2002... 617 lbs (280 kg)
    2003 .... 612 lbs (277.6 kg)
  FXDWG .... 612 lbs (277.6 kg)
  FXDL
    1999 .... 626 lbs (284 kg)
    2000 and later .... 614 lbs (278.5 kg)
  FXDX .... 619 lbs (281.1 kg)
  FXDXT .... 642 lbs (291.2 kg)
  FXDS-CONV .... 640.0 lbs (290.6 kg)
Seat height
  FXD .... 26.5 inches (673.1 mm)
  FXDL
    1999 through 2001... 26.5 inches (673.1 mm)
    2002 and later .... 25.2 inches (673.1 mm)
  FXDX
    2000 .... 27.00 inches (685.8 mm)
    2001 and later .... 27.25 inches (692.2 mm)
  FXDXT .... 27.88 inches (708.2 mm)
  FXDS-CONV .... 27.75 inches (704.9 m)
  FXDWG .... 26.75 inches (679.5 mm)

Touring models

Wheelbase........................ 63.5 inches (1613 mm)
Overall length
  FLHT .... 93.7 inches (2380 mm)
  FLHTC........................... 97.5 inches (2476 mm)
  FLHTCU .... 98.3 inches (2497 mm)
  FLHR, FLHRC .... 93.7 inches (2380 mm)
  FLTR .... 93.7 inches (2380 mm)
Overall width
  FLHT, FLHTC,
    FLHTCU .... 39.0 inches (990 mm)
  FLHR, FLHRC .... 34.45 inches (875 mm)
  FLTR .... 35.75 inches (908 mm)

Overall height
  FLHT, FLHTC, FLHTCU   61.0 inches (1549 mm)
  FLHR, FLHRC .... 55.06 inches (1398 mm)
  FLTR .... 5.0 inches (1397 mm)
Minimum ground clearance 5.12 inches (130 mm)
Dry weight
  FLHT
    1999 through 2001... 742 lbs (337 kg)
    2002 and later .... 758 lbs (344 kg)
  FLHTC
    1999 through 2001... 760 lbs (345 kg)
    2002 and later .... 776 lbs (788 mm)
  FLHTCU
    1999 through 2001... 772 lbs (350 kg)
    2002 and later .... 788 lbs (358 kg)
  FLHR
    1999 through 2001... 707 lbs (321 kg)
    2002 and later .... 723 lbs (328.2 kg)
  FLHRC
    1999 through 2001... 694 lbs (315 kg)
    2002 and later .... 710 lbs (322.3 kg)
  FLTR
    1999 through 2001... 715 lbs (324 kg)
    2002 and later .... 731 lbs (331.9 kg)
Seat height
  FLHT, FLHTC, FLHTCU
    1999 through 2001... 27.25 inches (69.2 mm)
    2002 and later .... 27.3 inches (693 mm)
  FLHR
    1999 through 2001... 27.25 inches (69.2 mm)
    2002 and later .... 27.3 inches 69.29 mm)
  FLHRC
    1999 through 2001... 26.94 inches (68.4 mm)
    2002 and later .... 26.9 inches (68.27 mm)
  FLTR
    1999 through 2001... 26.94 inches (68.4 mm)
    2002 and later .... 26.9 inches (682.7 mm)

Buying tools

A good set of tools is a fundamental requirement for servicing and repairing a motorcycle. Although there will be an initial expense in building up enough tools for servicing, this will soon be offset by the savings made by doing the job yourself. As experience and confidence grow, additional tools can be added to enable the repair and overhaul of the motorcycle. Many of the special tools are expensive and not often used so it may be preferable to rent them, or for a group of friends or motorcycle club to join in the purchase.

As a rule, it is better to buy more expensive, good quality tools. Cheaper tools are likely to wear out faster and need to be replaced more often, nullifying the original savings.

> ⚠ **Warning: To avoid the risk of a poor quality tool breaking in use, causing injury or damage to the component being worked on, always aim to purchase tools which meet the relevant national safety standards.**

The following lists of tools do not represent the manufacturer's service tools, but serve as a guide to help the owner decide which tools are needed for this level of work. In addition, items such as an electric drill, hacksaw, files, soldering iron and a workbench equipped with a vise, may be needed. Although not classed as tools, a selection of bolts, screws, nuts, washers and pieces of tubing always come in useful.

For more information about tools, refer to the Haynes *Motorcycle Workshop Practice Techbook* (Bk. No. 3470).

Manufacturer's service tools

Inevitably certain tasks require the use of a service tool. Where possible an alternative tool or method of approach is recommended, but sometimes there is no option if personal injury or damage to the component is to be avoided. Where required, service tools are referred to in the relevant procedure.

Service tools can be purchased from JIMS Tools (www.JIMUSA.com) or Motion Pro (www.MotionPro.com). Some of the commonly-used tools, such as rotor pullers, are available in aftermarket form from mail-order motorcycle tool and accessory suppliers.

Maintenance and minor repair tools

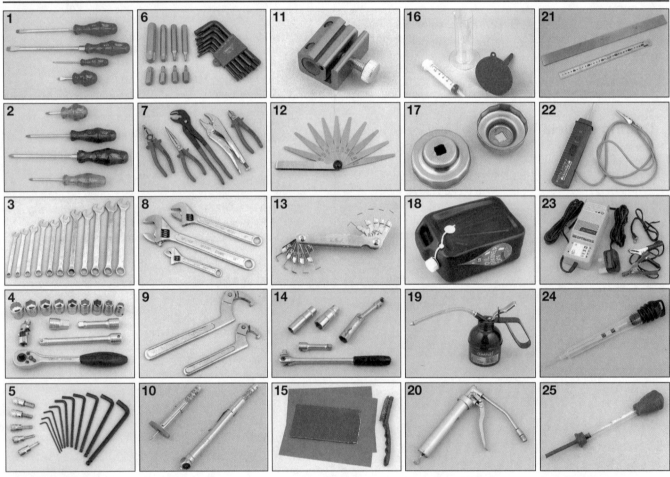

1 Set of flat-bladed screwdrivers	**6** Set of Torx keys or bits	**11** Cable oiler clamp	**16** Calibrated syringe, measuring cup and funnel	**21** Straight-edge and steel ruler
2 Set of Phillips head screwdrivers	**7** Pliers, cutters and self-locking grips (vise grips)	**12** Feeler gauges	**17** Oil filter adapters	**22** Continuity tester
3 Combination open-end and box wrenches	**8** Adjustable wrenches	**13** Spark plug gap measuring tool	**18** Oil drainer can or tray	**23** Battery charger
4 Socket set (3/8 inch or 1/2 inch drive)	**9** C-spanners	**14** Spark plug wrench or deep plug sockets	**19** Pump type oil can	**24** Hydrometer (for battery specific gravity check)
5 Set of Allen keys or bits	**10** Tread depth gauge and tire pressure gauge	**15** Wire brush and emery paper	**20** Grease gun	**25** Anti-freeze tester (for liquid-cooled engines)

Repair and overhaul tools

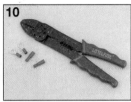

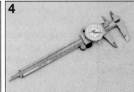

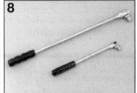

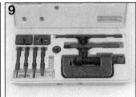

1 Torque wrench
(small and mid-ranges)
2 Conventional, plastic or
soft-faced hammers
3 Impact driver set

4 Vernier caliper
5 Snap-ring pliers (internal
and external, or
combination)
6 Set of cold chisels
and punches

7 Selection of pullers
8 Breaker bars
9 Chain breaking/
riveting tool set
10 Wire stripper and
crimper tool

11 Multimeter (measures
amps, volts and ohms)
12 Stroboscope (for
dynamic timing checks)
13 Hose clamp
(wingnut type shown)

14 Clutch holding tool
15 One-man brake/clutch
bleeder kit

Special tools

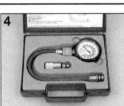

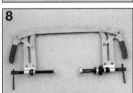
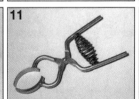

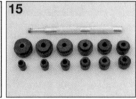

1 Micrometers
(external type)
2 Telescoping gauges
3 Dial gauge

4 Cylinder
compression gauge
5 Vacuum gauges (left) or
manometer (right)
6 Oil pressure gauge

7 Plastigage kit
8 Valve spring compressor
(4-stroke engines)
9 Piston pin drawbolt tool

10 Piston ring removal and
installation tool
11 Piston ring clamp
12 Cylinder bore hone
(stone type shown)

13 Stud extractor
14 Screw extractor set
15 Bearing driver set

1 Workshop equipment and facilities

The workbench

● Work is made much easier by raising the bike up on a ramp - components are much more accessible if raised to waist level. The hydraulic or pneumatic types seen in the dealer's workshop are a sound investment if you undertake a lot of repairs or overhauls (see illustration 1.1).

1.1 Hydraulic motorcycle ramp

● If raised off ground level, the bike must be supported on the ramp to avoid it falling. Most ramps incorporate a front wheel locating clamp which can be adjusted to suit different diameter wheels. When tightening the clamp, take care not to mark the wheel rim or damage the tire - use wood blocks on each side to prevent this.
● Secure the bike to the ramp using tie-downs (see illustration 1.2). If the bike has only a sidestand, and hence leans at a dangerous angle when raised, support the bike on an auxiliary stand.

1.2 Tie-downs are used around the passenger footrests to secure the bike

● Auxiliary (paddock) stands are widely available from mail order companies or motorcycle dealers and attach either to the wheel axle or swingarm pivot (see illustration 1.3). If the motorcycle has a centerstand, you can support it under the crankcase to prevent it toppling while either wheel is removed (see illustration 1.4).

1.3 This auxiliary stand attaches to the swingarm pivot

1.4 Always use a block of wood between the engine and jack head when supporting the engine in this way

Fumes and fire

● Refer to the Safety first! page at the beginning of the manual for full details. Make sure your workshop is equipped with a fire extinguisher suitable for fuel-related fires (Class B fire - flammable liquids) - it is not sufficient to have a water-filled extinguisher.
● Always ensure adequate ventilation is available. Unless an exhaust gas extraction system is available for use, ensure that the engine is run outside of the workshop.
● If working on the fuel system, make sure the workshop is ventilated to avoid a build-up of fumes. This applies equally to fume build-up when charging a battery. Do not smoke or allow anyone else to smoke in the workshop.

Fluids

● If you need to drain fuel from the tank, store it in an approved container marked as suitable for the storage of gasoline (see illustration 1.5). Do not store fuel in glass jars or bottles.

1.5 Use an approved can only for storing gasoline

● Use proprietary engine degreasers or solvents which have a high flash-point, such as kerosene, for cleaning off oil, grease and dirt - never use gasoline for cleaning. Wear rubber gloves when handling solvent and engine degreaser. The fumes from certain solvents can be dangerous - always work in a well-ventilated area.

Dust, eye and hand protection

● Protect your lungs from inhalation of dust particles by wearing a filtering mask over the nose and mouth. Many frictional materials still contain asbestos which is dangerous to your health. Protect your eyes from spouts of liquid and sprung components by wearing a pair of protective goggles (see illustration 1.6).

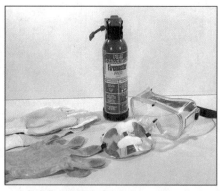

1.6 A fire extinguisher, goggles, mask and protective gloves should be at hand in the workshop

● Protect your hands from contact with solvents, fuel and oils by wearing rubber gloves. Alternatively apply a barrier cream to your hands before starting work. If handling hot components or fluids, wear suitable gloves to protect your hands from scalding and burns.

What to do with old fluids

● Old cleaning solvent, fuel, coolant and oils should not be poured down domestic drains or onto the ground. Package the fluid up in old oil containers, label it accordingly, and take it to a garage or disposal facility. Contact your local disposal company for location of such sites.

Note: It is illegal to dump oil down the drain. Check with your local auto parts store, disposal facility or environmental agency to see if they accept the oil for recycling.

2 Fasteners - screws, bolts and nuts

Fastener types and applications

Bolts and screws

● Fastener head types are either of hexagonal, Torx or splined design, with internal and external versions of each type (see illustrations 2.1 and 2.2); splined head fasteners are not in common use on motorcycles. The conventional slotted or Phillips head design is used for certain screws. Bolt or screw length is always measured from the underside of the head to the end of the item (see illustration 2.11).

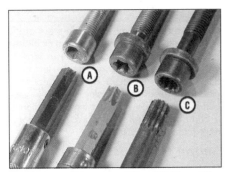

2.1 Internal hexagon/Allen (A), Torx (B) and splined (C) fasteners, with corresponding bits

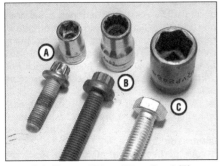

2.2 External Torx (A), splined (B) and hexagon (C) fasteners, with corresponding sockets

● Certain fasteners on the motorcycle have a tensile marking on their heads, the higher the marking the stronger the fastener. High tensile fasteners generally carry a 10 or higher marking. Never replace a high tensile fastener with one of a lower tensile strength.

Washers (see illustration 2.3)

● Plain washers are used between a fastener head and a component to prevent damage to the component or to spread the load when torque is applied. Plain washers can also be used as spacers or shims in certain assemblies. Copper or aluminum plain washers are often used as sealing washers on drain plugs.

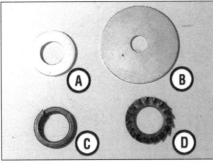

2.3 Plain washer (A), penny washer (B), spring washer (C) and serrated washer (D)

● The split-ring spring washer works by applying axial tension between the fastener head and component. If flattened, it is fatigued and must be replaced. If a plain (flat) washer is used on the fastener, position the spring washer between the fastener and the plain washer.

● Serrated star type washers dig into the fastener and component faces, preventing loosening. They are often used on electrical ground connections to the frame.

● Cone type washers (sometimes called Belleville) are conical and when tightened apply axial tension between the fastener head and component. They must be installed with the dished side against the component and often carry an OUTSIDE marking on their outer face. If flattened, they are fatigued and must be replaced.

● Tab washers are used to lock plain nuts or bolts on a shaft. A portion of the tab washer is bent up hard against one flat of the nut or bolt to prevent it loosening. Due to the tab washer being deformed in use, a new tab washer should be used every time it is removed.

● Wave washers are used to take up endfloat on a shaft. They provide light springing and prevent excessive side-to-side play of a component. Can be found on rocker arm shafts.

Nuts and cotter pins

● Conventional plain nuts are usually six-sided (see illustration 2.4). They are sized by thread diameter and pitch. High tensile nuts carry a number on one end to denote their tensile strength.

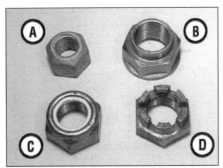

2.4 Plain nut (A), shouldered locknut (B), nylon insert nut (C) and castellated nut (D)

● Self-locking nuts either have a nylon insert, two spring metal tabs, or a shoulder which is staked into a groove in the shaft - their advantage over conventional plain nuts is a resistance to loosening due to vibration. The nylon insert type can be used a number of times, but must be replaced when the friction of the nylon insert is reduced, i.e. when the nut spins freely on the shaft. The spring tab type can be reused unless the tabs are damaged. The shouldered type must be replaced every time it is removed.

● Cotter pins are used to lock a castellated nut to a shaft or to prevent loosening of a plain nut. Common applications are wheel axles and brake torque arms. Because the cotter pin arms are deformed to lock around the nut a new cotter pin must always be used on installation - always use the correct size cotter pin which will fit snugly in the shaft hole. Make sure the cotter pin arms are correctly located around the nut (see illustrations 2.5 and 2.6).

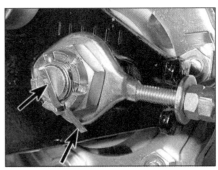

2.5 Bend cotter pin arms as shown (arrows) to secure a castellated nut

2.6 Bend cotter pin arms as shown to secure a plain nut

Caution: If the castellated nut slots do not align with the shaft hole after tightening to the torque setting, tighten the nut until the next slot aligns with the hole - never loosen the nut to align its slot.

● R-pins (shaped like the letter R), or slip pins as they are sometimes called, are sprung and can be reused if they are otherwise in good condition. Always install R-pins with their closed end facing forwards (see illustration 2.7).

2.7 Correct fitting of R-pin. Arrow indicates forward direction

Snap-rings (see illustration 2.8)

● Snap-rings are used to retain components on a shaft or in a housing and have corresponding external or internal ears to permit removal. Parallel-sided (machined) snap-rings can be installed either way round in their groove, whereas stamped snap-rings (which have a chamfered edge on one face) must be installed with the chamfer facing away from the direction of thrust load **(see illustration 2.9).**

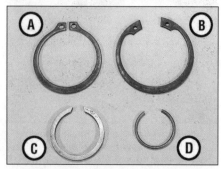

2.8 External stamped snap-ring (A), internal stamped snap-ring (B), machined snap-ring (C) and wire snap-ring (D)

● Always use snap-ring pliers to remove and install snap-rings; expand or compress them just enough to remove them. After installation, rotate the snap-ring in its groove to ensure it is securely seated. If installing a snap-ring on a splined shaft, always align its opening with a shaft channel to ensure the snap-ring ends are well supported and unlikely to catch **(see illustration 2.10).**

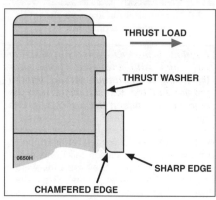

2.9 Correct fitting of a stamped snap-ring

THRUST LOAD
THRUST WASHER
SHARP EDGE
CHAMFERED EDGE
0650H

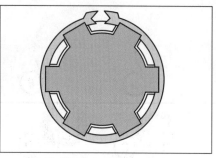

2.10 Align snap-ring opening with shaft channel

● Snap-rings can wear due to the thrust of components and become loose in their grooves, with the subsequent danger of becoming dislodged in operation. For this reason, replacement is advised every time a snap-ring is disturbed.

● Wire snap-rings are commonly used as piston pin retaining clips. If a removal tang is provided, long-nosed pliers can be used to dislodge them, otherwise careful use of a small flat-bladed screwdriver is necessary. Wire snap-rings should be replaced every time they are disturbed.

Thread diameter and pitch

● Diameter of a male thread (screw, bolt or stud) is the outside diameter of the threaded portion **(see illustration 2.11)**. Most motorcycle manufacturers use the ISO (International Standards Organization) metric system expressed in millimeters. For example, M6 refers to a 6 mm diameter thread. Sizing is the same for nuts, except that the thread diameter is measured across the valleys of the nut.

● Pitch is the distance between the peaks of the thread **(see illustration 2.11)**. It is expressed in millimeters, thus a common bolt size may be expressed as 6.0 x 1.0 mm (6 mm thread diameter and 1 mm pitch). Generally pitch increases in proportion to thread diameter, although there are always exceptions.

● Thread diameter and pitch are related for conventional fastener applications and the accompanying table can be used as a guide. Additionally, the AF (Across Flats), wrench or socket size dimension of the bolt or nut **(see illustration 2.11)** is linked to thread and pitch specification. Thread pitch can be measured with a thread gauge **(see illustration 2.12)**.

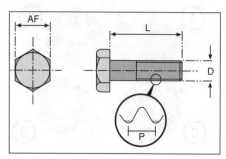

2.11 Fastener length (L), thread diameter (D), thread pitch (P) and head size (AF)

AF
L
D
P

2.12 Using a thread gauge to measure pitch

AF size	Thread diameter x pitch (mm)
8 mm	M5 x 0.8
8 mm	M6 x 1.0
10 mm	M6 x 1.0
12 mm	M8 x 1.25
14 mm	M10 x 1.25
17 mm	M12 x 1.25

● The threads of most fasteners are of the right-hand type, i.e. they are turned clockwise to tighten and counterclockwise to loosen. The reverse situation applies to left-hand thread fasteners, which are turned counterclockwise to tighten and clockwise to loosen. Left-hand threads are used where rotation of a component might loosen a conventional right-hand thread fastener.

Seized fasteners

● Corrosion of external fasteners due to water or reaction between two dissimilar metals can occur over a period of time. It will build up sooner in wet conditions or in countries where salt is used on the roads during the winter. If a fastener is severely corroded it is likely that normal methods of removal will fail and result in its head being ruined. When you attempt removal, the fastener thread should be heard to crack free and unscrew easily - if it doesn't, stop there before damaging something.

● A smart tap on the head of the fastener will often succeed in breaking free corrosion which has occurred in the threads **(see illustration 2.13)**.

● An aerosol penetrating fluid (such as WD-40) applied the night beforehand may work its way down into the thread and ease removal. Depending on the location, you may be able to make up a modeling-clay well around the fastener head and fill it with penetrating fluid.

2.13 A sharp tap on the head of a fastener will often break free a corroded thread

● If you are working on an engine internal component, corrosion will most likely not be a problem due to the well lubricated environment. However, components can be very tight and an impact driver is a useful tool in freeing them **(see illustration 2.14)**.

2.14 Using an impact driver to free a fastener

● Where corrosion has occurred between dissimilar metals (e.g. steel and aluminum alloy), the application of heat to the fastener head will create a disproportionate expansion rate between the two metals and break the seizure caused by the corrosion. Whether heat can be applied depends on the location of the fastener - any surrounding components likely to be damaged must first be removed **(see illustration 2.15)**. Heat can be applied using a paint stripper heat gun or clothes iron, or by immersing the component in boiling water - wear protective gloves to prevent scalding or burns to the hands.

2.15 Using heat to free a seized fastener

● As a last resort, it is possible to use a hammer and cold chisel to work the fastener head unscrewed **(see illustration 2.16)**. This will damage the fastener, but more importantly extreme care must be taken not to damage the surrounding component.

Caution: Remember that the component being secured is generally of more value than the bolt, nut or screw - when the fastener is freed, do not unscrew it with force, instead work the fastener back and forth when resistance is felt to prevent thread damage.

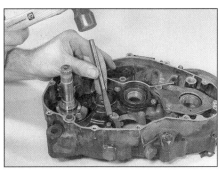

2.16 Using a hammer and chisel to free a seized fastener

Broken fasteners and damaged heads

● If the shank of a broken bolt or screw is accessible you can grip it with self-locking grips. The knurled wheel type stud extractor tool or self-gripping stud puller tool is particularly useful for removing the long studs which screw into the cylinder mouth surface of the crankcase or bolts and screws from which the head has broken off **(see illustration 2.17)**. Studs can also be removed by locking two nuts together on the threaded end of the stud and using a wrench on the lower nut **(see illustration 2.18)**.

2.17 Using a stud extractor tool to remove a broken crankcase stud

2.18 Two nuts can be locked together to unscrew a stud from a component

● A bolt or screw which has broken off below or level with the casing must be extracted using a screw extractor set. Centerpunch the fastener to centralize the drill bit, then drill a hole in the fastener **(see illustration 2.19)**. Select a drill bit which is approximately half to three-quarters the

2.19 When using a screw extractor, first drill a hole in the fastener . . .

diameter of the fastener and drill to a depth which will accommodate the extractor. Use the largest size extractor possible, but avoid leaving too small a wall thickness otherwise the extractor will merely force the fastener walls outwards wedging it in the casing thread.

● If a spiral type extractor is used, thread it counterclockwise into the fastener. As it is screwed in, it will grip the fastener and unscrew it from the casing **(see illustration 2.20)**.

2.20 . . . then thread the extractor counterclockwise into the fastener

● If a taper type extractor is used, tap it into the fastener so that it is firmly wedged in place. Unscrew the extractor (counter-clockwise) to draw the fastener out.

> ⚠ *Warning: Stud extractors are very hard and may break off in the fastener if care is not taken - ask a machine shop about spark erosion if this happens.*

● Alternatively, the broken bolt/screw can be drilled out and the hole retapped for an oversize bolt/screw or a diamond-section thread insert. It is essential that the drilling is carried out squarely and to the correct depth, otherwise the casing may be ruined - if in doubt, entrust the work to a machine shop.

● Bolts and nuts with rounded corners cause the correct size wrench or socket to slip when force is applied. Of the types of wrench/socket available always use a six-point type rather than an eight or twelve-point type - better grip

2.21 Comparison of surface drive box wrench (left) with 12-point type (right)

is obtained. Surface drive wrenches grip the middle of the hex flats, rather than the corners, and are thus good in cases of damaged heads **(see illustration 2.21)**.

● Slotted-head or Phillips-head screws are often damaged by the use of the wrong size screwdriver. Allen-head and Torx-head screws are much less likely to sustain damage. If enough of the screw head is exposed you can use a hacksaw to cut a slot in its head and then use a conventional flat-bladed screwdriver to remove it. Alternatively use a hammer and cold chisel to tap the head of the fastener around to loosen it. Always replace damaged fasteners with new ones, preferably Torx or Allen-head type.

A dab of valve grinding compound between the screw head and screw-driver tip will often give a good grip.

Thread repair

● Threads (particularly those in aluminum alloy components) can be damaged by overtightening, being assembled with dirt in the threads, or from a component working loose and vibrating. Eventually the thread will fail completely, and it will be impossible to tighten the fastener.

● If a thread is damaged or clogged with old locking compound it can be renovated with a thread repair tool (thread chaser) **(see illustrations 2.22 and 2.23)**; special thread

2.22 A thread repair tool being used to correct an internal thread

2.23 A thread repair tool being used to correct an external thread

chasers are available for spark plug hole threads. The tool will not cut a new thread, but clean and true the original thread. Make sure that you use the correct diameter and pitch tool. Similarly, external threads can be cleaned up with a die or a thread restorer file **(see illustration 2.24)**.

2.24 Using a thread restorer file

● It is possible to drill out the old thread and retap the component to the next thread size. This will work where there is enough surrounding material and a new bolt or screw can be obtained. Sometimes, however, this is not possible - such as where the bolt/screw passes through another component which must also be suitably modified, also in cases where a spark plug or oil drain plug cannot be obtained in a larger diameter thread size.

● The diamond-section thread insert (often known by its popular trade name of Heli-Coil) is a simple and effective method of replacing the thread and retaining the original size. A kit can be purchased which contains the tap, insert and installing tool **(see illustration 2.25)**. Drill out the damaged thread with the size drill specified **(see illustration 2.26)**. Carefully retap the thread **(see illustration 2.27)**. Install the

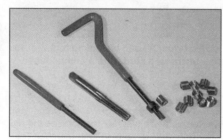

2.25 Obtain a thread insert kit to suit the thread diameter and pitch required

2.26 To install a thread insert, first drill out the original thread . . .

2.27 . . . tap a new thread . . .

2.28 . . . fit insert on the installing tool . . .

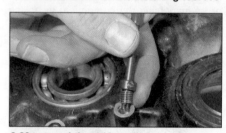

2.29 . . . and thread into the component . . .

2.30 . . . break off the tang when complete

insert on the installing tool and thread it slowly into place using a light downward pressure **(see illustrations 2.28 and 2.29)**. When positioned between a 1/4 and 1/2 turn below the surface withdraw the installing tool and use the break-off tool to press down on the tang, breaking it off **(see illustration 2.30)**.

● There are epoxy thread repair kits on the market which can rebuild stripped internal threads, although this repair should not be used on high load-bearing components.

Thread locking and sealing compounds

● Locking compounds are used in locations where the fastener is prone to loosening due to vibration or on important safety-related items which might cause loss of control of the motorcycle if they fail. It is also used where important fasteners cannot be secured by other means such as lockwashers or cotter pins.

● Before applying locking compound, make sure that the threads (internal and external) are clean and dry with all old compound removed. Select a compound to suit the component being secured - a non-permanent general locking and sealing type is suitable for most applications, but a high strength type is needed for permanent fixing of studs in castings. Apply a drop or two of the compound to the first few threads of the fastener, then thread it into place and tighten to the specified torque. Do not apply excessive thread locking compound otherwise the thread may be damaged on subsequent removal.

● Certain fasteners are impregnated with a dry film type coating of locking compound on their threads. Always replace this type of fastener if disturbed.

● Anti-seize compounds, such as copper-based greases, can be applied to protect threads from seizure due to extreme heat and corrosion. A common instance is spark plug threads and exhaust system fasteners.

3 Measuring tools and gauges

Feeler gauges

● Feeler gauges (or blades) are used for measuring small gaps and clearances (see illustration 3.1). They can also be used to measure endfloat (sideplay) of a component on a shaft where access is not possible with a dial gauge.

● Feeler gauge sets should be treated with care and not bent or damaged. They are etched with their size on one face. Keep them clean and very lightly oiled to prevent corrosion build-up.

3.1 Feeler gauges are used for measuring small gaps and clearances - thickness is marked on one face of gauge

● When measuring a clearance, select a gauge which is a light sliding fit between the two components. You may need to use two gauges together to measure the clearance accurately.

Micrometers

● A micrometer is a precision tool capable of measuring to 0.01 or 0.001 of a millimeter. It should always be stored in its case and not in the general toolbox. It must be kept clean and never dropped, otherwise its frame or measuring anvils could be distorted resulting in inaccurate readings.

● External micrometers are used for measuring outside diameters of components and have many more applications than Internal micrometers. Micrometers are available in different size ranges, typically 0 to 25 mm, 25 to 50 mm, and upwards in 25 mm steps; some large micrometers have interchangeable anvils to allow a range of measurements to be taken. Generally the largest precision measurement you are likely to take on a motorcycle is the piston diameter.

● Internal micrometers (or bore micrometers) are used for measuring inside diameters, such as valve guides and cylinder bores. Telescoping gauges and small hole gauges are used in conjunction with an external micrometer, whereas the more expensive internal micrometers have their own measuring device.

External micrometer

Note: *The conventional analogue type instrument is described. Although much easier to read, digital micrometers are considerably more expensive.*

● Always check the calibration of the micrometer before use. With the anvils closed (0 to 25 mm type) or set over a test gauge (for

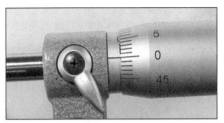

3.2 Check micrometer calibration before use

the larger types) the scale should read zero (see illustration 3.2); make sure that the anvils (and test piece) are clean first. Any discrepancy can be adjusted by referring to the instructions supplied with the tool. Remember that the micrometer is a precision measuring tool - don't force the anvils closed, use the ratchet (4) on the end of the micrometer to close it. In this way, a measured force is always applied.

● To use, first make sure that the item being measured is clean. Place the anvil of the micrometer (1) against the item and use the thimble (2) to bring the spindle (3) lightly into contact with the other side of the item (see illustration 3.3). Don't tighten the thimble down because this will damage the micrometer - instead use the ratchet (4) on the end of the micrometer. The ratchet mechanism applies a measured force preventing damage to the instrument.

● The micrometer is read by referring to the linear scale on the sleeve and the annular scale on the thimble. Read off the sleeve first to obtain the base measurement, then add the fine measurement from the thimble to obtain the overall reading. The linear scale on the sleeve represents the measuring range of the micrometer (eg 0 to 25 mm). The annular scale

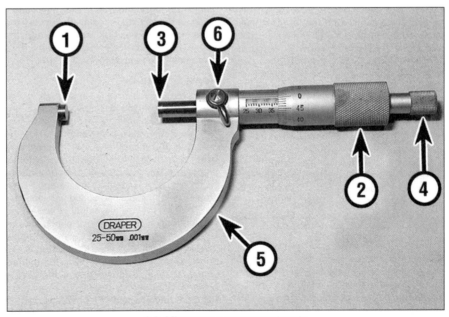

3.3 Micrometer component parts

1 Anvil	3 Spindle	5 Frame
2 Thimble	4 Ratchet	6 Locking lever

on the thimble will be in graduations of 0.01 mm (or as marked on the frame) - one full revolution of the thimble will move 0.5 mm on the linear scale. Take the reading where the datum line on the sleeve intersects the thimble's scale. Always position the eye directly above the scale otherwise an inaccurate reading will result.

In the example shown the item measures 2.95 mm **(see illustration 3.4)**:

Linear scale	2.00 mm
Linear scale	0.50 mm
Annular scale	0.45 mm
Total figure	**2.95 mm**

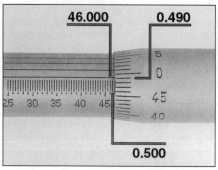

3.5 Micrometer reading of 46.99 mm on linear and annular scales . . .

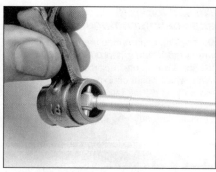

3.7 Expand the telescoping gauge in the bore, lock its position . . .

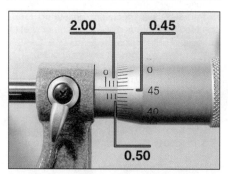

3.4 Micrometer reading of 2.95 mm

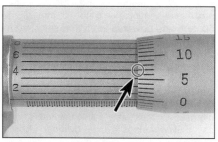

3.6 . . . and 0.004 mm on vernier scale

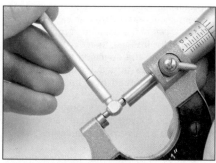

3.8 . . . then measure the gauge with a micrometer

Most micrometers have a locking lever (6) on the frame to hold the setting in place, allowing the item to be removed from the micrometer.
● Some micrometers have a vernier scale on their sleeve, providing an even finer measurement to be taken, in 0.001 increments of a millimeter. Take the sleeve and thimble measurement as described above, then check which graduation on the vernier scale aligns with that of the annular scale on the thimble **Note:** *The eye must be perpendicular to the scale when taking the vernier reading - if necessary rotate the body of the micrometer to ensure this.* Multiply the vernier scale figure by 0.001 and add it to the base and fine measurement figures.

In the example shown the item measures 46.994 mm **(see illustrations 3.5 and 3.6)**:

Linear scale (base)	46.000 mm
Linear scale (base)	00.500 mm
Annular scale (fine)	00.490 mm
Vernier scale	00.004 mm
Total figure	**46.994 mm**

Internal micrometer

● Internal micrometers are available for measuring bore diameters, but are expensive and unlikely to be available for home use. It is suggested that a set of telescoping gauges and small hole gauges, both of which must be used with an external micrometer, will suffice for taking internal measurements on a motorcycle.
● Telescoping gauges can be used to

measure internal diameters of components. Select a gauge with the correct size range, make sure its ends are clean and insert it into the bore. Expand the gauge, then lock its position and withdraw it from the bore **(see illustration 3.7)**. Measure across the gauge ends with a micrometer **(see illustration 3.8)**.
● Very small diameter bores (such as valve guides) are measured with a small hole gauge. Once adjusted to a slip-fit inside the component, its position is locked and the gauge withdrawn for measurement with a micrometer **(see illustrations 3.9 and 3.10)**.

Vernier caliper

Note: *The conventional linear and dial gauge type instruments are described. Digital types are easier to read, but are far more expensive.*
● The vernier caliper does not provide the precision of a micrometer, but is versatile in being able to measure internal and external diameters. Some types also incorporate a depth gauge. It is ideal for measuring clutch plate friction material and spring free lengths.
● To use the conventional linear scale vernier, loosen off the vernier clamp screws (1) and set its jaws over (2), or inside (3), the item to be measured **(see illustration 3.11)**. Slide the jaw into contact, using the thumbwheel (4) for fine movement of the sliding scale (5) then tighten the clamp screws (1). Read off the main scale (6) where the zero on the sliding scale (5) intersects it, taking the whole number to the left of the zero; this provides the base measurement. View along the sliding scale and select the division which

3.9 Expand the small hole gauge in the bore, lock its position . . .

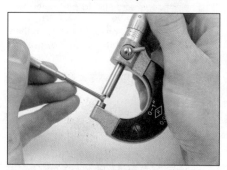

3.10 . . . then measure the gauge with a micrometer

lines up exactly with any of the divisions on the main scale, noting that the divisions usually represents 0.02 of a millimeter. Add this fine measurement to the base measurement to obtain the total reading.

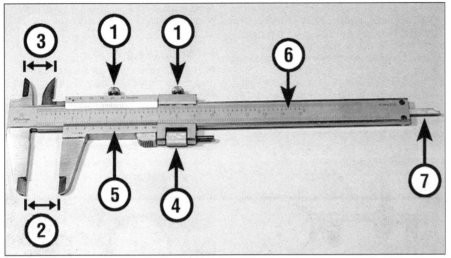

3.11 Vernier component parts (linear gauge)

1 Clamp screws	3 Internal jaws	5 Sliding scale	7 Depth gauge
2 External jaws	4 Thumbwheel	6 Main scale	

In the example shown the item measures 55.92 mm **(see illustration 3.12)**:

Base measurement	55.00 mm
Fine measurement	00.92 mm
Total figure	**55.92 mm**

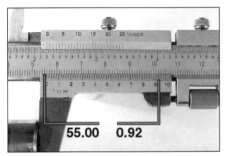

3.12 Vernier gauge reading of 55.92 mm

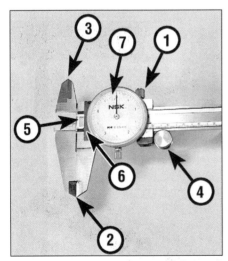

3.13 Vernier component parts (dial gauge)

1 Clamp screw	5 Main scale
2 External jaws	6 Sliding scale
3 Internal jaws	7 Dial gauge
4 Thumbwheel	

● Some vernier calipers are equipped with a dial gauge for fine measurement. Before use, check that the jaws are clean, then close them fully and check that the dial gauge reads zero. If necessary adjust the gauge ring accordingly. Slacken the vernier clamp screw (1) and set its jaws over (2), or inside (3), the item to be measured **(see illustration 3.13)**. Slide the jaws into contact, using the thumbwheel (4) for fine movement. Read off the main scale (5) where the edge of the sliding scale (6) intersects it, taking the whole number to the left of the zero; this provides the base measurement. Read off the needle position on the dial gauge (7) scale to provide the fine measurement; each division represents 0.05 of a millimeter. Add this fine measurement to the base measurement to obtain the total reading.

In the example shown the item measures 55.95 mm **(see illustration 3.14)**:

Base measurement	55.00 mm
Fine measurement	00.95 mm
Total figure	**55.95 mm**

3.14 Vernier gauge reading of 55.95 mm

Plastigage

● Plastigage is a plastic material which can be compressed between two surfaces to measure the oil clearance between them. The width of the compressed Plastigage is measured against a calibrated scale to determine the clearance.

● Common uses of Plastigage are for measuring the clearance between crankshaft journal and main bearing inserts, between crankshaft journal and big-end bearing inserts, and between camshaft and bearing surfaces. The following example describes big-end oil clearance measurement.

● Handle the Plastigage material carefully to prevent distortion. Using a sharp knife, cut a length which corresponds with the width of the bearing being measured and place it carefully across the journal so that it is parallel with the shaft **(see illustration 3.15)**. Carefully install both bearing shells and the connecting rod. Without rotating the rod on the journal tighten its bolts or nuts (as applicable) to the specified torque. The connecting rod and bearings are then disassembled and the crushed Plastigage examined.

3.15 Plastigage placed across shaft journal

● Using the scale provided in the Plastigage kit, measure the width of the material to determine the oil clearance **(see illustration 3.16)**. Always remove all traces of Plastigage after use using your fingernails.

Caution: Arriving at the correct clearance demands that the assembly is torqued correctly, according to the settings and sequence (where applicable) provided by the motorcycle manufacturer.

3.16 Measuring the width of the crushed Plastigage

Dial gauge or DTI (Dial Test Indicator)

● A dial gauge can be used to accurately measure small amounts of movement. Typical uses are measuring shaft runout or shaft endfloat (sideplay) and setting piston position for ignition timing on two-strokes. A dial gauge set usually comes with a range of different probes and adapters and mounting equipment.

● The gauge needle must point to zero when at rest. Rotate the ring around its periphery to zero the gauge.

● Check that the gauge is capable of reading the extent of movement in the work. Most gauges have a small dial set in the face which records whole millimeters of movement as well as the fine scale around the face periphery which is calibrated in 0.01 mm divisions. Read off the small dial first to obtain the base measurement, then add the measurement from the fine scale to obtain the total reading.

In the example shown the gauge reads 1.48 mm **(see illustration 3.17)**:

Base measurement	1.00 mm
Fine measurement	0.48 mm
Total figure	**1.48 mm**

3.17 Dial gauge reading of 1.48 mm

● If measuring shaft runout, the shaft must be supported in vee-blocks and the gauge mounted on a stand perpendicular to the shaft. Rest the tip of the gauge against the center of the shaft and rotate the shaft slowly while watching the gauge reading **(see illustration 3.18)**. Take several measurements along the length of the shaft and record the

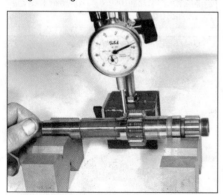

3.18 Using a dial gauge to measure shaft runout

maximum gauge reading as the amount of runout in the shaft. **Note:** *The reading obtained will be total runout at that point - some manufacturers specify that the runout figure is halved to compare with their specified runout limit.*

● Endfloat (sideplay) measurement requires that the gauge is mounted securely to the surrounding component with its probe touching the end of the shaft. Using hand pressure, push and pull on the shaft noting the maximum endfloat recorded on the gauge **(see illustration 3.19)**.

3.19 Using a dial gauge to measure shaft endfloat

● A dial gauge with suitable adapters can be used to determine piston position BTDC on two-stroke engines for the purposes of ignition timing. The gauge, adapter and suitable length probe are installed in the place of the spark plug and the gauge zeroed at TDC. If the piston position is specified as 1.14 mm BTDC, rotate the engine back to 2.00 mm BTDC, then slowly forwards to 1.14 mm BTDC.

Cylinder compression gauges

● A compression gauge is used for measuring cylinder compression. Either the rubber-cone type or the threaded adapter type can be used. The latter is preferred to ensure a perfect seal against the cylinder head. A 0 to 300 psi (0 to 20 Bar) type gauge (for gasoline engines) will be suitable for motorcycles.

● The spark plug is removed and the gauge either held hard against the cylinder head (cone type) or the gauge adapter screwed into the cylinder head (threaded type) **(see illustration 3.20)**. Cylinder compression is measured with the engine turning over, but not running - carry out the compression test as described in

3.20 Using a rubber-cone type cylinder compression gauge

Troubleshooting Equipment. The gauge will hold the reading until manually released.

Oil pressure gauge

● An oil pressure gauge is used for measuring engine oil pressure. Most gauges come with a set of adapters to fit the thread of the take-off point **(see illustration 3.21)**. If the take-off point specified by the motorcycle manufacturer is an external oil pipe union, make sure that the specified replacement union is used to prevent oil starvation.

3.21 Oil pressure gauge and take-off point adapter (arrow)

● Oil pressure is measured with the engine running (at a specific rpm) and often the manufacturer will specify pressure limits for a cold and hot engine.

Straight-edge and surface plate

● If checking the gasket face of a component for warpage, place a steel rule or precision straight-edge across the gasket face and measure any gap between the straight-edge and component with feeler gauges **(see illustration 3.22)**. Check diagonally across the component and between mounting holes **(see illustration 3.23)**.

3.22 Use a straight-edge and feeler gauges to check for warpage

3.23 Check for warpage in these directions

● Checking individual components for warpage, such as clutch plain (metal) plates, requires a perfectly flat plate or piece of plate glass and feeler gauges.

4 Torque and leverage

What is torque?

● Torque describes the twisting force around a shaft. The amount of torque applied is determined by the distance from the center of the shaft to the end of the lever and the amount of force being applied to the end of the lever; distance multiplied by force equals torque.
● The manufacturer applies a measured torque to a bolt or nut to ensure that it will not loosen in use and to hold two components securely together without movement in the joint. The actual torque setting depends on the thread size, bolt or nut material and the composition of the components being held.
● Too little torque may cause the fastener to loosen due to vibration, whereas too much torque will distort the joint faces of the component or cause the fastener to shear off. Always stick to the specified torque setting.

Using a torque wrench

● Check the calibration of the torque wrench and make sure it has a suitable range for the job. Torque wrenches are available in Nm (Newton-meters), kgf m (kilograms-force meter), lbf ft (pounds-feet), lbf in (inch-pounds). Do not confuse lbf ft with lbf in.
● Adjust the tool to the desired torque on the scale (see illustration 4.1). If your torque wrench is not calibrated in the units specified, carefully convert the figure (see *Conversion Factors*). A manufacturer sometimes gives a torque setting as a range (8 to 10 Nm) rather than a single figure - in this case set the tool midway between the two settings. The same torque may be expressed as 9 Nm ± 1 Nm. Some torque wrenches have a method of locking the setting so that it isn't inadvertently altered during use.

4.1 Set the torque wrench index mark to the setting required, in this case 12 Nm

● Install the bolts/nuts in their correct location and secure them lightly. Their threads must be clean and free of any old locking compound. Unless specified the threads and flange should be dry - oiled threads are necessary in certain circumstances and the manufacturer will take this into account in the specified torque figure. Similarly, the manufacturer may also specify the application of thread-locking compound.
● Tighten the fasteners in the specified sequence until the torque wrench clicks, indicating that the torque setting has been reached. Apply the torque again to double-check the setting. Where different thread diameter fasteners secure the component, as a rule tighten the larger diameter ones first.
● When the torque wrench has been finished with, release the lock (where applicable) and fully back off its setting to zero - do not leave the torque wrench tensioned. Also, do not use a torque wrench for loosening a fastener.

Angle-tightening

● Manufacturers often specify a figure in degrees for final tightening of a fastener. This usually follows tightening to a specific torque setting.
● A degree disc can be set and attached to the socket (see illustration 4.2) or a protractor can be used to mark the angle of movement on the bolt/nut head and the surrounding casting (see illustration 4.3).

4.2 Angle tightening can be accomplished with a torque-angle gauge . . .

4.3 . . . or by marking the angle on the surrounding component

Loosening sequences

● Where more than one bolt/nut secures a component, loosen each fastener evenly a little at a time. In this way, not all the stress of the joint is held by one fastener and the components are not likely to distort.
● If a tightening sequence is provided, work in the REVERSE of this, but if not, work from the outside in, in a criss-cross sequence (see illustration 4.4).

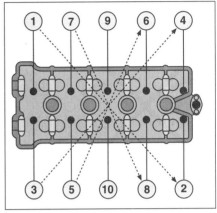

4.4 When loosening, work from the outside inwards

Tightening sequences

● If a component is held by more than one fastener it is important that the retaining bolts/nuts are tightened evenly to prevent uneven stress build-up and distortion of sealing faces. This is especially important on high-compression joints such as the cylinder head.
● A sequence is usually provided by the manufacturer, either in a diagram or actually marked in the casting. If not, always start in the center and work outwards in a criss-cross pattern (see illustration 4.5). Start off by securing all bolts/nuts finger-tight, then set the torque wrench and tighten each fastener by a small amount in sequence until the final torque is reached. By following this practice,

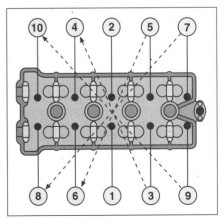

4.5 When tightening, work from the inside outwards

the joint will be held evenly and will not be distorted. Important joints, such as the cylinder head and big-end fasteners often have two- or three-stage torque settings.

Applying leverage

● Use tools at the correct angle. Position a socket or wrench on the bolt/nut so that you pull it towards you when loosening. If this can't be done, push the wrench without curling your fingers around it **(see illustration 4.6)** - the wrench may slip or the fastener loosen suddenly, resulting in your fingers being crushed against a component.

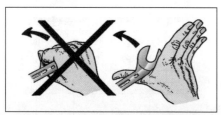

4.6 If you can't pull on the wrench to loosen a fastener, push with your hand open

● Additional leverage is gained by extending the length of the lever. The best way to do this is to use a breaker bar instead of the regular length tool, or to slip a length of tubing over the end of the wrench or socket.
● If additional leverage will not work, the fastener head is either damaged or firmly corroded in place (see *Fasteners*).

5 Bearings

Bearing removal and installation

Drivers and sockets

● Before removing a bearing, always inspect the casing to see which way it must be driven out - some casings will have retaining plates or a cast step. Also check for any identifying markings on the bearing and, if installed to a certain depth, measure this at this stage. Some roller bearings are sealed on one side - take note of the original installed position.
● Bearings can be driven out of a casing using a bearing driver tool (with the correct size head) or a socket of the correct diameter. Select the driver head or socket so that it contacts the outer race of the bearing, not the balls/rollers or inner race. Always support the casing around the bearing housing with wood blocks, otherwise there is a risk of fracture. The bearing is driven out with a few blows on the driver or socket from a heavy mallet. Unless access is severely restricted (as with wheel bearings), a pin-punch is not recommended unless it is moved around the bearing to keep it square in its housing.

● The same equipment can be used to install bearings. Make sure the bearing housing is supported on wood blocks and line up the bearing in its housing. Install the bearing as noted on removal - generally they are installed with their marked side facing outwards. Tap the bearing squarely into its housing using a driver or socket which bears only on the bearing's outer race - contact with the bearing balls/rollers or inner race will destroy it **(see illustrations 5.1 and 5.2)**.
● Check that the bearing inner race and balls/rollers rotate freely.

5.1 Using a bearing driver against the bearing's outer race

5.2 Using a large socket against the bearing's outer race

Pullers and slide-hammers

● Where a bearing is pressed on a shaft a puller will be required to extract it **(see illustration 5.3)**. Make sure that the puller clamp or legs fit securely behind the bearing and are unlikely to slip out. If pulling a bearing

5.3 This bearing puller clamps behind the bearing and pressure is applied to the shaft end to draw the bearing off

off a gear shaft for example, you may have to locate the puller behind a gear pinion if there is no access to the race and draw the gear pinion off the shaft as well **(see illustration 5.4)**.

> **Caution: Ensure that the puller's center bolt locates securely against the end of the shaft and will not slip when pressure is applied. Also ensure that puller does not damage the shaft end.**

5.4 Where no access is available to the rear of the bearing, it is sometimes possible to draw off the adjacent component

● Operate the puller so that its center bolt exerts pressure on the shaft end and draws the bearing off the shaft.
● When installing the bearing on the shaft, tap only on the bearing's inner race - contact with the balls/rollers or outer race will destroy the bearing. Use a socket or length of tubing as a drift which fits over the shaft end **(see illustration 5.5)**.

5.5 When installing a bearing on a shaft use a piece of tubing which bears only on the bearing's inner race

● Where a bearing locates in a blind hole in a casing, it cannot be driven or pulled out as described above. A slide-hammer with knife-edged bearing puller attachment will be required. The puller attachment passes through the bearing, and when tightened, expands to fit firmly behind the bearing **(see illustration 5.6)**. By operating the slide-hammer part of the tool the bearing is jarred out of its housing **(see illustration 5.7)**.
● It is possible, if the bearing is of reasonable weight, for it to drop out of its housing if the casing is heated as described opposite. If this

5.6 Expand the bearing puller so that it locks behind the bearing . . .

5.7 . . . attach the slide hammer to the bearing puller

method is attempted, first prepare a work surface which will enable the casing to be tapped face down to help dislodge the bearing - a wood surface is ideal since it will not damage the casing's gasket surface. Wearing protective gloves, tap the heated casing several times against the work surface to dislodge the bearing under its own weight **(see illustration 5.8)**.

5.8 Tapping a casing face down on wood blocks can often dislodge a bearing

● Bearings can be installed in blind holes using the driver or socket method described above.

Drawbolts

● Where a bearing or bushing is set in the eye of a component, such as a suspension linkage arm or connecting rod small-end, removal by drift may damage the component. Furthermore, a rubber bushing in a shock absorber eye cannot successfully be driven out of position. If access is available to a hydraulic press, the task is straightforward. If not, a drawbolt can be fabricated to extract the bearing or bushing.

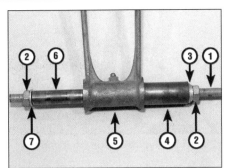

5.9 Drawbolt component parts assembled on a suspension arm

1 Bolt or length of threaded bar
2 Nuts
3 Washer (external diameter greater than tubing internal diameter)
4 Tubing (internal diameter sufficient to accommodate bearing)
5 Suspension arm with bearing
6 Tubing (external diameter slightly smaller than bearing)
7 Washer (external diameter slightly smaller than bearing)

5.10 Drawing the bearing out of the suspension arm

● To extract the bearing/bushing you will need a long bolt with nut (or piece of threaded bar with two nuts), a piece of tubing which has an internal diameter larger than the bearing/bushing, another piece of tubing which has an external diameter slightly smaller than the bearing/bushing, and a selection of washers **(see illustrations 5.9 and 5.10)**. Note that the pieces of tubing must be of the same length, or longer, than the bearing/bushing.
● The same kit (without the pieces of tubing) can be used to draw the new bearing/bushing back into place **(see illustration 5.11)**.

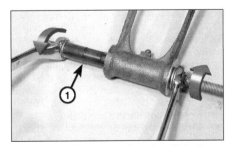

5.11 Installing a new bearing (1) in the suspension arm

Temperature change

● If the bearing's outer race is a tight fit in the casing, the aluminum casing can be heated to release its grip on the bearing. Aluminum will expand at a greater rate than the steel bearing outer race. There are several ways to do this, but avoid any localized extreme heat (such as a blow torch) - aluminum alloy has a low melting point.
● Approved methods of heating a casing are using a domestic oven (heated to 100°C/200°F) or immersing the casing in boiling water **(see illustration 5.12)**. Low temperature range localized heat sources such as a paint stripper heat gun or clothes iron can also be used **(see illustration 5.13)**. Alternatively, soak a rag in boiling water, wring it out and wrap it around the bearing housing.

> ⚠️ **Warning: All of these methods require care in use to prevent scalding and burns to the hands. Wear protective gloves when handling hot components.**

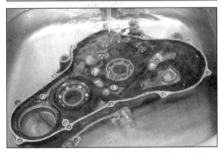

5.12 A casing can be immersed in a sink of boiling water to aid bearing removal

5.13 Using a localized heat source to aid bearing removal

● If heating the whole casing note that plastic components, such as the neutral switch, may suffer - remove them beforehand.
● After heating, remove the bearing as described above. You may find that the expansion is sufficient for the bearing to fall out of the casing under its own weight or with a light tap on the driver or socket.
● If necessary, the casing can be heated to aid bearing installation, and this is sometimes the recommended procedure if the motorcycle manufacturer has designed the housing and bearing fit with this intention.

● Installation of bearings can be eased by placing them in a freezer the night before installation. The steel bearing will contract slightly, allowing easy insertion in its housing. This is often useful when installing steering head outer races in the frame.

Bearing types and markings

● Plain shell bearings, ball bearings, needle roller bearings and tapered roller bearings will all be found on motorcycles **(see illustrations 5.14 and 5.15)**. The ball and roller types are usually caged between an inner and outer race, but uncaged variations may be found.

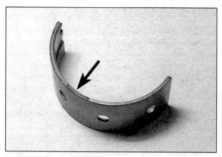

5.14 Shell bearings are either plain or grooved. They are usually identified by color code (arrow)

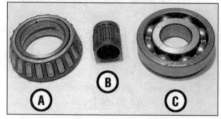

5.15 Tapered roller bearing (A), needle roller bearing (B) and ball journal bearing (C)

● Shell bearings (often called inserts) are usually found at the crankshaft main and connecting rod big-end where they are good at coping with high loads. They are made of a phosphor-bronze material and are impregnated with self-lubricating properties.
● Ball bearings and needle roller bearings consist of a steel inner and outer race with the balls or rollers between the races. They require constant lubrication by oil or grease and are good at coping with axial loads. Taper roller bearings consist of rollers set in a tapered cage set on the inner race; the outer race is separate. They are good at coping with axial loads and prevent movement along the shaft - a typical application is in the steering head.
● Bearing manufacturers produce bearings to ISO size standards and stamp one face of the bearing to indicate its internal and external diameter, load capacity and type **(see illustration 5.16)**.
● Metal bushings are usually of phosphor-bronze material. Rubber bushings are used in suspension mounting eyes. Fiber bushings have also been used in suspension pivots.

5.16 Typical bearing marking

Bearing troubleshooting

● If a bearing outer race has spun in its housing, the housing material will be damaged. You can use a bearing locking compound to bond the outer race in place if damage is not too severe.
● Shell bearings will fail due to damage of their working surface, as a result of lack of lubrication, corrosion or abrasive particles in the oil **(see illustration 5.17)**. Small particles of dirt in the oil may embed in the bearing material whereas larger particles will score the bearing and shaft journal. If a number of short journeys are made, insufficient heat will be generated to drive off condensation which has built up on the bearings.

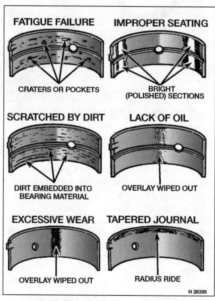

5.17 Typical bearing failures

● Ball and roller bearings will fail due to lack of lubrication or damage to the balls or rollers. Tapered-roller bearings can be damaged by overloading them. Unless the bearing is sealed on both sides, wash it in kerosene to remove all old grease then allow it to dry. Make a visual inspection looking to dented balls or rollers, damaged cages and worn or pitted races **(see illustration 5.18)**.
● A ball bearing can be checked for wear by listening to it when spun. Apply a film of light oil to the bearing and hold it close to the ear - hold the outer race with one hand and spin the inner

5.18 Example of ball journal bearing with damaged balls and cages

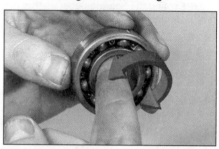

5.19 Hold outer race and listen to inner race when spun

race with the other hand **(see illustration 5.19)**. The bearing should be almost silent when spun; if it grates or rattles it is worn.

6 Oil seals

Oil seal removal and installation

● Oil seals should be replaced every time a component is dismantled. This is because the seal lips will become set to the sealing surface and will not necessarily reseal.
● Oil seals can be pried out of position using a large flat-bladed screwdriver **(see illustration 6.1)**. In the case of crankcase seals, check first that the seal is not lipped on the inside, preventing its removal with the crankcases joined.

6.1 Pry out oil seals with a large flat-bladed screwdriver

● New seals are usually installed with their marked face (containing the seal reference code) outwards and the spring side towards the fluid being retained. In certain cases, such as a two-stroke engine crankshaft seal, a double lipped seal may be used due to there being fluid or gas on each side of the joint.

● Use a bearing driver or socket which bears only on the outer hard edge of the seal to install it in the casing - tapping on the inner edge will damage the sealing lip.

Oil seal types and markings

● Oil seals are usually of the single-lipped type. Double-lipped seals are found where a liquid or gas is on both sides of the joint.
● Oil seals can harden and lose their sealing ability if the motorcycle has been in storage for a long period - replacement is the only solution.
● Oil seal manufacturers also conform to the ISO markings for seal size - these are molded into the outer.face of the seal **(see illustration 6.2)**.

6.2 These oil seal markings indicate inside diameter, outside diameter and seal thickness

7   Gaskets and sealants

Types of gasket and sealant

● Gaskets are used to seal the mating surfaces between components and keep lubricants, fluids, vacuum or pressure contained within the assembly. Aluminum gaskets are sometimes found at the cylinder joints, but most gaskets are paper-based. If the mating surfaces of the components being joined are undamaged the gasket can be installed dry, although a dab of sealant or grease will be useful to hold it in place during assembly.
● RTV (Room Temperature Vulcanizing) silicone rubber sealants cure when exposed to moisture in the atmosphere. These sealants are good at filling pits or irregular gasket faces, but will tend to be forced out of the joint under very high torque. They can be used to replace a paper gasket, but first make sure that the width of the paper gasket is not essential to the shimming of internal components. RTV sealants should not be used on components containing gasoline.
● Non-hardening, semi-hardening and hard setting liquid gasket compounds can be used with a gasket or between a metal-to-metal joint. Select the sealant to suit the application: universal non-hardening sealant can be used on virtually all joints; semi-hardening on joint faces which are rough or damaged; hard setting sealant on joints which require a permanent bond and are subjected to high temperature and pressure. **Note:** *Check first if the paper gasket has a bead of sealant*

impregnated in its surface before applying additional sealant.
● When choosing a sealant, make sure it is suitable for the application, particularly if being applied in a high-temperature area or in the vicinity of fuel. Certain manufacturers produce sealants in either clear, silver or black colors to match the finish of the engine. This has a particular application on motorcycles where much of the engine is exposed.
● Do not over-apply sealant. That which is squeezed out on the outside of the joint can be wiped off, whereas an excess of sealant on the inside can break off and clog oilways.

Breaking a sealed joint

● Age, heat, pressure and the use of hard setting sealant can cause two components to stick together so tightly that they are difficult to separate using finger pressure alone. Do not resort to using levers unless there is a pry point provided for this purpose **(see illustration 7.1)** or else the gasket surfaces will be damaged.
● Use a soft-faced hammer **(see illustration 7.2)** or a wood block and conventional hammer to strike the component near the mating surface. Avoid hammering against cast extremities since they may break off. If this method fails, try using a wood wedge between the two components.

Caution: If the joint will not separate, double-check that you have removed all the fasteners.

7.1 If a pry point is provided, apply gentle pressure with a flat-bladed screwdriver

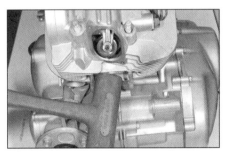

7.2 Tap around the joint with a soft-faced mallet if necessary - don't strike cooling fins

Removal of old gasket and sealant

● Paper gaskets will most likely come away complete, leaving only a few traces stuck on

Most components have one or two hollow locating dowels between the two gasket faces. If a dowel cannot be removed, do not resort to gripping it with pliers - it will almost certainly be distorted. Install a close-fitting socket or Phillips screwdriver into the dowel and then grip the outer edge of the dowel to free it.

the sealing faces of the components. It is imperative that all traces are removed to ensure correct sealing of the new gasket.
● Very carefully scrape all traces of gasket away making sure that the sealing surfaces are not gouged or scored by the scraper **(see illustrations 7.3, 7.4 and 7.5)**. Stubborn deposits can be removed by spraying with an aerosol gasket remover. Final preparation of

7.3 Paper gaskets can be scraped off with a gasket scraper tool . . .

7.4 . . . a knife blade . . .

7.5 . . . or a household scraper

7.6 Fine abrasive paper is wrapped around a flat file to clean up the gasket face

7.7 A kitchen scourer can be used on stubborn deposits

the gasket surface can be made with very fine abrasive paper or a plastic kitchen scourer **(see illustrations 7.6 and 7.7)**.

● Old sealant can be scraped or peeled off components, depending on the type originally used. Note that gasket removal compounds are available to avoid scraping the components clean; make sure the gasket remover suits the type of sealant used.

8 Chains

Breaking and joining final drive chains

● Drive chains for all but small bikes are continuous and do not have a clip-type connecting link. The chain must be broken using a chain breaker tool and the new chain securely riveted together using a new soft rivet-type link. Never use a clip-type connecting link instead of a rivet-type link, except in an emergency. Various chain breaking and riveting tools are available, either as separate tools or combined as illustrated in the accompanying photographs - read the instructions supplied with the tool carefully.

⚠ **Warning: The need to rivet the new link pins correctly cannot be overstressed - loss of control of the motorcycle is very likely to result if the chain breaks in use.**

● Rotate the chain and look for the soft link. The soft link pins look like they have been

8.1 Tighten the chain breaker to push the pin out of the link . . .

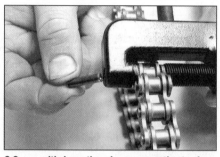

8.2 . . . withdraw the pin, remove the tool . . .

8.3 . . . and separate the chain link

deeply center-punched instead of peened over like all the other pins **(see illustration 8.9)** and its sideplate may be a different color. Position the soft link midway between the sprockets and assemble the chain breaker tool over one of the soft link pins **(see illustration 8.1)**. Operate the tool to push the pin out through the chain **(see illustration 8.2)**. On an O-ring chain, remove the O-rings **(see illustration 8.3)**. Carry out the same procedure on the other soft link pin.

Caution: Certain soft link pins (particularly on the larger chains) may require their ends to be filed or ground off before they can be pressed out using the tool.

● Check that you have the correct size and strength (standard or heavy duty) new soft link - do not reuse the old link. Look for the size marking on the chain sideplates **(see illustration 8.10)**.

● Position the chain ends so that they are engaged over the rear sprocket. On an O-ring

8.4 Insert the new soft link, with O-rings, through the chain ends . . .

8.5 . . . install the O-rings over the pin ends . . .

8.6 . . . followed by the sideplate

chain, install a new O-ring over each pin of the link and insert the link through the two chain ends **(see illustration 8.4)**. Install a new O-ring over the end of each pin, followed by the sideplate (with the chain manufacturer's marking facing outwards) **(see illustrations 8.5 and 8.6)**. On an unsealed chain, insert the link through the two chain ends, then install the sideplate with the chain manufacturer's marking facing outwards.

● Note that it may not be possible to install the sideplate using finger pressure alone. If using a joining tool, assemble it so that the plates of the tool clamp the link and press the sideplate over the pins **(see illustration 8.7)**. Otherwise, use two small sockets placed over

8.7 Push the sideplate into position using a clamp

8.8 Assemble the chain riveting tool over one pin at a time and tighten it fully

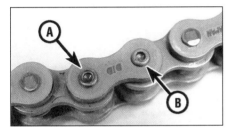

8.9 Pin end correctly riveted (A), pin end unriveted (B)

the rivet ends and two pieces of the wood between a C-clamp. Operate the clamp to press the sideplate over the pins.

● Assemble the joining tool over one pin (following the manufacturer's instructions) and tighten the tool down to spread the pin end securely **(see illustrations 8.8 and 8.9)**. Do the same on the other pin.

 Warning: Check that the pin ends are secure and that there is no danger of the sideplate coming loose. If the pin ends are cracked the soft link must be replaced.

Final drive chain sizing

● Chains are sized using a three digit number, followed by a suffix to denote the chain type **(see illustration 8.10)**. Chain type is either standard or heavy duty (thicker sideplates), and also unsealed or O-ring/X-ring type.

● The first digit of the number relates to the pitch of the chain, ie the distance from the center of one pin to the center of the next pin **(see illustration 8.11)**. Pitch is expressed in eighths of an inch, as follows:

8.10 Typical chain size and type marking

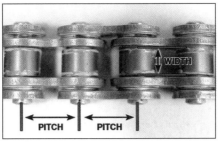

8.11 Chain dimensions

Sizes commencing with a 4 (for example 428) have a pitch of 1/2 inch (12.7 mm)

Sizes commencing with a 5 (for example 520) have a pitch of 5/8 inch (15.9 mm)

Sizes commencing with a 6 (for example 630) have a pitch of 3/4 inch (19.1 mm)

● The second and third digits of the chain size relate to the width of the rollers, for example the 525 shown has 5/16 inch (7.94 mm) rollers **(see illustration 8.11)**.

9 Hoses

Clamping to prevent flow

● Small-bore flexible hoses can be clamped to prevent fluid flow while a component is worked on. Whichever method is used, ensure that the hose material is not permanently distorted or damaged by the clamp.

a) A brake hose clamp available from auto parts stores **(see illustration 9.1)**.
b) A wingnut type hose clamp **(see illustration 9.2)**.

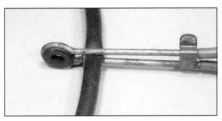

9.1 Hoses can be clamped with an automotive brake hose clamp . . .

9.2 . . . a wingnut type hose clamp . . .

c) Two sockets placed on each side of the hose and held with straight-jawed self-locking pliers **(see illustration 9.3)**.
d) Thick card stock on each side of the hose held between straight-jawed self-locking pliers **(see illustration 9.4)**.

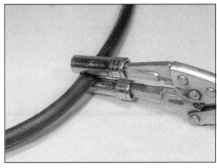

9.3 . . . two sockets and a pair of self-locking grips . . .

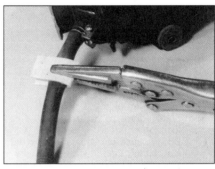

9.4 . . . or thick card and self-locking grips

Freeing and fitting hoses

● Always make sure the hose clamp is moved well clear of the hose end. Grip the hose with your hand and rotate it while pulling it off the union. If the hose has hardened due to age and will not move, slit it with a sharp knife and peel its ends off the union **(see illustration 9.5)**.

● Resist the temptation to use grease or soap on the unions to aid installation; although it helps the hose slip over the union it will equally aid the escape of fluid from the joint. It is preferable to soften the hose ends in hot water and wet the inside surface of the hose with water or a fluid which will evaporate.

9.5 Cutting a coolant hose free with a sharp knife

Conversion Factors

Length (distance)

Inches (in)	X	25.4	= Millimeters (mm)	X 0.0394	= Inches (in)
Feet (ft)	X	0.305	= Meters (m)	X 3.281	= Feet (ft)
Miles	X	1.609	= Kilometers (km)	X 0.621	= Miles

Volume (capacity)

Cubic inches (cu in; in^3)	X	16.387	= Cubic centimeters (cc; cm^3)	X 0.061	= Cubic inches (cu in; in^3)
Imperial pints (Imp pt)	X	0.568	= Liters (l)	X 1.76	= Imperial pints (Imp pt)
Imperial quarts (Imp qt)	X	1.137	= Liters (l)	X 0.88	= Imperial quarts (Imp qt)
Imperial quarts (Imp qt)	X	1.201	= US quarts (US qt)	X 0.833	= Imperial quarts (Imp qt)
US quarts (US qt)	X	0.946	= Liters (l)	X 1.057	= US quarts (US qt)
Imperial gallons (Imp gal)	X	4.546	= Liters (l)	X 0.22	= Imperial gallons (Imp gal)
Imperial gallons (Imp gal)	X	1.201	= US gallons (US gal)	X 0.833	= Imperial gallons (Imp gal)
US gallons (US gal)	X	3.785	= Liters (l)	X 0.264	= US gallons (US gal)

Mass (weight)

Ounces (oz)	X	28.35	= Grams (g)	X 0.035	= Ounces (oz)
Pounds (lb)	X	0.454	= Kilograms (kg)	X 2.205	= Pounds (lb)

Force

Ounces-force (ozf; oz)	X	0.278	= Newtons (N)	X 3.6	= Ounces-force (ozf; oz)
Pounds-force (lbf; lb)	X	4.448	= Newtons (N)	X 0.225	= Pounds-force (lbf; lb)
Newtons (N)	X	0.1	= Kilograms-force (kgf; kg)	X 9.81	= Newtons (N)

Pressure

Pounds-force per square inch (psi; lbf/in^2; lb/in^2)	X	0.070	= Kilograms-force per square centimeter (kgf/cm^2; kg/cm^2)	X 14.223	= Pounds-force per square inch (psi; lbf/in^2; lb/in^2)
Pounds-force per square inch (psi; lbf/in^2; lb/in^2)	X	0.068	= Atmospheres (atm)	X 14.696	= Pounds-force per square inch (psi; lbf/in^2; lb/in^2)
Pounds-force per square inch (psi; lbf/in^2; lb/in^2)	X	0.069	= Bars	X 14.5	= Pounds-force per square inch (psi; lbf/in^2; lb/in^2)
Pounds-force per square inch (psi; lbf/in^2; lb/in^2)	X	6.895	= Kilopascals (kPa)	X 0.145	= Pounds-force per square inch (psi; lbf/in^2; lb/in^2)
Kilopascals (kPa)	X	0.01	= Kilograms-force per square centimeter (kgf/cm^2; kg/cm^2)	X 98.1	= Kilopascals (kPa)

Torque (moment of force)

Pounds-force inches (lbf in; lb in)	X	1.152	= Kilograms-force centimeter (kgf cm; kg cm)	X 0.868	= Pounds-force inches (lbf in; lb in)
Pounds-force inches (lbf in; lb in)	X	0.113	= Newton meters (Nm)	X 8.85	= Pounds-force inches (lbf in; lb in)
Pounds-force inches (lbf in; lb in)	X	0.083	= Pounds-force feet (lbf ft; lb ft)	X 12	= Pounds-force inches (lbf in; lb in)
Pounds-force feet (lbf ft; lb ft)	X	0.138	= Kilograms-force meters (kgf m; kg m)	X 7.233	= Pounds-force feet (lbf ft; lb ft)
Pounds-force feet (lbf ft; lb ft)	X	1.356	= Newton meters (Nm)	X 0.738	= Pounds-force feet (lbf ft; lb ft)
Newton meters (Nm)	X	0.102	= Kilograms-force meters (kgf m; kg m)	X 9.804	= Newton meters (Nm)

Vacuum

Inches mercury (in. Hg)	X	3.377	= Kilopascals (kPa)	X 0.2961	= Inches mercury
Inches mercury (in. Hg)	X	25.4	= Millimeters mercury (mm Hg)	X 0.0394	= Inches mercury

Power

Horsepower (hp)	X	745.7	= Watts (W)	X 0.0013	= Horsepower (hp)

Velocity (speed)

Miles per hour (miles/hr; mph)	X	1.609	= Kilometers per hour (km/hr; kph)	X 0.621	= Miles per hour (miles/hr; mph)

Fuel consumption*

Miles per gallon, Imperial (mpg)	X	0.354	= Kilometers per liter (km/l)	X 2.825	= Miles per gallon, Imperial (mpg)
Miles per gallon, US (mpg)	X	0.425	= Kilometers per liter (km/l)	X 2.352	= Miles per gallon, US (mpg)

Temperature

Degrees Fahrenheit = (°C x 1.8) + 32

Degrees Celsius (Degrees Centigrade; °C) = (°F - 32) x 0.56

*It is common practice to convert from miles per gallon (mpg) to liters/100 kilometers (l/100km), where mpg (Imperial) x l/100 km = 282 and mpg (US) x l/100 km = 235

A number of chemicals and lubricants are available for use in motorcycle maintenance and repair. They include a wide variety of products ranging from cleaning solvents and degreasers to lubricants and protective sprays for rubber, plastic and vinyl.

• **Contact point/spark plug cleaner** is a solvent used to clean oily film and dirt from points, grime from electrical connectors and oil deposits from spark plugs. It is oil free and leaves no residue. It can also be used to remove gum and varnish from carburetor jets and other orifices.

• **Carburetor cleaner** is similar to contact point/spark plug cleaner but it usually has a stronger solvent and may leave a slight oily residue. It is not recommended for cleaning electrical components or connections.

• **Brake system cleaner** is used to remove brake dust, grease and brake fluid from the brake system, where clean surfaces are absolutely necessary. It leaves no residue and often eliminates brake squeal caused by contaminants.

• **Silicone-based lubricants** are used to protect rubber parts such as hoses and grommets, and are used as lubricants for hinges and locks.

• **Multi-purpose grease** is an all purpose lubricant used wherever grease is more practical than a liquid lubricant such as oil. Some multi-purpose grease is colored white and specially formulated to be more resistant to water than ordinary grease.

• **Gear oil** (sometimes called gear lube) is a specially designed oil used in transmissions and final drive units, as well as other areas where high friction, high temperature lubrication is required. It is available in a number of viscosities (weights) for various applications.

• **Motor oil**, of course, is the lubricant specially formulated for use in the engine.

It normally contains a wide variety of additives to prevent corrosion and reduce foaming and wear. Motor oil comes in various weights (viscosity ratings) from 5 to 80. The recommended weight of the oil depends on the seasonal temperature and the demands on the engine. Light oil is used in cold climates and under light load conditions; heavy oil is used in hot climates where high loads are encountered. Multi-viscosity oils are designed to have characteristics of both light and heavy oils and are available in a number of weights from 5W-20 to 20W-50.

• **Gasoline additives** perform several functions, depending on their chemical makeup. They usually contain solvents that help dissolve gum and varnish that build up on carburetor and inlet parts. They also serve to break down carbon deposits that form on the inside surfaces of the combustion chambers. Some additives contain upper cylinder lubricants for valves and piston rings.

• **Brake and clutch fluid** is a specially formulated hydraulic fluid that can withstand the heat and pressure encountered in break/clutch systems. Care must be taken that this fluid does not come in contact with painted surfaces or plastics. An opened container should always be resealed to prevent contamination by water or dirt.

• **Chain lubricants** are formulated especially for use on motorcycle final drive chains. A good chain lube should adhere well and have good penetrating qualities to be effective as a lubricant inside the chain and on the side plates, pins and rollers. Most chain lubes are either the foaming type or quick drying type and are usually marketed as sprays. Take care to use a lubricant marked as being suitable for O-ring chains.

• **Degreasers** are heavy duty solvents used to remove grease and grime that may accumulate on the engine and frame components. They can be sprayed or

brushed on and, depending on the type, are rinsed with either water or solvent.

• **Solvents** are used alone or in combination with degreasers to clean parts and assemblies during repair and overhaul. The home mechanic should use only solvents that are non-flammable and that do not produce irritating fumes.

• **Gasket sealing compounds** may be used in conjunction with gaskets, to improve their sealing capabilities, or alone, to seal metal-to-metal joints. Many gasket sealers can withstand extreme heat, some are impervious to gasoline and lubricants, while others are capable of filling and sealing large cavities. Depending on the intended use, gasket sealers either dry hard or stay relatively soft and pliable. They are usually applied by hand, with a brush or are sprayed on the gasket sealing surfaces.

• **Thread locking compound** is an adhesive locking compound that prevents threaded fasteners from loosening because of vibration. It is available in a variety of types for different applications.

• **Moisture dispersants** are usually sprays that can be used to dry out electrical components such as the fuse block and wiring connectors. Some types an also be used as treatment for rubber and as a lubricant for hinges, cables and locks.

• **Waxes and polishes** are used to help protect painted and plated surfaces from the weather. Different types of paint may require the use of different types of wax polish. Some polishes utilize a chemical or abrasive cleaner to help remove the top layer of oxidized (dull) paint on older vehicles. In recent years, many non-wax polishes (that contain a wide variety of chemicals such as polymers and silicones) have been introduced. These non-wax polishes are usually easier to apply and last longer than conventional waxes and polishes.

Preparing for storage

Before you start

If repairs or an overhaul is needed, see that this is carried out now rather than left until you want to ride the bike again.

Give the bike a good wash and scrub all dirt from its underside. Make sure the bike dries completely before preparing for storage.

Engine

● Remove the spark plug(s) and lubricate the cylinder bores with approximately a teaspoon of motor oil using a spout-type oil can **(see illustration 1)**. Reinstall the spark plug(s). Crank the engine over a couple of times to coat the piston rings and bores with oil. If the bike has a kickstart, use this to turn the engine over. If not, flick the kill switch to the OFF position and crank the engine over on the starter **(see illustration 2)**. If the nature of the ignition system prevents the starter operating with the kill switch in the OFF position, remove the spark plugs and fit them back in

their caps; ensure that the plugs are grounded against the cylinder head when the starter is operated **(see illustration 3)**.

> **Warning: It is important that the plugs are grounded away from the spark plug holes otherwise there is a risk of atomized fuel from the cylinders igniting.**

> **HAYNES HINT** *On a single cylinder four-stroke engine, you can seal the combustion chamber completely by positioning the piston at TDC on the compression stroke.*

● Drain the carburetor(s) otherwise there is a risk of jets becoming blocked by gum deposits from the fuel **(see illustration 4)**.

● If the bike is going into long-term storage, consider adding a fuel stabilizer to the fuel in the tank. If the tank is drained completely, corrosion of its internal surfaces may occur if left unprotected for a long period. The tank can be treated with a rust preventative especially for this purpose. Alternatively, remove the tank and pour half a liter of motor oil into it, install the filler cap and shake the tank to coat its internals with oil before draining off the excess. The same effect can also be achieved by spraying WD-40 or a similar water-dispersant around the inside of the tank via its flexible nozzle.

● Make sure the cooling system contains the correct mix of antifreeze. Antifreeze also contains important corrosion inhibitors.

● The air intakes and exhaust can be sealed off by covering or plugging the openings. Ensure that you do not seal in any condensation; run the engine until it is hot, then switch off and allow to cool. Tape a piece

Squirt a drop of motor oil into each cylinder

Flick the kill switch to OFF . . .

. . . and ensure that the metal bodies of the plugs (arrows) are grounded against the cylinder head

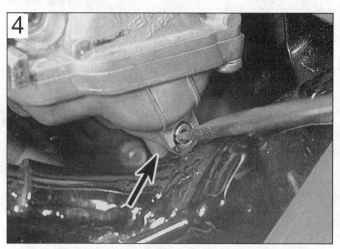

Connect a hose to the carburetor float chamber drain stub (arrow) and unscrew the drain screw

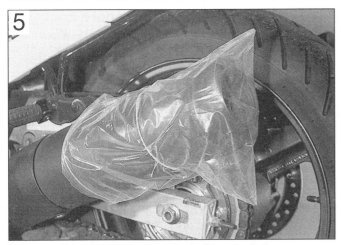

Exhausts can be sealed off with a plastic bag

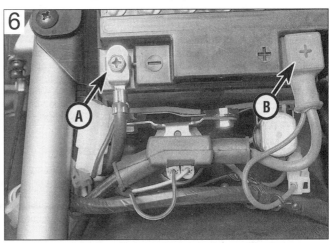

Disconnect the negative lead (A) first, followed by the positive lead (B)

of thick plastic over the silencer end(s) **(see illustration 5)**. Note that some advocate pouring a tablespoon of motor oil into the silencer(s) before sealing them off.

Battery

● Remove it from the bike - in extreme cases of cold the battery may freeze and crack its case **(see illustration 6)**.
● Check the electrolyte level and top up if necessary (conventional refillable batteries). Clean the terminals.
● Store the battery off the motorcycle and away from any sources of fire. Position a wooden block under the battery if it is to sit on the ground.
● Give the battery a trickle charge for a few hours every month **(see illustration 7)**.

Tires

● Place the bike on its centerstand or an auxiliary stand which will support the motorcycle in an upright position. Position wood blocks under the tires to keep them off the ground and to provide insulation from damp. If the bike is being put into long-term storage, ideally both tires should be off the

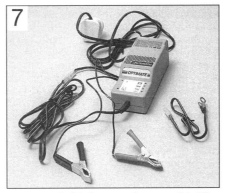

Use a suitable battery charger - this kit also assesses battery condition

ground; not only will this protect the tires, but will also ensure that no load is placed on the steering head or wheel bearings.
● Deflate each tire by 5 to 10 psi, no more or the beads may unseat from the rim, making subsequent inflation difficult on tubeless tires.

Pivots and controls

● Lubricate all lever, pedal, stand and

footrest pivot points. If grease nipples are fitted to the rear suspension components, apply lubricant to the pivots.
● Lubricate all control cables.

Cycle components

● Apply a wax protectant to all painted and plastic components. Wipe off any excess, but don't polish to a shine. Where fitted, clean the screen with soap and water.
● Coat metal parts with Vaseline (petroleum jelly). When applying this to the fork tubes, do not compress the forks otherwise the seals will rot from contact with the Vaseline.
● Apply a vinyl cleaner to the seat.

Storage conditions

● Aim to store the bike in a shed or garage which does not leak and is free from damp.
● Drape an old blanket or bedspread over the bike to protect it from dust and direct contact with sunlight (which will fade paint). Beware of tight-fitting plastic covers which may allow condensation to form and settle on the bike.

Getting back on the road

Engine and transmission

● Change the oil and replace the oil filter. If this was done prior to storage, check that the oil hasn't emulsified - a thick whitish substance which occurs through condensation.
● Remove the spark plugs. Using a spout-type oil can, squirt a few drops of oil into the cylinder(s). This will provide initial lubrication as the piston rings and bores comes back into contact. Service the spark plugs, or buy new ones, and install them in the engine.

● Check that the clutch isn't stuck on. The plates can stick together if left standing for some time, preventing clutch operation. Engage a gear and try rocking the bike back and forth with the clutch lever held against the handlebar. If this doesn't work on cable-operated clutches, hold the clutch lever back against the handlebar with a strong rubber band or cable tie for a couple of hours **(see illustration 8)**.
● If the air intakes or silencer end(s) were blocked off, remove the plug or cover used.
● If the fuel tank was coated with a rust

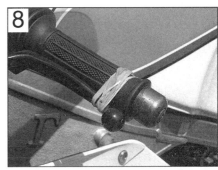

Hold the clutch lever back against the handlebar with rubber bands or a cable tie

preventative, oil or a stabilizer added to the fuel, drain and flush the tank and dispose of the fuel sensibly. If no action was taken with the fuel tank prior to storage, it is advised that the old fuel is disposed of since it will go bad over a period of time. Refill the fuel tank with fresh fuel.

Frame and running gear

● Oil all pivot points and cables.
● Check the tire pressures. They will definitely need inflating if pressures were reduced for storage.
● Lubricate the final drive chain (where applicable).
● Remove any protective coating applied to the fork tubes (stanchions) since this may well destroy the fork seals. If the fork tubes weren't protected and have picked up rust spots, remove them with very fine abrasive paper and refinish with metal polish.
● Check that both brakes operate correctly. Apply each brake hard and check that it's not possible to move the motorcycle forwards, then check that the brake frees off again once released. Brake caliper pistons can stick due to corrosion around the piston head, or on the sliding caliper types, due to corrosion of the slider pins. If the brake doesn't free after repeated operation, take the caliper off for examination. Similarly drum brakes can stick

due to a seized operating cam, cable or rod linkage.
● If the motorcycle has been in long-term storage, replace the brake fluid and clutch fluid (where applicable).
● Depending on where the bike has been stored, the wiring, cables and hoses may have been nibbled by rodents. Make a visual check and investigate disturbed wiring loom tape.

Battery

● If the battery has been previously removed and given top up charges it can simply be reconnected. Remember to connect the positive cable first and the negative cable last.
● On conventional refillable batteries, if the battery has not received any attention, remove it from the motorcycle and check its electrolyte level. Top up if necessary then charge the battery. If the battery fails to hold a charge and a visual check show heavy white sulfation of the plates, the battery is probably defective and must be replaced. This is particularly likely if the battery is old. Confirm battery condition with a specific gravity check.
● On sealed (MF) batteries, if the battery has not received any attention, remove it from the motorcycle and charge it according to the information on the battery case - if the battery fails to hold a charge it must be replaced.

Starting procedure

● If a kickstart is fitted, turn the engine over a couple of times with the ignition OFF to distribute oil around the engine. If no kickstart is fitted, flick the engine kill switch OFF and the ignition ON and crank the engine over a couple of times to work oil around the upper cylinder components. If the nature of the ignition system is such that the starter won't work with the kill switch OFF, remove the spark plugs, fit them back into their caps and ground their bodies on the cylinder head. Reinstall the spark plugs afterwards.
● Switch the kill switch to RUN, operate the choke and start the engine. If the engine won't start don't continue cranking the engine - not only will this flatten the battery, but the starter motor will overheat. Switch the ignition off and try again later. If the engine refuses to start, go through the troubleshooting procedures in this manual. **Note:** *If the bike has been in storage for a long time, old fuel or a carburetor blockage may be the problem. Gum deposits in carburetors can block jets - if a carburetor cleaner doesn't prove successful the carburetors must be dismantled for cleaning.*

● Once the engine has started, check that the lights, turn signals and horn work properly.

● Treat the bike gently for the first ride and check all fluid levels on completion. Settle the bike back into the maintenance schedule.

This Section provides an easy reference-guide to the more common faults that are likely to afflict your machine. Obviously, the opportunities are almost limitless for faults to occur as a result of obscure failures, and to try and cover all eventualities would require a book. Indeed, a number have been written on the subject.

Successful troubleshooting is not a mysterious 'black art' but the application of a bit of knowledge combined with a systematic and logical approach to the problem. Approach any troubleshooting by first accurately identifying the symptom and then checking through the list of possible causes, starting with the simplest or most obvious and progressing in stages to the most complex. Take nothing for granted, but above all apply liberal quantities of common sense.

The main symptom of a fault is given in the text as a major heading below which are listed the various systems or areas which may contain the fault. Details of each possible cause for a fault and the remedial action to be taken are given. Further information should be sought in the relevant Chapter.

1 Engine doesn't start or is difficult to start

- [ ] Starter motor doesn't rotate
- [ ] Starter motor rotates but engine does not turn over
- [ ] Starter works but engine won't turn over (seized)
- [ ] No fuel flow
- [ ] Engine flooded
- [ ] No spark or weak spark
- [ ] Compression low
- [ ] Stalls after starting
- [ ] Rough idle

2 Poor running at low speed

- [ ] Spark weak
- [ ] Fuel/air mixture incorrect
- [ ] Compression low
- [ ] Poor acceleration

3 Poor running or no power at high speed

- [ ] Firing incorrect
- [ ] Fuel/air mixture incorrect
- [ ] Compression low
- [ ] Knocking or pinging
- [ ] Miscellaneous causes

4 Overheating

- [ ] Engine overheats
- [ ] Firing incorrect
- [ ] Fuel/air mixture incorrect
- [ ] Compression too high
- [ ] Engine load excessive
- [ ] Lubrication inadequate
- [ ] Miscellaneous causes

5 Clutch problems

- [ ] Clutch slipping
- [ ] Clutch not disengaging completely

6 Gearchanging problems

- [ ] Doesn't go into gear, or lever doesn't return
- [ ] Jumps out of gear
- [ ] Overselects

7 Abnormal engine noise

- [ ] Knocking or pinging
- [ ] Piston slap or rattling
- [ ] Valve noise
- [ ] Other noise

8 Abnormal driveline noise

- [ ] Clutch noise
- [ ] Transmission noise
- [ ] Final drive noise

9 Abnormal frame and suspension noise

- [ ] Front end noise
- [ ] Shock absorber noise
- [ ] Brake noise

10 Oil pressure warning light comes on

- [ ] Engine lubrication system
- [ ] Electrical system

11 Excessive exhaust smoke

- [ ] White smoke
- [ ] Black smoke

12 Poor handling or stability

- [ ] Handlebar hard to turn
- [ ] Handlebar shakes or vibrates excessively
- [ ] Handlebar pulls to one side
- [ ] Poor shock absorbing qualities

13 Braking problems

- [ ] Brakes are spongy, don't hold
- [ ] Brake lever or pedal pulsates
- [ ] Brakes drag

14 Electrical problems

- [ ] Battery dead or weak
- [ ] Battery overcharged

1 Engine doesn't start or is difficult to start

Starter motor doesn't rotate

☐ Engine kill switch OFF.
☐ Fuse blown. Check main circuit breaker (Chapter 8).
☐ Battery voltage low. Check and recharge battery (Chapter 8).
☐ Starter motor defective. Make sure the wiring to the starter is secure. Make sure the starter solenoid clicks when the start button is pushed. If the solenoid clicks, then the fault is in the wiring or motor.
☐ Starter solenoid faulty. Check it according to the procedure in Chapter 8.
☐ Starter switch not contacting. The contacts could be wet, corroded or dirty. Disassemble and clean the switch (Chapter 8).
☐ Wiring open or shorted. Check all wiring connections and harnesses to make sure that they are dry, tight and not corroded. Also check for broken or frayed wires that can cause a short to ground (see wiring diagram, Chapter 8).
☐ Ignition (main) switch defective. Check the switch according to the procedure in Chapter 8. Replace the switch with a new one if it is defective.
☐ Engine kill switch defective. Check for wet, dirty or corroded contacts. Clean or replace the switch as necessary (Chapter 8).

Starter motor rotates but engine does not turn over

☐ Starter pinion gear defective. Inspect and repair or replace (Chapter 8).
☐ Damaged starter jackshaft. Inspect and replace the damaged parts (Chapter 8).

Starter works but engine won't turn over (seized)

☐ Seized engine caused by one or more internally damaged components. Failure due to wear, abuse or lack of lubrication. Damage can include seized valves, rocker arms, lifters, camshafts, pistons, crankshaft or connecting rod bearings. Refer to Chapter 2 for engine disassembly.

No fuel flow

☐ No fuel in tank.
☐ Fuel tank breather hose obstructed.
☐ Fuel filter is blocked (see Chapter 1).

Engine flooded

☐ Starting technique incorrect. Under normal circumstances the machine should start with little or no throttle. When the engine is cold, the choke should be operated (carburetor models) and the engine started without opening the throttle. When the engine is at operating temperature, only a very slight amount of throttle should be necessary.

No spark or weak spark

☐ Ignition switch OFF.
☐ Engine kill switch turned to the OFF position.
☐ Battery voltage low. Check and recharge the battery as necessary (Chapter 8).
☐ Spark plugs dirty, defective or worn out. Locate reason for fouled plugs using spark plug condition chart and follow the plug maintenance procedures (Chapter 1).
☐ Spark plug caps or secondary (HT) wiring faulty. Check condition. Replace either or both components if cracks or deterioration are evident (Chapter 4).

☐ Spark plug caps not making good contact. Make sure that the plug caps fit snugly over the plug ends.
☐ Ignition HT coils defective. Check the coils, referring to Chapter 4.
☐ ECM defective. Refer to Chapter 4 for details.
☐ Crankshaft or camshaft position sensor defective. Check the unit, referring to Chapter 4 for details.
☐ Ignition or kill switch shorted. This is usually caused by water, corrosion, damage or excessive wear. The switches can be disassembled and cleaned with electrical contact cleaner. If cleaning does not help, replace the switches (Chapter 8).
☐ Wiring shorted or broken between:

a) Ignition (main) switch and engine kill switch (or blown fuse)
b) ECM and engine kill switch
c) ECM and ignition HT coils
d) Ignition HT coils and spark plugs
e) ECM and crankshaft position sensor.

☐ Make sure that all wiring connections are clean, dry and tight. Look for chafed and broken wires (Chapters 4 and 8).

Compression low

☐ Spark plugs loose. Remove the plugs and inspect their threads. Reinstall and tighten to the specified torque (Chapter 1).
☐ Cylinder head not sufficiently tightened down. If the cylinder head is suspected of being loose, then there's a chance that the gasket or head is damaged if the problem has persisted for any length of time. The head bolts should be tightened to the proper torque in the correct sequence (Chapter 2).
☐ Cylinder and/or piston worn. Excessive wear will cause compression pressure to leak past the rings. This is usually accompanied by worn rings as well. A top-end overhaul is necessary (Chapter 2).
☐ Piston rings worn, weak, broken, or sticking. Broken or sticking piston rings usually indicate a lubrication or fuelling problem that causes excess carbon deposits or seizures to form on the pistons and rings. Top-end overhaul is necessary (Chapter 2).
☐ Piston ring-to-groove clearance excessive. This is caused by excessive wear of the piston ring lands. Piston replacement is necessary (Chapter 2).
☐ Cylinder head gasket damaged. If a head is allowed to become loose, or if excessive carbon build-up on the piston crown and combustion chamber causes extremely high compression, the head gasket may leak. Retorquing the head is not always sufficient to restore the seal, so gasket replacement is necessary (Chapter 2).
☐ Cylinder head warped. This is caused by overheating or improperly tightened head bolts. Machine shop resurfacing or head replacement is necessary (Chapter 2).
☐ Valve spring broken or weak. Caused by component failure or wear; the springs must be replaced (Chapter 2).
☐ Valve not seating properly. This is caused by a bent valve (from over-revving burned valve or seat (improper fuelling) or an accumulation of carbon deposits on the seat (from fuelling or lubrication problems). The valves must be cleaned and/or replaced and the seats serviced if possible (Chapter 2).

1 Engine doesn't start or is difficult to start (continued)

Stalls after starting

- ☐ Improper choke action (carburetor models). Make sure the choke linkage shaft is getting a full stroke and staying in the out position (Chapter 3).
- ☐ Ignition malfunction. See Chapter 4.
- ☐ Carburetor malfunction. See Chapter 3.
- ☐ Fuel contaminated. The fuel can be contaminated with either dirt or water, or can change chemically if the machine is allowed to sit for several months or more. Drain the tank (Chapter 3).
- ☐ Intake air leak. Check for loose intake manifold and damaged/disconnected vacuum hoses (Chapter 3).
- ☐ Engine idle speed incorrect. On carburetor models, turn idle adjusting screw until the engine idles at the specified rpm (Chapter 1).

Rough idle

- ☐ Ignition malfunction. See Chapter 4.
- ☐ Idle speed incorrect. See Chapter 1.
- ☐ Carburetor or EFI malfunction. See Chapter 3.
- ☐ Fuel contaminated. The fuel can be contaminated with either dirt or water, or can change chemically if the machine is allowed to sit for several months or more. Drain the tank (Chapter 3).
- ☐ Intake air leak. Check for loose intake manifold and damaged/disconnected vacuum hoses. Replace the intake ducts if they are split or deteriorated (Chapter 3).
- ☐ Air filter clogged. Replace the air filter element (Chapter 1).

2 Poor running at low speeds

Spark weak

- ☐ Battery voltage low. Check and recharge battery (Chapter 8).
- ☐ Spark plugs fouled, defective or worn out. Refer to Chapter 1 for spark plug maintenance.
- ☐ Spark plug cap or HT wiring defective. Refer to Chapters 1 and 4 for details on the ignition system.
- ☐ Spark plug caps not making contact.
- ☐ Incorrect spark plugs. Wrong type, heat range or cap configuration. Check and install correct plugs listed in Chapter 1.
- ☐ ECM faulty. See Chapter 3.
- ☐ Pick-up coil defective. See Chapter 3.
- ☐ Ignition coil defective. See Chapter 4.

Fuel/air mixture incorrect

- ☐ Pilot jet or air passage blocked. Remove and overhaul the carburetor (if equipped) (Chapter 3).
- ☐ Air filter clogged, poorly sealed or missing (Chapter 1).
- ☐ Air filter housing poorly sealed. Look for cracks, holes or loose clamps and replace or repair defective parts.
- ☐ Fuel tank breather hose obstructed.
- ☐ Intake air leak. Check for loose intake manifold and damaged/disconnected vacuum hoses. Replace the intake ducts if they are split or deteriorated (Chapter 3).

Compression low

- ☐ Spark plugs loose. Remove the plugs and inspect their threads. Reinstall and tighten to the specified torque (Chapter 1).
- ☐ Cylinder head not sufficiently tightened down. If the cylinder head is suspected of being loose, then there's a chance that the gasket and head are damaged if the problem has persisted for any length of time. The head bolts should be tightened to the proper torque in the correct sequence (Chapter 2).
- ☐ Cylinder and/or piston worn. Excessive wear will cause compression pressure to leak past the rings. This is usually accompanied by worn rings as well. A top-end overhaul is necessary (Chapter 2).
- ☐ Piston rings worn, weak, broken, or sticking. Broken or sticking piston rings usually indicate a lubrication or fuelling problem that causes excess carbon deposits or seizures to form on the pistons and rings. Top-end overhaul is necessary (Chapter 2).
- ☐ Piston ring-to-groove clearance excessive. This is caused by excessive wear of the piston ring lands. Piston replacement is necessary (Chapter 2).
- ☐ Cylinder head gasket damaged. If a head is allowed to become loose, or if excessive carbon build-up on the piston crown and combustion chamber causes extremely high compression, the head gasket may leak. Retorquing the head is not always sufficient to restore the seal, so gasket replacement is necessary (Chapter 2).
- ☐ Cylinder head warped. This is caused by overheating or improperly tightened head bolts. Machine shop resurfacing or head replacement is necessary (Chapter 2).
- ☐ Valve spring broken or weak. Caused by component failure or wear; the springs must be replaced (Chapter 2).
- ☐ Valve not seating properly. This is caused by a bent valve (from over-revving or improper valve adjustment), burned valve or seat (improper fuelling) or an accumulation of carbon deposits on the seat (from fuelling, lubrication problems). The valves must be cleaned and/or replaced and the seats serviced if possible (Chapter 2).

Poor acceleration

- ☐ Carburetor fault. Remove and overhaul the carburetor (Chapter 3).
- ☐ Electronic fuel injection system fault. Inspect the components (Chapter 3).
- ☐ Engine oil viscosity too high. Using a heavier oil than that recommended in Chapter 1 can damage the oil pump or lubrication system and cause drag on the engine.
- ☐ Brakes dragging. Usually caused by debris which has entered the brake piston seals, or from a warped disc or bent axle. Repair as necessary (Chapter 6).

3 Poor running or no power at high speed

Firing incorrect

☐ Air filter restricted. Clean or replace filter (Chapter 1).
☐ Spark plugs fouled, defective or worn out. See Chapter 1 for spark plug maintenance.
☐ Spark plug caps or HT wiring defective. See Chapters 1 and 4 for details of the ignition system.
☐ Spark plug caps not in good contact. See Chapter 4.
☐ Incorrect spark plugs. Wrong type, heat range or cap configuration. Check and install correct plugs listed in Chapter 1.
☐ ECM defective. See Chapter 4.
☐ Crankshaft or camshaft position sensor defective. See Chapter 4.
☐ Ignition coils defective. See Chapter 4.

Fuel/air mixture incorrect

☐ Carburetor fault. Remove and overhaul the carburetor (Chapter 3).
☐ Electronic fule injection system fault. Inspect the components (Chapter 3).
☐ Air filter clogged, poorly sealed, or missing (Chapter 1).
☐ Air filter housing poorly sealed. Look for cracks, holes or loose clamps, and replace or repair defective parts.
☐ Fuel tank breather hose obstructed.
☐ Intake air leak. Check for loose intake manifold and damaged/disconnected vacuum hoses. Replace the intake ducts if they are split or deteriorated (Chapter 4).

Compression low

☐ Spark plugs loose. Remove the plugs and inspect their threads. Reinstall and tighten to the specified torque (Chapter 1).
☐ Cylinder head not sufficiently tightened down. If the cylinder head is suspected of being loose, then there's a chance that the gasket and head are damaged if the problem has persisted for any length of time. The head bolts should be tightened to the proper torque in the correct sequence (Chapter 2).
☐ Cylinder and/or piston worn. Excessive wear will cause compression pressure to leak past the rings. This is usually accompanied by worn rings as well. A top-end overhaul is necessary (Chapter 2).
☐ Piston rings worn, weak, broken, or sticking. Broken or sticking piston rings usually indicate a lubrication or fuelling problem that causes excess carbon deposits or seizures to form on the pistons and rings. Top-end overhaul is necessary (Chapter 2).
☐ Piston ring-to-groove clearance excessive. This is caused by excessive wear of the piston ring lands. Piston replacement is necessary (Chapter 2).

☐ Cylinder head gasket damaged. If a head is allowed to become loose, or if excessive carbon build-up on the piston crown and combustion chamber causes extremely high compression, the head gasket may leak. Retorquing the head is not always sufficient to restore the seal, so gasket replacement is necessary (Chapter 2).
☐ Cylinder head warped. This is caused by overheating or improperly tightened head bolts. Machine shop resurfacing or head replacement is necessary (Chapter 2).
☐ Valve spring broken or weak. Caused by component failure or wear; the springs must be replaced (Chapter 2).
☐ Valve not seating properly. This is caused by a bent valve (from over-revving), burned valve or seat (improper fuelling) or an accumulation of carbon deposits on the seat (from fuelling or lubrication problems). The valves must be cleaned and/or replaced and the seats serviced if possible (Chapter 2).

Knocking or pinging

☐ Carbon build-up in combustion chamber. Use of a fuel additive that will dissolve the adhesive bonding the carbon particles to the crown and chamber is the easiest way to remove the build-up. Otherwise, the cylinder head will have to be removed and decarbonized (Chapter 2).
☐ Incorrect or poor quality fuel. Old or improper grades of fuel can cause detonation. This causes the piston to rattle, thus the knocking or pinging sound. Drain old fuel and always use the recommended fuel grade.
☐ Spark plug heat range incorrect. Uncontrolled detonation indicates the plug heat range is too hot. The plug in effect becomes a glow plug, raising cylinder temperatures. Install the proper heat range plug (Chapter 1).
☐ Improper air/fuel mixture. This will cause the cylinders to run hot, which leads to detonation. An intake air leak can cause this imbalance. See Chapter 3.

Miscellaneous causes

☐ Throttle valve doesn't open fully. Adjust the throttle grip freeplay (Chapter 1).
☐ Clutch slipping. May be caused by loose or worn clutch components. Refer to Chapter 2 for clutch overhaul procedures.
☐ Engine oil viscosity too high. Using a heavier oil than the one recommended in Chapter 1 can damage the oil pump or lubrication system and cause drag on the engine.
☐ Brakes dragging. Usually caused by debris which has entered the brake piston seals, or from a warped disc or bent axle. Repair as necessary.

4 Overheating

Firing incorrect

- [ ] Spark plugs fouled, defective or worn out. See Chapter 1 for spark plug maintenance.
- [ ] Incorrect spark plugs.
- [ ] ECM defective. See Chapter 4.
- [ ] Crankshaft or camshaft position sensor faulty. See Chapter 4.
- [ ] Faulty ignition coil. See Chapter 4.

Fuel/air mixture incorrect

- [ ] Carburetor fault. Remove and overhaul the carburetor (Chapter 3).
- [ ] Air filter clogged, poorly sealed, or missing (Chapter 1).
- [ ] Air filter housing poorly sealed. Look for cracks, holes or loose clamps, and replace or repair defective parts.
- [ ] Fuel tank breather hose obstructed.
- [ ] Intake air leak. Check for loose carburetor intake duct retaining clips and damaged/disconnected vacuum hoses. Replace the intake ducts if they are split or deteriorated (Chapter 3).

Compression too high

- [ ] Carbon build-up in combustion chamber. Use of a fuel additive that will dissolve the adhesive bonding the carbon particles to the piston crown and chamber is the easiest way to remove the build-up. Otherwise, the cylinder head will have to be removed and decarbonized (Chapter 2).
- [ ] Improperly machined head surface or installation of incorrect gasket during engine assembly.

Engine load excessive

- [ ] Clutch slipping. Can be caused by damaged, loose or worn clutch components. Refer to Chapter 2 for overhaul procedures.
- [ ] Engine oil level too high. The addition of too much oil will cause pressurization of the crankcase and inefficient engine operation. Check Specifications and drain to proper level (Chapter 1).
- [ ] Engine oil viscosity too high. Using a heavier oil than the one recommended in Chapter 1 can damage the oil pump or lubrication system as well as cause drag on the engine.
- [ ] Brakes dragging. Usually caused by debris which has entered the brake piston seals, or from a warped disc or bent axle. Repair as necessary.

Lubrication inadequate

- [ ] Engine oil level too low. Friction caused by intermittent lack of lubrication or from oil that is overworked can cause overheating. The oil provides a definite cooling function in the engine. Check the oil level (Chapter 1).
- [ ] Poor quality engine oil or incorrect viscosity or type. Oil is rated not only according to viscosity but also according to type. Some oils are not rated high enough for use in this engine. Check the Specifications section and change to the correct oil (Chapter 1).

Miscellaneous causes

- [ ] Modification to exhaust system. Most aftermarket exhaust systems cause the engine to run leaner, which makes it run hotter.

5 Clutch problems

Clutch slipping

- [ ] Clutch cable freeplay incorrectly adjusted (Chapter 1).
- [ ] Friction plates worn or warped. Overhaul the clutch assembly (Chapter 2).
- [ ] Metal plates warped (Chapter 2).
- [ ] Clutch diaphragm spring broken or weak. An old or heat-damaged (from slipping clutch) spring should be replaced with a new one (Chapter 2).
- [ ] Clutch pushrod bent. Check and, if necessary, replace (Chapter 2).
- [ ] Clutch center or housing unevenly worn. This causes improper engagement of the plates. Replace the damaged or worn parts (Chapter 2).

Clutch not disengaging completely

- [ ] Clutch cable freeplay incorrectly adjusted (Chapter 1).

- [ ] Clutch plates warped or damaged. This will cause clutch drag, which in turn will cause the machine to creep. Overhaul the clutch assembly (Chapter 2).
- [ ] Clutch spring tension uneven. Usually caused by a sagged or broken spring. Check and replace the diaphragm spring (Chapter 2).
- [ ] Engine oil deteriorated. Old, thin, worn out oil will not provide proper lubrication for the plates, causing the clutch to drag. Replace the oil and filter (Chapter 1).
- [ ] Engine oil viscosity too high. Using a heavier oil than recommended in Chapter 1 can cause the plates to stick together, putting a drag on the engine. Change to the correct weight oil (Chapter 1).
- [ ] Clutch housing bearing seized. Lack of lubrication, severe wear or damage can cause the bearing to seize on the input shaft. Overhaul of the clutch, and perhaps transmission, may be necessary to repair the damage (Chapter 2).

6 Gearchanging problems

Doesn't go into gear or lever doesn't return

- [ ] Clutch not disengaging. See above.
- [ ] Shift fork(s) bent or seized. Often caused by dropping the machine or from lack of lubrication. Overhaul the transmission (Chapter 2).
- [ ] Gear(s) stuck on shaft. Most often caused by a lack of lubrication or excessive wear in transmission bearings and bushings. Overhaul the transmission (Chapter 2).
- [ ] Gear shift drum binding. Caused by lubrication failure or excessive wear. Replace the drum and bearing (Chapter 2).
- [ ] Gear shift lever pawl spring weak or broken (Chapter 2).
- [ ] Gear shift lever broken. Splines stripped out of lever or shaft, caused by allowing the lever to get loose or from dropping the machine. Replace necessary parts (Chapter 2).
- [ ] Gear shift mechanism stopper arm broken or worn. Full engagement and rotary movement of shift drum results. Replace the arm (Chapter 2).
- [ ] Stopper arm spring broken. Allows arm to float, causing sporadic shift operation. Replace spring (Chapter 2).

Jumps out of gear

- [ ] Shift fork(s) worn. Overhaul the transmission (Chapter 2).
- [ ] Gear groove(s) worn. Overhaul the transmission (Chapter 2).
- [ ] Gear dogs or dog slots worn or damaged. The gears should be inspected and replaced. No attempt should be made to service the worn parts.

Overselects

- [ ] Stopper arm spring weak or broken (Chapter 2).
- [ ] Return spring post broken or distorted (Chapter 2).

7 Abnormal engine noise

Knocking or pinging

- [ ] Carbon build-up in combustion chamber. Use of a fuel additive that will dissolve the adhesive bonding the carbon particles to the piston crown and chamber is the easiest way to remove the build-up. Otherwise, the cylinder head will have to be removed and decarbonized (Chapter 2).
- [ ] Incorrect or poor quality fuel. Old or improper fuel can cause detonation. This causes the pistons to rattle, thus the knocking or pinging sound. Drain the old fuel and always use the recommended grade fuel (Chapter 3).
- [ ] Spark plug heat range incorrect. Uncontrolled detonation indicates that the plug heat range is too hot. The plug in effect becomes a glow plug, raising cylinder temperatures. Install the proper heat range plug (Chapter 1).
- [ ] Improper air/fuel mixture. This will cause the cylinders to run hot and lead to detonation. Blocked carburetor jets or an air leak can cause this imbalance. See Chapter 3.

Piston slap or rattling

- [ ] Cylinder-to-piston clearance excessive. Caused by improper assembly. Inspect and overhaul top-end parts (Chapter 2).
- [ ] Connecting rod bent. Caused by over-revving, trying to start a badly flooded engine or from ingesting a foreign object into the combustion chamber. Replace the damaged parts (Chapter 2).
- [ ] Piston pin or piston pin bore worn or seized from wear or lack of lubrication. Replace damaged parts (Chapter 2).
- [ ] Piston ring(s) worn, broken or sticking. Overhaul the top-end (Chapter 2).
- [ ] Piston seizure damage. Usually from lack of lubrication or overheating. Replace the pistons and cylinders, as necessary (Chapter 2).

- [ ] Connecting rod bearing clearance excessive. Caused by excessive wear or lack of lubrication. Replace worn parts.

Valve noise

- [ ] Hydraulic lifter worn or damaged. Inspect and replace as necessary (Chapter 2).
- [ ] Valve spring broken or weak. Check and replace weak valve springs (Chapter 2).
- [ ] Camshaft or rocker arms worn or damaged. Lack of lubrication at high rpm is usually the cause of damage. Insufficient oil or failure to change the oil at the recommended intervals are the chief causes. Inspect and replace as necessary. Rocker arm bushings can be replaced separately (Chapter 2).

Other noise

- [ ] Cylinder head gasket leaking.
- [ ] Exhaust pipe leaking at cylinder head connection. Caused by improper fit of pipe(s) or loose exhaust nuts. All exhaust fasteners should be tightened evenly and carefully. Failure to do this will lead to a leak.
- [ ] Crankshaft runout excessive. Caused by a bent crankshaft (from over-revving) or damage from an upper cylinder component failure. Can also be attributed to dropping the machine on either of the crankshaft ends.
- [ ] Engine mounting bolts loose. Tighten all engine mount bolts (Chapter 2).
- [ ] Crankshaft bearings worn (Chapter 2).
- [ ] Camchain, tensioner or guides worn. Replace according to the procedure in Chapter 2.

8 Abnormal driveline noise

Clutch and primary drive noise
- [ ] Clutch outer drum/friction plate clearance excessive (Chapter 2).
- [ ] Loose or damaged clutch pressure plate and/or bolts (Chapter 2).
- [ ] Loose or damaged primary chain (Chapter 1).

Transmission noise
- [ ] Bearings worn. Also includes the possibility that the shafts are worn. Overhaul the transmission (Chapter 2).
- [ ] Gears worn or chipped (Chapter 2).
- [ ] Metal chips jammed in gear teeth. Probably pieces from a broken gear or shift mechanism that were picked up by the gears. This will cause early bearing failure (Chapter 2).

- [ ] Transmission oil level too low. Causes a howl from transmission (Chapter 1).

Final drive noise
- [ ] Belt not adjusted properly (Chapter 1).
- [ ] Front or rear sprocket loose. Tighten fasteners (Chapter 6).
- [ ] Sprockets worn. Replace sprockets (Chapter 6).
- [ ] Rear sprocket warped. Replace sprockets (Chapter 6).

9 Abnormal frame and suspension noise

Front end noise
- [ ] Low fluid level or improper viscosity oil in forks. This can sound like spurting and is usually accompanied by irregular fork action (Chapter 5).
- [ ] Spring weak or broken. Makes a clicking or scraping sound. Fork oil, when drained, will have a lot of metal particles in it (Chapter 5).
- [ ] Steering head bearings loose or damaged. Clicks when braking. Check and adjust or replace as necessary (Chapters 1 and 5).
- [ ] Triple clamps loose. Make sure all clamp bolts are tightened to the specified torque (Chapter 5).
- [ ] Fork tube bent. Good possibility if machine has been dropped. Replace tube with a new one (Chapter 5).
- [ ] Front axle bolt or axle pinch bolts loose. Tighten them to the specified torque (Chapter 6).
- [ ] Loose or worn wheel bearings. Check and replace as needed (Chapter 6).

Shock absorber noise
- [ ] Fluid level incorrect. Indicates a leak caused by defective seal. Shock will be covered with oil. Replace shock (Chapter 5).
- [ ] Defective shock absorber with internal damage. This is in the body of the shock and can't be remedied. The shock must be replaced with a new one (Chapter 5).

- [ ] Bent or damaged shock body. Replace the shock with a new one (Chapter 5).

Brake noise
- [ ] Squeal caused by dust on brake pads. Usually found in combination with glazed pads. Clean using brake cleaning solvent (Chapter 6).
- [ ] Contamination of brake pads. Oil, brake fluid or dirt causing brake to chatter or squeal. Clean or replace pads (Chapter 6).
- [ ] Pads glazed. Caused by excessive heat from prolonged use or from contamination. Do not use sandpaper/emery cloth or any other abrasive to roughen the pad surfaces as abrasives will stay in the pad material and damage the disc. A very fine flat file can be used, but pad replacement is suggested as a cure (Chapter 6).
- [ ] Disc warped. Can cause a chattering, clicking or intermittent squeal. Usually accompanied by a pulsating lever and uneven braking. Replace the disc (Chapter 6).
- [ ] Loose or worn wheel bearings. Check and replace as needed (Chapter 6).

10 Oil pressure warning light comes on

Engine lubrication system
- [ ] Engine oil pump defective or failed relief valve. Inspect (Chapter 2).
- [ ] Engine oil level low. Inspect for leak or other problem causing low oil level and add recommended oil (Chapter 1).
- [ ] Engine oil viscosity too low. Very old, thin oil or an improper weight of oil used in the engine. Change to correct oil (Chapter 1).

Electrical system
- [ ] Oil pressure switch defective. Check the switch according to the procedure in Chapter 8. Replace it if it is defective.
- [ ] Oil pressure indicator light circuit defective. Check for pinched, shorted, disconnected or damaged wiring (Chapter 8).

11 Excessive exhaust smoke

White smoke

☐ Piston oil ring worn. The ring may be broken or damaged, causing oil from the crankcase to be pulled past the piston into the combustion chamber. Replace the rings with new ones (Chapter 2).

☐ Cylinders worn, cracked, or scored. Caused by overheating or oil starvation. Install a new cylinder (Chapter 2).

☐ Valve oil seal damaged or worn. Replace oil seals with new ones (Chapter 2).

☐ Valve guide worn. Perform a complete valve job (Chapter 2).

☐ Engine oil level too high, which causes the oil to be forced past the rings. Drain oil to the proper level (Chapter 1).

☐ Head gasket broken between oil return and cylinder. Causes oil to be pulled into the combustion chamber. Replace the head gasket and check the head for warpage (Chapter 2).

☐ Abnormal crankcase pressurization, which forces oil past the rings. Clogged breather is usually the cause.

Black smoke

☐ Air filter clogged. Clean or replace the element (Chapter 1).

☐ Carburetor flooding. Remove and overhaul the carburetor (Chapter 3).

☐ Main jet too large. Remove and overhaul the carburetor(s) (Chapter 3).

☐ Choke cable stuck (Chapter 3).

☐ Fuel level too high. Check the fuel level (Chapter 3).

12 Poor handling or stability

Handlebar hard to turn

☐ Steering head bearing adjuster nut too tight. Check adjustment as described in Chapter 5.

☐ Bearings damaged. Roughness can be felt as the bars are turned from side-to-side. Replace bearings and races (Chapter 5).

☐ Races dented or worn. Denting results from wear in only one position (e.g., straight ahead), from a collision or hitting a pothole or from dropping the machine. Replace races and bearings (Chapter 5).

☐ Steering stem lubrication inadequate. Causes are grease getting hard from age or being washed out by high pressure car washes. Disassemble steering head and repack bearings (Chapter 5).

☐ Steering stem bent. Caused by a collision, hitting a pothole or by dropping the machine. Replace damaged part. Don't try to straighten the steering stem (Chapter 5).

☐ Front tire air pressure too low (Chapter 1).

Handlebar shakes or vibrates excessively

☐ Tires worn or out of balance (Chapter 6).

☐ Swingarm bearings worn. Replace worn bearings (Chapter 5).

☐ Wheel rim(s) warped or damaged. Inspect wheels for runout (Chapter 6).

☐ Wheel bearings worn. Worn front or rear wheel bearings can cause poor tracking. Worn front bearings will cause wobble (Chapter 6).

☐ Handlebar clamp bolts loose (Chapter 5).

☐ Fork yoke bolts loose. Tighten them to the specified torque (Chapter 5).

☐ Engine mounting bolts loose. Will cause excessive vibration with increased engine rpm (Chapter 2).

Handlebar pulls to one side

☐ Frame bent. Definitely suspect this if the machine has been dropped. May or may not be accompanied by cracking near the bend. Replace the frame (Chapter 7).

☐ Wheels out of alignment. Caused by improper location of axle spacers or from bent steering stem or frame (Chapters 5 and 7).

☐ Swingarm bent or twisted. Caused by age (metal fatigue) or impact damage. Replace the arm (Chapter 5).

☐ Steering stem bent. Caused by impact damage or by dropping the motorcycle. Replace the steering stem (Chapter 5).

☐ Fork tube bent. Disassemble the forks and replace the damaged parts (Chapter 5).

☐ Fork oil level uneven. Check and add or drain as necessary (Chapter 1).

Poor shock absorbing qualities

Too hard:
a) Fork oil level excessive (Chapter 1).
b) Fork oil viscosity too high. Use a lighter oil (see the Specifications in Chapter 1).
c) Fork tube bent. Causes a harsh, sticking feeling (Chapter 5).
d) Shock shaft or body bent or damaged (Chapter 5).
e) Fork internal damage (Chapter 5).
f) Shock internal damage.
g) Tire pressure too high (Chapter 1).
Too soft:
a) Fork or shock oil insufficient and/or leaking (Chapter 1).
b) Fork oil level too low (Chapter 5).
c) Fork oil viscosity too light (Chapter 5).
d) Fork springs weak or broken (Chapter 5).
e) Shock internal damage or leakage (Chapter 5).

13 Braking problems

Brakes are spongy, don't hold

☐ Air in brake line. Caused by inattention to master cylinder fluid level or by leakage. Locate problem and bleed brakes (Chapter 6).
☐ Pad or disc worn (Chapters 1 and 6).
☐ Brake fluid leak. See paragraph 1.
☐ Contaminated pads. Caused by contamination with oil, grease, brake fluid, etc. Clean or replace pads. Clean disc thoroughly with brake cleaner (Chapter 7).
☐ Brake fluid deteriorated. Fluid is old or contaminated. Drain system, replenish with new fluid and bleed the system (Chapter 6).
☐ Master cylinder internal parts worn or damaged causing fluid to bypass (Chapter 6).
☐ Master cylinder bore scratched by foreign material or broken spring. Repair or replace master cylinder (Chapter 6).
☐ Disc warped. Replace disc (Chapter 6).

Brake lever or pedal pulsates

☐ Disc warped. Replace disc (Chapter 6).

☐ Axle bent. Replace axle (Chapter 6).
☐ Brake caliper bolts loose (Chapter 6).
☐ Wheel warped or otherwise damaged (Chapter 6).
☐ Wheel bearings damaged or worn (Chapter 6).

Brakes drag

☐ Master cylinder piston seized. Caused by wear or damage to piston or cylinder bore (Chapter 6).
☐ Lever binding. Check pivot and lubricate (Chapter 6).
☐ Brake caliper piston seized in bore. Caused by wear or ingestion of dirt past deteriorated seal (Chapter 6).
☐ Brake caliper mounting bracket pins corroded. Clean off corrosion and lubricate (Chapter 6).
☐ Brake pad damaged. Material separated from backing plate. Usually caused by faulty manufacturing process or from contact with chemicals. Replace pads (Chapter 6).
☐ Pads improperly installed (Chapter 6).

14 Electrical problems

Battery dead or weak

☐ Battery faulty. Caused by sulfated plates which are shorted through sedimentation. Also, broken battery terminal making only occasional contact (Chapter 8).
☐ Battery cables making poor contact (Chapter 8).
☐ Load excessive. Caused by addition of high wattage lights or other electrical accessories.
☐ Ignition (main) switch defective. Switch either grounds internally or fails to shut off system. Replace the switch (Chapter 8).
☐ Regulator/rectifier defective (Chapter 8).
☐ Alternator stator coil open or shorted (Chapter 8).
☐ Wiring faulty. Wiring grounded or connections loose in ignition, charging or lighting circuits (Chapter 8).

Battery overcharged

☐ Regulator/rectifier defective. Overcharging is noticed when battery gets excessively warm (Chapter 8).
☐ Battery defective. Replace battery with a new one (Chapter 8).
☐ Battery amperage too low, wrong type or size. Install manufacturer's specified amp-hour battery to handle charging load (Chapter 8).

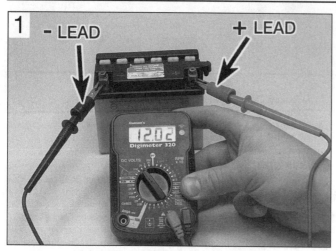

Measuring open-circuit battery voltage

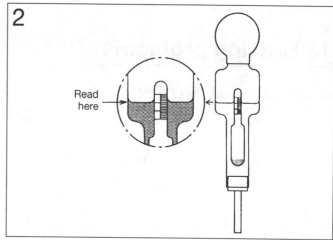

Float-type hydrometer for measuring battery specific gravity

Checking engine compression

● Low compression will result in exhaust smoke, heavy oil consumption, poor starting and poor performance. A compression test will provide useful information about an engine's condition and if performed regularly, can give warning of trouble before any other symptoms become apparent.

● A compression gauge will be required, along with an adapter to suit the spark plug hole thread size. Note that the screw-in type gauge/adapter set up is preferable to the rubber cone type.

● Compression testing procedures for the motorcycles covered in this manual are described in Chapter 2.

Checking battery open-circuit voltage

 Warning: The gases produced by the battery are explosive - never smoke or create any sparks in the vicinity of the battery. Never allow the electrolyte to contact your skin or clothing - if it does, wash it off and seek immediate medical attention.

● Before any electrical fault is investigated the battery should be checked.

● You'll need a dc voltmeter or multimeter to check battery voltage. Check that the leads are inserted in the correct terminals on the meter, red lead to positive (+), black lead to

negative (-). Incorrect connections can damage the meter.

● A sound, fully-charged 12 volt battery should produce between 12.3 and 12.6 volts across its terminals (12.8 volts for a maintenance-free battery). On machines with a 6 volt battery, voltage should be between 6.1 and 6.3 volts.

1 Set a multimeter to the 0 to 20 volts dc range and connect its probes across the battery terminals. Connect the meter's positive (+) probe, usually red, to the battery positive (+) terminal, followed by the meter's negative (-) probe, usually black, to the battery negative terminal (-) **(see illustration 1)**.

2 If battery voltage is low (below 10 volts on a 12 volt battery or below 4 volts on a six volt battery), charge the battery and test the voltage again. If the battery repeatedly goes flat, investigate the motorcycle's charging system.

Checking battery specific gravity (SG)

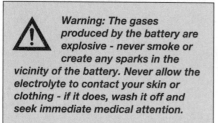 **Warning: The gases produced by the battery are explosive - never smoke or create any sparks in the vicinity of the battery. Never allow the electrolyte to contact your skin or clothing - if it does, wash it off and seek immediate medical attention.**

● The specific gravity check gives an indication of a battery's state of charge.

● A hydrometer is used for measuring specific gravity. Make sure you purchase one which has a small enough hose to insert in the aperture of a motorcycle battery.

● Specific gravity is simply a measure of the electrolyte's density compared with that of water. Water has an SG of 1.000 and fully-

charged battery electrolyte is about 26% heavier, at 1.260.

● Specific gravity checks are not possible on maintenance-free batteries. Testing the open-circuit voltage is the only means of determining their state of charge.

1 To measure SG, remove the battery from the motorcycle and remove the first cell cap. Draw some electrolyte into the hydrometer and note the reading **(see illustration 2)**. Return the electrolyte to the cell and install the cap.

2 The reading should be in the region of 1.260 to 1.280. If SG is below 1.200 the battery needs charging. Note that SG will vary with temperature; it should be measured at 20°C (68°F). Add 0.007 to the reading for every 10°C above 20°C, and subtract 0.007 from the reading for every 10°C below 20°C. Add 0.004 to the reading for every 10°F above 68°F, and subtract 0.004 from the reading for every 10°F below 68°F.

3 When the check is complete, rinse the hydrometer thoroughly with clean water.

Checking for continuity

● The term continuity describes the uninterrupted flow of electricity through an electrical circuit. A continuity check will determine whether an **open-circuit** situation exists.

● Continuity can be checked with an ohmmeter, multimeter, continuity tester or battery and bulb test circuit **(see illustrations 3, 4 and 5)**.

● All of these instruments are self-powered by a battery, therefore the checks are made with the ignition OFF.

● As a safety precaution, always disconnect the battery negative (-) lead before making checks, particularly if ignition switch checks are being made.

● If using a meter, select the appropriate

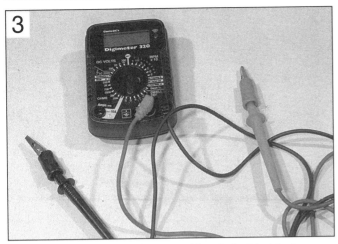

Digital multimeter can be used for all electrical tests

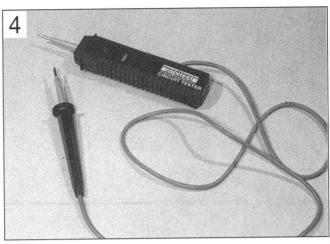

Battery-powered continuity tester

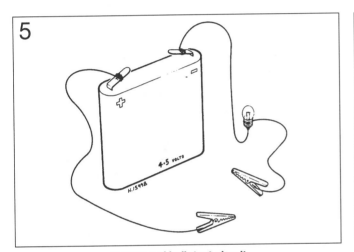

Battery and bulb test circuit

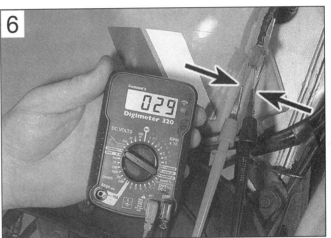

Continuity check of front brake light switch using a meter - note cotter pins used to access connector terminals

ohms scale and check that the meter reads infinity (∞). Touch the meter probes together and check that meter reads zero; where necessary adjust the meter so that it reads zero.

● After using a meter, always switch it OFF to conserve its battery.

Switch checks

1 If a switch is at fault, trace its wiring up to the wiring connectors. Separate the wire connectors and inspect them for security and condition. A build-up of dirt or corrosion here will most likely be the cause of the problem - clean up and apply a water dispersant such as WD40.

2 If using a test meter, set the meter to the ohms x 10 scale and connect its probes across the wires from the switch **(see illustration 6)**. Simple ON/OFF type switches, such as brake light switches, only have two wires whereas combination switches, like the ignition switch, have many internal links.

Study the wiring diagram to ensure that you are connecting across the correct pair of wires. Continuity (low or no measurable resistance - 0 ohms) should be indicated with the switch ON and no continuity (high resistance) with it OFF.

3 Note that the polarity of the test probes doesn't matter for continuity checks, although care should be taken to follow specific test procedures if a diode or solid-state component is being checked.

4 A continuity tester or battery and bulb circuit can be used in the same way. Connect its probes as described above **(see illustration 7)**. The light should come on to indicate continuity in the ON switch position, but should extinguish in the OFF position.

Wiring checks

● Many electrical faults are caused by damaged wiring, often due to incorrect routing or chaffing on frame components.

● Loose, wet or corroded wire connectors

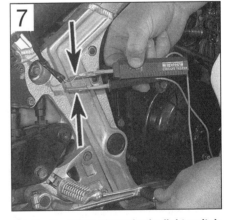

Continuity check of rear brake light switch using a continuity tester

can also be the cause of electrical problems, especially in exposed locations.

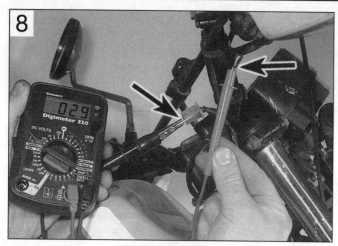

Continuity check of front brake light switch sub-harness

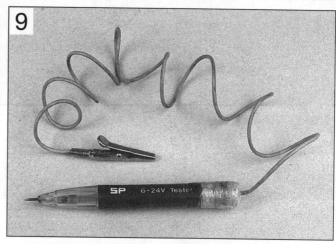

A simple test light can be used for voltage checks

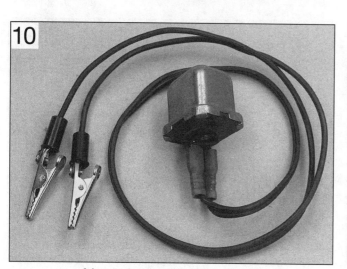

A buzzer is useful for voltage checks

Checking for voltage at the rear brake light power supply wire using a meter . . .

1 A continuity check can be made on a single length of wire by disconnecting it at each end and connecting a meter or continuity tester across both ends of the wire **(see illustration 8)**.

2 Continuity (low or no resistance - 0 ohms) should be indicated if the wire is good. If no continuity (high resistance) is shown, suspect a broken wire.

Checking for voltage

● A voltage check can determine whether current is reaching a component.

● Voltage can be checked with a dc voltmeter, multimeter set on the dc volts scale, test light or buzzer **(see illustrations 9 and 10)**. A meter has the advantage of being able to measure actual voltage.

● When using a meter, check that its leads are inserted in the correct terminals on the meter, red to positive (+), black to negative (-). Incorrect connections can damage the meter.

● A voltmeter (or multimeter set to the dc volts scale) should always be connected in parallel (across the load). Connecting it in series will destroy the meter.

● Voltage checks are made with the ignition ON.

1 First identify the relevant wiring circuit by referring to the wiring diagram at the end of this manual. If other electrical components share the same power supply (ie are fed from the same fuse), take note whether they are working correctly - this is useful information in deciding where to start checking the circuit.

2 If using a meter, check first that the meter leads are plugged into the correct terminals on the meter (see above). Set the meter to the dc volts function, at a range suitable for the battery voltage. Connect the meter red probe (+) to the power supply wire and the black probe to a good metal ground on the motor-cycle's frame or directly to the battery negative (-) terminal **(see illustration 11)**. Battery voltage should be shown on the meter with the ignition switched ON.

3 If using a test light or buzzer, connect its positive (+) probe to the power supply terminal and its negative (-) probe to a good ground on the motorcycle's frame or directly to the battery negative (-) terminal **(see illustration 12)**. With the ignition ON, the test light should illuminate or the buzzer sound.

4 If no voltage is indicated, work back towards the fuse continuing to check for voltage. When you reach a point where there is voltage, you know the problem lies between that point and your last check point.

Checking the ground

● Ground connections are made either

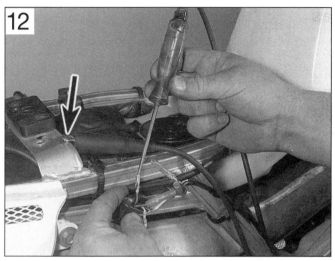

. . . or a test light - note the ground connection to the frame (arrow)

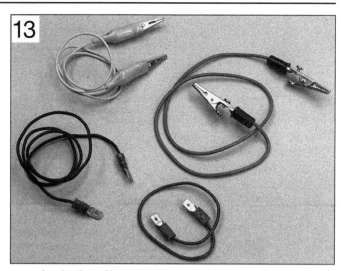

A selection of jumper wires for making ground checks

directly to the engine or frame (such as sensors, neutral switch etc. which only have a positive feed) or by a separate wire into the ground circuit of the wiring harness. Alternatively a short ground wire is sometimes run directly from the component to the motorcycle's frame.

● Corrosion is often the cause of a poor ground connection.

● If total failure is experienced, check the security of the main ground lead from the negative (-) terminal of the battery and also the main ground point on the wiring harness. If corroded, dismantle the connection and clean all surfaces back to bare metal.

1 To check the ground on a component, use an insulated jumper wire to temporarily bypass its ground connection **(see illustration 13)**. Connect one end of the jumper wire between the ground terminal or metal body of the component and the other end to the motorcycle's frame.

2 If the circuit works with the jumper wire installed, the original ground circuit is faulty. Check the wiring for open-circuits or poor connections. Clean up direct ground connections, removing all traces of corrosion and remake the joint. Apply petroleum jelly to the joint to prevent future corrosion.

Tracing a short-circuit

● A short-circuit occurs where current shorts to ground bypassing the circuit components. This usually results in a blown fuse.

● A short-circuit is most likely to occur where the insulation has worn through due to wiring chafing on a component, allowing a direct path to ground on the frame.

1 Remove any body panels necessary to access the circuit wiring.

2 Check that all electrical switches in the circuit are OFF, then remove the circuit fuse and connect a test light, buzzer or voltmeter (set to the dc scale) across the fuse terminals. No voltage should be shown.

3 Move the wiring from side to side while observing the test light or meter. When the test light comes on, buzzer sounds or meter shows voltage, you have found the cause of the short. It will usually shown up as damaged or burned insulation.

4 Note that the same test can be performed on each component in the circuit, even the switch.

Notes

A

ABS (Anti-lock braking system) A system, usually electronically controlled, that senses incipient wheel lockup during braking and relieves hydraulic pressure at wheel which is about to skid.

Aftermarket Components suitable for the motorcycle, but not produced by the motorcycle manufacturer.

Allen key A hexagonal wrench which fits into a recessed hexagonal hole.

Alternating current (ac) Current produced by an alternator. Requires converting to direct current by a rectifier for charging purposes.

Alternator Converts mechanical energy from the engine into electrical energy to charge the battery and power the electrical system.

Ampere (amp) A unit of measurement for the flow of electrical current. Current = Volts ÷ Ohms.

Ampere-hour (Ah) Measure of battery capacity.

Angle-tightening A torque expressed in degrees. Often follows a conventional tightening torque for cylinder head or main bearing fasteners **(see illustration)**.

Angle-tightening cylinder head bolts

Antifreeze A substance (usually ethylene glycol) mixed with water, and added to the cooling system, to prevent freezing of the coolant in winter. Antifreeze also contains chemicals to inhibit corrosion and the formation of rust and other deposits that would tend to clog the radiator and coolant passages and reduce cooling efficiency.

Anti-dive System attached to the fork lower leg (slider) to prevent fork dive when braking hard.

Anti-seize compound A coating that reduces the risk of seizing on fasteners that are subjected to high temperatures, such as exhaust clamp bolts and nuts.

API American Petroleum Institute. A quality standard for 4-stroke motor oils.

Asbestos A natural fibrous mineral with great heat resistance, commonly used in the composition of brake friction materials. Asbestos is a health hazard and the dust created by brake systems should never be inhaled or ingested.

ATF Automatic Transmission Fluid. Often used in front forks.

ATU Automatic Timing Unit. Mechanical device for advancing the ignition timing on early engines.

ATV All Terrain Vehicle. Often called a Quad.

Axial play Side-to-side movement.

Axle A shaft on which a wheel revolves. Also known as a spindle.

B

Backlash The amount of movement between meshed components when one component is held still. Usually applies to gear teeth.

Ball bearing A bearing consisting of a hardened inner and outer race with hardened steel balls between the two races.

Bearings Used between two working surfaces to prevent wear of the components and a build-up of heat. Four types of bearing are commonly used on motorcycles: plain shell bearings, ball bearings, tapered roller bearings and needle roller bearings.

Bevel gears Used to turn the drive through 90°. Typical applications are shaft final drive and camshaft drive **(see illustration)**.

BHP Brake Horsepower. The British measure-ment for engine power output. Power output is now usually expressed in kilowatts (kW).

Bevel gears are used to turn the drive through 90°

Bias-belted tire Similar construction to radial tire, but with outer belt running at an angle to the wheel rim.

Big-end bearing The bearing in the end of the connecting rod that's attached to the crankshaft.

Bleeding The process of removing air from a hydraulic system via a bleed nipple or bleed screw.

Bottom-end A description of an engine's crankcase components and all components contained therein.

BTDC Before Top Dead Center in terms of piston position. Ignition timing is often expressed in terms of degrees or millimeters BTDC.

Bush A cylindrical metal or rubber component used between two moving parts.

Burr Rough edge left on a component after machining or as a result of excessive wear.

C

Cam chain The chain which takes drive from the crankshaft to the camshaft(s).

Canister The main component in an evaporative emission control system (California market only); contains activated charcoal granules to trap vapors from the fuel system rather than allowing them to vent to the atmosphere.

Castellated Resembling the parapets along the top of a castle wall. For example, a castellated wheel axle or spindle nut.

Catalytic converter A device in the exhaust system of some machines which

Cush drive rubber segments dampen out transmission shocks

converts certain pollutants in the exhaust gases into less harmful substances.

Charging system Description of the components which charge the battery, ie the alternator, rectifer and regulator.

Clearance The amount of space between two parts. For example, between a piston and a cylinder, between a bearing and a journal, etc.

Coil spring A spiral of elastic steel found in various sizes throughout a vehicle, for example as a springing medium in the suspension and in the valve train.

Compression Reduction in volume, and increase in pressure and temperature, of a gas, caused by squeezing it into a smaller space.

Compression damping Controls the speed the suspension compresses when hitting a bump.

Compression ratio The relationship between cylinder volume when the piston is at top dead center and cylinder volume when the piston is at bottom dead center.

Continuity The uninterrupted path in the flow of electricity. Little or no measurable resistance.

Continuity tester Self-powered bleeper or test light which indicates continuity.

Cp Candlepower. Bulb rating commonly found on US motorcycles.

Crossply tire Tire plies arranged in a criss-cross pattern. Usually four or six plies used, hence 4PR or 6PR in tire size codes.

Cush drive Rubber damper segments fitted between the rear wheel and final drive sprocket to absorb transmission shocks **(see illustration)**.

D

Degree disc Calibrated disc for measuring piston position. Expressed in degrees.

Dial gauge Clock-type gauge with adapters for measuring runout and piston position. Expressed in mm or inches.

Diaphragm The rubber membrane in a master cylinder or carburetor which seals the upper chamber.

Diaphragm spring A single sprung plate often used in clutches.

Direct current (dc) Current produced by a dc generator.

Decarbonization The process of removing carbon deposits - typically from the combustion chamber, valves and exhaust port/system.

Detonation Destructive and damaging explosion of fuel/air mixture in combustion chamber instead of controlled burning.

Diode An electrical valve which only allows current to flow in one direction. Commonly used in rectifiers and starter interlock systems.

Disc valve (or rotary valve) An induction system used on some two-stroke engines.

Double-overhead camshaft (DOHC) An engine that uses two overhead camshafts, one for the intake valves and one for the exhaust valves.

Drivebelt A toothed belt used to transmit drive to the rear wheel on some motorcycles. A drivebelt has also been used to drive the camshafts. Drivebelts are usually made of Kevlar.

Driveshaft Any shaft used to transmit motion. Commonly used when referring to the final driveshaft on shaft drive motorcycles.

E

ECU (Electronic Control Unit) A computer which controls (for instance) an ignition system, or an anti-lock braking system.

EGO Exhaust Gas Oxygen sensor. Some-times called a Lambda sensor.

Electrolyte The fluid in a lead-acid battery.

EMS (Engine Management System) A computer controlled system which manages the fuel injection and the ignition systems in an integrated fashion.

Endfloat The amount of lengthways movement between two parts. As applied to a crankshaft, the distance that the crankshaft can move side-to-side in the crankcase.

Endless chain A chain having no joining link. Common use for cam chains and final drive chains.

EP (Extreme Pressure) Oil type used in locations where high loads are applied, such as between gear teeth.

Evaporative emission control system Describes a charcoal filled canister which stores fuel vapors from the tank rather than allowing them to vent to the atmosphere. Usually only fitted to California models and referred to as an EVAP system.

Expansion chamber Section of two-stroke engine exhaust system so designed to improve engine efficiency and boost power.

F

Feeler blade or gauge A thin strip or blade of hardened steel, ground to an exact thickness, used to check or measure clearances between parts.

Final drive Description of the drive from the transmission to the rear wheel. Usually by chain or shaft, but sometimes by belt.

Firing order The order in which the engine cylinders fire, or deliver their power strokes, beginning with the number one cylinder.

Flooding Term used to describe a high fuel level in the carburetor float chambers, leading to fuel overflow. Also refers to excess fuel in the combustion chamber due to incorrect starting technique.

Free length The no-load state of a component when measured. Clutch, valve and fork spring lengths are measured at rest, without any preload.

Freeplay The amount of travel before any action takes place. The looseness in a linkage, or an assembly of parts, between the initial application of force and actual movement. For example, the distance the rear brake pedal moves before the rear brake is actuated.

Fuel injection The fuel/air mixture is metered electronically and directed into the engine intake ports (indirect injection) or into the cylinders (direct injection). Sensors supply information on engine speed and conditions.

Fuel/air mixture The charge of fuel and air going into the engine. See Stoichiometric ratio.

Fuse An electrical device which protects a circuit against accidental overload. The typical fuse contains a soft piece of metal which is calibrated to melt at a predetermined current flow (expressed as amps) and break the circuit.

G

Gap The distance the spark must travel in jumping from the center electrode to the side electrode in a spark plug. Also refers to the distance between the ignition rotor and the pickup coil in an electronic ignition system.

Gasket Any thin, soft material - usually cork, cardboard, asbestos or soft metal - installed between two metal surfaces to ensure a good seal. For instance, the cylinder head gasket seals the joint between the block and the cylinder head.

Gauge An instrument panel display used to monitor engine conditions. A gauge with a movable pointer on a dial or a fixed scale is an analog gauge. A gauge with a numerical readout is called a digital gauge.

Gear ratios The drive ratio of a pair of gears in a gearbox, calculated on their number of teeth.

Glaze-busting see **Honing**

Grinding Process for renovating the valve face and valve seat contact area in the cylinder head.

Ground return The return path of an electrical circuit, utilizing the motorcycle's frame.

Gudgeon pin The shaft which connects the connecting rod small-end with the piston. Often called a piston pin or wrist pin.

H

Helical gears Gear teeth are slightly curved and produce less gear noise that straight-cut gears. Often used for primary drives.

Helicoil A thread insert repair system. Commonly used as a repair for stripped spark plug threads **(see illustration)**.

Installing a Helicoil thread insert in a cylinder head

Honing A process used to break down the glaze on a cylinder bore (also called glaze-busting). Can also be carried out to roughen a rebored cylinder to aid ring bedding-in.

HT (High Tension) Description of the electrical circuit from the secondary winding of the ignition coil to the spark plug.

Hydraulic A liquid filled system used to transmit pressure from one component to another. Common uses on motorcycles are brakes and clutches.

Hydrometer An instrument for measuring the specific gravity of a lead-acid battery.

Hygroscopic Water absorbing. In motorcycle applications, braking efficiency will be reduced if DOT 3 or 4 hydraulic fluid absorbs water from the air - care must be taken to keep new brake fluid in tightly sealed containers.

I

lbf ft Pounds-force feet. An imperial unit of torque. Sometimes written as ft-lbs.

lbf in Pound-force inch. An imperial unit of torque, applied to components where a very low torque is required. Sometimes written as inch-lbs.

IC Abbreviation for Integrated Circuit.

Ignition advance Means of increasing the timing of the spark at higher engine speeds. Done by mechanical means (ATU) on early engines or electronically by the ignition control unit on later engines.

Ignition timing The moment at which the spark plug fires, expressed in the number of crankshaft degrees before the piston reaches the top of its stroke, or in the number of millimeters before the piston reaches the top of its stroke.

Infinity (∞) Description of an open-circuit electrical state, where no continuity exists.

Inverted forks (upside down forks) The sliders or lower legs are held in the yokes and the fork tubes or stanchions are connected to the wheel axle (spindle). Less unsprung weight and stiffer construction than conventional forks.

J

JASO Japan Automobile Standards Organ-ization. JASO MA is a standard for motorcycle oil equivalent to API SJ, but designed to prevent problems with wet-type motorcycle clutches.

Joule The unit of electrical energy.

Journal The bearing surface of a shaft.

K

Kickstart Mechanical means of turning the engine over for starting purposes.

Only usually fitted to mopeds, small capacity motorcycles and off-road motorcycles.

Kill switch Handebar-mounted switch for emergency ignition cut-out. Cuts the ignition circuit on all models, and additionally prevent starter motor operation on others.

km Symbol for kilometer.

kmh Abbreviation for kilometers per hour.

L

Lambda sensor A sensor fitted in the exhaust system to measure the exhaust gas oxygen content (excess air factor). Also called oxygen sensor.

Lapping see **Grinding**.

LCD Abbreviation for Liquid Crystal Display.

LED Abbreviation for Light Emitting Diode.

Liner A steel cylinder liner inserted in an aluminum alloy cylinder block.

Locknut A nut used to lock an adjustment nut, or other threaded component, in place.

Lockstops The lugs on the lower triple clamp (yoke) which abut those on the frame, preventing handlebar-to-fuel tank contact.

Lockwasher A form of washer designed to prevent an attaching nut from working loose.

LT Low Tension Description of the electrical circuit from the power supply to the primary winding of the ignition coil.

M

Main bearings The bearings between the crankshaft and crankcase.

Maintenance-free (MF) battery A sealed battery which cannot be topped up.

Manometer Mercury-filled calibrated tubes used to measure intake tract vacuum. Used to synchronize carburetors on multi-cylinder engines.

Tappet shims are measured with a micrometer

Micrometer A precision measuring instru-ment that measures component outside diameters **(see illustration)**.

MON (Motor Octane Number) A measure of a fuel's resistance to knock.

Monograde oil An oil with a single viscosity, eg SAE80W.

Monoshock A single suspension unit linking the swingarm or suspension linkage to the frame.

mph Abbreviation for miles per hour.

Multigrade oil Having a wide viscosity range (eg 10W40). The W stands for Winter, thus the viscosity ranges from SAE10 when cold to SAE40 when hot.

Multimeter An electrical test instrument with the capability to measure voltage, current and resistance. Some meters also incorporate a continuity tester and buzzer.

N

Needle roller bearing Inner race of caged needle rollers and hardened outer race. Examples of uncaged needle rollers can be found on some engines. Commonly used in rear suspension applications and in two-stroke engines.

Nm Newton meters.

NOx Oxides of Nitrogen. A common toxic pollutant emitted by gasoline engines at higher temperatures.

O

Octane The measure of a fuel's resistance to knock.

OE (Original Equipment) Relates to components fitted to a motorcycle as standard or replacement parts supplied by the motorcycle manufacturer.

Ohm The unit of electrical resistance. Ohms = Volts 4 Current.

Ohmmeter An instrument for measuring electrical resistance.

Oil cooler System for diverting engine oil outside of the engine to a radiator for cooling purposes.

Oil injection A system of two-stroke engine lubrication where oil is pump-fed to the engine in accordance with throttle position.

Open-circuit An electrical condition where there is a break in the flow of electricity - no continuity (high resistance).

O-ring A type of sealing ring made of a special rubber-like material; in use, the O-ring is compressed into a groove to provide the sealing action.

Oversize (OS) Term used for piston and ring size options fitted to a rebored cylinder.

Overhead cam (sohc) engine An engine with single camshaft located on top of the cylinder head.

Overhead valve (ohv) engine An engine with the valves located in the cylinder head, but with the camshaft located in the engine block or crankcase.

Oxygen sensor A device installed in the exhaust system which senses the oxygen content in the exhaust and converts this information into an electric current. Also called a Lambda sensor.

P

Plastigage A thin strip of plastic thread, available in different sizes, used for measuring clearances. For example, a strip of Plastigage is laid across a bearing journal. The parts are assembled and dismantled; the width of the crushed strip indicates the clearance between journal and bearing.

Polarity Either negative or positive ground, determined by which battery lead is connected to the frame (ground return). Modern motorcycles are usually negative ground.

Pre-ignition A situation where the fuel/air mixture ignites before the spark plug fires. Often due to a hot spot in the combustion chamber caused by carbon build-up. Engine has a tendency to 'run-on'.

Pre-load (suspension) The amount a spring is compressed when in the unloaded state. Preload can be applied by gas, spacer or mechanical adjuster.

Premix The method of engine lubrication on some gasoline two-stroke engines. Engine oil is mixed with the gasoline in the fuel tank in a specific ratio. The fuel/oil mix is sometimes referred to as "petrol".

Primary drive Description of the drive from the crankshaft to the clutch. Usually by gear or chain.

PS Pferdestärke - a German interpretation of BHP.

PSI Pounds-force per square inch. Imperial measurement of tire pressure and cylinder pressure measurement.

PTFE Polytetrafluroethylene. A low friction substance.

Pulse secondary air injection system A process of promoting the burning of excess fuel present in the exhaust gases by routing fresh air into the exhaust ports.

Q

Quartz halogen bulb Tungsten filament surrounded by a halogen gas. Typically used for the headlight **(see illustration)**.

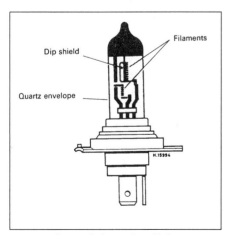

Quartz halogen headlight bulb construction

R

Rack-and-pinion A pinion gear on the end of a shaft that mates with a rack (think of a geared wheel opened up and laid flat). Sometimes used in clutch operating systems.

Radial play Up and down movement about a shaft.

Radial ply tires Tire plies run across the tire (from bead to bead) and around the circumference of the tire. Less resistant to tread distortion than other tire types.

Radiator A liquid-to-air heat transfer device designed to reduce the temperature of the coolant in a liquid cooled engine.

Rake A feature of steering geometry - the angle of the steering head in relation to the vertical **(see illustration)**.

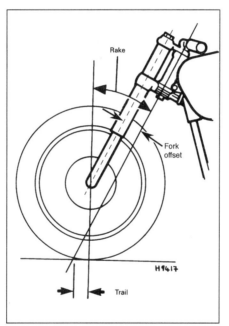

Steering geometry

Rebore Providing a new working surface to the cylinder bore by boring out the old surface. Necessitates the use of oversize piston and rings.

Rebound damping A means of controlling the oscillation of a suspension unit spring after it has been compressed. Resists the spring's natural tendency to bounce back after being compressed.

Rectifier Device for converting the ac output of an alternator into dc for battery charging.

Reed valve An induction system commonly used on two-stroke engines.

Regulator Device for maintaining the charging voltage from the generator or alternator within a specified range.

Relay A electrical device used to switch heavy current on and off by using a low current auxiliary circuit.

Resistance Measured in ohms. An electrical component's ability to pass electrical current.

RON (Research Octane Number) A measure of a fuel's resistance to knock.

rpm revolutions per minute.

Runout The amount of wobble (in-and-out movement) of a wheel or shaft as it's rotated. The amount a shaft rotates 'out-of-true'. The out-of-round condition of a rotating part.

S

SAE (Society of Automotive Engineers) A standard for the viscosity of a fluid.

Sealant A liquid or paste used to prevent leakage at a joint. Sometimes used in conjunction with a gasket.

Service limit Term for the point where a component is no longer useable and must be replaced.

Shaft drive A method of transmitting drive from the transmission to the rear wheel.

Shell bearings Plain bearings consisting of two shell halves. Most often used as big-end and main bearings in a four-stroke engine. Often called bearing inserts.

Shim Thin spacer, commonly used to adjust the clearance or relative positions between two parts. For example, shims inserted into or under tappets or followers to control valve clearances. Clearance is adjusted by changing the thickness of the shim.

Short-circuit An electrical condition where current shorts to ground bypassing the circuit components.

Skimming Process to correct warpage or repair a damaged surface, eg on brake discs or drums.

Slide-hammer A special puller that screws into or hooks onto a component such as a shaft or bearing; a heavy sliding handle on the shaft bottoms against the end of the shaft to knock the component free.

Small-end bearing The bearing in the upper end of the connecting rod at its joint with the gudgeon pin.

Snap-ring A ring-shaped clip used to prevent endwise movement of cylindrical parts and shafts. An internal snap-ring is installed in a groove in a housing; an external snap-ring fits into a groove on the outside of a cylindrical piece such as a shaft. Also known as a snap-ring.

Spalling Damage to camshaft lobes or bearing journals shown as pitting of the working surface.

Specific gravity (SG) The state of charge of the electrolyte in a lead-acid battery. A measure of the electrolyte's density compared with water.

Straight-cut gears Common type gear used on gearbox shafts and for oil pump and water pump drives.

Stanchion The inner sliding part of the front forks, held by the yokes. Often called a fork tube.

Stoichiometric ratio The optimum chemical air/fuel ratio for a gasoline engine, said to be 14.7 parts of air to 1 part of fuel.

Sulphuric acid The liquid (electrolyte) used in a lead-acid battery. Poisonous and extremely corrosive.

Surface grinding (lapping) Process to correct a warped gasket face, commonly used on cylinder heads.

T

Tapered-roller bearing Tapered inner race of caged needle rollers and separate tapered outer race. Examples of taper roller bearings can be found on steering heads.

Tappet A cylindrical component which transmits motion from the cam to the valve stem, either directly or via a pushrod and rocker arm. Also called a cam follower.

TCS Traction Control System. An electron-ically-controlled system which senses wheel spin and reduces engine speed accordingly.

TDC Top Dead Center denotes that the piston is at its highest point in the cylinder.

Thread-locking compound Solution applied to fastener threads to prevent loosening. Select type to suit application.

Thrust washer A washer positioned between two moving components on a shaft. For example, between gear pinions on gearshaft.

Timing chain See **Cam Chain**.

Timing light Stroboscopic lamp for carrying out ignition timing checks with the engine running.

Top-end A description of an engine's cylinder block, head and valve gear components.

Torque Turning or twisting force about a shaft.

Torque setting A prescribed tightness specified by the motorcycle manufacturer to ensure that the bolt or nut is secured correctly. Undertightening can result in the bolt or nut coming loose or a surface not being sealed. Overtightening can result in stripped threads, distortion or damage to the component being retained.

Torx key A six-point wrench.

Tracer A stripe of a second color applied to a wire insulator to distinguish that wire from another one with the same color insulator. For example, Br/W is often used to denote a brown insulator with a white tracer.

Trail A feature of steering geometry. Distance from the steering head axis to the tire's central contact point.

Triple clamps The cast components which extend from the steering head and support the fork stanchions or tubes. Often called fork yokes.

Turbocharger A centrifugal device, driven by exhaust gases, that pressurizes the intake air. Normally used to increase the power output from a given engine displacement.

TWI Abbreviation for Tire Wear Indicator. Indicates the location of the tread depth indicator bars on tires.

U

Universal joint or U-joint (UJ) A double-pivoted connection for transmitting power from a driving to a driven shaft through an angle. Typically found in shaft drive assemblies.

Unsprung weight Anything not supported by the bike's suspension (ie the wheel, tires, brakes, final drive and bottom (moving) part of the suspension).

V

Vacuum gauges Clock-type gauges for measuring intake tract vacuum. Used for carburetor synchronization on multi-cylinder engines.

Valve A device through which the flow of liquid, gas or vacuum may be stopped, started or regulated by a moveable part that opens, shuts or partially obstructs one or more ports or passageways. The intake and exhaust valves in the cylinder head are of the poppet type.

Valve clearance The clearance between the valve tip (the end of the valve stem) and the rocker arm or tappet/follower. The valve clearance is measured when the valve is closed. The correct clearance is important - if too small the valve won't close fully and will burn out, whereas if too large noisy operation will result.

Valve lift The amount a valve is lifted off its seat by the camshaft lobe.

Valve timing The exact setting for the opening and closing of the valves in relation to piston position.

Vernier caliper A precision measuring instrument that measures inside and outside dimensions. Not quite as accurate as a micrometer, but more convenient.

VIN Vehicle Identification Number. Term for the bike's engine and frame numbers.

Viscosity The thickness of a liquid or its resistance to flow.

Volt A unit for expressing electrical "pressure" in a circuit. Volts = current x ohms.

W

Water pump A mechanically-driven device for moving coolant around the engine.

Watt A unit for expressing electrical power. Watts = volts x current.

Wet liner arrangement

Wear limit see **Service limit**

Wet liner A liquid-cooled engine design where the pistons run in liners which are directly surrounded by coolant **(see illustration)**.

Wheelbase Distance from the center of the front wheel to the center of the rear wheel.

Wiring harness or loom Describes the electrical wires running the length of the motorcycle and enclosed in tape or plastic sheathing. Wiring coming off the main harness is usually referred to as a sub harness.

Woodruff key A key of semi-circular or square section used to locate a gear to a shaft. Often used to locate the alternator rotor on the crankshaft.

Wrist pin Another name for gudgeon or piston pin.

Notes

Note: *References throughout this index are in the form - "Chapter number"•"Page number"*

Notes